Everyday Law Kit For Dummies®

Steps for Preparing a Legally Binding Contract

- Make sure that all parties to the contract are legal adults — at least age 18 or 21, depending on the state.
- Be certain that all parties have the mental capacity to understand what they are doing in agreeing to the contract.
- Put the contract in writing.
- Use clear, concise language to describe the who, what, when, where, and how much of the contract.
- Spell out everyone's responsibilities, all deadlines, and any penalties for missing deadlines.
- Identify all of the things that could go wrong with your agreement and address them in the contract.
- If the agreement is important to you or involves a lot of money, hire an attorney to review and revise the contract to make sure it covers all the bases and adequately protects you.
- Have all parties to the contract sign it.

12 Basic Provisions to Include in a Contract

- Name and address of each party to the contract
- What each of you is agreeing to do or not do
- Date the contract begins and ends
- Whether the contract can be terminated early, under what circumstances termination can occur, and the process for ending the contract
- The consequences of early termination
- Under what circumstances a contract is considered breached or broken and the consequences for the party who breaks it
- How disputes are resolved — mediation, arbitration, or lawsuits
- How a mediator is chosen
- How an arbitrator is chosen
- Under what circumstances one party is responsible for paying the legal fees and expenses the other party might incur when getting the contract enforced
- All deadlines that apply

D1604980

For Dummies™: Bestselling Book Series for Beginners

BESTSELLING BOOK SERIES

Everyday Law Kit For Dummies®

Quick Reference Card

Dealer Lingo to Understand When You Shop for a New Car

- **Invoice sticker price.** (Also known as dealer invoice price or factory invoice price.) This is the price the dealer paid the manufacturer for the car, before any manufacturer rebates, discounts, or allowances the dealer might have been eligible for. It includes freight or "destination and delivery" costs. Focus on the invoice sticker price when you negotiate a purchase price.

- **Base price.** The price of the car with standard equipment and factory warranty, but with no options. This is the price listed on the Maroney sticker, which must be affixed to a new car's windshield.

- **Maroney sticker price.** (Also known as manufacturer's suggested retail price.) This sticker lists a car's base price, the manufacturer's installed options, the manufacturer's suggested retail price, the manufacturer's transportation cost, and the car's make, model, and vehicle identification number. This sticker also indicates the car's fuel economy — the average number of miles it gets per gallon of gas.

- **Dealer sticker price.** (Also known as the "mop and glow" sticker.) Usually, this price reflects the Maroney sticker price plus the suggested retail price for dealer-installed options. Ignore this sticker when you negotiate a purchase price. The dealer sticker is usually located next to the Maroney sticker.

Things to Find Out When You Shop for a Loan

- How long you have to repay the loan
- The amount of each monthly loan payment
- Whether your monthly payments stay the same over the life of the loan
- Whether you have to make a balloon payment at the end of the loan
- The loan's annual percentage rate (APR)
- The loan's total value — the amount of the loan plus interest and other loan-related costs
- Whether the interest rate on the loan increases if you are late with or miss a monthly payment
- How much you will pay in finance charges over the life of the loan
- What extra loan-related fees you must pay
- Whether buying credit insurance is a condition of the loan
- The size of the down payment, if any

Hungry Minds™

For Dummies™: Bestselling Book Series for Beginners

™

References for the Rest of Us!®

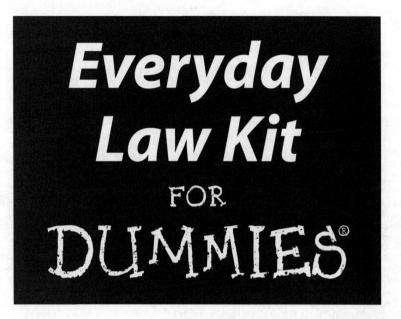

Everyday Law Kit FOR DUMMIES®

by John Ventura and Mary Reed

Hungry Minds™

HUNGRY MINDS, INC.

New York, NY ◆ Cleveland, OH ◆ Indianapolis, IN

Everyday Law Kit For Dummies®

Published by:
Hungry Minds, Inc.
909 Third Avenue
New York, NY 10022
www.hungryminds.com
www.dummies.com

Library of Congress Control Number: 00-108218

ISBN: 0-7645-5293-7

Printed in the United States of America

10 9 8 7 6 5 4 3 2 1

1B/RZ/QT/QR/IN

Distributed in the United States by Hungry Minds, Inc.

Distributed by CDG Books Canada Inc. for Canada; by Transworld Publishers Limited in the United Kingdom; by IDG Norge Books for Norway; by IDG Sweden Books for Sweden; by IDG Books Australia Publishing Corporation Pty. Ltd. for Australia and New Zealand; by TransQuest Publishers Pte Ltd. for Singapore, Malaysia, Thailand, Indonesia, and Hong Kong; by Gotop Information Inc. for Taiwan; by ICG Muse, Inc. for Japan; by Intersoft for South Africa; by Eyrolles for France; by International Thomson Publishing for Germany, Austria and Switzerland; by Distribuidora Cuspide for Argentina; by LR International for Brazil; by Galileo Libros for Chile; by Ediciones ZETA S.C.R. Ltda. for Peru; by WS Computer Publishing Corporation, Inc., for the Philippines; by Contemporanea de Ediciones for Venezuela; by Express Computer Distributors for the Caribbean and West Indies; by Micronesia Media Distributor, Inc. for Micronesia; by Chips Computadoras S.A. de C.V. for Mexico; by Editorial Norma de Panama S.A. for Panama; by American Bookshops for Finland.

For general information on Hungry Minds' products and services please contact our Customer Care department; within the U.S. at 800-762-2974, outside the U.S. at 317-572-3993 or fax 317-572-4002.

For sales inquiries and resellers information, including discounts, premium and bulk quantity sales and foreign language translations please contact our Customer Care department at 800-434-3422, fax 317-572-4002 or write to Hungry Minds, Inc., Attn: Customer Care department, 10475 Crosspoint Boulevard, Indianapolis, IN 46256.

For information on licensing foreign or domestic rights, please contact our Sub-Rights Customer Care department at 650-653-7098.

For information on using Hungry Minds' products and services in the classroom or for ordering examination copies, please contact our Educational Sales department at 800-434-2086 or fax 317-572-4005.

Please contact our Public Relations department at 212-884-5163 for press review copies or 212-884-5000 for author interviews and other publicity information or fax 212-884-5400.

For authorization to photocopy items for corporate, personal, or educational use, please contact Copyright Clearance Center, 222 Rosewood Drive, Danvers, MA 01923, or fax 978-750-4470.

Hungry Minds™ is a trademark of Hungry Minds, Inc.

About the Authors

John Ventura: John Ventura is an attorney and a nationally known expert on consumer law. As a boy, he wanted to become a Catholic priest so he could help people but later decided to pursue that dream by combining journalism with the law. He earned his law degree from the University of Houston. John operates three law offices in the Rio Grande Valley of Texas where he offers legal services in the areas of bankruptcy, consumer law, personal injury, and child support. His goal as an attorney is to make the law work for his clients, not against them. John is the author of nine books on consumer and small business financial and legal matters including two books in the *For Dummies* series, *Law For Dummies* and *Divorce For Dummies*. He writes a regular column on money and the law for a local business journal in Texas and hosts a weekly radio program on legal issues. He has also written about money and the law for a number of national magazines. John has been a guest on CNN, CNBC, the Fox News Channel, PBS, the Lifetime Network, and National Public Radio, as well as on many local TV and radio programs. He has also been interviewed by or mentioned in such publications as *Money, Kiplinger's Personal Finance Magazine, Newsweek,* and the *Wall Street Journal,* among other national publications. John and his family live on South Padre Island.

Mary J. Reed: Mary J. Reed co-authored *Divorce For Dummies* with John Ventura and has also ghost-written numerous books on consumer and small business legal and money matters. She has also written on those subjects for local as well as national publications. She has been a guest on local radio and TV programs and has been interviewed about personal finance and everyday legal topics for national magazines as well as local newspapers and Web sites. Mary is the owner of MRPR, a public relations firm, and Reed Books, a publishing intermediary. She has a Masters degree in business from Boston University.

In her free time, Mary spends time with her friends and family, travels, gardens, practices yoga, rides her race bike, helps run a neighborhood-based housing organization, takes care of her five cats, and reads both fiction and nonfiction. She and her husband live in a home they designed and built themselves.

Dedication

John: To Mary Ellen, my wife, who has never stopped believing in me.

Mary: To my sisters, Kay, Pat, and Beth, as a reminder that they are in my thoughts and in my heart each and every day.

Authors' Acknowledgments

First, thanks to Kathy Welton and Mark Butler for their patience and understanding during the evolution of *Everyday Law Kit For Dummies*. Second, thank you, thank you to Keith Peterson, our Project Editor. He helped us turn an overwhelming wealth of material into a book, making sage comments and suggestions along the way. Plus, he was unfailingly patient with our computer glitches. We also want to thank Tammy Castleman and Kris Simmons who polished our prose with diplomacy and a sense of humor. Thank you too to the research assistants who helped with this book. They include Alisa Perrotte, Ehren Ezzell, Chris Grandinetti, and Margo Garana. We couldn't have done it without you! There are others we also need to thank. At the top of our list are Aralyn Hughes, owner of Aralyn Hughes & Associates in Austin, Texas; Sam Listi; Rod Griffin, Manager of Consumer Communications for Experian in Allen, Texas; and Arthur McGuire, Vice President and General Counsel for Blumberg Excelsior in New York City. We also thank all of the businesses, organizations, and individuals who gave us permission to use their forms and information in *Everyday Law Kit For Dummies* and on its CD.

Publisher's Acknowledgments

We're proud of this book; please send us your comments through our Online Registration Form located at www.hungryminds.com

Some of the people who helped bring this book to market include the following:

Acquisitions, Editorial, and Media Development

Project Editor: Keith Peterson

Acquisitions Editor: Mark Butler

Copy Editors: Tammy Castleman, Kris Simmons

Acquisitions Coordinators: Lauren Cundiff, Jon Malysiak

Technical Editor: James T. Malysiak

Senior Permissions Editor: Carmen Krikorian

Media Development Specialist: Megan Decraene

Editorial Manager: Pam Mourouzis

Media Development Manager: Laura Carpenter

Editorial Assistants: Carol Strickland, Melissa Bennett

Production

Project Coordinator: Bill Ramsey

Layout and Graphics: Amy Adrian, Kristin Pickett, Jacque Schneider, Brian Torwelle, Jeremey Unger

Proofreaders: David Faust, Linda Quigley, York Production Services, Inc.

Indexer: York Production Services, Inc.

General and Administrative

Hungry Minds, Inc.: John Kilcullen, CEO; Bill Barry, President and COO; John Ball, Executive VP, Operations & Administration; John Harris, CFO

Hungry Minds Consumer Reference Group

   Business: Kathleen A. Welton, Vice President and Publisher; Kevin Thornton, Acquisitions Manager

   Cooking/Gardening: Jennifer Feldman, Associate Vice President and Publisher

   Education/Reference: Diane Graves Steele, Vice President and Publisher; Greg Tubach, Publishing Director

   Lifestyles: Kathleen Nebenhaus, Vice President and Publisher; Tracy Boggier, Managing Editor

   Pets: Dominique De Vito, Associate Vice President and Publisher; Tracy Boggier, Managing Editor

   Travel: Michael Spring, Vice President and Publisher; Suzanne Jannetta, Editorial Director; Brice Gosnell, Managing Editor

Hungry Minds Consumer Editorial Services: Kathleen Nebenhaus, Vice President and Publisher; Kristin A. Cocks, Editorial Director; Cindy Kitchel, Editorial Director

Hungry Minds Consumer Production: Debbie Stailey, Production Director

◆

The publisher would like to give special thanks to Patrick J. McGovern, without whom this book would not have been possible.

◆

Contents at a Glance

Cartoons at a Glance

By Rich Tennant

"I just don't know where the money's going."

page 73

"My portfolio's gonna take a hit for this."

page 331

"The first thing we should do is get you two into a good mutual fund. Let me get out the Magic 8-Ball and we'll run some options."

page 149

page 7

"Included with today's surgery, we're offering a manicure, pedicure, haircut, and ear wax flush for just $49.95."

page 295

"I swear, Frank, it's not a pyramid scam. You help a few guys with their home improvements and then, after you bring in ten friends, you'll be enjoying each and every Saturday as much as I do."

page 225

Cartoon Information:
Fax: 978-546-7747
E-Mail: richtennant@the5thwave.com
World Wide Web: www.the5thwave.com

Table of Contents

Introduction

*N*o doubt about it: Money makes our world go around. It greases the wheels of commerce, provides us with life's basics such as food and shelter, finances big-ticket items such as a home, a car, and our kids' college educations, and pays for special extras such as a family vacation. Where would we be without it? However, money has a dark side, too. It can be the root of countless problems in our lives, both big and small. As the poet Ralph Waldo Emerson so wisely said, "Money often costs too much." Here are some examples of the potential costs of spending money and entering into financial transactions:

- You are hounded by angry creditors and aggressive debt collectors and are living on the verge of bankruptcy because you can't pay your bills.

- You hired a contractor and paid him a big chunk of money up front, and now you can't get him to finish the job.

- That cute used convertible you snapped up after a quick ride around the block has turned out to be a clunker, and you can't rely on it to get you to and from work.

- You are turned down for a mortgage loan because your credit record contains too many negatives.

- Your former landlord keeps promising to return your security deposit, but three months after moving out of your old apartment, you still haven't received it.

- You filed a large claim with your insurance company, but it refuses to pay the claim.

When you come face to face with the dark side of money, you almost inevitably are dealing with the law. Laws at all levels of government define your rights and obligations when you spend money, use your credit cards, shop for a loan, use insurance, rent a place to live, and so on. Those laws also provide you with potential remedies, or solutions, to money-related problems. They can even help you avoid problems in the first place.

However, most people know very little about their legal rights and responsibilities when it comes to money matters, so they make mistakes. More often than not, what they do know they learn at the school of hard knocks, and that can be an expensive education! Your mistakes can cause you to miss opportunities, create costly legal hassles, and lose important assets such as your home and car.

How This Book Can Help

Everyday Law Kit For Dummies provides you with the information you need to take control of your financial life, to make wise decisions about financial matters, to avoid legal hassles, and to resolve hassles as quickly and cheaply as possible. It's an invaluable resource whether you're just beginning to make money and apply for credit or you've been spending money and using credit for years.

Using clear language — not legal mumbo-jumbo or bureaucratic doublespeak — *Everyday Law Kit For Dummies* covers the gamut, from getting and using credit, dealing with too much debt, and filing for bankruptcy to purchasing and using insurance, buying a car, shopping for a home mortgage, and surviving a real estate closing. This book also tells you about your ATM and debit card rights, explains how to put a stop to telemarketing calls, helps you protect your rights as a tenant, maps out your way through the Medicare maze, and a lot more.

This book can help you preserve the assets you acquire through hard work and maybe a little luck so that you can enjoy them while you're alive and pass them on to your loved ones when you die. For example, it educates you about the importance of estate planning and teaches you how to write a simple will and use other estate-planning tools, including a living will and a durable power of attorney.

Everyday Law Kit For Dummies also includes a CD full of sample letters, forms, checklists, directories, and agreements that you can use to protect your legal rights and resolve problems on your own. The book's text contains references to the materials on the CD, but for the big picture, check out the "About the CD" appendix at the end of the book. It provides an item-by-item outline of the CD's contents.

How This Book Is Organized

Everyday Law Kit For Dummies is organized into six parts. Here's the scoop on what you will find in each one.

Part 1: Law School Fundamentals

The first chapter in this part explains the important role that contracts play in nearly every aspect of your financial life and shows you how to use them to ensure that you get what you pay for and that your legal rights are protected. The next chapter explains why you should hold on to important financial records and legal documents and describes which ones to keep, how long to keep them, and where to store them. The last three chapters in this part focus on legal problem-solving. They show you how to resolve problems without using the courts; then, if all else fails, we offer information on filing a lawsuit in small claims court. For serious and complex legal matters, you need to retain an attorney. We show you the ins and outs of hiring and working with an attorney when your legal problem is not a small claims matter.

Part II: Credit Matters

This part of *Everyday Law Kit For Dummies* covers everything from getting and using credit cards and applying for a bank loan to understanding what your credit record says about you, dealing with too much debt, and filing for bankruptcy. It ends on a hopeful note by teaching you how to rebuild your credit after your money troubles are behind you.

Part III: Other Money Matters

The third part of *Everyday Law Kit For Dummies* deals with a wide range of legal topics. For example, it tells you how to buy a new or used car and what to consider if you decide to lease rather than buy. It also covers the ins and outs of buying and using insurance, offering specific advice and information about auto and homeowners insurance. Other chapters in this part tell you how to deal with tax problems and how to make telemarketers stop calling and introduce you to estate-planning basics.

Part IV: Home Matters

Home is where the heart is, but for many of us, our home also represents our biggest financial obligation and most important investment. To help you complete your real estate transaction, the first chapter in this part guides you through the home-buying process from start to finish and offers plenty of advice and information for sellers, too. Another chapter teaches you what you need to know about mortgages. The final chapters in this part tell you how to hire and work with a home contractor and cover issues important to renters, including leases, landlord problems, evictions, and security deposits.

Part V: Personal Matters

Taking care of ourselves and our loved ones is, for most people, the highest priority. Living our daily lives involves risks that could drastically change the quality of life for our families. Buying insurance can be a messy endeavor filled with confusing terminology and a miasma of regulations and fine print. Chapter 19 provides some clarity in the fog and helps make sense of life and health insurance. As you get older, you need to consider how you will fund your healthcare during retirement. Medicare, Medicaid, Medigap . . . oh my. Check out Chapter 20 for clear and understandable advice and explanations on these topics.

Part VI: The Part of Tens

The Part of Tens is a special feature of every . . . *For Dummies* book, and *Everyday Law Kit For Dummies* is no exception. This part includes three short chapters. One tells you about the ten best ways to learn more about the laws that affect your life. (Reading this book is one good way!) The second chapter introduces you to ten organizations that can help you cope when you have a money-related legal problem, and the third describes ten different legal Web sites that can assist, inform, and educate you about the laws that affect you.

Some Advice About Using This Book

You need to know a few things to get the most out of this book. *Everyday Law Kit For Dummies* focuses on the federal laws that affect your life because those laws apply to you no matter where you live. However, we let you know when your state might have its own laws related to a particular money matter and tell you how to discover what those laws are.

The information in this book and on the CD is not necessarily a substitute for a lawyer's advice and assistance. Although there are plenty of times when it's okay to address the law yourself, sometimes acting as your own lawyer can be downright dangerous. We let you know when an attorney's help is essential.

The steps we recommend that you take before you enter into an important transaction, such as renting an apartment, getting a mortgage, purchasing insurance, and choosing a credit card, represent an extremely thorough approach to financial decision-making. But we are realists, and we know that you may not have the time to follow every step; sometimes our advice may be impractical or even unnecessary given your particular circumstances. Therefore, we trust you to decide for yourself how much of it applies to you. However (and it's a big however), do not ignore our legal warnings and admonitions. Doing so could be damaging to your financial health.

Icons Used in This Book

As you read through the chapters in this book, you will notice funny little symbols in the margins of the pages. These symbols are called icons. Here's a rundown of what each icon in *Everyday Law Kit For Dummies* tells you.

Look here for special advice and information that can save you time, money, and legal headaches.

This icon reminds you about something important that's presented in an earlier chapter of the book.

When you want to find out as much as possible about a particular topic, read the information next to this icon.

Pay special attention to this icon! It alerts you to something you'd better do or not do if you want to stay out of trouble.

This icon refers you to sample forms, letters, legal documents, and more on the CD.

Part I
Law School Fundamentals

The 5th Wave   By Rich Tennant

"What's the chance of settling this without getting attorneys involved?"

HARVARD LAW SCHOOL ALUMNI PICNIC

ANTS, GNATS AND BEES

In this part . . .

Part I of this book introduces you to the fundamental concepts and skills you need to protect your legal rights when you spend your money. Chapter 1 shows you how to use contracts to formalize the important agreements and financial transactions you make throughout your life. Chapter 2 advises you about which legal documents and other records to hold on to and how long to keep them. Chapter 3 explains how to resolve problems without hiring a lawyer or filing a lawsuit. Chapter 4 tells you how to use small claims court to resolve problems that involve relatively small amounts of money, and Chapter 5 explains how to hire and work with an attorney if your legal matter does not qualify for small claims court.

Chapter 1

Contracts Rule!

· ·

In This Chapter

▶ Understanding what makes a contract legally binding

▶ Appreciating the value of a written contract

▶ Drafting your own contracts

▶ Dealing with contract problems

· ·

You may not realize it, but your life is full of contracts. Among other things, these legally binding agreements define and clarify the terms of your relationships with other people as well as with businesses and organizations, and they give you certain rights and responsibilities. Contracts can help keep you out of legal hot water and help you work things out when problems do develop.

This chapter provides a crash course in contracts. It shows you what makes a contract legally binding and why a written contract is usually better than an oral one. It provides advice for drafting your own contract, together with examples of common contracts, and tells you when to hire a lawyer to draft a contract for you. After finishing this chapter, you won't be a contracts expert; however, you will be more prepared to use contracts to protect yourself, and you will have a new appreciation of what to consider when you're asked to sign a contract that someone else has prepared.

Knowing a Contract When You See It

A *contract* is a legally binding, voluntary agreement between you and someone else. The term *legally binding* means that if a party to a contract you enter into violates the terms of the agreement, you have a legal right to enforce it, including by filing a lawsuit.

Some contracts are oral. For example, if you and the high school kid next door agree that he will mow your lawn once a month for $25, you have an oral contract with one another. Other contracts are written. Examples of written contracts include the paperwork you sign when you buy a home or car, rent an apartment, borrow money from a bank, or join a health club. Still other contracts are understood. For example, when you fill your shopping cart with groceries, you enter a tacit understanding between you and the store that for the right to shop there, you will pay for the items in your cart.

Making a Contract Legally Binding

Don't assume that every agreement you make in life is a legally binding contract. If you make such an assumption and problems develop later, you may discover that you don't have a legal leg to stand on. To be legally binding, your agreement must have certain characteristics. For example, legally binding contracts include the following:

- ✔ **Offer:** A specific, unambiguous statement of what's being agreed to.

- ✔ **Consideration:** An exchange of something of value between the parties. That something of value could be money, goods, services, giving up something, promising to do something, and so on. In the lawn-mowing example, the consideration is that the high school kid gets $25 and you get your lawn mowed.

- ✔ **Acceptance:** An agreement that there is a deal based on the offer and the consideration. The parties to a contract can verbally agree that they have a deal, or they can sign a written agreement. You can also have an acceptance agreement if the parties to a contract behave as though they have a deal. For example, if the high school kid never tells you one way or another whether he's willing to mow your lawn for $25, but on the day after you make him the offer, he mows your lawn, he demonstrates his acceptance, and you're obligated to pay him.

When you make an offer, the other party might give you a conditional acceptance. For example, if the high school kid accepts your offer with the condition that you will remove the tree limbs in your yard first, he is giving you a conditional acceptance. If you don't remove the limbs, you do not have a contract with one another. Three other things make a contract legally binding:

- ✔ All parties to it must be legal adults — age 18 or 21, depending on your state. Minors can enter into contracts for necessary items such as food and clothing, but not for extras or luxury items, such as a new car.

- ✔ All parties must have the mental capacity to appreciate the significance of the agreement. If you enter into a contract with a mentally incompetent person and the contract's validity is contested in court, the court will not uphold your agreement. The definition of "mental capacity" varies from state to state.

 ✔ The contract can't violate any local, state, or federal laws. In other words, a court will not help enforce a contract related to illegal drugs, illegal gambling, and the like.

Putting It Down in Black and White

Written contracts are almost always best, although most states enforce oral contracts. A written contract is essential if the subject of an agreement you're making is complex, it involves a lot of money, it extends for a long period of time, or the subject of the contract is particularly important to you. And by *written contract,* we don't mean words scribbled on the back of a cocktail napkin, although in some instances, courts have upheld cocktail napkin contracts.

It's important to put all but the simplest agreements in black and white because

 ✔ Writing things down helps clarify expectations and responsibilities and minimizes the potential for contractual problems in the future. When an agreement is oral, it's too easy to be casual about issues that could come back to haunt you later.

 ✔ You have something tangible to refer to in case confusion about the terms of your agreement arises. When confusion arises over an oral agreement, all you have to clear things up is your collective memories, and you can be almost certain that everyone's memory will differ.

 ✔ If you end up in a lawsuit over a contract, it's easier to sort things out when everything is in writing.

To protect against consumer fraud, most states require that contracts for certain transactions be in writing and signed. The federal law that covers these transactions is called *The Statute of Frauds.* The transactions covered are real estate transactions, including multiyear real estate leases; deals taking longer than one year to complete; buying or selling of goods worth more than $500 (in most states); and guaranteeing someone else's debt.

Drafting your own contracts

If the agreement you're making is simple and straightforward, it does not involve a lot of money, and you feel comfortable negotiating its terms, you can prepare your own legally binding written contract. To be enforceable, your contract does not have to be filled with legalese or span many pages.

However, it does need to conform to all the requirements for a legal contract. Here are some easy-to-follow guidelines for drafting a good contract:

- Use clear and concise language to describe what you're agreeing to. Use phrases like "I will" and "You will not" rather than "It would be nice if" and "I hope that you won't." Avoid promises to do something at an ill-defined date in the future.

- Address all the important details of your agreement — who, what, when, where, and how much. Spell out everyone's responsibilities, all applicable deadlines, and the penalties for missed deadlines.

- Don't assume that everything will go according to plan, even if you're entering into a contract with a friend or relative. Instead, when you're drafting a contract, identify all the things that could possibly go wrong with your deal and address each eventuality in the agreement. The contract checklist in the sidebar "Making a list and checking it twice" can help you make sure that your contract covers all the bases.

- Don't assume that your first contract draft will be your final contract. The other parties to your contract may want to add or subtract things, and getting everything right can take a couple of tries.

- Consider hiring an attorney to review and revise your draft. The lawyer can suggest things to add or delete and can fine-tune your language to ensure that the terms of the agreement are clear and that they protect your interests and rights. You should not have to pay a lot for this kind of legal help, and spending a little money on up-front legal help could save you a bucket of cash down the road.

- Once you have a final contract, make sure that the other party signs the contract. Depending on the laws of your state, the contract may have to be notarized, too. All parties to the contract should receive a copy of the signed contract. Keep the original for your files.

A sample form contract can help you get a jump-start on the drafting process. Although it may not apply to your situation word for word, it can provide you with a basic format to follow. The sidebar "Sources of sample contracts online" points out Web sites offering legal documents that you can print and use. The section "Getting Around the Limitations of a Form Contract" later in this chapter provides additional guidance about these types of contracts. For step-by-step help in drafting a basic contract, go to www.legaldocs.com/docs/gencon_1.mv.

Some contracts include a clause requiring that disputes related to the contract be resolved through arbitration rather than through mediation or lawsuit. *Arbitration* is a non-court method of dispute resolution that's less formal and less expensive than a trial. After a hearing in which both parties present their arguments, a neutral arbitrator decides how the dispute will be settled. *Mediation,* another form of dispute resolution, helps disputing parties work together to find a mutually acceptable resolution.

Warranty of words

A *warranty* is an implied or expressed guarantee of a product's quality and performance. Most new products and services come with written warranties. A warranty may be part of a contract, or it may be a separate contract. For example, when you purchase an extended warranty for your new car, that warranty is a contract separate and apart from the one you signed when you bought the car. Two basic types of warranties exist — *express* and *implied.*

✔ **Express warranty:** An express warranty can be conveyed verbally, in writing, or through advertising. It is a statement or a promise about what a product or service does or doesn't do. Written warranties for consumer goods are governed by the federal Magnuson-Moss Act. This law says that if a product comes with a written warranty, you must have an opportunity to read the warranty before you buy the product. It also says that the warranty must clearly indicate what the warranty covers, how long the warranty lasts, who is making the warranty (name and address of company), what to do if you have a problem with the warranty, and an overview of your legal rights. It also says that the warranty must indicate whether it is a full or limited warranty. A *full warranty* says that the product you purchase will be replaced or repaired at no cost to you during the warranty period. Most *limited warranties* cover parts only. If you're comparison-shopping for a product or service and it comes with a written warranty, don't make your purchase decision on price alone. Take the warranty details into consideration.

✔ **Implied warranty:** Products that do not come with written warranties usually carry implied warranties. The duration of these warranties depends on the laws of your state. Call the consumer protection office of your state attorney general's office to find out the specifics of the law in your state.

One type of implied warranty is a *warranty of merchantabililty,* which promises that a product you buy will do what it's supposed to do. For example, the refrigerator you bought will keep your food cold enough not to spoil; your new answering machine will record the messages that callers leave for you; and a certain model of car will tow your boat trailer.

Another kind of implied warranty is a *warranty of fitness.* This warranty applies when you purchase something because you have been told that it meets your particular needs. For example, a salesperson tells you that the portable heater you purchased for your greenhouse gives off enough heat to keep your plants from freezing when temperatures fall below zero.

If you purchase a product "as is," the seller does not make any promises about how well it works or whether it meets your needs. Some states prohibit the sale of certain types of products on an as-is basis.

The best way to protect your warranty rights is to save the printed copy of the warranty (if it's in writing) and to hold on to all receipts related to the product during the warranty period. Also, be sure that you meet your obligations vis-a-vis the warranty, or you risk voiding it. For example, if you purchase a new car, you must have it serviced on a particular schedule to maintain its warranty. If you have a problem with a warrantied product, talk to the company that sold you the product. It may be able to help you out. Otherwise, contact the maker of the product in writing according to the instructions in the warranty paperwork.

E-SIGNs of the times

Last year, Congress passed the Electronic Signatures in Global and National Commerce Bill, popularly known as the E-SIGN Bill. With a few exceptions, this bill gives the electronic contract you "sign" online the same legal weight as an old-fashioned paper contract. The new law covers such transactions as buying a car, getting a mortgage, purchasing insurance, and buying financial products, among other things.

The law also allows businesses to meet their legal obligation to provide you with certain legal notifications by sending them to you electronically rather than by mail, assuming you give your consent to receive them that way. However, the law also requires that businesses continue to send you paper notices about urgent matters such as the disconnection of your utilities, foreclosures, evictions, and defaults.

Although the concept of digital signatures may sound appealing, digital signatures present some potential drawbacks to consumers including the possibility of not reading an online contract as carefully and thoroughly as you would a paper contract. Therefore, you may agree to things you will regret later. Also, if you do not check your e-mail regularly, you may not read an important notice until it's too late.

Credit card companies, stock brokerages, banks, consumer finance firms, insurance companies, and HMOs often include a mandatory arbitration clause in their consumer contracts. The problem with this kind of clause is that it not only limits your problem-solving options to just arbitration, but it typically gives the company, not you, the right to select the arbitrator. The arbitrator the company chooses is apt to depend on the company for a steady stream of income and, therefore, is less likely to decide the dispute in your favor. Another drawback of arbitration is that it can be quite expensive. For additional information about mediation, arbitration, and mandatory arbitration clauses, see Chapter 3.

Sources of sample contracts online

The Internet is a good place to find sample contracts that you can use to draw up your own agreements. Some specific sites to visit are www.lawsmart.com. This Web site provides free forms and legal documents organized by legal topic. Also check out www.legaldocs.com. Use this Web site to prepare online, customized legal documents that you can print or download to your computer. Fees may apply if you decide to use certain documents, but you can preview all the documents for free. Visit legal-resource.com where after entering your name and e-mail address, you can gain access to an extensive number of sample legal documents.

Making a list and checking it twice

This laundry list of possible contract provisions can help you ensure that you don't overlook anything important when you're drafting a contract. An excellent list of provisions you need to address in a contract is on the CD on Form 1-6.

Creating a Contract to Loan Money

A written loan agreement or promissory note protects you when you loan someone money. If you're loaning someone a significant amount of money — more than $1,000 — or if you want the borrower to secure your loan by collateralizing it with real estate, hire an attorney to draft the agreement for you. Otherwise, you can draft the agreement yourself. Be sure that the borrower signs and dates it. Include the following information:

- Your name as the lender and the amount of money you're lending and the interest rate you're charging.

  Be reasonable about the rate of interest you charge. If the rate is excessive, you may violate your state's usury laws. Your state attorney general's can tell you what's reasonable.

- When the payments must begin, when the last payment is due, and to what address each payment should be sent.

- Whether a late loan payment carries a penalty and, if it does, when it will be assessed and how much it will be.

- Whether a bounced check carries a penalty and, if it does, the amount of the penalty.

- When the borrower will be in default of the loan and what will happen to the borrower's collateral, if there is any.

- Provisions related to prepayment. (If you charge interest on the loan and you want to maximize the amount of interest income you receive, you may want to prohibit prepayment or charge a penalty for prepayment to make up for the interest you will not receive.)

- Any other provisions you want to include. Refer to the sidebar "Making a list and checking it twice" for possible provisions to add.

Form 1-1 on the CD is a sample unsecured loan agreement. For an easy way to draft a simple promissory agreement, go to www.legaldocs.com/docs/note_1.mv.

Protecting yourself by securing your loan

When you lend someone a substantial amount of money, address the possibility that the borrower might default on your loan or might fail to repay it according to the terms of your agreement. You can provide yourself some security by requiring that the borrower give you a lien on an asset she owns. The lien gives you a legal claim to that asset, or the right to take the asset if the borrower doesn't live up to the agreement. The asset on which you place a lien should be comparable in value to the amount of your loan. Be sure to *perfect* your lien so that your claim will be official in the eyes of the court. Perfecting a lien involves filing certain paperwork with local, county, or state authorities.

When you place a lien on someone's property, you become a secured creditor. If the borrower later files for bankruptcy, that status makes it more likely that you will get at least some of the money you're owed. Unsecured creditors get little or nothing in most consumer bankruptcies.

Perfecting your lien

How to perfect your lien depends on whether the lien is on the borrower's personal property (such as furniture or computer equipment), real estate, a vehicle, or another titled asset such as a mobile home, boat, or motorcycle. Perfecting a lien on real estate can be tricky business! Don't try to do it without an attorney's guidance.

Perfecting a lien on personal property

Follow this advice to perfect a lien when it's on personal property. You may be able to find the form you need online. Get a Uniform Commercial Code 1 (UCC1) form from your secretary of state's office. Fill it out and file it with that office. You have to pay a filing fee. Although fees vary by state, you will pay less than $50. Form 1-2 on the CD provides a sample UCC1 form from Texas.

Perfecting a lien on real estate (otherwise known as a mortgage)

When you secure a loan with real estate, the process for perfecting the lien is a little more complicated. You should hire an attorney to draw up the lien paperwork and file a copy of your loan agreement and the real estate lien paperwork with the county where the property is located.

Perfecting a lien on the borrower's vehicle, motorcycle, and so on

When you're owed money for a vehicle such as a car or motorcycle, you need to follow some formal procedures that ensure you can get the vehicle back if the borrower fails to pay. To perfect such a lien, ask your state department of motor vehicles (or the motor vehicle department where the vehicle is registered) to issue a new title to the vehicle showing you as a lien holder. To do so, you need the vehicle's current title and a copy of the signed loan agreement.

Preparing a Contract to Sell Something

You do not need a contract, or *bill of sale,* when you sell something of relatively little value, such as a used lawn mower or miscellaneous books. However, if your transaction involves something more valuable, such as a motorcycle, a car, a set of furniture, artwork, jewelry, or computer equipment, protect yourself with a bill of sale.

Remember: Depending on the price of what you're selling, state law may require that you have a written contract. If you write your own bill of sale, be sure to include your name and address, the buyer's name and address, and a short description of what you're selling. Be specific — use exact numbers and avoid words such as *several* and *some.*

If your bill of sale is for a vehicle, be sure to include the VIN, or Vehicle Identification Number. This number is typically found inside the driver's side corner of the windshield or on the inside edge of the driver's side door.

If you're selling a car, a mobile home, a motorcycle, or anything else with a title, and if the buyer is going to pay you for the property over time, be sure to place a lien on that asset and perfect the lien according to the advice offered in the preceding section of this chapter.

- ✔ The price of the item you're selling and any guarantees you're making. Clearly state the guarantee.

- ✔ Whether you're selling an item as is. When you sell something as is, you make no promises about its condition or how well it performs or operates. On the bill of sale, make the words *as is* as conspicuous as possible by putting them in bold type, underlining them, or making the type larger than the rest of type in the bill of sale.

- ✔ Any special terms of sale that apply. For example, are you responsible for delivering the item to the buyer or for making repairs or improvements to the item?

Form 1-3 on the CD provides a sample bill of sale.

Getting Around the Limitations of a Form Contract

A *form contract* is a standardized contract with spaces for writing in the information that's specific to your situation. A lease is a common example of this kind of contract. This book's CD provides a variety of sample form contracts. You can find others at legal Web sites, at office supply stores, and in software programs.

Using a form contract can be a quick, easy alternative to writing a contract from scratch. However, it's important to understand the limitations with form contracts and to know how to deal with those limitations. To use a form contract effectively, follow these guidelines:

- Make sure that the form contract includes any provisions and language that your state requires. (Some form contracts are state-specific.) To find out about your state's requirements, call the office of the secretary of state or talk with an attorney.

  When provisions or language is missing, add it to the contract, assuming that there's enough space. Every party to the contract should initial each addition. If there isn't enough space, type the additions on a separate sheet of paper and attach the sheet to the contract as an addendum. The addendum as well as the contract should be signed.

- Read the contract carefully to make sure that it addresses all the issues of concern to you and that it's not missing provisions that are important to you. Many form contracts are quite general. If things are missing, add them to the contract or put them in an addendum. If you're unhappy with some of the contract's language or provisions, delete by lining out what you don't like and date and initial each change.

- Don't sign a form contract unless every blank is filled in. If you do, you might later discover that the blanks were filled in for you, and you may not be happy with what you have agreed to. If a blank relates to a provision that does not apply to your situation, write "N/A" in that space.

- Use pen, not pencil, when you fill in the blanks on a form contract. Someone can erase pencil to add different information.

Some form loan contracts have a place for indicating whether you want to purchase insurance on the loan. Insurance purchased this way is usually quite expensive. If you have to insure the loan, buy your own insurance — don't let the lender do it for you.

Knowing what to do before you sign someone else's contract

When you're asked to sign a contract that someone else drafted, read it carefully line by line to ensure that it meets your needs, protects your legal rights, and does not obligate you to do something you can't or don't want to do. Don't ignore the fine print; sometimes the most important information is buried there. You should also

- ✔ Ask questions about anything you do not understand so that you can be absolutely clear about what you're agreeing to. If you end up in court over a contract dispute, telling the judge that you didn't read what you signed, or that you didn't understand what you were agreeing to, doesn't make a convincing defense.

- ✔ Talk with the contract drafter about your concerns if you see things in the contract that you don't like. Suggest changes, deletions, and additions as appropriate. If you can't come to a meeting of the minds and your concerns are significant, don't sign the contract.

- ✔ Walk away from the deal if you're being pressured to sign a contract that you're unsure about.

- ✔ Refuse to sign a contract if it involves a lot of money, obligates you to its terms for a long period of time, or deals with something that is important to you, until an attorney reviews it for you. Another option is to hire an attorney to handle the contract from start to finish — from the first to the final negotiations.

Your state may require that you hire an attorney to represent you when you're negotiating the terms of certain kinds of contracts, such as a prenuptial agreement. Keeping all contract drafts and all correspondence related to a contract is a good idea. You may need them if a contract dispute arises.

Managing contracts with little or no wiggle room

Certain business contracts are so standardized, and give you so little room for negotiation, that they are best characterized as "take it or leave it" (also known as *adhesion* contracts) agreements. Credit card agreements, the paperwork you sign when you lease a rental car, and contracts to purchase insurance are common examples of these contracts.

Although usually you can do little or nothing to change the terms of these agreements, you should still read them carefully to find out what you're agreeing to. Among other things, you need to know under what circumstances you would be in violation of the agreement, the consequences, and whether you have a right to sue.

Modifying a contract

Once you enter into a contract, you may decide that you want to change some aspect of the agreement. For example, living up to the terms of the contract may become a hardship for you, perhaps because you move or because your income drops. Your first step should be to find out what your contract says about making modifications to it. If it's silent on the issue, amending the contract requires the agreement of all parties. If you can't come to an agreement, you're legally bound to live up to the contract unless you can get a court to declare it invalid.

If everyone agrees to the changes you want to make, and if those changes are quite minor, draft your own contract amendment. At a minimum, the amendment should indicate the date of the original contract; the parties to the contract; the subject of the contract; the specific changes you're making; a statement that all provisions in the original contract remain in force, except the changes detailed in the amendment; and a statement that the amendment prevails in any conflicts related to the original contract. You can find a sample contract modification agreement on Form 1-4 on the CD.

Don't rely on an oral agreement when you want to change a contract. Oral arguments don't give you the protection you need in a dispute. Put the changes in writing. If you're making a lot of changes to a contract, or if the changes are significant, you should cancel the first contract in writing and draft a new one. When you cancel the original contract, indicate that all provisions in the second contract supersede the first. Making a lot of changes to a contract can be risky. The other party to the contract may decide to make changes, too, and you may not like them.

Getting Out of a Contract

Generally, when you enter into a contract, you're legally obligated to live up to it even if you later regret that you made the agreement. After all, if everyone could cancel contracts at the slightest whim, the contracts wouldn't be worth the paper they were printed on.

Even so, you can sometimes cancel a contract. For example, when you buy something from a retailer, you often have the right to return your purchase for a refund or store credit, assuming that you do so within a certain period. Also, when you sign a contract in your home to purchase something, such as the proverbial set of encyclopedias, or to have your home repaired, you usually have the right to cancel the deal within a specific period. That right is called the *right of rescission.* (You can find out more about this right in subsequent chapters of this book.) You also have the right to cancel a contract when

- ✔ You can prove that the other party to your contract misled you or used fraud to get you to enter into the agreement, or you can prove that you were pressured into the contract or were *under duress.*

- ✔ The other party to the contract fails to live up to his contractual obligations.

- ✔ Circumstances make it impossible for you to live up to the contract. For example, after you hire a roofer to put a new roof on your home, the house burns to the ground.

- ✔ The contract you signed is "unconscionable" or "against public policy."

Sometimes, you can buy your way out of a contract. Get legal advice if you want to explore this option. Get legal help if you want to break a contract. An attorney can tell you whether you have a legal basis for canceling and, assuming that you do, can advise you about the best way to proceed. If you terminate a contract without a legal basis, or if you do not follow the appropriate process for canceling it, you could find yourself in a lawsuit for breach of contract.

Knowing when a contract is breached

Breach is a fancy word for *break.* It's also the legal term that describes what happens when someone doesn't live up to her contractual obligations. *Default* is the term used when someone fails to repay a loan according to the terms of a loan agreement. A contract is breached when

- ✔ A party to a contract fails to do what was promised. For example, if you hire a company to service your pool twice a month and the company never shows up, it has breached your contract.

- ✔ A party to a contract makes it impossible for the other party to live up to its terms. Returning to the pool-cleaning example, if the company keeps coming to your home to clean your pool according to your contract but can't do the job because you leave for work without unlocking the gate to your pool, then you have breached the contract. And if you fail to pay for the service in a timely manner, you have breached the contract.

- ✔ One party to a contract repudiates the contract or states that he has no intention to abide by it. For example, if you agree to sell something to someone for a certain price and work out all the details, and then you turn around and sell the item to someone else, you have repudiated your contract.

Dealing with a breached contract

When someone breaches a contract to which you're a party, your first step should be to read what the contract says about breaches. It may require that you go to mediation or arbitration, or it may allow you to use other legal means to resolve your problem, including filing a lawsuit. (Chapter 3 discusses how mediation and arbitration work.)

If the contract that has been breached involves a lot of money or is important to you for some other reason, hire an attorney to help you deal with your problem. If you're not limited in regard to how you can get the breach cured, consider this list of options:

✔ Send a polite letter to the party who has breached the contract. Your letter should clearly state what provision of the contract has been breached, provide the other party an opportunity to *cure* (or correct) the breach, and specify a date by which the breach must be cured. Unless you provide the party an opportunity to live up to her end of the bargain, you open yourself to the possibility that you will be accused of breaching the contract yourself! If your first letter gets nowhere, send a second letter. Keep copies of the letters you send and any letters you receive in response. A sample contract breach letter is Form 1-5 on the CD.

Don't assume that you can cure a breach by withholding payment. If you do, you risk breaching the contract yourself. Consult an attorney.

✔ Ask the party who breached the contract to agree to let you cure the breach and to reimburse you for any costs you incur in doing so. Another option is to deduct the cost of curing the breach from the dollar amount you owe him. If the party who breached the contract agrees to this arrangement, put it in writing. Both of you should sign the agreement. If it says that you will cure the breach, attach to your copy of the agreement all receipts for the expenses you incur in doing so.

✔ Ask the breaching party to resolve your differences by going to mediation or arbitration. (Making mediation or arbitration a contract requirement is a good idea.)

✔ File a lawsuit or walk away from the problem.

Document any contract problems as soon as they begin. Note the nature of the problem, the date it occurs, what you try to do about it, and how the other party responds.

There's a danger in creating a written record of what you do to try to resolve your contract problems. If you sue the other party to the contract, you could be legally required to share copies of your written record with the defendant.

Chapter 2

Filing It or Deep-Sixing It

In This Chapter
▶ Knowing which records to keep
▶ Understanding how long to keep your records
▶ Deciding where to store your records

Reading about record keeping is probably not going to keep you on the edge of your seat. However, having the right legal documents and records and being able to access them when you need them can be key to protecting your legal rights and nipping legal problems in the bud. For example, the right documents and information can help you get your money's worth out of a contract, avoid trouble with the IRS, and ensure that you receive the medical care and treatment you want when you're too ill or injured to speak for yourself.

The right documentation can also minimize the amount of capital gains taxes you pay when you sell your home, can ensure that your assets are transferred to the people you care about after your death, and can win lawsuits.

This chapter helps you get your documents and records in order. To do so, it outlines how long to keep certain information and where to keep it. The chapter also features a list that summarizes the basic legal documents you need, depending on the circumstances of your life.

Knowing What to Keep and How Long to Keep It

Most people know that hanging on to certain financial records, legal documents, and pieces of correspondence is important. However, many are unsure of which records to keep and how long to keep them. Some people decide to cover all their bases by saving years' worth of receipts, canceled checks, tax returns, loan documents, and so on in an ever-growing collection of bags, boxes, or file cabinets. Others save very little and get rid of what they do save regularly.

If you save everything, putting your fingers on what you need when you need it can be a major challenge; however, if you save very little, you risk getting rid of the wrong stuff. With either approach, you're unlikely to have the information you need to plan your finances and resolve problems. Therefore, this section helps clear up your confusion by giving you the lowdown on how long to hold on to important legal records and other information related to your taxes, your estate planning, and your home.

Your tax returns

After you file your federal tax return, hold on to it for at least ten years. After that time is up, except under unusual circumstances, the IRS cannot come after you to collect additional taxes and cannot audit your return. However, there's no time limit on how long after you file a return the IRS can come after you if it suspects that the return is false or fraudulent. Therefore, to be on the safe side, you may want to hold on to your returns forever.

Keep all backup information for each tax return for as long you keep the return itself. This information can include W-2s and 1099s, canceled checks, bank statements, charitable donation records, receipts for out-of-pocket medical expenses, payment records for contributions you make to a retirement account, proof of alimony and child support payments you make, and information documenting the amount of mortgage interest and property taxes you pay. If you have a home office, your backup data should also include anything that helps prove the home office deductions you claim.

Your home

Hold tight to the deed to your home until you sell the home. Also save all receipts and any other dated information that help document the amount of money you spend on capital improvements you make to your residence. *Capital improvements* are improvements that increase the home's value, not minor repairs and routine maintenance expenses. This information helps you minimize the amount of capital gains tax you pay on the sale of your home, assuming that you sell it for a profit. (If you're married, the first $500,000 of any gain is exempt from taxation; if you're single, it's the first $250,000.) After you sell your home, hold on to all the information for three more years.

Potential homebuyers may want to see your improvement receipts to help them justify paying your asking price. You might also want to save your home's utility bills for a year and maintain an inventory of your household items indefinitely for insurance purposes and for estate-planning purposes. Next to each item on your list, note its approximate value. Update your inventory as necessary.

Estate planning

Save indefinitely your will, healthcare directives (living will and durable power of attorney for healthcare), and any other estate-planning documents you have. Other estate-planning documents include your life insurance policy, trust agreements, power of attorney documents, and so on. Your executor should have a copy of your will. The trustee of any trust you set up should have a copy of the trust agreement, and the person with durable power of attorney for your healthcare should have a copy of your living will.

Other financial data

The financial records listed in this section may come in handy if there's any question about what you paid for by check or credit card, about your investments, or about your Social Security benefits, if you're eligible to receive them.

- **Canceled checks:** Toss your canceled checks after 24 months, assuming that they're not tax related and they don't relate to any improvements you make to your home. You can get rid of canceled checks for relatively routine items before that — assuming that you have the time to go through your canceled checks periodically.

- **Credit card statements:** Keep your monthly credit card statements for a year unless you need them to back up your tax return, or to prove payment on something really important.

- **Stocks and mutual funds:** Save stock and mutual fund purchase information (date purchased and the price you paid) as well as year-end summary information for at least four years after you sell a stock or mutual fund. The information can help you avoid paying more taxes than you should after you sell a stock or mutual fund for a profit.

- **Social Security information:** File indefinitely all your pension and Social Security information, including benefit information and correspondence related to your benefits.

- **IRAs:** Save indefinitely all records related to the contributions you make to your Individual Retirement Account (IRA) and to your withdrawals from it.

Family documents

Save all the following family-related documents indefinitely:

- Birth certificates
- Adoption papers
- Prenuptial and postnuptial agreements

- ✔ Marriage certificates
- ✔ Divorce decrees
- ✔ Military records
- ✔ Death certificates

Miscellaneous

Make room in your filing cabinet for the documents and records listed in this section. You never know when you'll need them.

- ✔ **Contracts:** Keep important contracts until they're no longer in effect or until enough time has passed that you feel sure neither you nor the other party can be accused of breaching it. For example, you may not discover that the work a contractor did for you was defective until months after the term of the contract has ended. Being able to refer to your contract is an important first step in resolving the matter with your contractor.

- ✔ **Vehicle titles:** Keep the titles to your vehicles until you sell them.

- ✔ **Receipts:** Retain receipts for your major purchases until you're sure that the item you bought is not defective or until its warranty runs out. Staple receipts for a warrantied item to the warranty itself.

- ✔ **Insurance:** Save your insurance policies for at least a year after they expire.

- ✔ **Medical bills:** Hold on to your medical bills and the canceled checks that correspond to them for a year. However, if the information relates to a serious medical problem, you may want to keep it indefinitely.

Maintain the following information indefinitely:

- ✔ Your bank account numbers and the names and addresses of your banks. If the IRS audits you sometime in the future, you may have to prove that you had accounts at these banks as well as what funds went into and out of those accounts. Being able to prove this can be particularly important if you own a small business or work out of your home.

- ✔ The name of your banker.

- ✔ Your credit card numbers and the address and telephone number of each company you have a credit card with.

- ✔ The location of all your important financial and legal documents.

- ✔ The location of your safe deposit box and its contents.

- ✔ A list of your insurance policies and contact information for each of your insurance beneficiaries.

- ✔ The name, address, and telephone number of your estate's executor.
- ✔ The name, address, and telephone number of anyone to whom you have given power of attorney.
- ✔ The name, address, and telephone number for the trustee of any trust you set up.
- ✔ The name, address, and telephone number of your lawyer.
- ✔ The name, address, and telephone number of your CPA.
- ✔ The name, address, and telephone number of your financial advisor.

Keeping Important Documents Safe

Store hard-to-replace items and other important documents in a home safe or in a bank safe deposit box. The fee for renting the safe deposit box depends on the size of the box, but even a large one doesn't cost much. Make copies of everything so you have easy access to the information at home. Be sure that someone besides you knows the location of the key to your bank safe deposit box as well as the combination to your home safe.

Depending on your state, access to your safe deposit box might be limited for a period of time after you die. Therefore, check with an estate-planning attorney before you store in this box anything that your executor and others might need immediately after your death.

You can keep most of the other documents and information mentioned in this chapter in your home in whatever kind of record-keeping system works for you and your family — a filing cabinet, a desk drawer, labeled cardboard boxes, plastic storage bins, or even paper bags. No matter what record keeping system you choose, it should be easy to use and update.

Computer software makes it easy to create and maintain important records. Quicken Basic and Quicken Deluxe (both published by Intuit) are two excellent and easy-to-use software programs that can help you organize your investing, banking, and tax information. Quicken has versions for Windows and the Mac.

Your home computer is a good place to keep lists of information, an extra copy of your will, and so on. However, make sure that the executor of your estate, the person with durable power of attorney, trusted family members, and so on know what documents and records are on your computer and how to find what they need. Also, be sure to back up the information on your computer and to keep a hard copy of everything as well. Computers are not fail-safe.

Knowing Which Legal Documents You May Need

Not everyone has or needs the same legal documents. What's right for you may be unnecessary for someone else — it all depends on the circumstances of your life. This list provides an overview of the basic legal documents you need, depending on your life circumstances. It also provides information about the healthcare-related documents everyone should have, no matter what your circumstances.

If you're a renter, keep a copy of your lease, a copy of your rental application, and your renter's insurance policy

If you're a landlord, keep your tenant's lease, your tenant's rental application, your rental property liability insurance policy, and the title to your rental property.

If you're a homeowner, keep the title to your home and all insurance policies related to your home and its contents

If you own real property and other assets, keep a will and maybe a trust as well and power of attorney for your finances

If you're the parent of minor children, keep a will designating a legal and a property guardian for your children.

No matter what your circumstances, you should keep a living will, a health-care power of attorney, and an organ donation card.

Chapter 3

Resolving Problems without Lawsuits

*T*V legal dramas would have you think that nearly every legal problem in life is resolved through a lawsuit and an emotionally charged courtroom battle. In fact, most problems are worked out by using cheaper, faster, and less stressful non-court methods. Those methods include friendly (or at least civil) conversations, polite letters, mediation, and arbitration. This chapter shows you how to use each of these methods effectively.

Talking It Out

It can be downright amazing what a calm, stick-to-the-point conversation can accomplish when you're having a problem with someone. Sometimes, simply sitting down together (or picking up the phone), stating your concerns, and listening to each other can clear the air and put an end to your trouble.

More often than not, when you talk things out, you discover that your problem is not the result of a deliberately malicious act, but rather the product of a simple misunderstanding or unrealistic expectations (a perfect example of why it's important to formalize important agreements with clearly written contracts). If your problem is with a business, it can also be due to a change of personnel, a lost document, a computer glitch, or some other innocent slip-up.

Preparing for your conversation

Spending even a short period planning for a problem solving conversation can reap dividends. Here are some suggestions for what you can do ahead of time to help make your conversation productive:

- ✓ Understand your legal rights and responsibilities. Don't ask for anything that you're not legally entitled to. If you have a written contract with the individual or business you're in conflict with, read what it says. Get educated by reading this book, checking out legal Web sites, calling the right government office, or talking with an attorney.

- ✓ Decide how you want to resolve your problem. If you come up with several options, write them all down and rank them from most acceptable to least acceptable.

- ✓ Think about what you're willing to give up to get what you want.

- ✓ Gather any receipts, check stubs, billing statements, and so on that relate to your problem.

- ✓ If your problem is with a business, find out who has the authority to help resolve it. That's the person you want to talk to. If the business is relatively small, you will probably talk with its owner or manager. For a large business, you're likely to deal with a staff person in the customer relations or consumer affairs office.

- ✓ If your problem is with an individual and your conversation will be face-to-face, agree on a neutral meeting place where you both feel comfortable, and that doesn't give either of you a psychological advantage over the other.

Consider inviting a neutral third party to sit in on your face-to-face conversation. She can help keep you focused on the problem you're trying to resolve and help calm everyone down if tempers start to flare.

If you come to an understanding

If your conversation resolves your problem, it's a good idea to put what you agree to in writing. Draft a statement of your agreement, and let the other party review it and make the necessary changes. Once your agreement is final, both of you should sign it and keep copies for your files. Form 3-1 on the CD provides a sample agreement that you can modify to fit your needs, depending on whether you're dealing with a business or an individual.

Talking tips

Talking things out is the cheapest and probably the fastest way to clear things up. Here are some tips on how to make the most of your conversation:

✔ Stay cool. If you yell, swear, or cry, you're apt to put the person you're talking with on the defensive and make him a lot less interested in working things out with you.

✔ Listen when the other person talks. Don't let your mind wander, and don't focus on what you want to say next. When you listen, you might hear the solution to your problem in the other person's words.

✔ Don't threaten or make accusations. If you do, you risk derailing the conversation.

✔ Don't yawn, look away, sigh, or drum your fingers on the table in a face-to-face conversation. Those kinds of behaviors may signal to the other person that you aren't really interested in what she's saying.

✔ Don't interrupt. Respect the other person's right to talk.

✔ Stay open to compromise, even if it means swallowing your pride and putting your ego on the back burner. A reasonable compromise can save you money, time, and hassle.

Harnessing the Power of the Pen

If talk gets you nowhere, try resolving your problem with a letter. Make your letter as specific as possible without going into needless details. Stick to the facts and avoid emotional rants or threats. If you want to express your frustration or anger, express it as a matter of fact rather than lash out. Here's an example of the wrong and right ways to do it:

> **Wrong:** "I am sick and tired of your pigheaded refusal to deal with this problem."

> **Right:** "I am growing increasingly frustrated by my inability to clear up this matter."

If any city, state, or federal laws apply to your problem, mention them in your letter and explain how they relate to what you're writing about. For example, if you're writing to your neighbor because she refuses to keep her dog from trampling through your gardens, and you know that your town has a law that prohibits dog owners from letting their dogs roam free, reference the law in your letter. If your problem involves a breach of contract, follow the advice in Chapter 1 for what to put in your letter.

Type your letter so it's readable. If you don't have access to a computer, print it neatly or take it to a typing service. After you have signed it, make a copy for your files. Make copies of any receipts, cancelled checks, billing statements, or other evidence you have that back up what you state in your letter and what you are requesting. Attach them to your letter.

To be sure that your letter reaches its destination, send it via certified mail and ask for a return receipt. You'll pay a little more than if you sent it regular mail, but the security of knowing that your letter got where you sent it can be worth the cost. Plus, you know who signed for the letter. If you have a bone to pick with a business, include the following information in your complaint letter:

- ✔ The date of your letter, the problem you're writing about, and when it occurred.

- ✔ What you have already done to resolve the problem and the outcome of your efforts to date.

- ✔ The names and titles of anyone you have spoken with so far.

- ✔ The outcome you're looking for. This could be getting a refund, an exchange, or a repair; getting something stopped; getting someone to do something; and so on.

- ✔ Applicable account numbers, serial, or model numbers.

- ✔ Warranty terms, if any.

- ✔ Your name, address, home and office numbers, and e-mail address.

- ✔ Date by which you would like a response. Within ten days is reasonable.

If you and the business have a written contract, be sure to refer to it in your letter. You can find a sample business complaint letter on page 34 of the *2001 Consumer Action Handbook* on the CD. If you get no response by the deadline stated in your letter, you can call to find out when you can expect a response or write a second letter, referencing your first one and setting a new deadline for a response.

If you're writing to a business, you may get faster action if you indicate in this second letter that you have sent a copy to your local Better Business Bureau, the trade or professional nonprofit organization to which the business belongs, or the appropriate government consumer protection office.

If you're writing to a local business that's part of a national company, let it know that a copy of your letter went to its national headquarters. Page 35 of the *2001 Consumer Action Handbook* on the CD provides contact information for more than 650 major corporations, including addresses, phone, and fax numbers for all and specific contact names and Web site addresses for many. If the national company you want to contact is not among those 650, find the information you need by searching the Internet or by using *The Standard & Poor's Register of Corporations, Directors, and Executives;* the *Dunn & Bradstreet Directory;* or a similar corporate directory. Your local library should have at least one of these reference books.

If you don't know the name of the national company you want to contact, you can find it on a product label or in your warranty information. Many local TV and radio stations have consumer-advocate reporters who expose the bad behavior of local businesses. Because most businesses do not like bad publicity, just knowing that they might be the subject of a negative news story can motivate them to work with you to resolve your problem.

Getting Help from the Better Business Bureau

The Better Business Bureau (BBB) is a nonprofit organization that's supported primarily by area businesses. There are BBB offices throughout the United States. When you're having a problem with a local business, you may want to file a complaint with your BBB. Assuming that your gripe is reasonable, the BBB contacts the business in an effort to get your problem worked out. If the business is not cooperative, your complaint is added to the BBB's database of local businesses with unresolved consumer complaints. Consumers often check this database before working with a business. When they discover that other consumers have complained about it and that the business has not been responsive, more often than not, the consumers look for another company to do business with.

The BBB you contact may suggest that you try to resolve your problem through its mediation or arbitration services. Because only some BBBs offers those services, contact the one in your area to find out whether it does. A list of BBBs across the country is found on page 117 of the *2001 Consumer Reference Handbook* on the CD.

Getting Help from the Government

Your city, county, or state government consumer-protection office can be helpful when you're having problems with a business. Among other things, these offices can mediate complaints, conduct investigations, prosecute those who violate consumer laws, and regulate and license a wide variety of professionals. Because different levels of government are responsible for enforcing different laws, the nature of your problem dictates which office to contact. Page 70 of the *2001 Consumer Resource Handbook* has a listing of state, county, and city government consumer protection offices.

The FTC: A federal agency you should know about

The Federal Trade Commission (FTC) is responsible for enforcing a wide range of consumer-oriented laws, including laws relating to credit, credit bureaus, debt collection, and borrowing money, as well as laws intended to protect consumers from fraud. It also enforces trade-regulation rules such as the Used Car Rule, the Mail Order Rule, and the Cooling Off Rule.

The FTC carries out its responsibilities in several ways, including by producing a variety of informative free brochures. These publications tell you about your consumer rights and how to protect them. Visit the FTC's Web site (www.ftc.gov) for a list of its publications, many of which you can read online. You can also get publication information from the FTC by calling 202-326-3650 or by writing the agency at

Office of Consumer and Business Education
Federal Trade Commission
Washington, DC 20580

The FTC maintains a database of consumer complaints about businesses and business practices. It advocates for new consumer-protection laws or for changes to existing laws. It takes legal action against businesses that violate the laws and rules it enforces. If the FTC receives many complaints about a particular business, it launches an investigation and can file a lawsuit against the business. To file a complaint with the FTC, you can write to the FTC at

Consumer Response Center
Federal Trade Commission
600 Pennsylvania Ave., NW
Washington, DC 20580

You can call its toll-free consumer complaint hotline at 877-FTC-HELP (877-382-4357). The line is open between 9 a.m. and 5 p.m. EST, Monday through Friday. If you have questions about filing a complaint, call the FTC at 202-326-2222. Another way to get help and information from the FTC is to contact the regional office for your area. Form 3-2 on the CD provides information about the FTC's regional offices, including their addresses.

If your problem is with an insurance company, a bank that's chartered by your state, a utility company, or an investment company or bank that sold you an investment product (including stocks, bonds, and mutual funds), state offices regulate and supervise their activities. These offices may be able to help you clear up your problem. A list of state banking authorities is available on the CD at page 87 of the *2001 Consumer Resource Handbook*.

A listing of federal agencies that might be able to provide information is located on the CD at page 107 of the *2001 Consumer Resource Handbook*.

Mediating Toward a Meeting of the Minds

When in-person conversations, telephone calls, and letters don't clear up your problem, mediation may be an option. *Mediation* is a highly effective method of non-court dispute resolution that uses talk, active listening, and give-and-take with the goal of achieving solutions that satisfy everyone involved.

Mediation can resolve civil matters but not criminal matters. The problems best suited to mediation include disputes with your neighbors, family, or friends; simple real estate issues, landlord-tenant issues, or business-consumer complaints. Mediation works only when everyone involved in the problem agrees to give it a try. No one can be forced to settle their differences through mediation. However, a court can order you to go to mediation.

You can try mediation even after you're involved in a lawsuit. In fact, many judges require that the parties to a lawsuit give mediation a try before they can get a trial date. This is a common requirement when divorcing couples can't resolve child-custody issues.

Assessing the advantages of mediation

Using mediation to resolve your problems has many advantages. For example:

- ✔ **It's relatively cheap.** On average, the services of a private mediator cost between $60 and $100 per hour, depending on where you live and the mediator's experience. Ordinarily, the participants split the cost of mediation equally.

   Many communities have nonprofit dispute-resolution centers. If you work with a mediator at one of these centers, you pay only a nominal fee for his services, and maybe even less if your income is low.

- ✔ **It's relatively fast.** Getting a court date and getting through a trial can take months, even if your case is settled outside of court. On the other hand, a mediation session can usually be scheduled within a couple of weeks, and it's conceivable that your dispute could be settled after just a few hours of give and take.

- ✔ **It's relatively convenient.** Many mediators work in the evenings and on weekends. On the other hand, most courts and lawyers do business only during normal business hours, Monday through Friday.

- ✔ **You have control.** You're in the driver's seat during mediation because crafting a solution to your problem is up to you. You may not get everything you want, but you might get more than you would if you filed a lawsuit and it went all the way to trial. In that situation, a judge or jury decides your fate, and you might not like the decision. Although trials have winners and losers, the goal of mediation is to devise a solution that leaves everyone feeling as if he won something.

✔ **You can be creative.** Mediation gives you the freedom to come up with an imaginative solution to your problem that's beyond the scope of the court. The decisions of a judge or jury, however, are constrained by the laws that apply to your case. In mediation, you're under no obligation. You don't have to accept an agreement you don't like; you have the right to say no.

✔ **It's private.** Anyone who wants to can attend your court trial and hear your personal business. But during mediation, the only people in the room besides you and the mediator are whoever else you want there. Those other people could be your lawyer, your spouse, a real estate agent, your CPA, a home contractor, and so on. It's confidential. Your final mediation agreement does not become part of the public record. A judge or jury's decision does.

✔ **Mediation is less emotionally taxing than a lawsuit and trial.**

In some states, under limited circumstances, the things you say during mediation can be admissible in court. In other words, if your mediation fails and you end up in a trial, what you say during mediation could be used as evidence for or against you. However, no state treats an offer to settle made during mediation as admissible.

To be extra sure that everything discussed during your mediation session remains private, work with a mediator who requires all participants to sign an up-front confidentiality agreement. Confidentiality can also be stipulated in your final mediation agreement, assuming that you come to an agreement.

✔ If you don't like the way your mediation is going, you can end it at any time.

✔ **It's likely that everyone involved will comply with the agreement you work out.** History shows that when people in conflict work together to resolve their problem, they're more apt to uphold their end of the bargain than when someone else imposes a resolution on them.

✔ You can use mediation not only to resolve a problem but also to decide how to implement the solution you choose.

✔ **You preserve your options.** If mediation doesn't work for you, you can try arbitration, file a lawsuit, or go to trial if you already have a lawsuit on file.

Knowing when mediation does not make sense

Despite the many advantages of mediation, it may not be the best option for you, depending on your situation. Going to mediation is not a good idea when you are no longer able to think calmly and rationally about your problem; when you feel intimidated by whomever you're having a dispute with. Mediation works best when everyone feels on equal footing and therefore can be frank and honest with one another. Going to mediation may also be a bad idea if you have difficulty speaking your mind and standing up for yourself, if you fear that the person you have a dispute with might harm you physically, or if you are closed to compromise. A successful mediation requires give and take.

Understanding the mediator's role

A mediator is a trained, neutral third party, often an attorney. During your mediation, he does not act as a judge or jury and resolve your problem for you. That's your job. However, a mediator does

- ✔ Clarify the issues involved in your dispute so that you can focus your discussion.
- ✔ Spell out the ground rules for discussion and hold you to them.
- ✔ Help articulate each side's priorities, perspectives, and concerns.
- ✔ Explain what the law says and help negotiate the details of an agreement.
- ✔ Keep everyone on track and suggests possible solutions.
- ✔ Formalize the agreement by putting it on paper and having everyone sign it. A signed mediation agreement is legally enforceable because it is a contract.

If your mediator's services do not include putting your agreement in writing, hire an attorney to do so for you. However, be sure that during mediation, everyone agrees on what attorney to use and how they will share the attorney's cost.

Deciding what kind of mediator you need

Two basic types of mediators exist. Some mediate a variety of problems, and others focus on specific types of legal disputes. For example, members of the Academy of Family Mediators specialize in mediating divorce-related issues as well as other types of family-related disputes. (For a list of mediators who are members of the Academy, call 800-292-4236.)

Although a specialist might charge more than a generalist, it can be money well spent if the issue you want to resolve is complicated or requires special knowledge. A specialist might get you faster results and might also help you develop an overall better mediation agreement than a generalist.

Finding a mediator

To find a mediator, ask an attorney you know for a referral. You can also talk with friends or relatives who have used mediation, or check out the Yellow Pages under "Mediation."

✔ Call your local or state bar association for a referral to mediators in your area. Form 3-3 on the CD lists the addresses and phone numbers for the bar associations in all 50 states and for the District of Columbia, Puerto Rico, and the Virgin Islands.

✔ If your problem is with a business, and if that business is a member of a trade or professional organization, the organization might offer mediation services to its members and to the consumers they're in conflict with.

✔ If your dispute is with a local business, find out whether the BBB in your area offers mediation services.

Page 129 of *the 2001 Consumer Action Handbook* on the CD provides a list of many larger trade and professional associations that might offer dispute-resolution services. If you don't see the association you're looking for, your local library should be able to help you locate contact information.

✔ Contact national mediator organizations that make referrals. Here are two worth contacting:

• The Society of Professionals in Dispute Resolution, 202-783-7277.

• National Center for Dispute Resolution, 202-466-4764.

If money is a concern, look for a mediator who charges on a sliding scale according to income, or for one who will take your case on a *pro bono* basis. Nonprofit dispute-resolution centers are also a source of low-cost or no-cost mediation services.

Knowing what to ask a mediator

After you identify some mediators you may want to work with, ask them to send you background information about themselves, including their training and experience, how they charge, and so on. Then set up meetings with the mediators who most interest you. These meetings give you an opportunity to ask questions and to assess how comfortable you feel with the mediators. If a face-to-face meeting is not possible, schedule a time to talk by telephone.

Note: If a court orders you into mediation, the judge will probably give you a list of mediators to choose from.

Mediation is a waste of time if you don't trust the mediator you work with. If you don't have confidence in the mediator's skills or don't feel comfortable sharing certain information with the mediator, you may go into mediation with a negative attitude toward the process. Here are some things to find out about each mediator you talk with:

- ✔ How long has he been working as a mediator and has he ever handled similar situations?
- ✔ How much formal mediation training has he received?
- ✔ Will he draft a written agreement for you if your mediation is successful?
- ✔ How does he charge? (Mediators can charge by the hour, by the day, or on a flat-fee basis.) And does he provide references?

When you talk with each mediator, also note whether the mediator makes you feel comfortable or uncomfortable. Does she convey neutrality? Does she demonstrate an understanding of and an interest in your problem? Does she ask you questions and respond to your questions with answers you can understand?

After everyone involved in your dispute agrees on the mediator you will work with, the mediator asks each of you to sign and return a mediation agreement. The mediator may also want to receive payment up front. If the mediator charges a flat fee, she may expect to be paid the entire amount up front.

Preparing for mediation

If you spend time preparing for mediation, you increase the likelihood that it will be productive. Here are some things you can do to prepare:

- ✔ Gather documents related to your problem, including contracts, letters, receipts, medical records, and so on.
- ✔ Prepare a timeline of the history of your problem, if appropriate.
- ✔ Develop a game plan. Decide what you want out of mediation and what compromises you will make to get it. Know your bottom line. Although mediation is about give and take, you're not obligated to make compromises you don't like.
- ✔ Put your emotions aside. Your emotions can be your worst enemy when you're involved in a dispute. They can cloud your thinking and make you less open to reasonable solutions. However, putting your emotions aside does not mean that at the mediation session you shouldn't state your position with confidence and let the other party know what you feel most strongly about.
- ✔ Meet with an attorney to make sure that you have a firm grasp of the legal issues related to your dispute. The attorney can also help you identify possible options for settling your disagreement.

Using a lawyer during mediation

When you participate in mediation, you can have a lawyer by your side every step of the way. The lawyer can help you evaluate your options, assess any offers the other side makes, suggest a counteroffer, advise you about your legal rights and obligations, and explain the legal consequences of a possible agreement. You can also ask your accountant, real estate agent, insurance agent, or any other professional who has special knowledge regarding the subject of your dispute to be available to consult during your mediation.

If you want your lawyer to do the talking and negotiating for you, you must give him the authority to settle your dispute on your behalf. When the problem being mediated is the subject of a lawsuit and you are represented by a lawyer, it's advisable to give your lawyer this authority.

If you don't bring a lawyer to mediation, you can consult with one if you reach a tentative agreement. The lawyer can advise you about the legal pros and cons of accepting or rejecting the agreement and can also suggest changes you may want to push for. This kind of legal assistance is probably not necessary if your dispute is relatively straightforward and you're clear about the laws that apply to it. But if you have a lot at stake or if the subject of your dispute is technical, getting legal advice before and after mediation is essential. Better yet, have an attorney by your side, or hire an attorney to negotiate for you.

For a summary of how your mediation will likely proceed, Check out Form 3-4 on the CD.

Arbitrating Your Differences

Arbitration is another method of non-court dispute resolution. You may want to use arbitration if you try mediation and it fails. Or you may want to have your dispute arbitrated if using mediation is not practical — maybe because the parties involved have such broad differences of opinion that no amount of talk can bridge the chasm that divides you, or because emotions are running so high that compromise seems impossible.

Sometimes, going to arbitration is a requirement, not an option. For example, to reduce their legal expenses, a growing number of companies are making mandatory arbitration a standard part of their consumer contracts. These companies include stock brokerages, banks, credit card companies, consumer finance firms, insurance companies, and HMOs.

When you agree to a contract that makes arbitration mandatory, you give up your right to sue or to use mediation. This is the case even if you didn't have an opportunity to negotiate the terms of the contract. A credit card agreement is an example of this type of contract.

Understanding how arbitration and mediation differ

Although mediation and arbitration are both non-court methods of dispute resolution, and although they both tend to be cheaper and faster than filing a lawsuit and going to trial, their similarities end there. Arbitration is more formal than mediation. In fact, it's very much like a mini-trial conducted outside of a courtroom. The arbitrator acts as a judge; the arbitration process follows formal rules and procedures; records can be subpoenaed; and you (or more likely your lawyer) present evidence and question witnesses.

Given the trial-like nature of arbitration, you should hire an attorney to represent you. In arbitration, the arbitrator, not you, decides how your dispute is settled after hearing from all sides. You can't end arbitration unless everyone involved agrees to it. And, an arbitrator's decision is usually legally binding and can be appealed only in exceptional circumstances. *Binding arbitration* means that the decision has the force of law, and you must abide by it. Sometimes, however, if everyone agrees to it, arbitration can be *nonbinding*, which means that you can reject the arbitrator's decision.

Working out the terms of your arbitration

When you're headed to arbitration, you have decisions to make regarding the arbitration process. These decisions are important because they can affect the outcome of the arbitration. Although you may not have the right to be involved in every decision, the more you have input into, the better. The decisions can include determining who the arbitrator is, where the arbitration takes place, what some of the rules are for the arbitration, and what kind of evidence can be presented.

When a contract you have signed forces you into arbitration, you may have little input into these decisions. In fact, the deck may be stacked against you. For example, many of the businesses that include mandatory arbitration clauses in their consumer contracts retain the right to choose the arbitrator or arbitration company that conducts the arbitration. If the arbitrator or arbitration company is financially dependent on the business you're in conflict with, it's possible that the outcome of arbitration will not favor you. In fact, some courts have struck down mandatory arbitration clauses because they're so consumer-unfriendly.

Mandatory arbitration clauses can also be a bad deal for consumers because you may have to pay an arbitrator a substantial up-front fee — as much as a couple of hundred dollars — *and* a fee for each hour of the arbitrator's time. These expenses can add up. In fact, in the end, the arbitration may cost you more than you stand to gain if the arbitrator decides in your favor.

Obviously, when arbitration is mandatory, it pays to assess whether it's worth your while or a waste of your time and money. Depending on how the arbitration session will be structured and how much it will cost you, you may be better off simply dropping your dispute. Here are some questions that can help you make that assessment:

- ✔ How much will the arbitration cost you? And what do you stand to gain if the arbitrator decides in your favor?

- ✔ If the arbitrator decides in your favor, can you get reimbursed for your arbitration expenses?

- ✔ Can you help select the arbitrator? If you can't, how is the arbitrator selected, and how much can you find out about her?

- ✔ What are the rules of the arbitration, and what kind of evidence can you present?

- ✔ Will the company you're feuding with give you any of the documents you might need to help support your case?

Chapter 4

Filing a Lawsuit

· ·

In This Chapter

▶ Deciding when to file a small claims lawsuit

▶ Beginning your lawsuit

▶ Preparing for your day in court

▶ Understanding what will happen in the court room

▶ Collecting your money if you win your lawsuit

· ·

*Y*ou followed the advice in Chapter 3 without success. You still have a legal problem. Now what? Tear your hair out? Have a good old-fashioned cry? Maybe it's time to file a lawsuit. This chapter tells you how to file and what happens if you do. We focus most of our attention on suing in small claims court, because that's the court where people can resolve a variety of everyday legal problems quickly and without an attorney's help. The chapter also gives you questions to answer so you can be sure that filing in small claims court is a good idea.

This chapter tells you how to collect your money if you sue and win. This is important information because the defendant in your lawsuit probably won't write you a check for the full amount of your judgment right there on the spot. Instead, you have to get your judgment enforced, which can take a lot of effort.

The last part of this chapter highlights the challenges you face if your legal problem does not qualify for small claims court and you have to file in a higher court. It also explains why you should hire an attorney in that case and outlines how an attorney can help you.

Using the People's Court

Small claims court may be just the place for you if your legal problem involves a relatively small amount of money, between $1,000 and $10,000, depending on your state, and if you're willing to act as your own lawyer. Depending on your state, the small claims court in your area may be called a justice-of-the-peace court, justice court, or municipal court.

The rules and procedures in small claims court are informal. The judges use little if any legalese. Unlike trials in higher courts, a small claims court trial is usually quite brief — often under an hour. Plus, as an added convenience, many small claims courts offer evening and weekend hours.

Depending on where you file your lawsuit, the small claims court may allow you to be represented by an attorney. However, when you're suing for a small amount of money, hiring a lawyer is not sensible unless the lawyer is willing to take his fee from the judgment you win against the defendant. For helpful state-by-state information about suing in small claims court, go to `consumer.findlaw.com/lawyers/self/small.html`. By clicking on your state, you can find small claims forms that you can download.

You can file a lawsuit against an individual or a business in small claims court. The majority of small claims lawsuits relate to property damage issues, landlord-tenant problems (including evictions in some states), and debt-collection matters. You may be able to sue over an auto accident in small claims court, depending on your state.

Ordinarily, you can sue for monetary damages only in small claims court. These damages represent compensation for the financial harm you believe a defendant has caused you.

Small claims courts in some states do not hear cases related to motor vehicle accidents. You can't use small claims court to sue for punitive damages; however, a few states do allow it. *Punitive damages* provide plaintiffs with additional compensation for the harm the defendant caused them. Courts order punitive damages to punish defendants when they have done something wrong and to deter them from repeating the wrong in the future. Additionally, you can't use small claims court to make someone do or not do something. That requires a court injunction.

Asking Yourself Ten Important Questions Before You File a Lawsuit

Just because you have a legal problem that qualifies for small claims court, don't assume that filing a lawsuit is a good use of your time or your money. Answering the following ten questions can help you make up your mind. If you conclude that small claims court is not for you, you may decide to sue in a higher court or not sue at all.

1. **Have I sent the defendant a final demand letter?** Send this letter before you file a money-related lawsuit in any court. Send it via certified mail, return receipt requested, and keep a copy of the letter for your files.

You can find four different sample demand letters on the CD. Form 4-1 demands reimbursement for the cost of the medical care and treatment you received as a result of a personal injury. Form 4-2 requests reimbursement for property damage related expenses. Form 4-3 demands the return of a rental deposit. And Form 4-4 demands payment for a bad debt. Tailor these letters to your own needs.

2. **Does the dollar amount I want to sue for exceed the court's limit?** If the amount of your claim is just a little over the court's maximum, you may want to forfeit the excess dollars and sue for the remainder. If you want to sue for the full amount, you can't file in small claims court.

3. **Am I filing my lawsuit within the statue of limitation?** This is the amount of time you have according to state law to file a lawsuit. Once the statue of limitation elapses, you're out of luck; it's too late to sue. Each state establishes its own statutes of limitation and sets different limitations for different types of legal matters.

4. **Do I have enough evidence to prove my case?** Sometimes, even though you know you have been wronged, you may not have what you need to build a winning case. If you don't, filing a lawsuit is a waste of time. The evidence you need might include copies of correspondence, receipts, contracts, cancelled checks, photographs, bills, and so on.

5. **Is the law on my side?** You will lose your lawsuit if you're not legally entitled to what you ask for.

6. **Do I have time to prepare for a small claims court trial?** When you represent yourself, all the preparation rests on your shoulders. Your preparation might include locating evidence, creating a chronology of events, lining up witnesses, deciding what you will say when you present your case in court, and so on.

7. **Am I comfortable speaking in public?** If your tongue gets tied and you can't think straight when you do any kind of public speaking, representing yourself in small claims court can be a losing and highly stressful proposition.

8. **Will I forfeit any future legal options by suing in small claims court?** In some states, you might limit your right to appeal and lose the opportunity to sue later for any additional damages that come to your attention after your small claims lawsuit is over. To answer this question, consult with an attorney.

9. **Do I risk damaging important relationships in my life if I proceed with my lawsuit?** These could include relationships with family members, business associates, clients, and so on. Also, will the lawsuit damage your reputation in your community? If you answer "yes" to either of these questions, weigh the potential benefit of winning your lawsuit (and remember, the benefit is only "potential" — there's no guarantee that you and the court will see eye-to-eye) against the potential drawbacks of suing.

10. **What are the chances that I will see the money I'm entitled to if I win my lawsuit?** Unless the defendant voluntarily pays up (don't hold your breath!), you have to collect whatever money the court awards you. If the defendant is *judgment proof,* collecting is an impossible task unless the defendant's situation changes at some point. A defendant is judgment proof if the defendant owns no assets or if all the defendant's assets are exempt assets and therefore are protected from the collection process. (Exempt assets are not a concern if the defendant is a corporation.) You can find out about exempt assets in the section "Avoiding those exempt assets" later in this chapter. A defendant is also considered judgment proof if they are unemployed or insolvent.

Getting Your Lawsuit Going

You initiate a lawsuit by filling out and filing a legal form called a *petition,* a *complaint,* a *statement of plaintiff,* or something else, depending on the court you're filing in. The petition should come with instructions for how to complete it.

Form 4-5 on the CD is a sample small claims court notice form. Because different courts use different petition forms, be sure to get your form from the small claims court that will hear your case. Usually, that court is in the county where the defendant lives or does business. However, you may also be able to file in the county where your personal property was damaged or where you were injured, or in the county where you entered into a contract with the defendant. If you're not sure what court to sue in, ask your local small claims court clerk. If you have several options for where to file, pick the small claims court that's closest to you — it will be more convenient to use.

Get a copy of the court's rules and procedures at the same time you obtain a petition form. Among other things, this tells you how much it costs to file a lawsuit and whether you can have witnesses and experts testify on your behalf, and it provides an overview of your rights and responsibilities in small claims court. If you don't live close to the court where you're filing your lawsuit, the court clerk will mail the forms and information to you, and you can mail them back after you fill everything out.

Filling out the paperwork

When you fill out the petition, you must indicate why you're filing your lawsuit and how much you're suing for. You must also provide basic information about the defendant in your case. Here's a general rundown on the specific information you must provide about the defendant, depending on whether you're suing an individual or a business:

Knowing the order of the courts

State court systems, including the system for the District of Columbia, comprise a confusing maze of court names, structures, and jurisdictions. No two systems are alike. This confusion can make figuring out what court to file in particularly difficult if the defendant in your lawsuit lives or does business in a state other than yours.

By and large, most states have a three- to four-tiered court system. The courts at the lowest tiers are *trial courts*. Courts within these two tiers hear specific types of cases. Also, certain courts can hear only lawsuits that relate to a limited amount of money. Courts at the upper tiers are *appeals* or *appellate courts*. Plaintiffs and defendants use these courts to appeal the outcomes of cases tried in lower courts.

States also have *specialized courts*. They commonly include traffic, family, probate, and juvenile courts. Small claims court is a type of specialized court. Some states also have courts devoted to landlord-tenant matters. Although your state's system may not look quite like this, here is an overview of what your state's court structure is apt to look like.

- **Courts of limited jurisdiction:** Cases heard at this level involve, among other things, disputes over limited amounts of money. Courts at this tier may be called justice-of-the-peace courts, magistrate courts, district courts, or county courts.

- **Courts of general jurisdiction:** Next within a state's court system, courts at this tier can be referred to as district courts, county courts, chancery courts, circuit courts, courts of common pleas, probate courts, or superior courts. There's no limit on the amount of money you can sue for at this level, and you can usually opt for either a jury or a bench trial — a trial decided by a judge.

- **State courts of appeal or intermediate appellate courts:** These courts hear appeals from the lower courts. They can uphold a lower court's decision, reverse it, modify the decision, or order a new trial.

- **State supreme courts:** Courts at this level are the pinnacle of a state's court system. They decide cases that are on final appeal. Sometimes, although rarely and only when an important federal issue is involved, a state supreme court decision can be appealed or petitioned to the U.S. Supreme Court.

Although most civil lawsuits are heard in state courts, there are exceptions. For example, bankruptcies are heard in federal court. Generally, cases heard in federal courts involve matters related to the U.S. Constitution or to federal law; residents of different states and claims for more than $50,000; disputes between U.S. citizens and residents of other countries; disputes that involve both federal and state law.

- If you sue an individual, you need the defendant's full name (no nicknames allowed) and current address. If you sue more than one person in the same lawsuit, even if the defendants are married or living together, you have to list each name. For example, you can't list them as Mr. and Mrs. Jack Smith or Mr. and Ms. Frank Welby.

- If you sue over a motor vehicle accident, you need the name of the driver of the vehicle that hit you, as well as the name of the person the car is registered to. If a business owns the vehicle, you need the name of the business.

TIP

If you're missing some of the information you need related to an auto accident, you may be able to get it from the police accident report or from the department of motor vehicles' vehicle registration database. To get it, you have to provide the department with the vehicle's license plate number. You may also have to pay a small fee.

- If the defendant named in your lawsuit is a sole proprietorship, you need the name of the owner and the name of the business. Those names may be the same, or the business may have a DBA, which stands for "doing business as." An example is Susan Smith, doing business as Susan Smith Design.

- If you sue a partnership, you should have the names of all the partners in the business, even if your beef is with only one of them. Each partner is personally liable for the debts, contractual obligations, and actions of the partnership. Therefore, if you win your lawsuit and you have listed all the partners on the petition, you increase the likelihood that you will get the money you're entitled to because you can go after all the partners.

- If you sue a corporation, you need the business's legal name and the name of its registered agent for service. A *registered agent* is a person designated by a corporation to receive notices of lawsuits.

In many states, if you don't provide complete and accurate information on the petition, your lawsuit can't move forward. Therefore, if you have questions about how to fill it out, talk to the small claims court clerk.

Playing business name detective

You can find out the legal name of a business by contacting the appropriate government office. Which office depends on where the business is located and whether you're suing a sole proprietorship, a partnership, or a corporation. Here's a list of the government offices that may be able to help you. It may take a couple calls before you find the right one:

- **For all businesses:** The local, county, or state tax office. You may need a business's address to get its legal name from one of these offices.

- **For sole proprietorships:** The county clerk's office in the county where the business is

located. It can tell you whether the business has a DBA.

- **For incorporated businesses:** The secretary of state's office or the office of corporations in the state where the business is located.

- **For licensed businesses:** Doctors and attorneys must be licensed. Other professionals, such as electricians, mechanics, building contractors, plumbers, exterminators, and air conditioning repair people, are commonly required to be licensed. Call the appropriate city, county, or state licensing office for more information.

Don't assume that you know the actual, legal name of the business you're suing. The name on the outside of its office or retail outlet, or the name listed on its letterhead or invoice, may not be its legal name. For example, although the apartment complex you want to sue may be called Ridgefield Hollow, the owner of the complex might be Apartments For Rent, Inc.

Paying the fee

You must pay a small fee to file your petition with the small claims court. The amount of the fee is between $20 and $50 in most states (although some states have higher and lower fees). Some states set small claims filing fees based on the amount of money in controversy. If you win your lawsuit, the judge might add this fee to the total amount of your judgment. After you pay the fee, the clerk gives you a case or docket number. You might get a date for your trial at the same time. Otherwise, the date is assigned after the defendant has been officially notified about your lawsuit.

If you have a low income, you can apply to the court for a waiver of your filing fee.

Knowing what to do if you can't claim in small claims court

If your legal problem does not qualify for small claims court, you can file a lawsuit in a higher court. But before you do that, consider this:

- ✔ Getting a trial date could take months.

- ✔ You will spend a considerable amount of money — at least in the four figures, but maybe even more, depending on the nature of your lawsuit and how it progresses. The legal processes and procedures in higher courts are much more formal and structured than they are in small claims court. Therefore, to help your manage your lawsuit, you should hire an attorney, and as you know, attorneys cost money! However, she takes care of all the confusing legal details, develops a strategy for winning your case, argues your case in court if necessary, and so on.

  Working with someone who knows her way around a courthouse can mean the difference between winning and losing your lawsuit. Chapter 6 tells you everything you need to know about how to hire and work with an attorney.

- ✔ Even if you have an attorney, your lawsuit takes up your time.

- ✔ Many lawsuits start out as relatively simple disputes but over time become much more complicated and expensive. For example, the other party may try to force you to respond to legal motions and requests for discovery, which will increase the cost of your lawsuit.

- ✔ The more you have at stake, the more stress you will almost certainly feel.

- ✔ You have no assurance that the outcome of your trial will be to your liking. When all is said and done, you may have spent a lot of money and have nothing to show for it.

Breaking the News to the Defendant

After you file your petition, the defendant in your lawsuit must be officially notified about your action. The defendant is served with a *summons*. If you sue multiple defendants, each of them must be served individually. You may be able to get the cost of service included in your judgment if you win your lawsuit. Form 4-6 on the CD provides a sample summons.

Courts have specific rules about how service must be accomplished and about how many days before a trial a defendant must be served. The small claims court can fill you in on the rules that apply to your lawsuit. Follow those rules, or the progress of your lawsuit will be delayed. Following are the usual options for service, but every court is different, so don't make any assumptions about what is required:

- ✔ **Service by certified mail:** The court clerk might do this for you (for a fee, of course). The drawback to this method is that a high percentage of defendants do not accept certified letters (especially if they already know that they're about to be sued). Therefore, you risk having the summons returned to the court and then having to serve the defendant in some other way.

- ✔ **Service by a sheriff, marshal, or constable:** These uniformed county officers can serve a defendant in person at home, work, and so on. However, they can accomplish service only in their particular county. Although the cost of service by one of these officers varies, you will probably spend between $20 and $30. If the officer is able to serve the defendant, he sends proof of service to the court. If he is unable to serve the defendant, he sends the form to you.

- ✔ **Service by a private process server:** Private process servers also serve defendants in person. They can work across county lines. On average, expect to pay between $35 and $60 for service by a private process server. Rushed service costs more.

In a few states, a disinterested adult — that does not mean you — can serve the defendant with a summons. If you sue an individual, the summons can be hand-delivered to the defendant at home, at work, or wherever you can find him. The same is true if you sue the owner of a sole proprietorship or a partner in a partnership. However, if you sue a corporation, serve the corporation's agent of record. To get that person's name and address, call the secretary of state's office or the office of corporations in the state where the business is located.

Reporting back to the court

Before your lawsuit can move forward, the court must receive confirmation that the defendant has been served. That's easy if the court clerk mails the summons for you because the clerk is the one to receive a signed receipt in the mail if the defendant accepts the summons. If you send the summons to the defendant via certified letter and the signed receipt is returned to you, file it with the small claims court as proof that the defendant was served. If you use a peace officer or a private process server to serve the summons, make sure that she signs a *proof of service* form. You can get that form from the small claims clerk.

Tracking the progress of your case to ensure that all the right paperwork is filed and so on is your responsibility, not the court's.

Anticipating the defendant's reaction

The defendant may respond to your lawsuit by

✔ **Offering to settle with you out of court in exchange for getting the lawsuit dismissed:** If you reach an out-of-court settlement, be sure to write down the terms of your agreement. You can draft the agreement yourself or get an attorney's help. Form 4-7 provides a sample letter of agreement that you can file with the court. After all parties to the agreement have signed it, attach it to your complaint and file everything with the court clerk.

- If the defendant agrees to pay you money as part of the settlement, ask to be paid in cash or with a money order, not with a check. That way, you don't have to worry about being paid with a bad check.

- If you agree to dismiss your lawsuit, you may have to file a motion for dismissal with the court or simply write a letter to the court clerk informing the court that you have decided not to pursue your lawsuit. Form 4-8 provides a sample request for dismissal. Form 4-9 provides a sample *motion to dismiss*.

- The defendant might grow more interested in an out-of-court settlement as the day of your trial nears. He may realize that he is apt to lose the lawsuit and decide that he doesn't want a court judgment on his credit record.

✔ **Not responding:** If the defendant does not respond after being served and then fails to show for the trial, the judge will probably give you a default judgment. Most likely, the judgment will cover the full amount of money you asked for in your petition, as well as your court costs and cost of service.

✔ **Filing a written** *answer* **or** *response:* Your state may require that the defendant do this if she wants to contest what you put in your petition. The defendant can deny some or all of the allegations in your petition, move to end your lawsuit immediately or to narrow its focus, or even file a counterclaim or a separate lawsuit against you.

If the court dismisses your lawsuit, or if you lose your lawsuit, neither of those events affects the defendant's counterclaim. In other words, if the defendant decides to pursue a counterclaim, your legal hassles and expenses may be just beginning.

✔ **Just showing up:** Most states allow defendants to show up for their hearings without filing any formal paperwork ahead of time.

In some courts, a defendant can send the court a letter stating that she does not dispute the plaintiff's claim but can't afford to pay what the plaintiff is asking in a single lump sum. The judge may let the defendant pay it in installments.

Helping Yourself Win Your Suit

Before your day in court arrives, spend some time thinking about the best way to convince the judge or jury that you're entitled to what you're asking for. How will you tell your story? What evidence should you present? What arguments do you think the defendant will make, and how can you counter them? Just winging it when trial begins is usually not a good idea. To win most civil lawsuits, you must prove your case by a *preponderance of the evidence.* In other words, your challenge is to prove to the court that your version of the facts is more convincing and credible than the defendant's.

To build a winning case, you need a logical argument, a basic understanding of the law that applies to your case, and solid evidence such as a valid legal contract, correspondence, receipts, check stubs, photographs, telephone records, warranties, police accident reports, and your date book. Depending on the court, you may have to present original copies or certified copies, not photocopies, of some evidence, and you may have to send the defendant photocopies of your evidence prior to the trial date. You also need witnesses unless your case is extremely simple and straightforward. You may need expert witnesses; however, experts rarely testify in small claims matters.

Subpoenas are rarely used in small claims court, but if you don't have access to certain documents or other printed or written evidence that you consider critical to your case, you can obtain what you need by using a *Subpoena Duces Tecum*. Examples of evidence you might want to subpoena include the defendant's bank records, telephone records, financial data, hospital records, and so on. Form 4-10 on the CD provides a sample *Subpoena Duces Tecum*. The particular subpoena form used by the court where you file your lawsuit may look different than this one but all *Subpoena Duces Tecum* forms ask for similar information.

Ask the small claims court clerk for the form you must fill out to get this subpoena. To complete it, you need the name of the person in charge of the evidence you want, because that's who must be served with the subpoena. Some small claims courts do not have these forms. In that case, you need to write out what you want and give it to the court clerk. Ask the clerk exactly what you need to include in your written request for a *Subpoena Duces Tecum*.

Your presentation should begin with what you're asking for from the court and then an explanation of why you believe you're legally entitled to it. To increase your courtroom confidence, visit the small claims court where your case will be heard to see what the courtroom looks like and to watch the judge in action.

Consider buying an hour or two of an attorney's time if you're suing for a relatively significant amount of money by small claims standards. Having an attorney explain the basic points of law relating to your lawsuit and give you tips on how to argue your case can be a worthwhile investment of your time and money.

Working with witnesses

When you're preparing your case, you may decide that it would be helpful to have certain people who know about your legal problem act as witnesses on your behalf. If you do, tell them about your lawsuit and explain why you want them to testify for you. Be sure to tell them that the defendant may cross-examine them or ask them questions that can make them uncomfortable, put them on the defensive, or even make them angry. Keep in mind that friends and family members are generally less credible witnesses than individuals who don't have personal relationships to you.

Generally, a witness can't testify regarding things about which he has no direct, personal knowledge. When a witness testifies about secondhand information learned from someone else, or about things she did not personally observe, hear, or experience, the testimony is considered *hearsay* evidence, and it may not be admissible in court. Before your trial date, review with your witnesses the questions you will ask them, talk to them about what you want them to say, and prepare them for what you think the defendant may ask them. This kind of witness preparation is perfectly legal. What is not legal is asking a witness to lie for you.

If a witness can't be in court to testify for you, some small claims courts allow you to introduce their testimony by using an *affidavit* or *declaration*. This is a notarized, out-of-court statement by a witness. Form 4-11 provides a sample declaration affidavit.

It's rarely done in a small claims lawsuit, but you can ask the court to subpoena a reluctant witness to testify, assuming that the witness lives or does business within a certain distance from the courthouse. The distance varies by state. Obtain the subpoena form from the court, fill it out, and take it back to the court. After the clerk issues the subpoena, it's your responsibility to have it served. Don't forget to provide the court with proof of service. If a subpoenaed witness fails to appear in court as ordered, the judge can order the sheriff, marshal, or constable to bring the witness to court. A witness who ignores a subpoena can face jail time.

It's best if your witnesses testify because they want to, not because they were forced to. An angry or resentful witness may not be helpful to you and can even harm your case.

Just the facts, ma'am

Discovery is the legal term for the fact-finding phase of a lawsuit. Most lawsuits filed outside of small claims court involve some amount of formal discovery. Attorneys use the discovery process to learn as much as they can about the facts of a case. Depending on the complexity of your case and on how much you and the defendant can afford to spend, there can be a lot or a little discovery in your lawsuit. The lawyers for both sides can file motions to limit discovery or to force compliance with a discovery request. The most common tools of discovery are

- **Depositions:** Attorneys use these to compel potential witnesses for the other side to testify under oath outside of court. As a witness responds to questions, a court reporter records the answers. Sometimes, a videographer videotapes the witnesses.

- **Interrogatories:** Attorneys serve these written requests to potential witnesses for the other side. The witnesses must respond to the interrogatories in writing while under oath.

- **Motions or requests to produce documents:** These motions can help attorneys get certain documents related to a case. They can include bank records for the other side, financial data, correspondence, medical evidence, photographs, and so on.

- **Requests for admissions:** Attorneys use these to try to get the other side to admit that certain facts are true so that the facts do not have to be proven. These requests can help decrease the amount of discovery in a lawsuit and can shorten the entire lawsuit process.

Using expert witnesses

Experts are witnesses who have special expertise. Although experts rarely testify in small claims trials, using one might help you make your case with a judge. For example, you may need an auto mechanic to testify about how much it will cost to repair your car, or someone from your local nursery to testify about the dollar value of the damage the house painter did to your landscaping. If you want an expert to testify in your trial, check with the court to make sure that experts are allowed. Be aware that some experts charge a fee to testify in court and to prepare to testify.

Awaiting Judgment Day

The day of your small claims trial has arrived. Dress nicely and show up on time. Other lawsuits are scheduled to be heard for the same time as yours. Before any of them is heard, the judge checks to make sure that the plaintiffs and defendants in each lawsuit are in the courtroom. If you aren't there when your name is read, your case may be dismissed or dropped from the day's schedule. Then you have to start your lawsuit all over again.

A couple of days before your day in court arrives, call the court clerk to make sure that your trial is still on as scheduled. There may be a glitch, or the defendant may have asked for a delay. Here's a rundown on the likely sequence of your trial if your case moves forward:

1. **The judge reviews courtroom procedures and guidelines with you and the defendant and may explain proper courtroom decorum.** Listen carefully, and respect the judge's wishes. Stand up when you address the judge, and address the judge as "Your Honor."

2. **As the plaintiff, you present your side of the case first.** Start by making it clear to the judge exactly what your lawsuit is about. Present any evidence you have, and let the judge know whether you will be calling experts or other witnesses to testify. Present your case in a simple and straightforward manner, and be as brief as possible. If you go on too long, you risk losing the judge's attention and may even alienate her. Remember, many small claims plaintiffs have won their lawsuits with presentations that lasted no more than five minutes. During your presentation, the judge might interrupt with questions or comments or wait to talk until you've finished.

If a key witness can't be in court on the day of your trial, let the judge know at the start of the proceedings, and ask whether your trial can be rescheduled. The judge will probably agree to it. However, if you request another delay to the start of your trial at your next court date, don't expect the judge to be quite so accommodating.

The defendant in your lawsuit may question or cross-examine you and your witnesses to discredit your testimony or to get you to say things that might help his own defense. You can do the same to the defendant and the defendant's witnesses when it comes time for the defendant to present his case.

At the end of your presentation, let the judge know how much you have spent on court costs and other expenses. Your costs could include filing fees, attorney fees, and the cost of service. Ask the judge to add these costs to the total amount of the judgment if you win your lawsuit.

3. **The defendant presents her side of the story.** While the defendant is talking, don't interrupt, and don't be rude or argumentative if he puts you on the witness stand to ask you questions.

The judge may render her verdict at the end of your trial, or you may have to wait for the decision to arrive in the mail. If you win, the judge issues a judgment in your favor for a specific amount of money, and you receive a copy.

Say it isn't so

In most states, if you don't like what a judge decides about your case, you can appeal the decision to a higher court. However, a few states do not permit small claims appeals, and a handful, including California and Massachusetts, allow only defendants to file appeals.

Each state has specific rules for what you can ask for when you appeal a small claims court decision. For example, in some states, you can ask for a whole new trial. In others, you can ask for only a review of how the judge applied the law to your particular case. Non-lawyers face an uphill battle when they try to win an appeal on that basis because their arguments must reflect an appreciation of the technicalities of the law.

If the defendant in your lawsuit appeals the judge's ruling and wins on appeal, you may end up having to pay for the defendant's court costs and attorney fees as well. States also have different rules regarding how quickly you must file an appeal. You could have anywhere from just a few days to 30 days, but usually the deadline is 10 days from the date that a judgment is entered.

If you know that you will miss the deadline for filing an appeal, ask the court clerk for an extension. If you have a good excuse, you may get one. When you file your appeal, be prepared to pay more than you did when you filed your complaint in small claims court. With a higher court comes more costs, not to mention more legal formalities.

Collecting the judgment

Unless the defendant in your lawsuit pays you on the spot, you have to take special steps to enforce your judgment and collect your money. But before you do anything, wait to see whether the defendant appeals the court's decision. The defendant has a limited period of time to do so. If no appeal is filed, or if an appeal is denied, you get to put on a new hat and become a *judgment creditor*. The defendant, meanwhile, becomes a *judgment debtor*.

As a judgment creditor, your first move should be to write the debtor a polite letter asking for payment. Attach a copy of your judgment to the letter, send everything to the defendant via certified mail, and request a return receipt. The sample letter in Form 4-12 on the CD gives you an idea of how to phrase your demand letter. Some states require that a defendant send payment to the court, which in turn pays you.

If your demand letter gets you nowhere, be prepared for the possibility of a long struggle. Getting the money you're legally entitled to could take longer than your small claims court trial took from start to finish.

Using collection tools

Depending on how much money you want to collect and the number of obstacles in your way, hiring a lawyer to help you may be a good idea. The attorney will probably agree to work with you on a contingent fee basis. A lawyer's help can be particularly valuable if the judgment debtor owns property in a state other than the one where you obtained your court judgment. Collecting on a judgment when that's the case may be more than you can handle on your own.

If you're not owed a large amount of money, you still might want to talk to a lawyer to get detailed information about your collection options and to find out how to obtain the information you need about the debtor's assets. The lawyer can also give you an idea of how much it might cost to use certain collection tools. In some cases, the cost is considerable. However, if you're able to enforce your judgment and get the money you're entitled to, you can usually get your collection costs back from the debtor. Here's a rundown of the collection tools that may be available to you and how to use them:

✔ **Place a lien.** Placing a lien on the judgment debtor's real property — home and land — means that the debtor can't do anything with the property without paying the judgment. If the debtor sells the property, the sale proceeds go toward the judgment. (Usually, you're notified of the pending sale.) If he tries to refinance the property, the lender who is providing the refinancing loan will probably make him pay off your lien as a condition of getting the loan.

If other creditors already have liens on the judgment debtor's real property, they're in line to get their money before you. In fact, you could end up with nothing when all is said and done, depending on the value of the property that's encumbered by the lien and how much money the other creditors are legally entitled to.

In many states, a lien is automatically placed on any of the judgment debtor's real property located in the county where the judgment is made. Otherwise, you want to get an *abstract of judgment* from the small claims court that heard your case and file it with the deeds of records for the county where the real property is located. You have to pay a small fee to file the abstract. Also, the deed recorder asks you for the defendant's address so the recorder can notify the defendant about what has been done.

✔ **Force the sale of the property.** When you place a lien on property, you can force a sale of the property in order to be paid from the proceeds. Be aware, however, that a forced sale can be a costly proposition. First, you may have to put up a large deposit to cover its cost. Then, after the sale occurs, you must reimburse the office of the sheriff, constable, or marshal for the costs involved. If you put up a deposit, those expenses are paid out of the deposit. Then, before you get any money, the sale proceeds are used to help pay off any mortgage balances on the property and any other loan balances related to the property, as well as to satisfy judgment liens placed on the property before yours. In the end, for all your time and money, you can end up with little or nothing.

To force a sale, you must get a *writ of execution* from the court. You fill out a special form that asks for your name and address as the judgment creditor, the name and address of the judgment debtor, your small claims case number, and the amount of your judgment, among other things. On a separate piece of paper, write specific instructions regarding the real property you want seized and sold. Then give the writ to the sheriff, constable, or marshal in the county where the debtor's property is located. You have to pay a fee to get the writ. The cost varies, but it could be more than $100.

There may be a time limit to obtain a writ of execution after you get a court judgment. Check with the court.

✔ **Levy against the judgment debtor's personal property.** You can take possession of a debtor's personal property, such as the money in his savings or checking account, a vehicle, computer equipment, and so on. Again, you need a writ to do so. Give the writ to the sheriff, marshal, or constable, together with specific written information about the asset you want seized, so that the county law officer knows exactly where to find it. You must provide that information in writing.

If you want the debtor's bank account seized, you must provide the bank account number, as well as bank's name and location. It you want a vehicle seized, the county law officer needs its license plate number, make, and location. If you want a business's cash, inventory, equipment, and so on taken, you must provide equally specific information about those assets. The county law officer can tell you exactly what information you need to provide.

Form 4-13 on the CD provides an example of a writ of execution form. Use the sample letter on Form 4-14 to write your own request to levy a judgment debtor's bank account.

The county law official serves the judgment debtor with a *Notice of Intent to Levy,* giving the debtor a chance to pay the judgment or to file a timely claim stating that the assets to be levied against are exempt from collection. The debtor can also formally protest the sale of the property. The law official takes the assets assuming that the judgment debtor does not pay the judgment, if the claim is denied after a hearing, or the protest is overturned. If he takes cash, you get whatever is left after the cost of the seizure is deducted from the deposit you paid to get the writ executed. If the county law officer seizes other kinds of property, the property is sold at a public auction, often for much less than it's worth. Then, after the court deducts the cost of the auction from the sale proceeds, the remaining money goes toward satisfying your judgment.

✔ **Apply for a wage garnishment.** *Wage garnishment* is a special kind of levy that involves getting the court to order the defendant's employer to withhold from his paychecks as much as 25 percent of his wages. You receive the garnished wages until your judgment has been satisfied. Ordinarily, to initiate a wage garnishment, you must get a writ of execution, complete an application and order for wage garnishment, and then get the order served on the judgment debtor's employer. Employers who do not comply with an order for wage garnishment can be held liable for the amount of money that should have been garnished.

You can view a sample application for wage garnishment on Form 4-16 of the CD.

Avoiding those exempt assets

Remember, if the defendant in your lawsuit is an individual, a sole proprietorship, or a partner in a business, you can't collect your judgment by going after his exempt assets — the assets that are legally protected from the collection process. Therefore, if all the debtor's assets are exempt, getting a judgment from the court is an exercise in futility because you have a judgment that you can't enforce.

Each state has its own list of exempt assets. Some are more generous than others. For example, Texas and Florida provide many more exemptions than other states. The most common exemptions are

- A homestead — the residence that someone uses as his primary residence. Generally, only a certain amount of the equity is exempt, not the entire value of the home.
- An automobile, up to a certain dollar value.
- Household furnishings, household goods, clothing, appliances, books, and so on, up to a certain dollar value.
- Jewelry, up to a certain dollar value.
- Farm implements, tools, and professional books used by a debtor in the normal course of business, up to a certain dollar value.
- Life insurance contracts that have not matured or the dividend, interest, or loan value of an unmatured contract, up to a certain dollar value. Also, stock bonuses, pensions, profit-sharing, annuities, IRAs, Social Security and veteran's benefits, unemployment compensation, and public assistance payments.

Chapter 5

Using an Attorney

Attorneys are like dentists and doctors: You may not like paying money to see them, but sometimes their services are indispensable. This chapter clues you in about when to get legal help and shows you how to find an attorney who meets your needs and who won't put too big of a dent in your bank account. We also provide advice for cutting your legal costs and working effectively with your attorney, as well as describe your options in case your relationship with your lawyer gets rocky.

Knowing When to Hire an Attorney

The best time to hire an attorney is before you really need one — before you're in legal trouble. An attorney's up-front advice and assistance can help you protect your legal rights, secure your financial interests, and avoid messy and potentially expensive legal entanglements. An attorney's help is essential if you're negotiating something important that could affect your life for years to come or that involves a lot of money.

Yes, an attorney costs you money, but the money you spend getting up-front help is a drop in the bucket compared to how much you could fork over later if your decision not to get help and information lands you in legal hot water. For example, you want to use a lawyer when

✔ You're buying or selling a home or you have tax problems.

✔ You're getting divorced, and you and your spouse must divide assets of significant value, you want spousal support, or you and your spouse share minor children.

> ✔ Your fiancé wants you to sign a prenuptial agreement, you've experienced financial problems, or have been injured in an accident.
>
> ✔ You want to write a complex will or set up a trust.

A lawyer's help is also indispensable when you're involved in a lawsuit outside of small claims court. Self-representation is nothing short of foolhardy.

Deciding What Kind of Attorney You Need

First things first: Before you hire an attorney, you must decide what kind of attorney you need.

Some attorneys are generalists. They deal with a wide variety of everyday legal matters. They're qualified to draft simple contracts, negotiate simple divorces, draft simple wills, and so on. If your legal matter is straightforward, a generalist may fit the bill.

If your legal matter is complex or involves a significant amount of money, hire a specialist. This type of attorney focuses most if not all of his practice on a specific type of law, such as personal injury, bankruptcy, estate planning, real estate, or family law. Some specialists are also state board certified in their practice areas. Usually, to become board certified, an attorney must pass a special state test. To maintain his certification, he may have to attend periodic classes on topics related to his area of legal expertise. About half of all the states board-certify attorneys who have experience in certain areas of the law, such as bankruptcy and civil trial law.

Board certification means that an attorney is especially experienced in a certain type of law. It does not necessarily mean that the attorney is best qualified to represent you. You not only need to have confidence in your attorney's legal abilities, but you also must believe that the attorney sincerely wants to help you solve your problem.

Next, familiarize yourself with the following list of attributes that describe a good attorney. If your legal problem is complicated or you need help with a lawsuit, working with a lawyer who embodies as many of these attributes as possible is particularly important. These attributes are less important if you need an attorney to perform a relatively simple task, such as writing a letter or reviewing a simple contract.

✔ **A legal track record:** Ideally, you want a seasoned attorney, not one who just passed the bar exam. You also want an attorney with specific experience in handling legal matters like yours. Practice makes perfect!

✔ **Good communication skills:** You want an attorney who can use plain English to clarify a law, interpret a contract, or define a legal term. When you're involved in a lawsuit, you encounter many new and confusing legal terms and procedures. Working with a lawyer who can explain everything to you makes the lawsuit less overwhelming. Most important, perhaps, a lawyer who is a good communicator usually has an edge when negotiating out-of-court settlements and arguing cases in court.

✔ **A comfortable personality:** You may have to share personal information with your lawyer — maybe even something that is embarrassing to you. Therefore, you want a lawyer you feel comfortable confiding in.

✔ **An interest in your problem:** An attorney who is genuinely interested in your legal problem is more motivated to help you. An attorney who is working with you only for the money is apt to cut corners, deliver results slowly, and provide you with inferior legal help. Luckily, most lawyers are caring professionals who want to get the best results possible for their clients.

Your attorney is not your therapist. If you need help dealing with the emotional aspects of your legal problem, see a mental health professional.

✔ **Familiarity with the court and the court personnel:** When it comes to filing paperwork, getting court dates scheduled, and so on, it helps to work with an attorney who's familiar with the procedures of the court where your lawsuit will be heard and who's liked and respected by the court personnel and judges.

✔ **Affordability:** The fees of most attorneys are negotiable, so there's no reason to pay more than you have to for legal services. However, don't base your choice of a lawyer on cost alone. A lawyer's inexpensive fees can reflect inexperience, incompetence, or both.

Finding a Lawyer Who Fits the Bill

The best way to find a lawyer who meets your needs is to talk with at least two attorneys. Comparison-shopping for an attorney can make you feel confident that you're hiring the best lawyer for the job. Of course, the amount of time and energy you devote to shopping for a lawyer should be commensurate with the significance of your legal needs. In other words, it's more important to interview multiple lawyers when your legal need is complex or involves a lot of money than when your legal need is simple and straightforward.

Hiring an attorney

When you're suing (or being sued) outside of small claims court, not having legal help is downright foolish — and sometimes even dangerous. Here are some of the most important reasons you should have legal representation:

✔ Your attorney can help you determine which court is best if you have the option of filing your lawsuit in more than one court. He knows the strategic reasons for filing in one court rather than another.

✔ Your attorney can use the *discovery* process to help build a winning case for you by getting at the facts of your dispute. It's difficult, if not impossible, to effectively use the discovery process yourself. The sidebar "Just the facts, ma'am" later in this chapter provides an overview of the tools of discovery.

✔ If your case goes to trial, you usually have the option of a judge or a jury trial. Your attorney can help you decide which is best for your case.

✔ From the perspective of your pocketbook, you'll spend more money if you go with a jury trial because jury trials take longer than bench trials. Simply selecting a jury can take days.

✔ A jury's decision is called a *verdict*; a judge's is called a *decision*. Regardless of who decides the outcome of your case, the decision must be based on the facts of your case and on the law that applies to it. Once

the judge or jury reaches its decision, the judge who presided over your trial issues a judgment. A *judgment* is a formal written statement of the decision.

✔ It may be easier to negotiate an out-of-court settlement with the defendant. Your attorney can help you objectively assess the strengths and weaknesses of your case (which can be hard to do on your own) and work with the opposing attorney to negotiate a resolution that's acceptable to you. By the way, most lawsuits are settled out of court.

✔ Your attorney can prepare you for the kinds of questions the defendant's attorney may ask you and can poke holes in the defendant's case with effective questioning.

✔ Your attorney can use various legal maneuvers to prevent the other side from introducing damaging evidence during your trial.

If your attorney raises an objection to a question you're asked while on the witness stand, do not answer the question until the judge rules on the objection. If the judge overrules your attorney's objection, you must answer the question. If the judge sustains the objection, do not answer the question.

✔ An attorney can help calm your nerves and ease your fears by explaining what's going on, filling out the legal paperwork, and monitoring and meeting the court's deadlines.

Sources for attorney referrals can include

✔ **Friends and family members:** Friends and family can be good sources for recommendations of attorneys they've worked with on legal issues similar to yours.

✔ **Local or state bar:** Although having her name on a bar association's referral list is no guarantee that the lawyer is right for you, a local or state bar can be a good source for attorneys. Go to the American Bar Association's Web site at www.abanet.org/referral/home.html to link up to local and state bar association lawyer referral services for each state.

✔ **Lawyer referral services:** Although these services can provide you with the names of lawyers in your area, they make no claim about the lawyers' legal skills or experience. Some services refer only lawyers who practice a particular kind of law — family law or estate-planning law, for example — and others refer lawyers from a wide range of practice areas.

✔ **Other lawyers:** Lawyers often have the inside scoop on who is and isn't a good attorney.

✔ **Lawyer ads:** You can find these ads in the Yellow Pages, in the weekly television listings section of your local newspaper, and on TV and radio. They can be a good starting place for developing a list of attorneys you may want to work with.

✔ **Lawyer Web sites:** These Web sites typically provide more detailed information about a lawyer and the firm he works for than other types of lawyer advertising. Some also provide basic information about the law and links to other legal resources.

✔ **Legal Web sites:** Many legal Web sites include a lawyer database. Usually, you can search the database by location and by legal specialty. The sidebar "Online resources for finding a lawyer" lists some Internet lawyer databases you may want to check out.

Lawyers who are part of a Web site's database might pay to be included in it. Being part of a database does not necessarily mean that a lawyer is well qualified.

✔ **Your insurance company:** If your legal problem is covered by your insurance policy — for example, the driver of the car you hit sues you — the company that issued the policy might provide you with an attorney.

Whittling down your list

Once you have a list of attorneys, call each of their offices to ask some initial screening questions. These questions help you determine which lawyers you want to meet in person. If your list is lengthy, meeting every lawyer face-to-face can take a lot of time, so screening by telephone is a time-saver. Ideally, you'll speak with the attorney when you call, but in many instances, you'll talk to the lawyer's assistant or the office receptionist.

To screen potential attorneys, be sure to ask how long they've been practicing law, whether they often handle matters like yours, and whether they offer a free initial consultation.

If your legal matter is straightforward and simple, ask how much each lawyer charges to provide the legal help you need. With that information, you may feel prepared to make a hiring decision. However, if you want to be 100 percent certain about your choice, or if your legal matter is complex, face-to-face meetings are essential.

Online resources for finding a lawyer

Here's a sampling of Web sites that you can use to locate an attorney. Don't forget: Being listed at one of these Web sites does not speak to a lawyer's abilities. You have to check that out for yourself.

✔ www.attorneypages.com provides state-by-state contact information for lawyers in 70 different practice areas.

✔ www.attorneyfind.com lets you query the lawyers in its database about their fees and legal experience.

✔ www.lawyers.com profiles more than 42,000 attorneys and their firms. You can search for an attorney by legal specialty and by location.

Getting down to the nitty-gritty

After you finish your phone screenings and narrow down your list to between three and five lawyers, schedule a meeting with each one. These meetings give you an opportunity to discuss your legal needs in detail, find out how you would be charged, and assess the attorneys up close and personal.

Each initial consultation will probably last about an hour. Deciding ahead of time what questions you want to ask and bringing them to your meetings help you use your consultation time efficiently. Don't hesitate to jot down each attorney's answers along with your impressions. These notes come in handy when you're ready to make a hiring decision.

The following questions represent a range of things you may want to ask during your meetings. However, not all of them are appropriate for every legal need. Choose from these questions to develop a list that's right for you.

✔ What is your legal background and experience?

✔ How many cases like mine have you handled?

✔ How many cases like mine have you tried? (Not all lawyers have experience in the courtroom, and many lawyers actually avoid it. If you need help with a lawsuit, look for an attorney who enjoys the give-and-take of trials and who has experience with them.)

✔ From what you know so far, what are the strengths and weaknesses of my case?

✔ What are the potential outcomes for my case?

✔ What steps would you take to resolve my problem?

✔ Is mediation or arbitration an option for my case?

✔ What issues should I be thinking about?

✔ What is your hourly rate?

✔ How will I be billed for your services? (You can find out about billing options in the section "Managing Money Matters" later in this chapter.)

✔ Are your fees negotiable?

✔ Can you estimate about how many hours it will take to resolve my legal problem and how much it will cost?

✔ What expenses will I be liable for, and how much do you estimate they will amount to? (Expenses can include filing fees, long-distance calls, postage and overnight delivery service, copying, courier services, and a lot more if you're involved in a complicated lawsuit that goes all the way to trial.)

✔ Would I have any control over how much you spend on legal expenses related to my case? (Possible options include setting a ceiling on expenses or requiring that your lawyer get your approval for expenses over a certain dollar amount. Asking to set limits on expenses is a reasonable request when resolving your legal problem is likely to take a long time.)

✔ How often will I be billed?

✔ Can I see a sample written fee agreement? (The section "Managing Money Matters" later in this chapter provides sample agreements.)

✔ How will I be kept informed of your progress on my case? (If you're hiring an attorney to represent you in a lawsuit, you should expect to receive monthly progress reports. Read them carefully, and ask about anything you don't understand.)

✔ Who else in your office will work on my case? What are their hourly rates?

Having a paralegal or junior attorney work on your case under the supervision of your lawyer can save you money, assuming that you're billed at their hourly rates rather than at your attorney's higher hourly rate.

✔ If I am your client, what will you expect of me?

✔ How quickly will you return my calls?

✔ Will you provide me with references of other clients you have worked with who had legal needs similar to mine?

The attorneys you meet will probably have questions of their own for you. Their questions may be intended to clarify things you say, get additional information, help decide how to charge for their services, and determine whether working with you might pose a conflict of interest with any of their current clients.

Most attorneys pick and choose their clients. Therefore, if you come across as a potentially demanding or difficult client, or if you act distrustful of attorneys in general, you may have a hard time finding a good lawyer who's willing to take your case.

Signing the Letter of Agreement

After you have decided on an attorney, ask her to formalize the terms of your relationship with a contract or letter of agreement. It should be written in language you can understand, not in legalese. If you have questions about the agreement, don't sign it or pay the attorney any money until you get them answered.

The agreement is relatively brief if you're hiring a lawyer to provide a narrowly focused legal service, such as drafting your will. However, if you're hiring a lawyer to help you with a more complicated legal matter, and you will be working together for a prolonged period, the agreement will be longer and more detailed. At a minimum, the agreement should spell out the fee arrangement, how you will be billed, the services the lawyer is to provide, and how expenses are to be handled.

Also included should be the attorney's hourly rate, and the hourly rates of anyone else who will work on your case; how frequently you will receive written reports on the status of your legal problem. (You don't need this information if your lawyer won't be working for you for an extended period. For example, if your lawyer is writing a will for you, you probably won't need periodic written updates on how he is progressing.); and anything else you and the attorney agreed to.

Managing Money Matters

There's no doubt about it: Quality legal help doesn't come cheap. But understanding how lawyers charge and the pros and cons of each fee option can help you keep your legal bill from reaching into the stratosphere. Lawyers charge for their services by the hour, on a retainer basis, by flat fee, or by a contingent fee arrangement.

Paying by the hour

Attorneys most often charge by the hour. Their hourly rate is usually based on the following three factors:

- **Their experience and reputation:** Attorneys with a lot of experience under their belts or big reputations (Johnny Cochran comes to mind) can, and usually do, charge more than other attorneys.

- **The size of their law firm:** Big firms tend to have big overheads, and the lawyers who work for them pass that expense on to their clients.

>
> ✔ **Their geographic location:** Lawyers practicing law in major markets such as New York, Chicago, Houston, and Los Angeles usually have higher hourly rates than comparable attorneys in smaller markets.

When an attorney bills you by the hour, you will probably be asked to pay money up front. This money, called a *retainer,* is a down payment on the total cost of the attorney's legal services. You can find out more about retainers in the sidebar "A rundown on retainers" later in this chapter.

To prepare for what might appear in your lawyer's retainer agreement, see the sample hourly retainer agreement on Form 5-1 of the CD.

To ensure that your legal bill doesn't spin out of control when an attorney is going to charge you on an hourly basis, ask for a provision in your agreement that limits the number of hours the attorney can bill you without your okay to bill more.

Before you agree to pay by the hour, clarify how the lawyer charges for partial hours. For example, does he bill in 15-minute increments, 25-minute increments, or something else? If he spends just 5 minutes doing something related to your case but bills you as though he spent 25 minutes, you'll pay more for legal help than if he treated that 5 minutes as 15 minutes.

Paying a flat fee

If your legal need is simple, it has a clear beginning and end, and the likelihood of complications is slim, a lawyer might agree to charge a flat fee for her services based on her hourly rate. For example, you may be charged a flat fee to have your will drafted, have a straightforward divorce agreement drawn up, or have your attorney handle your bankruptcy. You may have to pay the attorney a retainer to begin work on your case.

The advantage of a flat fee is obvious: You know exactly how much your lawyer is going to cost you. The downside is that if your legal matter takes more time to handle than your attorney anticipated, you may end up having to pay more than the flat fee. However, most lawyers tell you up front under what circumstances you will be charged more. Make sure to confirm that a lawyer's flat fee includes all expenses, such as copying, filing fees, delivery charges, and so on.

Form 5-2 on the CD provides an example of the kind of flat fee agreement your lawyer may ask you to sign.

A rundown on retainers

As your attorney works on your case, he charges the cost of that time, based on his hourly rate, against the amount you paid as a retainer. The more work your lawyer does for you, and the higher the lawyer's hourly rate, the quicker your retainer is depleted. Other lawyers who might work on your case, as well as your lawyer's support staff, also charge their time against the retainer. Depending on your legal problem, an attorney might want a separate retainer for expenses.

When you work out the terms of your relationship with a lawyer, clarify exactly who will be billing against the retainer and what their hourly rates are. Make sure that any lawyers who are junior to the one you hire, as well as all support staff, bill their time at their hourly rate and not at your lawyer's higher rate. Also, find out under what conditions you can get back whatever is left of your retainer. For example, if your attorney finishes all work on your case without depleting the retainer, you should get back whatever money is left.

Paying contingency fees

When you need a lawyer to help you collect money you're entitled to, the lawyer will probably propose working on a contingent fee basis. This means that he gets paid by taking a percentage of whatever money he collects for you. Most lawyers take 30 percent of what they collect before litigation, and up to 50 percent of what they collect through a lawsuit. Debt collection, personal injury, and medical malpractice cases are often billed on a contingent fee basis. You can find a sample contingent fee agreement on Form 5-3 on the CD.

The advantage of a contingent fee arrangement is that it lets you minimize your up-front legal costs and gives your lawyer a strong incentive to work hard for you. No results, no money! However, unless you negotiate something different, you must reimburse your lawyer for the expenses associated with your case whether you win or lose.

When you and your lawyer work out the terms of your contingent fee agreement, make sure that the agreement clearly spells out the percentage your lawyer will take and how expenses are handled. Many states require lawyers to provide their clients with written agreements when they work for them on a contingent fee basis.

To keep a lid on your expenses, you may be able to negotiate a ceiling on the total of expenses you're liable for, or an attorney may be willing to take her cut of any money collected after expenses are deducted.

Knowing how to proceed when money is tight

If you don't have a lot of money to spare but you need legal services, look for an attorney who will let you pay over time or who will charge you less than usual. Don't be bashful about presenting your situation in a sympathetic manner and asking to work out special payment arrangements if you need a financial break.

Another option is to check out the low-cost or no-cost legal resources in your community. Depending on where you live, you might find help at a law school clinic, through the state or local bar association, or from Legal Aid. Legal Aid is a federally sponsored program designed to assist low-income people. It tends to focus on landlord-tenant problems, credit issues, problems with utility companies, foreclosures, and simple divorces. To find a Legal Aid office near you, look in your local phone book, call your local bar association, or call the Legal Services Corporation in Washington, D.C., at 202-336-8800.

Money-saving advice

You don't want to pay more than you have to for legal help. To keep your legal costs under control, follow the money-saving advice given here. Most of this advice can also help you build a positive relationship with your lawyer:

- Ask your lawyer what you can do to minimize your legal costs, and then follow that advice.

- Provide your lawyer with as much information as you can and avoid needless calls to your lawyer. They cost you money if your lawyer charges you for the time she spends on the phone with you.

- Let your lawyer know as soon as possible when new developments relate to your case. The information can change how your

lawyer approaches your case and can save your lawyer time.

- Find out whether you can handle any of the tasks related to your legal problem — copying, making deliveries, filing court documents, and even performing simple research.

- Make brevity your motto. The more of your lawyer's time you take up, the more your lawyer costs you, unless she's working for a contingent fee. Even then, respect your lawyer's time.

- Review your lawyer's bill to make sure that you haven't been overcharged and to keep tabs on your legal expenses.

Resolving Complaints and Disputes

Are you angry with your attorney? If you're upset over a relatively minor matter, call your lawyer and talk about it. The root of your dissatisfaction may be just a misunderstanding. If your gripe is more serious, put your concerns in writing and ask for a face-to-face meeting.

Whether you're upset with your lawyer over something big or something little, make sure that your unhappiness is justified before you do anything about it. For example, review the contract or letter of agreement you have with your lawyer. You may find that you really have no cause to gripe.

Also, make sure that you have realistic expectations of your lawyer. Although you have a right to expect your phone calls to be returned in a timely manner (within 24 hours is reasonable unless you have an emergency) and to be kept up-to-date on the progress of your case, you don't have the right to expect your attorney to spend hours on the phone with you or to spend full-time working on your legal matter.

If your dissatisfaction is legitimate, and if your lawyer is unresponsive to your requests and concerns, it may be time to send her a dismissal letter. (Form 5-4 on the CD provides a sample lawyer-dismissal letter.) Then you can hire a new lawyer. However, depending on the terms of your agreement, be prepared to pay for the services your lawyer has provided to you up to the point of dismissal and for all his expenses up to then as well.

Part II
Credit Matters

The 5th Wave   By Rich Tennant

"I just don't know where the money's going."

In this part . . .

We can prepare you to be a responsible credit card consumer and to make wise decisions when you apply for a bank loan. Chapter 6 briefs you on the various types of credit you may want, tells you how creditors evaluate you, and discusses the credit-related federal laws that protect you. Chapter 7 tells you how to protect your valuable financial information and credit history. If you're feeling buried in debt and you wonder about the best way to dig out, read Chapter 8. It provides get-out-of-debt strategies and offers important advice about how to deal with your car and home loans when you can't keep up with your payments. Chapter 9 tells you what happens if you file a Chapter 7 or Chapter 13 bankruptcy, prepares you for the decisions you have to make, and warns you against taking certain steps in the months just prior to your bankruptcy. Because bankruptcy and other serious money troubles destroy your credit, Chapter 10 brings you full circle by showing you how to rebuild your credit once those troubles are behind you.

Chapter 6

Consumer Credit: It's the American Way

onsumer credit lets you buy now and pay later. Although using credit can be a matter of convenience, it's usually a necessity if you want to buy a big-ticket item such as a home or a car or pay for your kid's college education. Consumer credit also provides an invaluable financial safety net if an unexpected emergency throws you for a loop.

Consumer credit has some downsides, however. For one thing, when you purchase something with credit, you end up paying more than if you purchase it with cash, because the creditor charges you interest. Another downside of credit is that it can be all too easy to overuse. Worst case scenario, you could be forced to file for bankruptcy and maybe lose the very assets that the credit helped you acquire.

Although using credit is a double-edged sword, the advice and information in this chapter can help you make credit work *for* you, not against you. For example, we educate you about your rights during the credit application and review process. We also tell you about the basic types of credit, what to consider when you apply for credit, and how to deal with credit card billing problems, among other things.

Getting the Credit You Deserve

Creditors won't extend credit to just anyone. They have their standards! When you apply for credit, the creditor determines whether it wants to work with you by evaluating how you measure up against the three Cs: character, capacity, and collateral. Some creditors also check your credit score.

Knowing the three Cs

Character, capacity, and *collateral:* These three C words represent the criteria that most creditors use when they evaluate a credit application. Unless you score well on all three, you may be denied the credit you want, or you may have to pay a higher interest rate than other people do.

Creditors judge your *character* by looking at the way you've handled your debts in the past. Have you paid your debts on time? Have you ever defaulted on a loan? Have you ever filed for bankruptcy?

Capacity relates to your ability to repay your debt. Bankcard issuers, banks, mortgage companies, and other creditors don't want to extend credit to someone who can't afford to repay them.

Usually, lenders care about *collateral* only if you ask to borrow a substantial amount of money. They want you to guarantee the credit they extend to you by letting them have a lien on one of your assets. Being able to put up collateral can make the difference between getting your credit application approved or denied.

Creditors generally measure you against the three Cs by using these three tools:

- ✔ **Your credit application:** The application may be short or long, but the more money you apply for, the longer it usually is. For example, you have to provide a lot more information when you apply for a mortgage loan than when you apply for a credit card.
- ✔ **Your credit history:** This is a record of your use of credit over time. For detailed information about credit histories and how to find out about your own history, turn to Chapter 7.
- ✔ **Your credit score:** This is a numeric indicator of your credit worthiness.

Knowing your score

We bet you don't know your credit score. In fact, you may not even know that you have one! Yet a growing number of creditors are relying less on the information in your credit record and more on how you score when they evaluate your credit worthiness.

A *credit score* is an automated number derived from information in your credit record. The score ranges from 300 to 900, the higher the score, the better. It sometimes takes into account such things as your job or occupation, the length of your employment, and whether you own your home. This information is evaluated in light of five different factors. From most important to least important, those factors are

- ✔ **Your debt payment history:** A history of on-time payments raises your score.

- ✔ **The amounts and the types of your debts:** Having too much debt or certain types of debt is commonly viewed as a sign of money troubles. A finance company loan, for example, hurts your credit score.

- ✔ **The length of your credit history:** A relatively brief history works against you because you don't have a long track record as a consumer.

- ✔ **The amount of new credit you have applied for recently and the amount of new credit you have been approved for:** Moderation boosts your credit score.

The Equal Credit Opportunity Act

It doesn't matter whether you're applying for a bank loan, a Visa or Master-Card, or a retail store charge; when you go through the credit application and review process, you're protected by the federal Equal Credit Opportunity Act (ECOA). Among other things, this law limits what a creditor can ask you and consider when it evaluates your application. For example, the law says when you apply for credit, creditors can't ask you about your sex, your race, your national origin, and whether you're single, married, separated, or divorced (unless you're applying for joint credit).

If you apply for separate, unsecured credit, in most states you can't be asked about your marital status. However, that's not the case if you're married, you live in a community property state, and you apply for separate, unsecured credit. Arizona, California, Idaho, Louisiana, New Mexico, Texas, and Washington are all community property states.

When applying for credit, the ECOA also prohibits creditors from asking you about your plans to have children, your religion, or whether you receive child support, alimony, or separate maintenance.

If you apply for a real estate loan, the creditor can ask you to disclose all this stuff voluntarily, except your religion. The information helps the federal government enforce its anti-discrimination laws.

The ECOA also says that when a creditor is deciding whether to give you the credit you ask for, it can't consider your sex, race, national origin, marital status, or religion; whether you have a telephone listed in your name.

(However, the creditor can ask if you have a phone.) And a creditor can't consider tour age, unless you're too young to enter into a contract (under age 18 in most states). However, if you're at or near retirement age, a creditor can consider such things as how long your retirement income will continue or how long it will be until you reach retirement age.

Getting back to you

Once a creditor has all the information it needs to make a decision about your credit application, the ECOA says that you must be told in writing whether your application has been approved or denied. If you're turned down for credit, the notice you receive is called an *adverse action letter*. It must either provide you with the main reasons for the denial or tell you how to find out. If the reasons are stated in the letter, they must be specific — "Your income is not sufficient" or "You do not have a long enough work history," for example. The creditor can't simply give you a vague excuse like, "You don't meet our standards."

If a creditor's so-called specific reason for denying you credit is vague and confusing, call the creditor and ask for an explanation. If the letter tells you to contact the creditor to find out why you weren't approved, you must do so within 60 days. These same rights apply when one of your creditors sends you a notice that it has closed your account or downgraded the terms of the account. These rights also apply when you're offered credit at less favorable terms than the credit you applied for, unless you accept those other terms.

If the creditor reviewed your credit record as part of its decision-making process, the federal Fair Credit Reporting Act (FCRA) says that it must provide you with the name and address of the credit bureau that supplied your credit record information. You can use that information to order a free copy of your record from that credit bureau. You must request that free copy within 60 days of learning that you were rejected for credit. Chapter 7 tells you how to order a free copy of your credit record.

If your credit record contains errors that could have contributed to your being denied credit, correct it by following the process outlined in Chapter 9 and then reapply for the credit.

Knowing what to do when your ECOA rights have been violated

Do you think that a creditor has trampled on your ECOA rights? If you do, your first step should be to write the creditor a complaint letter, explaining what happened and why you believe that your ECOA rights have been violated. Form 6-1 on the CD provides a sample complaint letter.

Special ECOA protections for women

The Equal Credit Opportunity Act (ECOA) has special importance to women because it includes provisions that help married women develop their own credit records separate and apart from their spouses'. Then, if the women later become widowed or divorced, they have access to the credit they need to rebuild their lives. Among other ECOA rights, the law says that as a woman, you have the right to have credit in your birth or maiden name, in your first married name, or in a name that combines both last names. You also have a right to have your credit application judged on its own merits, based on your income and credit history; have all your income considered when your credit application is evaluated, regardless of whether the income is from part-time or full-time work, public assistance, child support, alimony, and so on; and not be asked about your husband when you apply for credit, unless you must rely on his alimony or child support payments to help you qualify for the credit.

Additional protections for women in the ECOA include protection from being asked about your marital status when you apply for unsecured credit, unless you live in a community property state. However, if you apply for secured credit, the creditor can use your marital status to deny your credit and to limit the amount of credit you're approved for; not be asked about your plans to have children or about your birth control method when you apply for credit; getting unsecured credit without having your spouse as a co-signer, assuming you meet the creditor's standards. However, if you apply for secured credit, your spouse can be asked to sign the ownership documents. Also, if you live in a community property state, the lender can require your spouse to co-sign for the credit even if you qualify for it on your own; and the right to keep accounts in your own name after you're married, change your name, reach a certain age, or retire, unless a creditor has evidence that you can't afford to or are unwilling to pay on the account.

If the letter doesn't clear up the problem, you can meet with an attorney who has experience in handling ECOA disputes to discuss the feasibility of suing the creditor. You can sue for actual damages as well as punitive damages of up to $10,000. If you win your lawsuit, you can be reimbursed for your attorney's fees and court costs.

Some states have their own equal credit opportunity laws. If your state does, the lawyer you meet with may recommend suing under that law, not under the federal law. In addition to writing a protest letter and filing a lawsuit against the creditor who ignores your ECOA rights, you should file a complaint against the creditor with your state attorney general's office of consumer protection. You should then report the creditor to the appropriate government agency. Although many of these agencies will not intervene on your behalf, they may take action against a creditor if they receive enough complaints about the company.

Who ya gonna call?

When you want the federal government to know that your ECOA rights have been violated, it's important to send your complaint to the right government agency. This sidebar gives you a rundown on which federal office oversees which kind of complaint. By the way, you can use the information in this sidebar when you have a complaint about a creditor that has violated *any* of the federal consumer credit laws, not just when you have an ECOA-related beef.

✔ **Federal Trade Commission (FTC):** Contact this agency if the creditor is a retail store, a department store, a small loan or finance company, a mortgage company, an oil and gas company, a public utility, a state credit union, a government lending program, or a travel and entertainment credit card. Write to Federal Trade Commission, Consumer Response Center, 600 Pennsylvania Ave. NW, Washington, DC 20580.

✔ **Comptroller of the Currency:** This is the agency to write to if your problem concerns a nationally chartered bank. The word *National* or the abbreviation *N.A.* in a bank's

title tells you that it has a national charter. Direct your complaint letter to Comptroller of the Currency, Compliance Management, Mail Stop 7-5, Washington, DC 20219.

✔ **Federal Deposit Insurance Corporation (FDIC):** Write to this office if you have a complaint about a state-chartered bank that's insured by the FDIC. Your letter should go to Federal Deposit Insurance Corporation, Consumer Affairs Division, Washington, DC 20429.

✔ **Office of Thrift Supervision:** If your complaint concerns a federally chartered or federally insured savings and loan association, write to Office of Thrift Supervision, Consumer Affairs Program, Washington, DC 20552.

✔ **National Credit Union Administration:** This is the agency to contact if you believe that a federally chartered credit union has violated your credit rights. Write to National Credit Union Administration, Consumer Affairs Division, Washington, DC 20456.

Understanding What You're Applying For

The federal Truth in Lending Act (TLA) requires creditors to provide applicants with the terms and conditions of the credit they apply for. Unfortunately, most of this information may be buried in an application's fine print. However, don't disregard this information because of the size of the words. Reading the terms and conditions information is the only way to know whether a particular credit offer is a good deal or a bad deal for you, and it's the only way to compare credit offers and options.

Applying the TLA to credit cards

If you apply for a credit card, the TLA says that a creditor must tell you the card's

✔ **Annual percentage rate, or APR:** This is the rate of interest you pay over a year's time on your card's balance. The APR is either fixed or variable. If it's variable, it goes up or down depending on the performance of certain economic indicators. If the credit card you're offered has a variable APR, the card issuer must tell you that and must also tell you how the rate is determined.

✔ **Periodic rate:** This is the interest rate that you pay on your card balance in a given month. The periodic rate is 1/12 of a card's APR. For example, if a card has an APR of 18 percent, the periodic or monthly rate is 1.5 percent. The higher the rate, the more it costs you to maintain a balance on the card.

✔ **Balance calculation method:** Different creditors use different methods to calculate the amount of interest they charge you each month. Some methods cost more than others. Creditors can apply the periodic rate to

- **The *adjusted daily balance* on your credit card:** This method adds up to the lowest monthly finance charge. Therefore, it's your most advantageous balance calculation method.

- **The *average daily balance* on your credit card:** This is the balance calculation method that credit card issuers use most often. It may or may not take into account new charges you make during a billing period, but it's better for you if it doesn't.

- **The *previous balance* on your credit card:** This method does not take into account any payments or charges you make during the billing period.

Pay close attention to a card's balance computation method. Even though two card offers may have the same APR and periodic rate, one card may cost significantly more than the other, depending on the method used to calculate finance charges.

When you receive a low-interest introductory offer for a credit card, don't sign up without knowing how long that rate of interest lasts; sometimes it lasts only a few months. Also, find out whether the low rate applies only to balance transfers or to purchases as well.

✔ **Grace period:** This is the amount of time that you have between the end of a billing cycle and the due date to pay the account in full and avoid finance charges. Most grace periods are between 20 and 25 days. However, some cards give you no grace period, which means that you're charged interest even if you pay your bill in full as soon as you receive it.

When your credit card gives you a grace period, the card issuer is legally obligated to give you enough time to pay your bill and avoid finances by mailing your bill to you at least 14 days before your account payment is due.

✔ **Annual fees:** Some cards charge a yearly fee for the privilege of using them.

> ✔ **Other fees:** Depending on the card, you may have to pay a fee whenever you exceed your credit limit, every time you use it to get a cash advance, and every time you're late with your payment. With some cards, you even have to pay a fee each time you use them. Ouch!

Card issuers are prohibited from sending you a credit card that you haven't asked for. They can, however, send you an application for a credit card, call to ask whether you're interested in one, and send you a preapproved offer of credit.

Considering some important points when applying for credit

Now that you know about the laws that protect you when you apply for credit, it's time to get down to the nitty-gritty of choosing and using credit. First come credit cards, and then come loans.

The credit cards in your wallet might all look the same to you, but they may differ from one another in important ways. For starters, they may have very different terms of payment. For example, bankcards such as Visa, MasterCard, and some retail store and gas cards let you maintain a balance on your account from month to month, up to your credit limit, as long as you pay at least the minimum due each month. You're charged interest on your account balance, and you're charged a late fee if you make your monthly payment after the due date. Credit cards such as these are categorized as *revolving* or *open-end credit*.

Bankcards can be secured or unsecured. If you don't have a good credit history or you're just starting to build one, a secured card may be the only kind of card you qualify for. For information about credit histories, read Chapter 7. If you want to read more about *secured credit cards,* which you collateralize with money in a bank account or with a CD, turn to Chapter 10.

Most merchants accept Visa and MasterCard, which tend to offer terms of credit that are a lot more attractive than those associated with retail store charge cards. Usually, you're better off charging retail store purchases on Visa or MasterCard, not on a retail store card.

Dealing with Credit Card Problems

When you use a credit card, your problems may not be limited to not being able to make your account payments on time or to pay at least the minimum due on your account each month. Your problems can also include statement errors, defective, shoddy, or incomplete products or services, and unauthorized charges on your account. The federal Fair Credit Billing Act (FCBA) applies to each of these problems.

Fixing errors

Billing statement errors covered by the FCBA include being charged for things that you did not purchase or authorize to have purchased with your credit card; an incorrect date of a purchase or the amount of the purchase; being charged for goods or services that you did not accept. For example, the couch you ordered arrives damaged, and you tell the delivery person to take it back; math errors in your statement; or a payment to your account not being reflected.

The FCBA also covers credit card account problems that are triggered because your monthly account statement is not delivered to the proper mailing address. However, to be protected by the FCBA, be sure to provide your creditor with your change-of-address information when you move at least 20 days before the end of the account billing cycle.

The FCBA does not protect you if you make purchases with the cash advance checks that your bankcard company sends you. Write to the card issuer as soon as you find an error in your credit card account statement. (Note that a telephone call does *not* activate the protections of the FCBA. Only a letter does.) Your letter should indicate your name, address, and account number; the dollar amount of the error; and the date of the error. It should also provide a clear and concise statement of why you believe your statement is wrong. If you have receipts, cancelled checks, or other documents that help make your point, attach copies of them to the letter. Make a copy of the letter for your files.

Form 6-2 on the CD provides a sample FCBA account statement dispute letter. Direct your letter to the address on your account statement for *billing inquiries* or *billing errors*. Do not send it in the same envelope you use to mail your account payment. If you do, your dispute letter may get lost in the shuffle, and the person who can help deal with your problem may never receive it.

Send your letter via certified mail and ask for a return receipt so you know when your creditor receives it and who signs for it. The letter should arrive no later than 60 days after the creditor first mailed you the incorrect bill.

Waiting for the creditor to act

After the creditor receives your letter, the FCBA gives the creditor 30 days to acknowledge receipt in writing. Then the creditor has two billing cycles or 90 days, whichever is less, to investigate the errors in your letter.

Dealing with debit cards

A debit card can make your daily life easier. You can use it as an ATM card together with your personal identification number (PIN) to obtain cash from your account, or you can use it like a check to pay for purchases.

You should use your debit card with caution — when you use a debit card, you are not protected by the Fair Credit Billing Act (FCBA). You cannot put a stop payment on a debit card purchase as you can when you pay with a check. If your debit card is lost or stolen, federal law gives you less legal protection against unauthorized purchases and withdrawals than you have when your credit card is lost or stolen.

The Electronic Funds Transfer Act (EFTA) gives you limited protection against unauthorized purchases and withdrawals made with your debit card. The law says that if your debit card is lost or stolen and you let the issuing bank know what happened within two business days of the card's disappearance, you are liable for only the first $50 of unauthorized withdrawals or purchases. If you wait until later to notify your bank, you could be held legally responsible for up to $500 in unauthorized withdrawals or purchases, assuming the bank can prove that you knew the card was lost or stolen and you didn't bother to report that fact right away.

When you get your bank statement, you might discover bank errors related to your debit card withdrawals or purchases. If you do, get in touch with your bank right away. (According to the EFTA, you have 60 days after the error was made to dispute it; however, the sooner you do, the easier it will be for you and the bank to sort things out.) Generally, once you have notified it about the problem, the bank has 10 business days to conduct an investigation. It must report its conclusion to you in writing within three business days of completing the investigation. If your bank concludes that it made an error, it must correct the problem within one business day of discovering it. If your bank needs more time to conduct its investigation, it can have up to 45 more days. However, it must credit your account for the total amount of money you are questioning and notify you of the credit.

While the investigation is taking place, you don't have to pay the amount in dispute or any related charges, but you must continue paying on the rest of your account. In addition, while the creditor is conducting its investigation, the FCBA says that the creditor can't take steps to collect the money in dispute or any related charges. The creditor also can't report to credit bureaus that your account is past due because you have not paid the amount in dispute. It can, however, report that you are disputing your bill. The creditor also can't close your account or restrict your use of the account. However, the dollar amount in dispute can be applied toward your credit limit.

And the answer is . . .

If your creditor concludes that your account statement is wrong, it must notify you in writing and tell you how the error will be corrected. However, if your creditor concludes that your account billing statement is correct, it must explain in writing why it arrived at that decision and send you a statement of what you owe.

If you dispute a charge on your credit card statement and the card issuer credits your account for that amount, the credit must include the amount of the charge and all related finance charges, late fees, and so on.

The FCBA gives you options when a creditor tells you that your account billing statement is correct and you disagree. You can

✔ Within your usual grace period, pay the amount in dispute as well as any related finance charges. If your account doesn't have a grace period, you have ten days after hearing from your creditor to pay up. If you don't pay by the deadline, your creditor can report to credit bureaus that your account is past due.

✔ Notify your creditor within your usual grace period that you continue to dispute your bill and that you will continue withholding payment. If you have no grace period, make this notification within ten days of your creditor's contact. This response has two downsides:

    • The creditor has the right to begin collection action against you.

    • The creditor can report to credit bureaus that your account is delinquent. If it does, the creditor must also report that you are disputing the fact that your account is past due. In addition, the FCBA says that the creditor must provide you with the name and address of each credit bureau it reports to, as well as the name and address of anyone else who saw your credit file with the notation that your account is in dispute. The creditor also must notify them if you settle your dispute.

If a creditor does not follow the FCBA's rules for investigating billing errors, it can't collect the money you're disputing or any related finance charges — up to $50 — even if you really do owe that money. You can also sue the creditor in federal court.

Handling Problem Goods and Services

Suppose the merchandise or services you buy with a credit card end up being defective. Maybe they're never delivered, or they're not provided according to the terms of your agreement. The FCBA can help you. Just how much depends on the kind of credit card you use. If you used a national bankcard or a travel and entertainment card such as American Express to purchase the problem merchandise or service, the FCBA applies only if the cost of your purchase exceeds $50 and you made the purchase in your home state or within 100 miles of your current mailing address.

If the FCBA applies to you, write to the creditor to give the business an opportunity to clear up the problem. Model your letter after Form 6-3 on the CD. While the creditor is looking into your problem, it cannot close your account or report it as late to credit bureaus. However, it can report your account as in dispute.

If your letter does not resolve your problem, the FCBA gives you the right to withhold payment from the creditor. If you do, however, the company can take steps to collect its money, ranging from turning your account over to a collection agency to suing you.

If the credit card company sues you to collect the money in dispute, the lawsuit could end up damaging your credit record.

Knowing what to do when someone else uses your credit card

According to the FTC, credit fraud costs consumers hundreds of millions of dollars. The fraud is due to stolen credit cards and account numbers. If one of your cards turns up missing, call the creditor immediately. If you make the call before someone else uses your card, the Fair Credit Billing Act says that you are not liable for any unauthorized charges. Otherwise, the most you can be responsible for is $50.

Paying for credit loss protection is a rip-off. Not only does the FCBA protect you from the financial effects of a lost or stolen credit card — assuming that you notify your creditor — but also the FCBA's protection costs you nothing.

If you believe that one of your creditors has violated the FCBA, write another letter to the credit card company, but this time, send it to the company's legal department. Call first to get the name of the individual responsible for ensuring that the company complies with the FCBA. In your letter, briefly describe the history of your problem, why you believe that the company has violated the law, and what you want done about your problem. Provide a date by which you expect to receive a response. Be sure to let the lawyer know that you're sending a copy of the letter to the federal government agency that regulates the credit card company. (The sidebar "Who ya gonna call?" provides the name and address of that agency.)

If you don't hear from the credit card company, or if the company's response doesn't satisfy you, meet with an attorney who has experience in resolving FCBA-related problems. The lawyer can advise you about the pros and cons of suing a credit card company and about the strengths and weaknesses of your case. If you decide to sue and you win your case, you will be awarded actual damages plus twice the amount of any applicable finance charges, but no more than $1,000 and no less than $100. Your creditor will also have to pay your attorney's fees and court costs.

If the damages you want to sue for are relatively small, you may want to sue in small claims court, where your expenses will be a lot lower.

If a lawyer will not take your case on a contingent fee basis, compare before you hire him to file a lawsuit the likely cost of the suit, how much you stand to gain if you win, and the likelihood that you will win. Chapter 5 explains how contingent fees work.

Other fair credit billing rights

The FCBA imposes additional obligations on creditors. It says that your creditors must give you written notice of your right to dispute billing errors when you open a new account. Creditors must also provide you with a billing statement every month you owe at least $1 on the account, or every month the creditor owes you at least $1.

Additionally, creditors must credit your account payment on the day it's received unless crediting the payment later will not cause you to be penalized in any way. And they must promptly credit your account or issue you a refund when you overpay on your account, assuming that you're entitled to more than $1.

Getting the Lowdown on Consumer Loans

Credit cards are a convenient but expensive source of credit. Therefore, when you want to finance the purchase of something big — something that costs more than $1,000 — it's best to get a loan rather than pay for the item with a credit card. And you simply can't buy some things with a credit card — a home or a car, for example. Therefore, unless you have the cash to pay for those things, you need to finance them with a loan.

The loan you apply for may be *unsecured* or *secured.* The bigger the loan, the more likely it is that the loan will be secured. Here are the key differences between the two types of loans:

✓ **Personal or unsecured loan:** If you have a good relationship with your bank and a solid credit history, you may qualify for a personal loan. However, the loan will probably be for just a few thousand dollars. To borrow more, you have to secure, or *collateralize,* your loan, which means that you have to allow the lender to place a lien on an asset you own. Then, if you default on the loan, the lender can take the asset and sell it to get the money to pay off your loan.

✔ **Secured loan:** If your credit record isn't top-grade, and/or if you want to borrow a substantial amount of money, you collateralize the loan with an asset. Car loans and debt-consolidation loans are common examples of secured loans.

✔ **Mortgage:** A mortgage is a special type of loan for a home, secured by the home itself. We cover mortgages in detail in Chapter 16.

✔ **Home equity loan:** This type of loan lets you borrow against the *equity* — the difference between the current value and how much you still owe — on your home. Your home acts as collateral for this oan.

In addition to knowing the basic terms and conditions of a loan that the TLA says a lender must tell you about, answer the following questions before you sign a loan application.

✔ How long do you have to repay the loan?

✔ Will the monthly payment change over the life of the loan?

✔ Will you have to make a *balloon payment?* A balloon payment is a large payment due at the end of a loan after you've made a series of smaller payments.

✔ Do you pay any penalties if you pay the loan off early?

✔ Will the interest rate on the loan increase if you miss a payment or make a payment late?

✔ Is credit insurance a condition of the loan, and if so, is the cost of the insurance included in the cost of the loan?

Don't initial or sign anything saying that you're buying voluntary credit insurance unless you really want to buy that insurance.

Try negotiating the terms of a loan as a way to decrease its cost. For example, ask for a lower interest rate or APR, or ask the lender to lower or eliminate some of the penalties or fees. (You usually do this when you're negotiating in person with a lender. You don't need to put your request in writing unless the loan officer asks you to do so.) Don't be afraid to ask for better terms — all a loan officer can say is no. The TLA says that when you apply for a loan, the creditor must indicate the following in writing:

✔ The total amount of money you're borrowing and the size of the down payment, if any.

✔ The amount of each loan payment, and the total number of payments necessary to pay off the loan.

✔ The loan's *total value,* which is the loan amount, interest on the loan, and any other loan-related costs, such as insurance.

✔ The loan's annual percentage rate, or APR. The APR reflects the interest rate as well as mortgage broker fees, points, and other charges (depending on the kind of loan you apply for).

✔ The total amount of the finance charges you'll pay over the life of the loan, as well as any extra charges you'll pay. Depending on the loan, extras may include late fees, service charges, and appraisal fees.

Most states have *usury laws*. These laws limit the amount of interest that a lender can charge you for a loan. Businesses that violate these laws may have to forfeit either all the interest you paid them or the right to collect future interest from you. Depending on your state's law, if you're a victim of usury, you may have the right to collect twice the amount of interest you paid to the creditor, plus your attorney's fees and court costs. Usury laws are very complicated. Therefore, you're usually best off scheduling an appointment with a consumer law attorney if you suspect that you're a victim. Signs that a lender may be violating your state's usury law include being asked to pay an unusually large number of loan-related fees and an interest rate that seems particularly high.

Avoiding the Wrong Lender

Most lenders are on the up and up. But if you don't have a stellar credit record and you're eager to get a loan, a lender with questionable ethics may offer you one. Watch out! Here are some signs that a lender is not someone with whom you should do business:

✔ The lender pressures you into applying for a loan or tells you to lie on your loan application. For example, an unscrupulous lender may tell you to pad your income so you can qualify for the loan you want. This tactic is most likely to happen when you have to collateralize the note; the lender is gambling that you will borrow more than you can afford to repay and that it will be able to take your collateral in the end.

✔ The lender tells you to sign loan documents that aren't complete, promising to fill in the blanks later.

✔ The lender doesn't provide you with legally required disclosures, such as a loan's APR and other information, or tells you that they aren't important enough to read.

✔ The lender promises you one set of terms when you apply for a loan, but then at closing, the actual terms of the loan are much less attractive.

If you end up doing business with a shady lender, contact your state banking commission, local Better Business Bureau, and the FTC. Depending on the kind of lender you're dealing with, you may also want to contact one of the federal regulatory offices listed in this chapter's "Who ya gonna call?" sidebar.

Special Information about Home Equity Loans

Home equity loans let you benefit from the appreciated value of your home and are a relatively easy and quick way to obtain cash. However, because home equity loans involve giving a lender a lien on your home, understanding how they work is very important. If you can't repay the loan, you may be forced to sell your home.

The right to change your mind

With a home equity loan, your home collateralizes the loan; therefore, after you've been approved, the lender must give you the *right of rescission* — three days to change your mind about going through with the loan. You have this right whenever a lender takes an interest in your home.

These three days begin after you've signed the loan agreement, after the lender provides you with a Truth in Lending disclosure form, and after the lender has given you two copies of a notice about your right of rescission. The three days end at midnight on the third business day after you sign the loan agreement. Sundays and legal holidays don't count as one of the three days; however, Saturdays do.

You can waive your right of rescission if you have a bona fide financial emergency. However, if you do waive your right, you must go through with the credit transaction. During these three days, if you have a change of heart, you must let the creditor know in writing that you want to cancel the loan. Within 20 days of receiving your letter, the creditor must return to you any money or property you paid as part of the credit transaction and must release any security interest it has in your home. If you decide that you don't want to go through with a home equity loan, model your letter to the creditor after the one on Form 6-4 on the CD.

Being aware of credit insurance tricks

Credit insurance guarantees that the payments on your credit account are made if you're too sick or injured to work and/or if you die leaving a balance on your account. A creditor may offer to sell you this insurance when you apply for a credit card or loan or after you've had the credit for a while.

When a creditor offers to sell you credit insurance, it must tell you how much the insurance costs and whether having the insurance is a condition of approval for the credit. Usually it isn't. If it is a condition, however, the APR the lender quotes you must reflect the cost of the insurance.

Although having credit insurance is rarely a condition of getting credit, unscrupulous creditors may make it sound like you have to buy it. They may use scare tactics to try to convince you that you need credit insurance. For example, they may try to persuade you by using worst-case scenarios, like unexpected incapacitation or sudden unemployment. The best way to deal with scare tactics is to ignore them.

If credit insurance is a requirement, compare the cost of buying it directly from an insurance company rather than through the lender. If you're worried about how your loan or your credit card bills will get paid if you can't work or if you die, consider these alternatives to credit insurance: You can purchase life insurance, buy disability insurance, build up your savings, and minimize your debt. Chapter 19 discusses life and disability insurance.

Cosigning Conundrum

Your best friend is going through financially tough times and has asked you to cosign the loan she needs to help her pay her bills for the next six months. Your 20-something daughter wants a bank loan so she can furnish her first apartment. Your sister just got divorced and has asked you to cosign on the loan she needs to get back on her feet. Talk about being between a rock and a hard place! You want the people you care about to have the things they need, but you really aren't sure that you want to tie their iffy finances to yours. Your misgivings are right on.

Cosigning a note can be risky business. Here's why: You're being asked to take a risk that a professional lender was unwilling to take. In most states, when a loan is past due, the creditor can try to collect from the cosigner before trying to collect from the borrower.

Call your state attorney general's Office of Consumer Protection to find out whether your state has a law governing cosigners. If the borrower falls behind on the loan payments and the lender sues to collect its money, suddenly you're part of a lawsuit, and that means you'll have to pay money to defend yourself. And if the lender wins, the judgment against you and the borrower will include not only the amount of the past-due payments but probably the late charges, the lender's attorney's fees, and court costs as well. Additionally, if you or the borrower can't pay the judgment, your wages, property, and credit history are at risk.

Potential creditors view a loan you cosign as your credit obligation. Therefore, depending on the overall state of your finances, that extra debt may make getting the credit you need for yourself a difficult task. If you decide to cosign a loan despite the risks, the following advice can help you minimize the downsides of being a cosigner:

✔ Don't cosign a loan that you can't afford to repay. Remember, to save your credit record, you may end up having to make the loan payments.

✔ Ask the lender to agree in writing to notify you if the borrower misses a single loan payment. If you rely on the borrower, the loan could be seriously past due before you find out that it's in arrears.

✔ Ask the lender to negotiate the specific terms of your obligation as a cosigner and have those terms added to the loan agreement. For example, you will only be responsible for paying a certain amount if the borrower defaults on the loan.

Ask the lender to provide copies of all loan documents. If the lender won't give them to you, ask the borrower for copies. Sign a separate agreement with the borrower. Use the sample agreement on Form 6-5 on the CD to protect yourself when you cosign a loan.

Chapter 7

Dealing with Credit Bureaus and Protecting Your Financial Information

• •

• •

*T*he information in your credit record is vital to you and your family. If your credit record contains substantial amounts of negative information, your ability to get a job, buy insurance, or secure more credit could be seriously affected. Your credit rating is your key to securing loans at reasonable rates — for most people, a reasonable line of credit is what allows them to buy their dream home, afford reasonable transportation, or rent a decent apartment.

When it comes to opportunities for you and your family, the ability to get credit is often critical to realizing your dreams. The fate of your credit may hinge on the information held by the three national credit-reporting agencies or credit bureaus: Equifax, Experian, and Trans Union. To get the credit you want and need, keep a close eye on your personal and financial information stored with these companies. Read on to see how to order a copy of your credit record from each of these companies, how to decipher and interpret your credit record, and how to correct any problems you find in your record.

This chapter also fills you in on the federal Fair Credit Reporting Act (FCRA). This important federal law regulates the activities of credit bureaus, as well as the companies and organizations that supply them with information about you and other consumers. The FCRA also helps protect the privacy of your credit record and gives you certain rights and responsibilities in regard to that record.

Understanding Credit Reporting

No matter how much you know about your credit record and your credit record rights, good money management is still critical to maintaining an excellent credit rating. If you don't manage your money well, your record will be full of negatives, which makes qualifying for credit at reasonable terms or getting a job that involves responsibility for a large sum of money difficult, if not impossible.

Meet Equifax, Experian (formerly TRW), and Trans Union. These three national credit-reporting agencies dominate the credit-reporting industry and maintain vast computerized databases on nearly every consumer in the United States — including you. Other, smaller credit bureaus exist, but these three companies own or are affiliated with most of them.

The information in your credit record creates a portrait of how well (or how poorly) you manage your credit. This portrait is also called a *credit history* or *credit file.* Among other things, your credit record provides information about your credit accounts, including credit cards and some loans, how often you've been late in making your account payments, how much you owe on each account, whether you've filed for bankruptcy in the last ten years, and whether you have a tax or judgment lien on any of your assets.

Your goal should be to build and maintain a pristine credit record — one that opens doors for you. To achieve that goal, you must pay your bills on time, keep your debt to a minimum, avoid applying for a lot of credit, and review your credit record regularly to make sure that everything in it is correct.

If your credit record contains a great deal of negative information, don't despair. Negative information, other than bankruptcies and unpaid tax liens, can remain in your credit record for only seven years. After that, it must be deleted. Bankruptcies, however, can linger for ten years, and unpaid tax liens can stick around for 15 years.

Things you should know about the Fair Credit Reporting Act

The federal Fair Credit Reporting Act (FCRA) was passed in 1970 to regulate the activities of credit bureaus and to give consumers rights regarding their credit records and dealings with credit bureaus. The law was amended in 1996 to provide consumers additional rights. The following list provides a quick summary of the law's most important provisions. The FCRA says that you have the right to

✔ Know what's in your credit record. Under certain circumstances, you also have the right to know what's in an investigative report that's prepared about you.

✔ Obtain a free copy of your credit record if you've been denied credit, insurance, employment, or a place to rent, and the denial was in whole or in part due to information in that record.

✔ Have most negative information removed from your credit record after seven years; ten years for bankruptcies, and 15 years for unpaid tax liens.

✔ Have an employer obtain your written permission to review your credit record before looking at it as part of its hiring, firing, or promotion process.

✔ Have an employer provide you with a free copy of your credit report if you're fired or denied a job or promotion in whole or in part because of negative information in your credit record.

✔ Have a credit bureau investigate information in your credit record that you believe is inaccurate or out-of-date.

✔ Have information in your credit record corrected if a credit bureau investigation concludes that it's wrong.

✔ Receive a free copy of your credit report if information in it is corrected and if you request that free copy within 60 days.

✔ Prepare a written statement of no more than 100 words explaining the reason for the negative information in your credit record — assuming that your reason is sympathetic. (For example, you fell behind on your credit card payments because you were ill and unable to work.) You also have the right to have the written statement made a permanent part of your credit record when a credit bureau's investigation does not result in a correction to your credit report. Some creditors may read your written statement and be willing to extend you credit once they understand the reason for the negative information in your record.

✔ Have a credit bureau send a corrected copy of your credit report to employers who reviewed your uncorrected credit record in the past two years and to anyone else who looked at it in the past six months. However, the FCRA does not require those employers to offer you the position you were denied or an equivalent position.

✔ Sue a credit bureau in state or federal court.

Getting the information: Where credit companies scrounge the dirt

Equifax, Experian, and Trans Union, as well as the smaller guys, get their consumer credit record information from several sources. They draw information from subscribers — companies that offer credit to customers. These companies report consumer credit data to the Big Three monthly. The Big Three also scrounge public records such as tax liens, judgments, and bankruptcies. They draw information from collection agencies and from you any time you fill out a credit application with your name, address, and social security number on the form.

The three major credit-reporting agencies, as well as the smaller ones, maintain the consumer information they collect in computerized databases and then sell it to credit card companies, banks, mortgage companies, savings and loans, credit unions, finance companies, retailers, and so on. These companies use the information to decide whether they should give you new or additional credit, change the terms of the credit you already have, or cancel your account.

Credit-reporting agencies also sell information to insurance companies who want to check out what your credit file says before they sell you a policy or write the terms of your policy. If you already have insurance, the company may review your credit record to decide whether it should raise your premium or cancel your policy.

In addition, credit bureaus provide some landlords — mostly the owners/managers of larger multiunit rental properties — with information about the consumers who apply to be their tenants. Therefore, consumers with a number of negatives in their credit files may find renting more difficult because landlords don't want to lease to people with debt problems.

Finally, a growing number of employers are reviewing consumer credit record data as part of their hiring, firing, and promotion processes. Therefore, having quite a bit of negative information in your credit record could work against you in the work world. The sidebar "When an employer looks at your credit record" provides information about your FCRA legal rights when an employer uses your credit record information in its decision-making.

Credit-reporting agencies may not report medical information about you to creditors, insurers, or employers without your written permission. Here are others whom the FCRA says have a legal right to peek at your credit record:

✔ **Government agencies:** These agencies may use your credit record to help them decide whether to grant you a professional license, a security clearance, or government benefits such as welfare.

✔ **Attorneys:** Attorneys can view your credit record if they're trying to collect on a debt you owe.

✔ **Private investigators:** Private investigators can view your credit record if they're acting as debt collectors.

✔ **Child support enforcement agencies:** These agencies can use your credit record to help them collect the past-due child support you owe.

✔ **Someone with a judgment against you:** If someone wants to collect on that judgment, she can use your credit record.

✔ **Creditors:** Creditors who want to make you a firm offer of credit, as well as insurance companies who want to make a firm offer to sell you insurance.

✔ **Anyone with a legitimate business need:** As long as the need relates to a business transaction you initiated, this person can view your credit record.

✔ **Anyone you authorize.**

Checking out your own credit record

The FCRA says that you have a right to know what's in your credit record. Therefore, at least once a year, take advantage of that right by ordering a copy so you know what your record says about you and so you can be sure that it doesn't contain incorrect information that could jeopardize your chances of getting credit, employment, or insurance. A problem-free credit record with one credit bureau is no guarantee that your record with the other two won't include errors or inaccuracies.

Make it a rule to take a gander at your credit record before you apply for important credit, employment, or insurance. That way, you won't be surprised by problems you were unaware of and didn't have a chance to correct. Credit-reporting agencies aren't obligated to give you information about the credit scores that may be a part of your credit file.

Your credit report should arrive about two weeks after you mail your request letter. If you made your request because you were turned down for credit, insurance, employment, or a place to rent due to information in your credit file, you should receive your report even sooner. For more information about getting a copy of your credit record under those circumstances, see the section "Free reports" in this chapter. If sufficient time passes and your credit report has not arrived, call the credit bureau you ordered from to make sure that your letter was received and to check on the status of your order.

Each credit bureau has specific requirements about what kind of information it wants you to include in your credit report request letter. Omitting any of the information will delay delivery of your report. Therefore, here's a bureau-by-bureau rundown on what to include in your letters and where to send them. When you finish drafting your letters, refer to these lists to make sure that you haven't left anything out. Be sure to sign your credit report request letter, too. Credit bureaus need your signature to process your request.

Equifax

Include the following in the credit report request letter you write to Equifax. Model your letter to Equifax after the sample letter on Form 7-1 of the CD.

- ✔ Your full name, including your middle initial and Jr., Sr., II, III; your date of birth and phone number.

- ✔ Your current address, as well as any other addresses at which you have lived during the past five years.

Mail the letter to Equifax, Equifax Consumer Information Service Center, P.O. Box 740241, Atlanta, GA 30374. To order an Equifax credit report online, go to www.econsumer.equifax.com/equifax.app/Welcome. The online form asks you to provide information the credit bureau needs to locate you in its database. This information also helps Equifax ensure that you are who you say you are, and not a stranger trying to get an unauthorized look at your credit record. When you order online, you must pay with a national credit card, like Visa or MasterCard.

Experian

When you write to Experian, include the following in your request letter. Model your letter after the one you find on Form 7-2 on the CD.

- ✔ Your full name, including your middle initial and Jr., Sr., II, III; your date of birth and Social Security number.

- ✔ Your spouse's first and last names. Experian asks for this information to help it verify that you are who you say you are and to be sure that the information in your credit record applies to you and not to someone with a similar last name.

- ✔ Your current home address, including apartment number when applicable, and your zip code. Also, your home addresses for the past five years.

If you've moved during the last six months, attach two proofs of residence to your request letter. These can include a copy of your utility bill, telephone bill, driver's license, or bank statement.

Send your letter and any attachments to Experian, National Consumer Assistance Center, P.O. Box 2104, Allen, TX 75013-2104. If you're requesting a copy of your credit report because you've been denied credit, insurance, rental housing, or employment and were notified that information in your report contributed to the denial, send your letter to Experian, National Consumer Assistance Center, P.O. Box 9595, Allen, TX 75013-0036.

As a shortcut to writing a request letter, you can go to Experian's Web site at `www.experian.com/product/consumer/orderform.html` and print a credit report order form. Complete the form and then mail it to Experian. (You can't order your Experian credit report online.) Another option is to call 888-397-3742 for Experian's automated ordering system.

Trans Union

You can model your Trans Union letter after Form 7-3 on the CD. Credit report request letters for Trans Union should include the following information:

- ✔ Your full name, including your middle initial and Jr., Sr., II, III; your date of birth, telephone number, and Social Security number.

- ✔ Your current address, as well as any other addresses at which you may have lived during the past two years.

- ✔ The name of your current employer. Trans Union uses this information to help it confirm that you are who you say you are and that the information in your report belongs to you, not to someone else.

Send your Trans Union letter to Trans Union Consumer Disclosure Center, P.O. Box 1000, Chester, PA 19022. To order a Trans Union credit report online, go to `www.transunion.com/CreditReport/CreditFileinfo.asp`.

As an alternative to going online or mailing your request, you may be able to order your report by using Trans Union's telephone interactive voice response system. The number to call is 800-888-4213. However, you can use this number to order only if you have been denied credit, employment, or insurance during the last 60 days and the company that turned you down reviewed your Trans Union credit report in its decision-making, or if you are a resident of Colorado, Georgia, Massachusetts, Maryland, New Jersey, or Vermont.

Credit report costs

If you're not entitled to a free copy of your credit report, a copy will cost you between $2 and $10, plus applicable state tax. Your cost depends on your state of residence — some states mandate a lower price. All credit reports ordered online cost $8 plus tax, regardless of your circumstances. Your credit report will cost you nothing — nada — under certain circumstances:

- ✔ **You're denied credit, insurance, employment, or rental housing because of information in your credit report.** The company you applied to must give you the name, address, and phone number of the credit bureau that provided the information about you so you know from whom to order your free credit report.

  You must request a free credit report within 60 days of your denial.

- ✔ **An adverse action is taken against you because of information in your credit record.** For example, your credit limit was decreased or your insurance premium was increased.

- ✔ **You certify in writing that any of the following circumstances applies to you:**

  - You are unemployed and intend to apply for a job within 60 days.

  - You believe that your credit report is inaccurate because of credit fraud.

  - You are receiving welfare payments.

- ✔ **You live in a state that gives you the right to receive a free credit report.** Residents of Colorado, Maryland, Massachusetts, New Jersey, and Vermont are entitled to receive one free credit report per year from Equifax, Experian, and Trans Union. Residents of Georgia are entitled to receive two copies of their credit reports from the three national credit bureau companies each year.

Understanding What Your Credit Report Says about You

Ordering your credit report is the easy part of the job. After you receive it, you have to understand what it says. The FCRA says that credit bureaus must have people on staff to answer your questions. To reach one of these people, call the credit bureau's phone number listed on your credit report. All credit reports include four basic categories of information: *identifying information, credit account information, public record information,* and *inquiries.*

Identification information: The identification information includes your name and generation — whether you are a Jr. Sr., II, III; your Social Security number, current and recent past addresses, and date of birth; your spouse's name; and your current and past employers.

Credit account information: For each account in your credit report, you usually find the name of the creditor and the account/loan number; whether the credit is revolving, installment, individual, or joint; the type of loan — mortgage, home equity, student loan, and so on; the account's credit limit, current balance, monthly payment amount, date the account was opened, and the number of late payments you have made; and whether the account/loan is in collections and whether you or the creditor has closed the account.

Your credit report may not provide a comprehensive portrait of your finances. That's because not all creditors report consumer account information to credit bureaus, and those that do may report their information more regularly than others. For example, some creditors may report account payment information every month, while others report only a default or when an account is sent to collections.

Public record information: Information in the public record is also a standard part of each report. That information may include outstanding tax liens or judgments as well as bankruptcies that were filed during the past ten years. If you're behind on your court-ordered child support payments, that fact may also show up on your credit record.

You can find a sample Experian credit report, along with explanations of each element on the report, on Form 7-4 of the CD. If you order your credit report from Equifax and Trans Union, they'll look quite different from this one.

Inquiries: The Inquiries section of a credit report tells who has looked at or asked about your credit history in the past two years. The FCRA says that inquiries related to employment must remain in your credit report for at least two years, and that all other inquires must stay for a minimum of six months.

By law, a credit bureau must give you the address and phone number of any business listed in the Inquiries section of your credit report if you request the information in writing.

A creditor listed in this section may have the letters PRM next to it. These letters stand for *Promotional.* Usually, PRM means that the creditor did not actually review your credit record; instead, it provided the credit bureau with a set of criteria, asked the credit bureau to review its database for consumers who matched the criteria, and you were one of the consumers who did. Therefore, you received a pre-approved offer of credit from that creditor. Another creditor may have the letters AM or AR next to it. Those letters stand for *account monitoring* or *account review,* which means that one of your existing creditors probably checked out your credit report to decide whether it should raise or lower your credit limit or cancel your account. If you order a copy of your own report, that request shows up in this section as a *consumer inquiry.*

Having a lot of inquiries in your credit record is a strike against you, because when you apply for the credit you really need, the creditor may interpret the inquiries as a sign that you are short of cash or are applying for more credit than you can handle. Even credit applications that you submit online count as inquiries. However, promotional, employment-related, and account monitoring and review inquiries are not provided to credit report users and therefore do not affect your credit record.

Looking for Errors

As you read your credit report, be on the lookout for errors and misinformation. Following are some of the most common errors:

- ✔ Incorrect information about one of your accounts.

- ✔ Someone else's information shows up, or *commingles,* in your credit record. Commingling is most apt to happen if your name is very similar to someone else's. For example, a father and son may have the same names and not consistently use Jr., Sr., or another generational designation to distinguish themselves when applying for credit or signing other documents. As a result, the son's information may end up in the father's credit file and vice versa.

- ✔ An account that you don't recognize appears on your credit report.

- ✔ Your credit report doesn't reflect that you had a tax or judgment lien released.

- ✔ Wrong address or incorrect social security number.

- ✔ Information relating to a former spouse shows up in your credit record. Remember, though, that any joint accounts you opened during your marriage rightfully belong in your and your former spouse's credit records.

Dealing with Credit Record Problems

If your review of your credit record turns up any negative but true information, nothing but time can change or remove it.

Some credit repair companies boast that they can make negative information in your credit record disappear. However, the techniques they use to do so are illegal, and if you fall for their offers, you're committing a crime for which you can be prosecuted.

Now for the good news: If you discover negative but inaccurate or outdated information in your credit record, you have a legal right to get it removed. The following sections show you how to do that.

Step 1: Get in touch with the company that generated the report

Get in touch with the company that generated the credit report and ask it to investigate the information you believe doesn't belong there. The exact way to go about triggering an investigation depends on which credit bureau you're dealing with.

If the research request form you received doesn't address your credit record problem, or if the form doesn't give you enough space to explain the problem, put the additional information in a letter and attach the letter to the form. Be sure to date your letter and to make a copy of the letter and the completed form for your files.

Step 2: Make copies of any receipts, cancelled checks, and correspondence that help prove your point

Attach these copies to the investigation form or letter. Make a copy of your credit report, circle or highlight the items you're disputing, and attach it to the form or letter. Send the same information to the creditor that provided the incorrect information to the credit bureau, along with a copy of your letter or a copy of your completed research request or investigation request form.

Step 3: Mail everything to the address on your credit report or on the research request form

Send your letter and any copies you've made via certified mail, return receipt requested. That way, you know when the credit bureau received your request. Having that information is important because by law and in most instances, the credit bureau must respond to you within 30 days of receiving your research request.

What a credit bureau does after it gets your request for an investigation

After a credit bureau receives your request to investigate an alleged error in your credit record, the FCRA requires the company to take certain actions to determine whether there really is an error and to report its findings to you. The FCRA also establishes very specific deadlines by which the credit bureau must complete each step of its investigation.

Within five business days of receiving the request, the credit bureau must ask the provider of the information you're disputing to certify in writing whether the information is accurate. If the credit bureau can't verify the accuracy of that information, it must delete the information. And if the credit bureau's research shows that the information in your credit record is incomplete, it must add the missing information. If the information provider determines that the information you dispute is inaccurate, it must correct its own records within 30 days and must let all the other credit bureaus to which it reports know about the error so that the bureaus can correct their records. The same holds true if you, and not a credit bureau, contact the information provider directly about a problem in your credit record.

Because each of the three major credit bureaus notifies the other two about any errors it identifies in your credit record, you don't have to make that notification yourself. However, after a while, you should order a copy of your credit reports from all three bureaus to make sure that each of them has corrected its information about you.

Credit bureaus do not investigate research requests they believe are frivolous. Generally, *frivolous requests* are ones for which you provide little or no justification. The credit bureau must send you a free copy of your corrected credit report. It also must send you a notice of your legal right to ask the credit bureau to send a corrected version of your report to any employer who reviewed your file in the past two years and to anyone else who reviewed it in the past six months. You may be charged for each report you have sent.

Sometimes, due to a human error or a computer glitch, credit record problems that you thought were corrected can reappear. Therefore, to make sure that a problem stays gone for good, request another copy of your credit record a few months after it has been corrected.

Disagreeing with a credit bureau that says that your credit record is accurate

When a credit bureau concludes that your credit record is complete and accurate, the information remains in your record until the law says it must be removed. If you continue to see a problem in your credit record despite the credit bureau's conclusion, you can try to find new information that may cause the credit bureau to change its mind, or you can contact the provider of the incorrect information. Model your letter to the information provider after the one on Form 7-5 on the CD.

If you can prove that the information is wrong or incomplete, the provider is legally obligated to notify the credit bureau(s) it reports to, and those bureaus must correct your credit record. To make sure that the correction happens, ask to be copied on any notices the information provider sends to the credit bureau. Then, a couple of months later, order a copy of your credit record from the credit bureau that received the notice to make sure that your credit record was corrected.

You have a right to ask the credit bureau for the name and address of the information provider it contacted to verify the accuracy of the information in your credit record. Another option when a credit bureau's investigation doesn't turn out the way you hoped is to write a statement in 100 words or less explaining why you believe your credit record is inaccurate. If you send it to the credit bureau, the FCRA says that statement must become a part of your credit record so anyone who looks at the record can read your statement. You can also ask the credit bureau to send your statement to anyone who reviewed your credit record recently, but you may have to pay for this service.

Computers are reviewing a growing number of credit applications. When a computer evaluates your credit application, it may not consider your written statement. Additionally, the credit rating services marketed by Equifax, Experian, and Trans Union are diluting the value of written statements. Creditors who use these services evaluate your credit worthiness based on a numerical credit rating derived from the information in your credit file, not on an actual review of the information in that record. To ensure that potential creditors, employers, insurers, and landlords who use credit record information as part of their decision-making processes actually read your written statement, attach a copy of it to your application.

Filing lawsuits related to your credit report

The FCRA gives you the right to file a civil lawsuit against a credit-reporting agency, a user of information in your credit report, and, in some instances, an information provider if you believe that it has violated the law. You can sue for actual damages and, in some cases, for punitive damages as well. If you win your lawsuit, you're also entitled to a reimbursement for your attorney fees and court costs.

These kinds of lawsuits are complicated and tough to win. Therefore, don't even consider going it alone. Hire an attorney who has experience with law suits related to credit report problems. The attorney can also decide whether you should sue in state or federal court.

Your lawsuit can allege willful noncompliance or negligent noncompliance with the FCRA. *Willful noncompliance* means that you think the credit bureau or information user deliberately violated the law. If you sue for *negligent noncompliance,* you're alleging that a company was negligent in meeting the FCRA's requirements — it didn't have the appropriate systems in place, its employees were not thoroughly trained about the FCRA requirements, and so on.

Recognizing Identity Theft

A new kind of thief — one who could cause you to lose your good credit, cost you money, and generally generate a heap of trouble for you — is out there. This person is an identity thief. These crooks steal your personal information — your bank and credit card account numbers, your Social Security number, your income information, your name, address, and phone number — in order to commit fraud or theft. An identity thief may get this information by stealing your wallet, purse, mail, trash, or change of address forms. The thief may obtain your business or personal records at work. Yes, you may work with an identity thief! The thief may also find your personal information at your home. A repairperson, a cleaning person, and even someone you know might do this. A thief may steal personal information you share on the Internet or may buy your personal information from people who know something about you and are willing to sell it, or who have access to information about you that appears on an application you filled out.

Identity thieves have many uses for your personal information. Those uses have the potential to do serious damage to your credit record. They may go on a spending spree at your expense, open bank accounts in your name, and even buy cars on your tab. These ruthless crooks may even file for bankruptcy in your name to avoid eviction or to avoid having to pay the bills they have run up. The nerve! Form 7-9 on the CD has a list of useful tips for protecting your identity.

Dealing with an identity crisis

Act immediately if you think that someone is using your identity. Keep track of all the things you do by using the chart on Form 7-6 of the CD. The information on the chart may come in handy if the identity thief is prosecuted or if the companies or agencies you contact don't take swift action. Start by contacting each of the fraud departments of the three national credit bureaus to request that a fraud alert be placed in your credit file. Also include a statement requesting that before a creditor opens a new account in your name or makes any changes to an existing account, the creditor contact you. Call Equifax at 800-525-6285, Experian at 888-397-3742, or Trans Union at 800-680-7239.

Also ask each credit bureau for a copy of your credit report so you can make sure that no accounts have been opened in your name and no unauthorized changes have been made to your existing accounts. If the Inquiries section of your report includes companies that opened fraudulent accounts in your name, contact the credit bureaus to ask that those accounts be removed, and then request copies of your reports a few months later to verify that your request was honored and that no additional fraudulent activity has taken place.

If your credit record shows that someone has opened an account in your name used or has tampered with an existing account, contact the creditors involved by calling their fraud or security departments. Then follow up with a letter, which is the only way to ensure that the federal Fair Credit Billing Act (FCBA) will protect you from problems in your account billing statements. (Chapter 6 tells you all about the FCBA.) Close all accounts that have been used or tampered with, and then open new ones. Pick new personal identification numbers and passwords. Contact your local police or the police in the community where the identity theft occurred, and get a copy of the police report in case you run into trouble when you apply for new credit.

Getting help from the government

The federal government is cracking down on identity thieves. For example, in 1998, the federal Identity Theft and Assumption Deterrence Act was passed, making identity theft a federal crime. Violations of the law are investigated by the Secret Service, the FBI, the postal service, and the Social Security Administration's Office of the Inspector General and prosecuted by the Department of Justice. Generally, a conviction carries a maximum penalty of 15 years in prison, a fine, and the forfeiture of any personal property used or intended to be used to commit the crime. Identity theft may also involve other federal crimes.

Many states have passed their own identity theft laws, and others are considering legislation. Visit www.consumer.gov/idtheft on the Web to find out whether your state is one of them. Government agencies are also working hard to combat this crime. Many have special numbers you can call to report instances of identity fraud.

  ✔ **FTC:** Call the FTC's Identity Theft Hotline at 877-438-4338 to report a crime. Although the FTC will not prosecute on your behalf, it will help you resolve any financial problems that have developed as a result of the identity theft. To report an identity theft to the FTC, you can also file a complaint online at www.ftc.gov or write Federal Trade Commission, Identity Theft Clearinghouse, 600 Pennsylvania Ave. NW, Washington, DC 20580.

- ✔ **Social Security Administration (SSA):** If you think that someone has used your personal information to apply for a job, report it to the SSA's Fraud Hotline at 800-269-0271. You should also verify the accuracy of the earnings reported on your Social Security number and request a copy of your Social Security statement. You can do both by calling 800-772-1213.

- ✔ **Postal service:** Let your local Postal Inspector know if you believe that someone has stolen your mail in order to steal your identity. Your area post office can tell you how to reach the Inspector, or you can go to this Web site to find out: `www.usps.gov/websites/depart/inspect`.

- ✔ **Federal Communications Commission (FCC):** This office can help you if you're unable to get fraudulent phone charges removed from your long-distance bill or your cell phone bill. You can reach the FCC by going to `www.fcc.gov/ccb/enforce/complaints.html` on the Web or by calling 888-CALL-FCC.

- ✔ **Bankruptcy court:** If you believe that someone has filed for bankruptcy in your name, write to the U.S. Trustee for the federal bankruptcy court where you believe the bankruptcy was filed. (Use the sample letter on Form 7-7 of the CD.) Your letter should describe your situation and include proof of your identity. Use the U. S. Department of Justice Trustee Locator at `www.usdoj.gov/ust/regional_links.htm` to get the name, address, and phone number of the Trustee to contact. If you provide sufficient documentation and the Trustee believes that a crime has occurred, your problem will be referred to the appropriate authorities.

Going online: Special privacy concerns

You're especially vulnerable to identity fraud when you go online because no matter what you do, you can't keep your information private. Without your knowledge, information is collected about you every time you use the Internet. You leave electronic fingerprints everywhere you go, and there's no telling who is picking them up and what they will do with that information. Even Web companies who claim to keep your information private may not be doing a very good job of following through on their promises.

Although the future may bring greater protections to consumers when they surf the Web, for now it's pretty much up to you to do what you can to keep your personal information private when you use the Internet. Form 7-9 contains a list of helpful tips on protecting your identity in Cyberspace.

Chapter 8

Drowning in Debt

· ·

In This Chapter

▶ Getting your debt under control

▶ Dealing with debt collectors

▶ Negotiating with your creditors

▶ Handling your past-due car and home loans

· ·

Recent research shows that too much debt not only hurts your pocket-book and your credit record, but also may be harmful to your health. Yikes! Taking on too much debt can destroy your credit record and land you in a heap of legal trouble, too. Worst-case scenario, you may find yourself struggling to pay your bills and to keep the roof over your head and your wheels on the road.

This chapter tells you how to nip money troubles in the bud and lays out your options should your problems grow more serious. We also explain how the home foreclosure and auto repossession processes work.

Knowing How Much Is Too Much

You may know that you owe too much money because the state of your finances is too hard to ignore. For example, more often than not, you can't afford to pay all your bills, so you're constantly juggling between who to pay now and who to pay later. You may also be receiving threatening letters from your creditors or have debt collectors pounding on your door.

On the other hand, you may be feeling pretty good about the state of your finances. After all, you pay the minimum due on each of your credit cards each month! But in fact, you too may have taken on too much debt, and whether or not you realize it, you're flirting with disaster. With little or no money left over each month to put into savings, all it will take to destroy your illusion of financial well-being is a sudden job loss, an expensive illness, or an unexpected and substantial expense.

Facing facts about your financial situation

When your finances are spinning out of control, taking decisive steps to stabilize and then improve your situation is critical. If you don't, things will inevitably go from bad to worse. For example, credit card companies may change your terms of credit, either increasing your interest rate or decreasing your credit limit. Consequently, your credit record will deteriorate, and getting new or additional credit at reasonable terms will be difficult, if not impossible. Even worse, your money troubles could destroy your credit, causing you to lose all the credit you once had — but not your credit balances.

Other potential results of being head over heels in debt include calls from debt collectors, home foreclosure, eviction, car repossession, wage garnishment, and the potential loss of valuable assets other than your home and car. You ultimately may be forced to declare bankruptcy.

Stemming the money flow

Put a tourniquet on your spending by figuring out where your money is going and what expenses you can reduce. Start by tracking your spending for at least one month. Record all the checks you write, all the charges you make, and all the cash you spend, even if the amounts are very small. All those small amounts add up over time. Try to record your expenditures daily so that you're less likely to overlook anything. Tedious though it may be, this exercise is almost always revealing.

Record your spending information in a small spiral notebook, on a pad of lined paper, or, better yet, on a computer. You can create your own computer data-collection form, or you can record your information by using a budgeting and financial management software program such as Quicken.

Form 8-1 on the CD is an example of how to organize your spending data. This form can help you highlight your biggest and smallest spending items and point out where you can cut back. You can also use it as a budget or household spending plan.

Once you have a month's worth of spending data, compare the total amount that you spent to your monthly net income (your take-home income). If your expenses exceed your income, review your spending record to identify expenses that you can reduce or eliminate. A list of money saving tips is in Form 8-2 on the CD.

Heading off disaster

As soon as you realize that too much debt is causing your finances to go downhill, take these six steps right away:

1. **Stop charging!** If resisting the urge to say, "Charge it," is going to be difficult, freeze your credit cards in a container of water. By the time the water melts and you can get to your cards, the urge may have passed.

2. **Cancel all your credit cards except the one with the best terms of credit.** Chapter 6 tells you how to evaluate terms of credit.

3. **Determine where your money is going and then develop and live with a realistic spending plan (a nice name for a budget).**

4. **Prioritize your debts and pay the ones at the top of your list first.** We tell you how to do so in the "Prioritizing bills" section of this chapter.

5. **Familiarize yourself with your debt-collection legal rights.** The "Dealing with Debt Collectors" section of this chapter tells you what your rights are.

6. **Find a life raft.** Assess your long-term options for dealing with your debt, and then choose the best ones. The longer you wait to address your debt problem, the fewer options you'll have.

Prioritizing bills

If you can't pay everything you owe, prioritize your bills and pay the bills with the highest priority first. This strategy can help you keep the assets that are most important to you and your family, that help you earn a living, or both. The following bills should be at the top of your list:

- ✔ **Your mortgage:** If you fall behind on your mortgage, the mortgage holder may try to take back your home by beginning the foreclosure process. A foreclosure can be much like a freight train barreling down the tracks straight toward you — hard to stop. (We discuss foreclosures in more detail later in this chapter.)

- ✔ **Your rent:** Your landlord will evict you if you ignore your rent obligation. We talk more about evictions in Chapter 18.

    If you're renting a storage facility and you fall behind on your rental payments, the owner of the facility has the right to sell the items you're storing to get the money you owe in past-due rent.

- ✔ **Your utility bills:** You need electricity, gas, water, and telephone service to live safely and comfortably in your home or apartment. Most utility companies work with you if you can't pay the full amount of a utility bill or are behind on your payments. Also, during periods of the year when temperatures are especially hot or cold, many utilities offer breaks for consumers who are struggling financially to keep their utilities on.

- ✔ **Your home equity loan, or any other debts that you *collateralized* (offered as security for the loan) with an asset that you don't want to lose:** If you're making your mortgage payments but not your home equity loan payments, your home equity lender has a legal right to foreclose on you. Therefore, if you want to hold on to your home, be sure to stay current on your home equity loan as well as your mortgage.

- ✔ **Your car loan, especially if you need your vehicle to make a living:** The company that's financing your car will take it back if you fall too far behind on your payments. We discuss repossessions in more detail later in this chapter.

- ✔ **Your auto liability insurance:** In most states, driving without liability insurance is illegal. If you let your auto insurance lapse because you can't pay it, the company financing your vehicle may purchase new insurance for you and pass the expense on to you. That insurance could be much more expensive than the insurance you used to have.

- ✔ **Other secured loans, such as a furniture loan.**

- ✔ **Child support:** You're only adding to your problems if you ignore your child support obligation. Both the federal and state governments have increased their efforts to crack down on people who ignore their legal obligation to pay child support. In fact, you could be put in jail for not living up to your legal obligation to help support your kids. Also, the parent of your minor children may hire a private company or an attorney to force you to pay what you owe. If you can't pay your child support, ask the court that issued your child support court order to reduce your obligation to an amount you can afford to pay.

- ✔ **Your taxes:** When you get behind on your taxes, you not only create the potential for legal problems in your life, but your tax debt also increases day-by-day due to penalties and interest. Chapter 11 tells you what to do if you can't pay your taxes.

Pay your unsecured debts last, if you have any money left over. Those debts include your credit card bills, unsecured loan payments, and medical bills.

Dealing with Debt Collectors

At some point after one of your debts becomes past due, the creditor will probably turn it over to a debt-collection agency or a lawyer who collects debts. Debt collectors are paid for their efforts by taking a percentage of whatever they collect. Therefore, they have an incentive to be persistent — maybe a little too persistent sometimes.

Although most debt collectors are reputable and don't cross the line between persistent-but-polite efforts to collect what you owe and harassment, some do. Therefore, if you have debt problems, you need to understand your legal rights according to the federal Fair Debt Collection Practices Act (FDCPA) and to be familiar with what the law requires of debt collectors.

Debt collector do's and don'ts

When a debt collector is trying to collect a debt, the FDCPA says that he must do certain things. For example, a debt collector must send you written information about your debt within five days after contacting you for the first time through the mail, in person, by telephone, or by telegram. This information must include the amount of money you owe, to whom you owe the money, and what you should do if you don't believe you owe the money.

The debt collector also must give you the name of the creditor he is working for; tell you the amount of the debt he is trying to collect; let you know that you have 30 days to dispute the debt; and inform you of your legal right to request written verification of the debt. You must make this request within five days of the debt collector's initial contact with you. Make this request in writing, and save a copy for your files. That way, in the event that you do not receive written verification, or if the debt collector takes additional steps to collect what you owe without responding to your letter first, you have a record of your request and the date on which you made it. The FDCPA also says that a debt collector cannot

- Use a postcard to contact you about your debt, or use an envelope that mentions your debt or that indicates in any way that you are being contacted about a debt. You have a right to privacy when it comes to the money you owe.

- Send you a letter that looks like it is from a government agency or from a court when it isn't.

- Contact you before 8 a.m. or after 9 p.m., or anytime on a Sunday.

- Contact you at work after you have told the debt collector that your employer doesn't want you to be contacted during working hours.

- Contact your employer about your debt, unless the debt collector is trying to collect past-due child support you owe.

- Call you repeatedly or let your telephone ring and ring or use obscene, insulting, or abusive language.

- Threaten to harm you, your property, or your reputation if you don't pay up. However, the law says that a debt collector can threaten to sue you or take your property if he intends to act on that threat.

✔ Threaten to put you in jail. Debtors' prisons are a thing of the past. However, you can end up behind bars for not paying your child support.

✔ Tell you that you owe more money than you really do or falsely imply that he is a government official.

✔ Order you to accept his collect calls or to pay for his telegrams.

What to do when a debt collector contacts you

How to respond to a debt collector depends on whether you believe you owe the money, whether you can pay your debt, and what you stand to lose if you ignore the debt collector's demands. You can

✔ Work out an arrangement for paying the debt if you agree that you owe it and have the money to pay it.

✔ Ask for written verification of your debt. Take this option if you aren't sure that the debt collector is accurate about how much money you owe, or if you want to buy yourself time to figure out what to do about your debt. Form 8-3 on the CD provides a sample debt verification letter.

✔ Tell the debt collector that you don't owe the debt and that you don't want to be contacted about it again. You must send this letter within 30 days of the debt collector's initial contact. The letter halts the debt collector's collection activities. However, if the collector sends you proof of the debt, he can renew his efforts to collect the money you owe.

✔ Write the debt collector a letter asking him to stop contacting you simply because you don't want to get debt-collection calls and letters. After receiving your letter, the debt collector must respect your wishes, although he can contact you to confirm that you won't be contacted again or to let you know about a specific collection action he plans to take.

Telling a debt collector not to contact you again does not mean that the collector's collection efforts will cease. Quite the opposite. If you tell a debt collector to stop contacting you and the size of your debt is relatively small, your creditor may opt to write off the debt rather than continue trying to collect. However, the fact that the creditor tried to collect the debt and you refused to pay it may end up in your credit record, which will cause serious damage. Chapter 7 tells you all about credit records.

Hire a lawyer to help you deal with your debt problem. If you owe a considerable amount of money, getting legal help is a good idea, especially if an important asset is being threatened. Plus, after you let a debt collector know that you've hired an attorney, the debt collector must contact the lawyer, not you, about your debt.

Responding to a debt collector who violates the law

Consult with a lawyer if you believe that a debt collector has violated the FDCPA. If your case is a strong one, you can probably find an attorney willing to take your case on a *contingent fee basis.* An attorney who charges on this basis takes a percentage of what money she is able to win for you as payment for her services. If she doesn't win your case, you don't have to pay her for her legal services, although you will probably have to reimburse her for any expenses she incurs on your behalf. Chapter 5 tells you more about how contingent fees work.

If your state has its own debt-collection law, the lawyer can help you decide whether it would be better to sue under your state's debt collection law or under the FDCPA. Many state laws impose stiffer penalties than the federal law. Suing a debt collector usually comes with a one-year statute of limitations.

Under the FDCPA, you can sue for the actual damages you have suffered because of a debt collector's actions as well as up to $1,000 for each of the debt collector's legal violations. You can also ask to be reimbursed for your court and attorney costs. You can sue for lost wages, assuming you can prove that the debt collector's actions caused you to miss work, and for medical expenses, mental anguish, or both if you can prove that the debt collector triggered those problems.

When a debt collector violates the law, file a complaint with the Federal Trade Commission and with the consumer affairs office of your state attorney general. Chapter 3 tells you how to file a complaint.

Finding a Life Raft When You Can't Pay Your Bills

One of the key actions you should take to get your finances under control when you're drowning in debt is to find a debt-control life raft. The sooner you do so, the more options you'll have. If you wait too long, your only option will be bankruptcy, an emotionally and financially difficult step. Plus, you'll experience its repercussions for years to come.

Here are your basic options are to borrow money to pay off as much of your debt as possible; negotiate new, more affordable debt repayment plans with your creditors; or file for bankruptcy. (See Chapter 9.)

Borrowing money

Taking on more debt to get out of debt may sound like strange advice. But if you're sure that your finances are fundamentally sound and that your cash crunch is temporary, it can be a smart move. Potential sources of borrowed money include

✔ **A loan from a friend or relative:** To protect the lender, sign a written agreement that spells out the terms of the loan and, if possible, collateralize the loan. That way, if you end up in bankruptcy, your friend or relative will be a secured creditor and will have a stronger position in your bankruptcy. Form 8-4 on the CD provides a sample loan agreement.

Don't borrow money from someone you know unless you're certain that you can repay the loan. Adding to your troubles by angering friends or relatives with a broken promise makes no sense.

✔ **A debt consolidation loan:** A debt consolidation loan gives you money to pay off some or all of your current debts and lets you trade multiple debt payments for just one. Not only is writing one check more convenient than writing several checks, but you're also less apt to run up late penalties. Depending on the amount of money you want to borrow and your financial situation, the lender may require that you collateralize the debt consolidation loan.

For a debt consolidation loan to make financial sense, your monthly payment on the loan should be less than the total amount you're paying now on all the debts the loan would pay off. Also, the interest rate on the loan should be lower than the average rate associated with those debts. If you're already neck-deep in debt, getting a debt consolidation loan with good terms is probably impossible.

Avoid a debt consolidation loan that comes with big fees or substantial closing costs, because those expenses add to the cost of the loan. Also, don't assume that the best loan is the one with the lowest monthly payments and the longest repayment period. The longer you take to pay off the loan, the more you'll pay in interest charges. Your goal should be to pay off the loan as quickly as you can.

✔ **A home equity loan:** A home equity loan lets you tap into the *appreciated value* of your home, which is the difference between its current market value and the amount you owe on your mortgage. Your home secures the loan. This kind of loan is attractive because it usually comes with a lower interest rate than other types of loans and because getting one is relatively easy. Also, the interest you pay over the life of the loan is tax deductible up to a certain dollar amount.

If you default on a home equity loan, you risk losing your home. Therefore, don't apply for one unless you're sure that you can afford to repay the loan. Steer clear of finance company loans or loans that promise you quick money. More often than not, these loans comes with a very high rate of interest and other terms of credit that make them bad deals for consumers with money troubles.

Asking creditors for a break

Another option when you're overwhelmed by debt is to contact your creditors about the possibility of reducing your monthly debt payments and extending the amount of time you have to pay off your debt. If you discuss this option with your creditors early enough, quite a few of them are likely to be amenable to your proposal. They'd rather have you take longer to meet your financial obligations than have to spend time and money trying to collect what you owe after you default on your debt. To protect your collateral, contact your secured creditors before your unsecured creditors.

Contact your creditors about more affordable debt-payment plans *before* they begin taking collection against you — not after. If you're going through a relatively brief credit crunch and you have a good payment history, some of your creditors may let you pay just the interest due on your debt rather than interest and principal for a while. Others may be willing to let you make reduced payments for a limited time. However, after that period is up, you must resume paying according to the original terms of your agreement.

Figure out what you can afford

Before you approach any of your creditors, figure out exactly how much you can afford to pay each month on your debts. Your goal should be to pay as much as you can without agreeing to larger debt payments than you can afford. If you can't live up to what you agree to, don't expect a second chance.

Meet face-to-face with your creditors when possible to discuss your need for financial relief. Turning you down may be harder if you're sitting across from one another. Explain that you're having trouble paying your bills and outline what you are and will be doing to get your financial situation under control. Reassure each of your creditors that you want to meet your financial obligations, but to do so, you need more time and lower payments. When you propose a new, lower monthly debt payment to a creditor, offer less than what you can really afford. That way, you leave room for bargaining.

If you use a letter to propose the renegotiation of your debt, call the creditor you're writing to and ask for the credit manager's name. Direct your letter to that person. After you send the letter, call to discuss your request. Form 8-5 on the CD is an example of what to say in your letter.

If the creditor seems uninterested in working with you, don't shout or make threats. Instead, remind the creditor that you really want to pay your debt, but that to achieve that goal, you need to lower your monthly payments.

Get it in writing

After you and a creditor agree on a new debt payment plan, let the creditor know that you want the agreement to be put in writing. If the creditor tells you that preparing the agreement is your responsibility, clearly restate in the letter your understanding of exactly what you agreed to and then send the letter to the creditor. Form 8-6 on the CD is an example of what to put in the letter.

After the agreement is final, wait a month or so and then order a copy of your credit report from the credit bureau to which the creditor reports. (Chapter 7 tells you how to order a copy of your credit report.) Review it to make sure that the account information the creditor is reporting reflects your agreement. If it doesn't, write the creditor a letter referencing your agreement and attach a copy of the agreement to the letter.

Get negotiation help

If you don't feel confident in doing your own negotiating, these organizations can help you:

- **Consumer Credit Counseling Service (CCCS):** This office is part of a national network of CCCS offices, all of which are members of the National Foundation for Consumer Credit. The National Foundation is a nonprofit organization that advises and educates consumers on how to use credit wisely. CCCS offices provide consumers with low-cost/no-cost money management help and education. Among other things, it can help you establish a realistic spending plan and negotiate new debt-repayment plans with your creditors. Because CCCS offices have established relationships with many creditors, they have a high rate of negotiation success.

  To locate the CCCS office nearest you, go to the National Foundation for Consumer Credit Web site, www.nfcc.org. If you have questions, call your local office or the NFCC at 800-388-2227.

- **Myvesta.org** (www.dca.org/special/sp_debtective.htm): Myvesta. org is a nonprofit online financial help organization. Among the services it offers is *DebtTectives,* which can help you negotiate debt-payment plans with your creditors as well as dispute amounts on your account statements and look into debts you don't think you owe. Although you have to pay $200 per account for this service, the charge may be worth it to you.

Avoiding Disaster: Two Kinds of Loans That Deserve Special Attention

Getting behind on your home mortgage or your car loan is risky business with serious potential consequences. You may lose your car in a repossession or lose your home in a foreclosure. Therefore, this section of the chapter discusses how repossessions and foreclosures work and explains your options for dealing with them.

Losing your home in a foreclosure

When you're at risk of losing your home because you haven't been making your mortgage payments, you'll probably have considerably more opportunities to get caught up than when you're behind on your car payments. For example, in most states, when your mortgage is in default, your creditor will give you several months to cure it, although some states give considerably less time.

You have the best chance of holding on to your home if foreclosures in your state are judicial, not statutory. In a *judicial foreclosure,* the mortgage holder must sue you to get the court's permission to take back your home. A good lawyer can use the court process to slow the foreclosure and buy you time to come up with the money you need to keep your home, and may even be able to stop the foreclosure completely. The consumer protection office of your state attorney general's office can tell you whether your state has judicial or statutory foreclosures.

Be alert for scam artists who offer to help you out of your jam with a loan. This scam is called *equity skimming.* Usually, they promise to help you qualify for a loan by getting you a cosigner and telling you that the loan proceeds will be used to pay the past-due amount on your mortgage and to make your mortgage payments while you stabilize your finances. After that, you must take over the loan payments. What you don't realize when you go for this kind of loan is that you're actually selling your home for below market value and that you're living in your home as a renter, not an owner. Although the loan gives you a buy-back option, the terms of that option are usually so onerous that you can't exercise it. So, ultimately, you end up losing your home and all your equity as well.

The main danger with a *statutory foreclosure* is that the foreclosure can be over and done with quite quickly. The court isn't involved, and the mortgage holder has to take just a few straightforward steps to take back the home. At a minimum, the mortgage holder must take out a legal notice in your area newspaper advertising that your home is for sale. They also must send you a certain number of written notices about its foreclosure plans. Finally, they must give you an opportunity to catch up on your loan so that you won't lose your home.

No matter what type of foreclosure process your state requires, after a couple of missed payments — usually between three and four — your mortgage holder will begin the foreclosure process. The missed payments may be consecutive, or they may be payments you have missed over the life of your mortgage. If you have missed several payments, you can expect to receive a *Notice of Default* — usually the first warning you receive that you're about to lose your home. This notice tells you the number of mortgage payments you have missed and indicates the total dollar amount of those payments. At this point, contacting your lender and arranging to catch up on your mortgage is usually all it takes to stop a foreclosure, because lenders don't like to take back a home. You may be able to get your payments reduced for a period, or the lender may even agree to refinance your home at more affordable terms.

If you don't respond to the Notice of Default, or if you're unable to come to an understanding with your lender about getting caught up, you will receive a *Notice of Acceleration*. This notice warns you that the *full amount* of your mortgage balance is due, not just the past-due amount.

Hire an attorney right away if you receive a Notice of Acceleration! You have no time to waste if you want to hold on to your home. If the foreclosure is judicial and you don't pay the balance on your loan, your mortgage lender will file a lawsuit against you. If the foreclosure is statutory, the lender will take the steps outlined earlier.

What to do when you're about to lose your home

When you lose your home, you lose not only your right to live there but also all the money you have invested in it. Get legal help right away if the fore-closure process moves forward and you face the loss of your home. Losing your home means saying good-bye not only to the single most valuable asset you probably own, but also to an asset that represents security and well-being to your family. A lawyer can assess your situation and advise you about your options. Those options include

- ✔ **Cure your default by paying all the money your mortgage holder says you owe in back payments along with all the lender's foreclosure expenses.** In some states, if you offer to cure your default after the loan has been accelerated, the lender can refuse to accept your offer and proceed with the foreclosure.

- ✔ **If you believe that the amount of money that the Notice of Default says you owe is wrong, send your mortgage holder a check or money order for what you believe is the right amount.** Include with it a letter that explains what the money is for. The letter should also state that by accepting the money, the lender is agreeing that you have fully satisfied your past-due mortgage obligation. The lender can reject your offer by returning your check or money order. However, your lawyer may be able to use the fact that your offer was rejected to strengthen your position with the court. Your lawyer will write the letter for you.

✔ **Delay the foreclosure process.** A delay gives you more time to figure out how to deal with your problem and may even buy you the time you need to put together enough money to bring the foreclosure to a halt. You can read about delay tactics in the section of this chapter called "Stalling for time."

✔ **Deed your home back to your mortgage lender.** You lose your home, but you also minimize the amount of foreclosure expenses you owe to your lender. Plus, by giving your home back, you avoid having a fore-closure on your credit record.

If you deed your home back to the lender, find out whether it will clean up your credit record in return for your saving it the time and expense of a foreclosure and sale. Some lenders are willing to do that — it never hurts to ask.

✔ **Sell your home.** Ideally, you will sell it for a high enough price that you can pay off your mortgage and maybe even get back some of the equity you have in it. Your lender is apt to put the foreclosure process on hold if you let it know that you will sell the house, because it's apt to net more from a private sale than from a public auction. As a condition of releasing the mortgage lien, your lender may require that you reimburse it for its foreclosure costs.

✔ **File for bankruptcy.** You may be able to keep your home, depending on the kind of bankruptcy you file (see Chapter 9). At the very least, filing for bankruptcy delays foreclosure.

Stalling for time

You can't delay the foreclosure of your home on a whim. You must have a legal basis for the delay — something your lawyer can figure out. If the foreclosure is judicial, your lawyer will argue before the court for the delays as part of the lawsuit filed by your mortgage lender. However, if the foreclosure is statutory and you want to use delay tactics, you must sue your mortgage holder.

Losing your home: Desperate straits

If your mortgage holder gets the right to take back your home, you'll receive a Notice of Sale telling you when your home will be sold, regardless of whether the foreclosure is judicial or statutory. If you haven't yet gotten legal help with your problem, run, don't walk, to a lawyer's office. You may still be able to keep your home!

In a few states, you have the right to get your house back after it's sold. If the mortgage holder takes back title to your home, your home will be sold in a public auction. The sale proceeds will go toward paying off your mortgage loan balance and toward the mortgage holder's costs of foreclosure. If any money is left over and other creditors have liens on your home, the money is applied toward their loans next. If anything is left after that, you get it. For a limited time, depending on your contract, you may have the right to buy your home back after it's been sold.

Once your home has been sold, you'll receive some notices from your mortgage holder, including notices telling you who bought your home and how much it sold for. If your home was sold for less than your mortgage balance, you will also receive a notice informing you of the shortfall, or *deficiency,* and asking you to pay that amount. The notice will also let you know how the lender intends to collect the deficiency if you don't pay it.

Car crisis: The repo man cometh

Getting behind on your car payments is like playing with fire. With little or no warning, you can lose control of your situation, with disastrous results. In most states, the creditor can take your car back without giving you any prior notice and without getting the court's permission. Therefore, if you're behind on your car payments, you may wake up one morning, or leave work one afternoon, and discover that your vehicle is gone. The *repo man* — your creditor or an employee of a company in the business of doing repossessions — will have taken it so that it can be sold, usually in a public auction.

You will probably be notified about when and where the auction will take place, so you can try to buy back your car — assuming that you have the cash. Some states place restrictions on creditors' repossession and sales methods. Call your state attorney general's office to find out whether your state is one of them.

 Every creditor has its own policy for when it will take back a vehicle for non-payment. The policy that applies to your loan is probably spelled out in the contact you signed when you financed your car. Although your contract may say something different, most creditors begin the repossession process after you haven't made your car payments for three consecutive months, but sometimes that time frame is much shorter. The creditor can legally repossess if you default on the loan by one day unless the contract says otherwise.

Even if you get caught up on your past-due car payments, your loan agreement may give your creditor the right to *call* the loan, which means that you must pay the loan's full balance immediately or lose your vehicle.

Losing the stuff in your car

If you're afraid that your car is going to be repossessed, remove your personal property from it. That includes your dry cleaning, CDs, maps, cell phone, spare tires, sporting goods, and so on.

If your car is repossessed before you're able to remove your things, send your creditor a letter asking that those things be returned to you. The creditor must comply with the request. However, don't be surprised if the creditor says that nothing was in your car when it was taken. Form 8-8 on the CD features an example of the letter to write.

If you installed a radio, CD player, TV, or a VCR in your car after you bought it, your creditor may argue that those things are integral parts of your vehicle even though you paid for them. Therefore, the creditor will tell you that you can't get them back. You'll probably need legal help to resolve this problem.

Knowing what to do when your car is being repossessed

The law in every state says that when your car is physically repossessed, the repo man can't breach the peace. Although each state defines "breaching the peace" differently, generally, the repo man can't use physical force or threats to take your car, and he can't ignore your verbal objections to what he's doing. He also can't show up to repossess your vehicle with a police officer or another government official, unless the officer or official has a court order to seize your car. Also, the repo man can't break into your locked garage to take your car. However, the repo man is legally entitled to come onto your property to get your car.

In some states, hiding your car to try to prevent it from being repossessed is illegal.

After your car has been repossessed

After your car is taken from you, your creditor will make plans to sell it. More often than not, it will be sold in a public auction. Then your creditor will apply the sale proceeds toward your loan balance, as well as toward the expense of taking back your car, storing it, and selling it.

Your car will most likely sell for much less than what you owe on it. Therefore, your creditor will look to you to make up the difference, or *deficiency*. If you don't pay the deficiency within a certain period, the creditor may turn it over to a debt-collection agency or sue you for the money.

Preventing repossession

If you believe that repossession is inevitable, you don't have to sit back and wonder when it will happen. You may not be able to keep your car, but you can save yourself some money by exercising one of the following options:

> ✔ **Sell your car if you owe less than what it's worth, and give the sale proceeds to your creditor.** You will almost certainly net more money by selling the car yourself than by letting it be sold at a public auction.

✔ **Give your car back to your creditor voluntarily.** This option benefits your credit record somewhat because the repossession will be reported as a voluntary, not an involuntary, repossession. Also, giving your car back costs you less because you're not liable for your creditor's repossession costs. However, you may still have a deficiency to pay.

When you let your creditor know that you intend to give your car back, push the creditor for some concessions because you're saving it the time and expense of a repossession. If your creditor agrees to any concessions, get them in writing before you give back your car.

✔ **File for bankruptcy.** In a Chapter 13 bankruptcy, you can stop the repossession, pay the present value of your vehicle, and reduce your car payments by stretching them out over as many as five years. Plus, you don't have to come up with your missed payments. Chapter 9 tells you all about bankruptcy.

Chapter 9

Bankruptcy: The Last Resort

. . . .

In This Chapter

▶ Filing a Chapter 13 bankruptcy to reorganize your debts

▶ Using Chapter 7 bankruptcy to wipe out most of your debts

▶ Knowing what to expect at your creditors' meeting

▶ Filling out the bankruptcy paperwork

▶ Understanding how your debts are dealt with in bankruptcy

. . . .

*W*hen your financial situation is going downhill fast and your efforts to improve it have failed, it's time to consider bankruptcy. Bankruptcy is usually your best bet when you're in danger of losing an important asset because you have defaulted on the loan that the asset secures or when you owe so much money in relation to your income that you're falling behind on all your debts. Another sign that your situation is critical is that the IRS is breathing down your neck because you owe it money.

Bankruptcy is a legal process that takes the pressure off by halting your creditors' collection efforts, giving you time to decide how to deal with them. Federal bankruptcy law governs the bankruptcy process, and your bankruptcy is heard in federal bankruptcy court. There are no state bankruptcy laws.

You should know, however, that filing for bankruptcy has its downside. For one thing, the federal Fair Credit Reporting Act (FCRA) says that a bankruptcy can remain on your credit record for up to ten years. During this time, it will be difficult for you to get new credit at reasonable terms. Plus, filing for bankruptcy is a hassle — even with an attorney's help — because there is lots of paperwork to fill out and creditors to deal with. Some of those creditors may be upset with you for not paying your bills and for filing for bankruptcy. And filing for bankruptcy will cost you money — typically between $500 and $2,500 if you file a Chapter 7 and between $1,000 and $3,000 for a Chapter 13 bankruptcy. Exactly how much your bankruptcy will cost depends on the complexities of your case.

When considering bankruptcy, most consumers consider two options: a Chapter 13 reorganization bankruptcy or a Chapter 7 liquidation bankruptcy. A Chapter 13 bankruptcy gives you the opportunity to restructure your debts by lowering your monthly payments and extending the amount of time you have to pay your creditors. Your goal when you file this kind of bankruptcy is to pay as much on your debts as you possibly can. When you file a Chapter 7 bankruptcy, however, most of your debts are wiped out. A bankruptcy attorney can help determine which type of bankruptcy is more appropriate for you.

Reorganizing with Chapter 13 Bankruptcy

Chapter 13 Bankruptcy allows you to keep your creditors at bay while you create a plan for repaying what you owe. You may pay 100 percent of the claims against you or less, depending on what you can afford. When you're developing your Chapter 13 debt-reorganization plan, you should have three goals:

- ✔ Keep your debt payments affordable.
- ✔ Satisfy your creditors.
- ✔ Get your reorganization plan approved by the bankruptcy court.

Your creditors and the trustee who oversees your bankruptcy want you to pay as much as you can on your debts, but don't agree to pay more than you can afford. If you fall behind on your payments or stop making them, your bankruptcy case will be dismissed, and you're back at the mercy of your creditors.

Your attorney prepares your plan, addressing your priority debts first and then your secured debts. Your lawyer deals with your unsecured debts last. The law says that over the life of your reorganization plan, you must pay your unsecured creditors as much as they would have received if you had filed Chapter 7. But the court expects you to pay more than that if you can afford to.

Thirty days after you file your debt-repayment plan with the court, along with your petition and schedules, the automatic stay is invoked. Thirty days after the plan is filed, you must begin making the debt payments that you proposed in the plan, even though you don't know yet whether the court will approve or disapprove it. You don't make those payments directly to your creditors, but instead to a trustee.

The bankruptcy court appoints a bankruptcy trustee to oversee your case. He collects your debt payments, distributes them to your creditors, and monitors whether you live up to your reorganization plan.

Your Chapter 13 trustee does more than receive your debt payments, disburse the money to your creditors, and monitor the progress of your bankruptcy. Some trustees also advise you about the development of your reorganization plan and remain available to answer your financial questions throughout your bankruptcy. Others even require that you attend financial management programs.

Meanwhile, your lawyer contacts your creditors to resolve any objections they have about how your reorganization plan treats them. Ideally, every-thing is resolved before the day of your creditors' meeting. However, some of them might file motions to take back their collateral and motions objecting to the confirmation or approval of your reorganization plan. They can file these motions before or after the creditors' meeting. If you and your creditors can't work out your differences, court hearings are scheduled. After hearing from both sides, a judge decides what should happen.

Meeting with your creditors

Forty to sixty days after you file your bankruptcy petition, your creditors' meeting takes place. Any of your creditors can attend the meeting, but your secured creditors are more apt to show up than your unsecured creditors. At the meeting, the trustee asks questions to determine whether the plan you're proposing is feasible, and your creditors can ask questions or negotiate how they're being treated in your plan.

Knowing what to expect from the confirmation hearing

The confirmation hearing can be held on the same day as the creditors' meet-ing or about a month later, depending on the procedure used by the court that's hearing your bankruptcy. If any of your secured creditors is still object-ing to your reorganization plan, the judge rules on the remaining objections and then either approves or disapproves the plan. If the judge rejects your plan, you have an opportunity to revise it and submit a new plan for approval.

If you can't get your Chapter 13 reorganization plan approved, you can con-vert to a Chapter 7. If your plan is confirmed, you must continue sending your payments to the trustee according to the terms of the plan until the plan is up — after three or five years. Once your plan is completed, the court discharges all your remaining debt, and your bankruptcy is over. Yippee!

What to do if you can't live up to the terms of your reorganization plan

Contact your attorney if you begin having trouble making the debt payments you promised in your reorganization plan. Depending on your circumstances, your attorney can file a motion asking the bankruptcy judge to give you permission to

- ✔ Reduce your payments for a limited time, assuming that the reason for your problem is temporary — you lose your job, for example.

- ✔ Change your plan if the reason for your payment problems appears fairly permanent.

- ✔ Convert your Chapter 13 bankruptcy to a Chapter 7. However, you can't do so if you have received a Chapter 7 discharge within the past six years.

  If you convert your bankruptcy to a Chapter 7, you have to give to the trustee all the nonexempt property you own.

- ✔ Refile your bankruptcy after the judge dismisses your first case. In both a Chapter 7 and a Chapter 13 bankruptcy, if your case is not dismissed "with prejudice," you have the right to refile and try again.

Under certain circumstances — usually circumstances that are beyond your control, such as a debilitating illness or accident — if you are unable to complete your reorganization plan, you can ask the bankruptcy court for a hardship discharge. If your request is granted, the debts that remain are wiped out. Usually, however, before this request can be granted, you must pay each of your creditors at least as much as they would have received if you had filed a Chapter 7. Also, there must be no chance of your being able to make payments even if you modified your reorganization plan.

Chapter 13 is a good option if you have a stable job and a steady income. However, to be eligible for Chapter 13, your total unsecured debt must be less than $269,250, and your total secured debt less than $807,750.

Your goal in a Chapter 13 is to hold on to your property and pay as much of your debt as you can over a three- to five-year period according to your debt-repayment plan, which the court must approve. Your bankruptcy is over after you have completed the plan.

Federal law says that a bankruptcy can remain in your credit record for up to ten years, not for seven years as with other negative information. However, the three major credit bureaus report Chapter 13 bankruptcies for just seven years. You can file Chapter 13 as many times as you want throughout your life.

To file or not to file

The following are reasons to file Chapter 13:

✔ You can keep all your property — exempt and nonexempt.

✔ You get three to five years to pay as much as you can afford on your debts.

✔ You can reduce the total amount of money you pay to your secured creditors.

✔ You are protected against the loss of your home through foreclosure.

✔ Your cosigners are protected from your creditors as long as your debt-repayment plan provides for full repayment of your joint debts. If it doesn't, the creditors can come after your cosigners for the balance of the debt after getting the court's permission.

✔ Chapter 13 stops a foreclosure as long as you continue making your current mortgage payments and you are paying the past-due mortgage amount according to your plan.

The following reasons are arguments against filing Chapter 13:

✔ You're involved with the bankruptcy court for a three- to five-year period.

✔ After your bankruptcy is over, some of your debts remain, and you must repay them.

✔ Filing a Chapter 13 is more expensive than filing a Chapter 7.

Going Bankrupt with Chapter 7

Filing a Chapter 7 Bankruptcy is less complicated than filing a Chapter 13. It's also your best option when you have so much debt that you have little or no chance of paying what you owe over time.

In a Chapter 7, you don't have to prepare a debt-reorganization plan as you do in a Chapter 13. Instead, the bankruptcy trustee in charge of your bankruptcy takes control of your nonexempt assets, liquidates them, and gives the money to your creditors. You can be in and out of a Chapter 7 in a matter of months. However, after you file this kind of bankruptcy, you can't file another Chapter 7 for six years.

Before filing Chapter 7, you have to make some important decisions that your lawyer helps you make. These decisions affect how much debt you repay and what assets you keep. Here's an overview of the decisions you face:

> ✔ **What property do you want to exempt from your bankruptcy?** If you owe money on any of these assets, your lawyer must contact your creditors to negotiate payment arrangements if you have fallen behind in payments.

✔ **Do you want to keep any of your nonexempt property?** If you do but you have a lot of equity in any of them, the trustee liquidates those assets to pay your debts, and you don't get to keep them. However, if the assets you want to keep have little or no value, the trustee lets you hold on to them. If you still owe money on any of those debts, you have to either reaffirm the debt or buy the assets back from your creditors.

If you're behind on your payments on the assets you want to keep, your lawyer contacts your creditors to work out agreements regarding how you will catch up and stay current on future payments at the same time. Although most creditors will work with you, some may demand that you catch up immediately if you want their cooperation.

✔ **Are there any nonexempt assets that you want to buy back from the trustee or redeem from a creditor?** If so, you and your creditors must agree on what they're worth, and you must be able to pay that amount of money to your creditors. If you and a creditor can't agree on a price, your lawyer can file a motion to redeem the property. At a court hearing, the judge decides how much you must pay to buy back the asset.

Most attorneys charge extra to file a motion to redeem and to represent you at the hearing. Before you fight for an asset, decide whether the asset is really worth the cost of the battle.

✔ **Do you want to reaffirm any of your debts?** Reaffirming a debt lets you keep the asset that collateralizes it in exchange for continuing to pay the debt. Assuming your creditor is amendable to the reaffirmation, you sign a debt-reaffirmation agreement promising to pay all that you owe even though you have filed for bankruptcy. In return, your creditor promises not to take back the collateral as long as you live up to the agreement. If you don't live up to the agreement after your bankruptcy is over, the creditor can take back the asset, sell it, and come after you to make up any deficiency.

Form 9-1 on the CD provides a sample reaffirmation agreement. After you sign the agreement, you have 60 days to change your mind and give the asset back. If you do, formally rescind the agreement by writing your creditor a letter, and let your lawyer know about your plans. Form 9-2 on the CD provides you with a sample rescission letter to a creditor.

Debts you can't discharge in a Chapter 7

When you file a Chapter 7 to wipe out most of your debt, some debts remain your responsibility to pay. Those debts include secured debts, spousal support and child support debts, and student loans. Other loans that are not dischargeable include the following:

✔ Taxes. However, in certain circumstances, some kinds of taxes can be discharged through bankruptcy.

✔ Personal injury damages that you owe to someone because you were driving drunk.

✔ Criminal penalties, such as the restitution you owe because you were found guilty of fraud, larceny, or embezzlement, as well as the money you owe because a court found you guilty of assault, libel, and so on. If any of your creditors think that you committed fraud, they must go to bankruptcy court and have the bankruptcy judge determine whether the debt will be considered as nondischarged — still your responsibility.

✔ Government penalties and fines.

✔ Debts that you did not list on your bankruptcy schedules.

Knowing what to expect from the creditors' meeting

Before your debts can be discharged through bankruptcy, you must attend a creditors' meeting. Your attorney will be there with you. The trustee who is overseeing your bankruptcy and any creditors who show up will ask you about your finances.

The creditors' meeting takes place about six to eight weeks after you file Chapter 7. Although any of your creditors can attend the meeting, as in a Chapter 13 creditors' meeting, your secured creditors are more apt to show up because they want to know what you plan to do with their collateral.

Exempt and nonexempt property in a Chapter 7

When you file for a Chapter 7 bankruptcy, you get to declare some of your property as exempt. Those assets are unaffected by your bankruptcy and protected from your creditors. In other words, you don't have to give them up in your bankruptcy, and when your bankruptcy is over, you still own them. Be sure that you take full advantage of all your potential exemptions.

Thirteen states let you decide whether you want to use the exemptions allowed by the federal bankruptcy code or the exemptions allowed by the law of your state. Your state law might provide more generous exemptions than federal law. Florida, California, and Texas have the most generous exemption laws.

Regardless of which set of exemptions you choose, there is a dollar limit on how much property you can exempt. The dollar amount varies widely from state to state. Whatever property you do not declare as exempt is considered nonexempt. Those assets are sold during your bankruptcy to pay off your debts.

Among other things, this meeting gives the trustee an opportunity to make sure that you were 100 percent honest when you filled out the bankruptcy schedules. She wants to be sure that you haven't overlooked or tried to conceal nonexempt property that could be sold to pay off your debt. Also, the trustee wants to be certain that you have a true appreciation of how filing a Chapter 7 affects you financially and legally. To get at these and other issues, the trustee may ask you the questions in the next section.

Preparing for the questions

Your lawyer gets a list of the questions ahead of time and reviews them with you before the meeting.

- ✔ Why did you file for bankruptcy?

- ✔ Have you listed all your assets and debts on the schedules? Tell the trustee if you know that you left some out. You will not be penalized. However, if you pretend that your schedules are accurate and the trustee learns later that they aren't, you could be charged with bankruptcy fraud.

- ✔ How did you determine the value of the assets on your schedules? If the trustee is not satisfied with your answers, he can hire an independent appraiser to value them.

- ✔ Have you been in an accident in the past year? The trustee wants to make sure that if you are entitled to compensation for the damages you may have suffered in an accident, the amount of that compensation is reflected on your asset schedule.

- ✔ Are you entitled to a tax refund? Once again, the trustee wants to make sure that you include it on your asset schedule.

- ✔ Are you entitled to an inheritance, or is there a chance that you might be receiving an inheritance within six months of your bankruptcy filing? Although you must record inheritance information on your schedules, the court can allow you to exempt it.

Your creditors can also ask you questions during the meeting. For example, secured creditors want to know what you plan to do with their collateral. Do you want to pay them for it so you can keep the collateral, or are you planning to give it back? Secured creditors who do not want you to keep their collateral will file motions to lift the automatic stay. If the judge grants their motions after a hearing, they can take back their collateral.

Your attorney will try to negotiate everything with your secured creditors prior to the creditors' meeting. Unsecured creditors who attend your creditors' meeting will want to know whether they're going to get anything in your bankruptcy. If your bankruptcy is like most Chapter 7s, they will get little or nothing. After the creditors' meeting, your creditors have 60 days to file objections to the discharge of your debt. Their objections are heard in a court hearing.

To file or not to file a Chapter 7

The following are reasons to file a Chapter 7:

✔ You can still file a Chapter 13 after your Chapter 7 discharge to pay off any remaining liens.

✔ After your nonexempt assets are liquidated and used to pay as much of your debt as possible, whatever debt remains is wiped out, or discharged.

✔ Filing a Chapter 7 is relatively cheap.

✔ Your bankruptcy will probably take no longer than six months.

The following are reasons not to file a Chapter 7:

✔ You can lose your nonexempt property.

✔ Unlike Chapter 13, you can't modify, or reduce your secured debt, but you can buy it back at present value, which is usually a lot less than what you owe on it.

✔ Chapter 7 delays but does not stop a foreclosure.

✔ Some debts will be waiting for you at the end of your bankruptcy — such as your mortgage.

✔ Creditors can come after your cosigners to collect your joint debts.

Your discharge hearing occurs about 80 to 120 days after the creditors' meeting. At this hearing, all your debts are discharged, except those that can't be erased through bankruptcy and those that you have agreed to pay or reaffirm. This hearing represents the end of your bankruptcy.

You may or may not have to attend this hearing — it depends on the practices and procedures of the court hearing your case. After you receive your discharge order, keep it in a safe place in case a creditor has a short memory or does not understand bankruptcy law and begins trying to collect from you again. If that happens, send the creditor a copy of your discharge order along with a letter stating that the debt was discharged and can no longer be collected. Form 9-3 on the CD provides you with a sample letter.

Once you have your discharge order in hand, send each of the big three credit bureaus a copy of that order, along with a copy of your debt schedules. Also send a letter asking to have your credit record reflect that all the debts listed on the schedules have been discharged. Doing so helps you rebuild your credit.

Getting Legal Help

Consult with a bankruptcy attorney as soon as you begin thinking that filing for bankruptcy may be something you should do. (Chapter 5 tells you how to find a good attorney.) An attorney can determine whether there is a better way to deal with your financial woes, and assuming there isn't, can advise you about your bankruptcy options. The attorney will also advise you about what you should *not* do prior to filing — actions that could negatively affect the final outcome of your bankruptcy. You can find out more about them later in this chapter.

Your lawyer fills out all the legal forms required by the bankruptcy court and deals with your creditors. Going through a bankruptcy can be stressful, but a bankruptcy attorney can help you rest easier.

Avoiding pre-bankruptcy no-no's

During the months leading up to your bankruptcy, certain things you do could complicate your bankruptcy, land you in legal trouble, and leave you with a lot of debt to pay once your bankruptcy is over. For example, prior to filing:

- ✔ Don't give your creditors post-dated checks. If the checks bounce, you could be charged with a criminal offense. Bankruptcy does not protect you from criminal prosecution.

- ✔ Don't hide your assets from the bankruptcy court by transferring them to other people. If the bankruptcy trustee learns about the transfer, she will take the property back and include those assets in your bankruptcy, which means that you may lose them. You may also be accused of fraud.

- ✔ Don't charge more than $1,000 in luxury items and services with a single creditor 60 days or less prior to filing for bankruptcy. Your bankruptcy does not wipe out those charges if a creditor objects to the charges and wins. The IRS views as luxury items such things as taking a cruise, buying a sailboat or snowmobile for recreation, and spending money on anything that's not essential to your life.

- ✔ Don't obtain a cash advance of more than $1,000 60 days or less prior to filing.

- ✔ Don't pay one creditor at the expense of another 90 days or less prior to filing for bankruptcy. If you do, the trustee can cancel the payment, take the money back, and distribute it more fairly among your creditors.

Taking the pressure off

No matter what kind of bankruptcy you choose, to initiate it you must file a petition with the federal bankruptcy court in your district, together with a series of *schedules,* or forms, which your lawyer fills out for you. You can look at a sample bankruptcy petition by checking out Form 9-4 on the CD. If you file a Chapter 13 bankruptcy, you must file a copy of your debt-reorganization plan with the petition. You must also pay a filing fee. It costs $200 to file a Chapter 7 and $185 to file a Chapter 13.

After your petition has been filed, the court issues an automatic stay. Now you can breathe a sigh of relief, because the stay orders all your creditors to cease their collection efforts immediately. That means repossessions and foreclosures are put on hold; lawsuits are stopped; your creditors can't try to enforce a judgment against you; your wages can't be garnished; and the IRS can't continue a legal proceeding against you that it has already initiated.

As powerful as an automatic stay is, it *can't* call a halt to some things, including an ex-spouse's efforts to establish the right to receive spousal support (alimony) from you or to collect the support you're legally obligated to pay; the efforts of the other parent of your minor child to establish your obligation to help support that child; criminal proceedings against you; and an IRS audit

Filling out the paperwork

Initiating a bankruptcy, regardless of whether you're filing a Chapter 7 or a Chapter 13, involves filling out a lot of forms related to your assets and debts. Your attorney completes them for you by using the information you provide. Those forms are filed with the court along with your bankruptcy petition. Most of the forms are the same regardless of whether you file a Chapter 7 or a Chapter 13 bankruptcy. However, with a Chapter 13, you also have to prepare and file a Chapter 13 Plan.

Here's a list of most of the forms you must fill out and a description of the kinds of information each one requires. You can find a sample of each form on the CD.

- **Schedule A:** On this form, you describe each piece of real property you own (your home, other buildings, and raw land) and give an address for each. You also indicate the nature of your interest in each property — you have title to the property or have invested money in it — and the current market value of your interest in the property. If the asset collateralizes a loan, you must indicate the loan balance. You can find Schedule A on Form 9-5 of the CD.

- **Schedule B:** This form asks you to describe all your personal property, including their locations and the current market value of your interest in each asset. Your personal property can include cash, the money in your checking and savings accounts, household goods, clothing, books, jewelry, investment interests (IRA, SEP, pension sharing plan, and so on), automobiles, boats, hobby equipment, insurance policies, and more. Schedule B is Form 9-6 of the CD.

- **Schedule C:** When you file a Chapter 7 bankruptcy, you indicate the assets you want to exempt from the bankruptcy on this form. Chapter 4 explains exempt and nonexempt assets, but the sidebar "Exempt and nonexempt property in a Chapter 7" provides a brief refresher course on the topic as it relates to bankruptcy. Check out Schedule C on Form 9-7 of the CD.

✔ **Schedule D:** List on this form all your secured creditors, their addresses, and how much you owe to each secured creditor. You can find this schedule on the CD on Form 9-8.

✔ **Schedule E:** This form is for providing information about all the unsecured creditors with priority claims in your bankruptcy, including their names and the amount you owe to each. They can include the persons to whom you owe past-due alimony or child support, the IRS, and certain student loans. This schedule is Form 9-9 on the CD.

✔ **Schedule F:** On this form, you list all the creditors with unsecured nonpriority claims against you and the amount of each claim. These creditors include credit card companies and unsecured loans. Schedule F is on the CD as Form 9-10.

The difference between priority and nonpriority claims becomes clear in the section "Realizing that all debts are not created equal" later in this chapter.

✔ **Schedule G:** On this form, you provide information about the leases and other contracts you are a party to. Find Schedule G on the CD as Form 9-11

✔ **Schedule H:** If any of your debts are joint, use this form to provide the name and address of each of your codebtors. You also indicate the name and address of the creditors to whom you owe money and the amount of each debt. You can see what Schedule H looks like by going to Form 9-12 on the CD.

✔ **Schedule I:** Use this form to list your income. List all sources of income, including your take-home pay, commissions, interest and dividends, rental income, and so on. If your spouse has income, include that information on this schedule as well. This schedule is Form 9-13 on the CD.

✔ **Schedule J:** Use this form to itemize your monthly living expenses — the amount you spend on housing, food, clothing, recreation, insurance, utilities, and so on. You can find Schedule J on Form 9-14 on the CD.

✔ **Statement of financial affairs:** The purpose of this statement is to uncover any assets you own that you did not list on the schedules and to determine whether you made any illegal financial transactions before you filed for bankruptcy. The trustee carefully examines each of your responses on this statement. To see what a statement of financial affairs looks like, go to Form 9-15 on the CD.

✔ **Chapter 13 Plan:** If you're filing a Chapter 13 bankruptcy, you use this form to detail how you intend to deal with each of your debts. You can find a Chapter 13 Plan on Form 9-16 of the CD.

Make sure that all your debts are listed on the schedules your attorney files with the court. If a debt is left off, it is not discharged through your bankruptcy. Therefore, it continues to be your debt — something you must pay.

Realizing that all debts are not created equal

In a bankruptcy, some debts are more important than others. How they're treated in a bankruptcy depends on the type of bankruptcy you file. The most important debts are priority debts, which include unpaid taxes, including income and property taxes, unpaid spousal support, maintenance, and child support, and criminal fines

In a Chapter 13, you must pay off these debts either according to the terms of your reorganization plan or by selling some of your assets. If you file a Chapter 7, you can't discharge or wipe out most priority debts. If you own any nonexempt assets, the court sells them to help pay your priority debt. Otherwise, the creditors to which you owe money will be waiting for you when your bankruptcy is over, and they can begin trying to collect their money again.

Secured debts are next in importance. These are debts that you have collateralized with an asset. They include your home mortgage, home equity loan, other substantial bank loans, your car loan, and so on.

In a Chapter 13 bankruptcy, you have several ways to deal with your secured debt. You can return the collateral to your creditor or

- ✔ Modify the debt. You can change the way you pay back your secured debts so that your debt payments are more affordable. You may also be able to repay just the value of the collateral rather than the full amount of a debt you owe. This approach usually works to your advantage when you want to hold on to your car and you still owe money on it. Most likely, the car is worth less than your loan balance. To do this, you have to pay the creditor the value of the collateral over the life of your reorganization plan, with some interest added.

  You can't modify the balance on your mortgage loan. You can pay off the past-due balance over the life of your reorganization plan, but you have to pay your current mortgage payments at the same time.

- ✔ Pay your creditor the full amount of your debt according to your contract, assuming that the value of the collateral is worth more than what you owe.

If you file Chapter 7, you have fewer options for dealing with your secured debts. For example, when a debt secures a nonexempt asset, the trustee can take the decision away from you by selling the asset to help pay your debts. But if the trustee is not interested in the asset, you can buy it back from the trustee if you have the money. If you have, say, a piece of land that isn't your homestead and is worth more than what you still owe on it, the trustee can sell it and get the equity out to pay your debts. Or you could pay the trustee the equity and keep the property if you can come up with the money you need.

In the eyes of the law, your unsecured debts are the least important. Therefore, in both a Chapter 13 and a Chapter 7 bankruptcy, unsecured debts are handled last. More often than not, your unsecured creditors get little or nothing because there simply isn't enough money to pay them. Once your bankruptcy is over, all your unpaid unsecured debts are discharged.

When you're preparing your Chapter 13 reorganization plan, the court expects that you will pay your unsecured creditors as much as you can, even if you can afford to pay them only cents on the dollar. No matter what you do, however, you must treat all your unsecured creditors equally.

Chapter 10

Life After Debt: Making a Fresh Start

*W*hen money troubles damage your credit history, you may worry whether you will ever be able to get credit at reasonable terms again. Your worries are understandable. After all, a damaged or destroyed credit record limits your opportunities in life. Buying a home, affording a college education for your children, purchasing adequate insurance, and even getting the job you want may be difficult, if not impossible.

Furthermore, if your credit history is so damaged that you no longer have a bankcard, renting a car, reserving a hotel room, making airline reservations, buying things online, and so on will be difficult as well.

Take heart! You can improve and even rebuild your credit record and create a brighter future for yourself and your family. This chapter tells you how to do so. It provides you with an overview of the credit rebuilding process when you have no credit at all, as well as giving advice about how to improve your credit record when it's damaged but you still have a credit card or two. It also warns you about credit scams to steer clear of, including bogus credit repair firms and "guaranteed" credit offers.

Rebuilding Your Credit

Building a new, problem-free credit history that puts you back in the credit mainstream isn't a complicated process. Quite simply, it's a matter of applying for a limited amount of new credit and making your credit payments on time.

However, rebuilding your credit record takes time. Once you begin the process, you most likely won't qualify for an unsecured MasterCard or Visa for two to three years. (More about secured and unsecured credit cards later in this chapter.) Qualifying for a mortgage will take a couple of years more. Therefore, as soon as the money troubles that landed you in credit record chaos are behind you, you should get the credit rebuilding process underway.

If you have a bankruptcy on your record, you will have to wait a little longer than other consumers to begin the rebuilding process. Without a bankruptcy, you can begin rebuilding as soon as you're financially stable again. If a bankruptcy is a part of your credit history, you usually must wait six to twelve months after the bankruptcy is over to start rebuilding. Filing for bankruptcy is a serious step, and creditors want to be sure that you have had time to stabilize your finances before they will give you new credit. (Chapter 9 explains how bankruptcy works.)

No one way is the "right" way to rebuild your credit history; however, here is the process we recommend:

1. **Check the record.**

   Order a copy of your credit record from each of the three national credit bureaus. Make sure that all the information they're reporting about you is current and accurate. Chapter 7 tells you how to order a copy of your record from each of the major credit bureaus and how to correct any problems you find.

2. **Become a saver.**

   Start saving, even if it's only $5 a week. Something is better than nothing. When you put money in a savings account, you're creating a financial safety net for yourself that you can use to help pay for emergencies and other unexpected expenses. Also, having money in savings can help you qualify for a bank loan and for a secured credit card.

3. **Get a loan.**

   After you have $500 to $1,000 in savings, ask your bank for a small loan. You may have to secure or collateralize the loan with the money in your savings account. (Chapter 6 tells you how secured loans work.) If your bank turns down your loan application, apply for a loan with other banks in your area.

   Having a person-to-person meeting with a consumer loan officer before you apply for a loan can increase the chances of your application being approved. Sit down with the loan officer, explain your situation and what you have done or are doing to stabilize and improve it, and tell the officer why you want a loan.

4. **Make all your loan payments on time.**

   Falling behind on your loan builds a new negative credit history — and that's definitely not what you want.

5. **Get another loan.**

   After you pay off the first loan, get a second loan if your first one was secured. If the loan was unsecured, move on to the next step in the credit rebuilding process.

6. **Apply for a Visa or MasterCard.**

   Just one card will do. Get the card with the best possible terms. If you don't qualify for a regular unsecured credit card, apply for a secured card. Whether your card is secured or unsecured, the issuing bank will report your card payment history to one or more of the three national credit bureaus, helping you rebuild your credit record.

   MasterCard and Visa are the best types of cards to apply for because most businesses accept them and because they're relatively easy to qualify for. You may want to apply for an American Express card later, but it isn't as widely accepted and has more stringent qualification standards than MasterCard and Visa do.

   Avoid retailer credit cards. Their terms of credit are not as attractive as those on a MasterCard or Visa card, and the business that issues you a store credit card may not report your card payment history to credit bureaus. Furthermore, most businesses that offer their own cards also accept Visa and MasterCard, so a retailer credit card is unnecessary.

Gathering the secrets to success

When you're rebuilding your credit history, keep the following credit rebuilding advice in mind. This advice will help you increase the likely success of your rebuilding efforts and will decrease your chances of new money troubles in the future.

- ✔ **Go slowly.** Don't fill out every credit card application that comes in the mail. Fill out the one with the best terms of credit. Chapter 6 tells you how to choose the best credit card.

- ✔ **Limit the number of credit cards you own to one or two at the very most.** The more cards you have, the bigger your risk of taking on too much debt. Also, creditors don't like to work with consumers with multiple credit cards, even if some of them are paid off.

- ✔ **Be proactive.** Don't wait for offers to come to you. Use these resources to find a good card:

  - Myvesta.org, an Internet-based nonprofit organization that provides information, services, and online counseling to people who are dealing with too much debt or with the repercussions of too much debt. This organization was formerly known as Debt Counselors of America. If you visit its Web site, you can download a free list of secured credit cards. You can also call Myvesta.org at 800-680-3328.

- • **CardTrack** offers information on a variety of types of credit cards, including secured cards. You can easily compare the secured card you're considering with other secured cards by visiting www.cardtrack.com or by calling 301-631-9100.

✔ **Don't use your credit card for frivolous purchases.** Use it to pay for something relatively expensive that you really need, and then pay off the balance over time. Another credit rebuilding strategy is to use your card to make small purchases each month and then to pay off each card balance in full. Either way, your goal is to build a history of on-time payments.

✔ **Make all your debt payments on time.** Late payments won't help you achieve your credit rebuilding goal.

✔ **Pay more than the monthly minimum.** Try to pay more than the minimum due when you make credit card payments, but always pay at least that much. Your goal should be to pay off your credit balance as quickly as possible. The longer it takes, the higher your cost of credit because you pay more in interest and because you are more likely to pay late and be charged a late fee.

✔ **Work with the right creditors.** Don't work with creditors who won't report your payment history to the major credit bureaus. Chapter 7 tells you which types of creditors tend to report to credit bureaus and which don't.

✔ **Avoid finance company loans.** Although the image of these companies is improving, a finance company loan is an expensive source of credit given the high rates of interest usually charged. Also, traditional creditors may be reluctant to work with you if you have a finance company loan on your credit record.

✔ **Don't open a rent-to-own account.** Rent-to-own companies prey on people with bad credit and charge exorbitant rates of interest. Working with one won't improve your credit record, either.

✔ **Steer clear of advance fee loans.** These loans charge you a fee up front. They are bad news for your credit and should be avoided. We tell you more about these loans later in this chapter.

Improving but not rebuilding a damaged credit rating

When you go through financially difficult times, your credit history may be damaged, but not destroyed. Therefore, although you may still have some credit, you'll probably have a tough time getting new and additional credit at reasonable terms unless you improve your credit record. This section offers some tips for how to do that.

If you fell behind on payments for one of your accounts but are all caught up now and have since been making your account payments on time, write your creditor a polite letter asking the company to remove the negative information from your credit record and to report the "corrected" information instead. In your letter, briefly explain why you got behind and point out your recent history of on-time payments. The creditor may be willing to cooperate if

✔ Your reasons for getting behind are credible: You lost your job, someone in your family was seriously ill or injured, and so on.

✔ You weren't behind on your payments for a long time — between six and twelve months.

✔ Your overall account payment history has been positive.

✔ The creditor has not signed an agreement with the credit bureaus it reports to that prevents the creditor from making the changes you're asking for.

Direct your letter to the manager of consumer accounts, the credit manager, or someone in a similar position. Get a specific name. Send the letter via certified mail, return receipt requested. Then call to determine whether your request will be granted. If your creditor agrees to your request, draft an agreement and send it to the creditor. Again, use certified mail and ask for a return receipt. To be sure that the creditor has lived up to the terms of the agreement, request a copy of your credit report from the credit bureau a couple of months later. If you see no change in your credit record, write a second letter to your creditor referencing the agreement and attach a copy of the agreement.

Form 10-1 on the CD provides you with a sample request letter, and Form 10-2 offers a sample draft agreement. Model your follow-up letter after the one on Form 10-3 of the CD.

Sending a stamped, self-addressed envelope to your creditor along with the agreement may get you faster action. Ask your creditor to send you a copy of the corrected information it sends to the credit bureau(s) it reports to. That way, you can be sure that the creditor has complied with your request.

If you've been paying on accounts for some time that aren't part of your credit record, write each of the three national credit bureaus and ask them to add that information to your record. Attach a copy of your most recent account statement to the letter, as well as a summary of your account payment history. (Most creditors will provide you with a written copy of that history, although you may have to pay for it.) The credit bureau doesn't have to honor your request, but it may. Check out Form 10-4 on the CD for an example of the kind of letter to write.

Your story in 100 words or less

If the story behind your credit problem is a sympathetic one — health problems, a job loss, the financial repercussions of a divorce, or a house fire — take advantage of the opportunity to include a written statement in your credit record. The federal Fair Credit Reporting Act (FCRA) gives you the right to write a 100-word (or fewer) explanation of why your credit problems occurred and to have that explanation be made a part of your credit record. Be sure that your explanation is clearly written, and if you have receipts, legal documents, or other records to back up your statement, note that you will share them with any creditor who wants to review them. The FCRA requires credit bureaus to make your written statement a part of your credit record. That way, if a potential creditor, insurer, or employer reviews your record, the business can appreciate the human story behind your money troubles and can take that information into account when deciding whether to give you credit.

Note: Computers, not human beings, are reading a growing number of credit histories to determine who is and isn't credit worthy. When they do, they won't take the written statement in your credit record into account.

Losing ground with advanced fee loans

Your finances may start looking down, not up, if you apply for a guaranteed or advanced fee loan. To get this loan, you have to pay an up-front fee, possibly as much as a couple hundred dollars. More often than not, if you fall for the offer, you'll never get a loan, and the company or loan broker that promised one to you in exchange for your money will be nowhere to be found.

Guaranteed loans are often advertised on TV and radio, in print ads, on posters and flyers, via e-mail, and at Web sites. These ads may tell you to call a toll-free number or a 900 pay-per-minute number. Someone claiming to be a loan broker may also offer you a guaranteed loan.

The federal Telemarketing Sales Rule says that if a company or loan broker offers to give you a loan or even implies that you can get a guaranteed loan, it can't take any money from you until you actually have the loan.

If you need to finance the purchase of a new car, avoid companies that advertise loans for people with bad credit. Your loan will almost certainly come with an extremely high interest rate, or APR, and it will also require that you pay a larger than usual down payment. A high APR not only increases the cost of your loan but also increases the likelihood that if you sell your car before the loan is paid off, what you get for it won't cover your loan balance. (For an APR refresher, read Chapter 6.)

If a car dealer offers financing, don't take the car salesperson's information at face value. He is apt to earn a commission on new car financing and therefore has a financial incentive to make dealer financing sound as good as possible.

Secured Card, Regular Card: What's the Difference?

When you want a MasterCard or Visa and your credit history is not stellar, you may have to apply for a secured card and prove that you can use it responsibly in order to qualify for a regular unsecured card.

Secured and unsecured cards may look the same and serve the same purpose, but they differ in some important ways. The bank that issues you a secured credit card requires that you deposit with it a certain amount of money, often between $500 and $1,000. You won't have access to this money because it collateralizes the purchases you make with your card. However, if you fall behind on your payments, the bank probably won't tap the collateral, but instead will send your account to collections. Usually, the only time your collateral is used is to pay an unpaid balance if your account is closed.

Secured credit cards often come with less attractive terms of credit. For example, their credit limits tend to be lower, they have higher interest rates, and they have larger late penalties than the typical unsecured card.

Comparing secured credit card offers

Secured credit cards and regular unsecured cards have at least one thing in common: Some have better terms of credit than others. Therefore, when you shop for a secured credit card, carefully read *all* the information that explains your responsibilities as a cardholder and the card issuer's rights. When you do, remember that much of the information — certainly most of the information that's in large print — is written to make the credit card sound like a good deal. The really important details are probably buried in the small print. So read them, too — even if you have to use a magnifying glass!

When you're trying to distinguish between a good and a not-so-good secured card, consider these questions:

- Do you have to pay a fee to apply for the card? If so, how much?
- If you don't qualify for the card, can you get your application fee back?
- How much money do you have to put up as collateral? Remember, you can't use this money.
- What rate of interest will your collateral earn? The higher, the better.
- Can you put your collateral in a CD or money market account rather than in a lower-yielding savings account?
- What is the card's credit limit? Usually, the limit is between 50 and 100 percent of the collateral. The higher the percentage, the better.

✔ If you maintain a balance on the secured card, what rate of interest will you be charged?

✔ Does the card come with a late fee? If so, how much is it?

✔ Do you have a grace period for credit card payments? The longer, the better, because a long grace period means that you're less apt to make your card payments late and to have to pay late charges. Remember, being late will show up as a negative on your credit record.

✔ What other fees are associated with the card? How much are they? The other fees could include an application fee, a bounced check fee, a fee for going over your credit limit, and a fee for closing the account.

✔ After you establish a good payment history, can you increase your credit limit without increasing the collateral?

✔ How soon after you obtain the card can you increase your credit limit?

✔ Can you convert the card to an unsecured card? If you can, what are the conditions of conversion, and how soon can you convert?

✔ When does the credit card company have the right to tap into your collateral?

✔ If you close the account, under what conditions and how soon can you get your collateral back?

✔ Do you have to pay any fees to close the account?

✔ Will the card company report your account payments to at least one of the major credit bureaus? This question is important because many disreputable secured card companies issue cards but don't report payment information to the credit bureaus. The following section tells you about these companies and how to spot one.

Watching out for shady secured card deals

Most secured credit card companies are reputable. In fact, most of them are established banks that also issue traditional bankcards. However, some secured card companies are in the business of preying on people with credit problems. They commonly market to these consumers by telling them that a national credit card is "just a phone call away." Many imply and even promise that they can guarantee you a credit card.

If you hear the words *guaranteed credit* or something similar, an alarm should go off in your head. No reputable company will promise you any kind of credit card, secured or unsecured, without looking at your credit history first.

Here are two other dead giveaways that the company offering you a secured credit card is less than reputable:

✔ Neither the promotional materials for the card nor the card application mentions the name of the bank issuing the card. Why? Because no bank is involved. Therefore, if you pay money to apply, the card you applied for will never arrive, and you're out the money.

✔ The promotional literature for the secured card says that you can use it only to order things from a catalog provided by the card issuer.

Some offers are little more than promotions for a list of banks that may send you a secured card application. You pay money, you get the list, but the companies on that list may or may not give you the credit you want.

A shady secured credit card company may direct you to call a 900 number to learn more about its credit card offer. If you do, you're charged for the call on a per-minute basis. The company may not tell you how a 900 call works or how much you'll be charged for each minute, much less that a part of what you pay to make the call will go into its pockets. The company may also not mention that your application fee — which can be substantial — is nonrefundable. To top it off, for all your expense and effort, you may end up with no card at all, or a secured card with very bad terms of credit.

Hiring Someone to Repair Your Credit

Rebuilding your credit history or improving a damaged history isn't difficult, but if you're like some consumers, you may want to hire a credit repair firm to do the job for you. Many of these firms are legitimate, but many are not. In fact, some of these firms use illegal methods that could put you on the wrong side of the law.

Credit repair firms often charge a lot for their services. Yet they can't do anything that you can't do for yourself — for free — under the provisions of the federal Fair Credit Reporting Act (FCRA). Chapter 7 discusses this law in detail.

Bogus credit repair companies often claim that they can speed up the credit building process by — presto-chango! — making the negative information in your credit record disappear. To accomplish that feat, these credit "magicians" use tactics that skirt the law or are illegal.

Familiarize yourself with the federal Credit Repair Organizations Act (CROA) before you hire a company to help you rebuild or improve your credit history. By understanding what the law requires, you can be more certain that the firm you choose is on the up and up. Among other things, the CROA says that a credit repair firm must

✔ Provide you with a written and dated contract that spells out the services it will provide to you and the total cost of those services. A credit repair firm contract that doesn't comply with the requirements of the CROA is legally unenforceable.

✔ Provide all the services spelled out in its contract before it takes any money from you.

✔ Provide you with a written statement titled *Your Consumer Credit File Rights Under State and Federal Law* before it enters into a contract with you. This information explains that you can dispute inaccurate or out-of-date information in your credit record yourself without professional help. It also tells you that you don't need outside help to obtain a copy of your credit record. The statement must also spell out your rights according to the CROA.

✔ Not make statements that are intended to deceive you in any way.

✔ Not encourage you to alter your credit identity in order to get new credit.

If you sign a contract with a credit repair firm, the CROA gives you three days to cancel it. You must cancel by sending the firm the cancellation form that it's legally required to give you when you sign its contract. The credit repair firm can't provide you with any services until the three days are up. If a credit repair firm violates the CROA, you can sue the firm for actual damages, or for the amount of money that you have paid so far — whichever is greater. You may also be able to sue the firm for punitive damages and collect your attorney's fees and court costs if you win.

Part III
Other Money Matters

The 5th Wave   By Rich Tennant

"The first thing we should do is get you two into a good mutual fund. Let me get out the 'Magic 8-Ball' and we'll run some options."

In this part . . .

Stop here for the lowdown on a wide variety of everyday money topics, some big and some small. Chapter 11 offers helpful advice about using debit cards and tackles a tough subject to love: taxes. Find out what to do when you can't pay or when the IRS says you owe more than you think you do. Chapter 12 helps you avoid the perils and pitfalls of buying or leasing a new or used car so that you can get a good deal. Chapter 13, by providing specific information related to auto and homeowner's insurance, explains how insurance works and how to shop for a policy. Chapter 14 discusses writing a will, trusts, and estate taxes and covers other end-of-life issues such as living wills and durable healthcare powers of attorney.

Chapter 11

Tackling Telemarketers and Taxes

*T*his chapter deals with two subjects that aggravate most people to no end — telemarketers and taxes. New federal legislation gives you the right to control when telemarketers call you and spells out your other telemarketing rights. Few experiences are as taxing as your taxes. This chapter helps illuminate your rights and responsibilities when it comes to dealing with or avoiding conflicts with the IRS.

Telemarketing Trauma: Making Them Stop!

Does this sound familiar? It's dinnertime and the phone rings just as you sit down to your meal. When you say, "Hello," you're greeted by an overly friendly stranger who mispronounces your name and immediately tries to engage you in conversation. It's another telemarketer trying to sell your something you probably don't want.

Is there anything you can do to stop these calls? Yes, thank goodness. Gain greater control over telemarketers by activating the protections of the federal Telemarketing Sales Rule. This rule makes it illegal for a telemarketer to continue contacting you after you tell him that you do not want to be called. It also restricts telemarketing calls to between 8 a.m. and 9 p.m.

More telemarketing protections

Most telemarketers are honest people selling legitimate products and services. However, some telemarketers try to rip off unsuspecting consumers by selling them too-good-to-be-true business opportunities, easy credit, bogus investments, phony travel packages, the chance to win "free" prizes, and so on. In fact, the federal government estimates that each year, telemarketing fraud costs consumers $40 billion. Therefore, it pays to know what the Telemarketing Sales Rule requires of telemarketers. That way, if a telemarketer doesn't live up to the letter of this law, you know that the caller is probably a shyster and someone with whom you do not want to do business.

The Telemarketing Sales Rule also applies to calls you place in response to a postcard indicating that you have won a prize or contest or to a print, TV, or radio ad that directs you to call a phone number for more information.

The Telemarketing Sales Rule says that telemarketers must tell you up front that they're calling to sell you something. They must be clear about what they're selling, and they must give you the name of the company they're calling for. Telemarketers who are marketing prize promotions must also let you know that to enter their contests, you do not need to pay or purchase anything.

Telemarketers must be honest about what they're selling, the prize you could win, the profits you could make, the risks associated with the business opportunity they're marketing, and so on. And telemarketers must indicate up front the total cost of what they're selling. They must also tell you about any restrictions and whether the sale is final or the payment nonrefundable. If they're trying to get you to participate in a contest, they must tell you your odds of winning and indicate any restrictions or conditions on your receiving the prize if you do.

If a telemarketer violates the terms of the rule, contact the consumer affairs office of your state attorney general. State law enforcement officials have the right to prosecute fraudulent telemarketers whether they're calling from your state or another state.

Going on defense when a telemarketer calls

Many telemarketers are experienced salespeople who are good at talking people out of their money. Therefore, if a telemarketer's sales pitch sounds interesting to you, listen with a skeptical ear and keep this advice in mind:

- Don't do business with anyone who tries to pressure you into buying and who won't take "no" for an answer.
- Don't do business with anyone who tells you that you must act quickly or the offer will expire.

- ✔ Don't agree to pay money to a telemarketer without first seeing printed information about exactly what you would be buying.

- ✔ Don't give the caller any financial information about yourself, including your checking and savings account numbers and your credit card numbers. Also, keep your Social Security number to yourself.

- ✔ Don't send a telemarketer money by courier or via overnight delivery, and don't wire money to one who insists on being paid right away. Reputable businesses do not operate this way.

If you think that a telemarketer is not on the up and up, contact your local Better Business Bureau and the consumer protection office of your state attorney general before you pay the telemarketer any money or sign anything. It's also a good idea to call the National Fraud Information Center (NFIC) at 800-876-7060.

If you believe that you're the victim of telemarketing fraud, or if you have information about a fraudulent telemarketer, file a complaint with Project KNOW FRAUD, a joint effort of the Federal Trade Commission (FTC) and several nonprofit and government organizations. Use the online form available at www.consumer.gov/knowfraud to file your complaint. The FTC will review your complaint and may post it in an electronic database that's available to more than 200 law enforcement organizations across the United States and in Canada. Although the FTC will not take action against a telemarketer on your behalf, if it gets enough complaints about the company, it may prosecute on behalf of all consumers who have been victimized by that telemarketer. It will immediately report your information to federal and state enforcement agencies and consumer protection offices around the country.

Reducing telemarketing calls

If you want to cut down on the number of telemarketing calls you receive, check out the suggestions in this section. Although you won't reduce the calls to zero, you should notice a decrease.

Whenever you have the option of being removed from a credit card company's marketing list, do so. Your own credit card company might sell the list to other companies that use the information for telemarketing purposes.

Contact companies that sell consumer information, including your information, and ask that they take you off their lists. The following large companies sell consumer information: Doubleclick at www.doubleclick.com, Donnelley Marketing at 888-633-4402, Polk Company at 800-873-7655, and Abacus Direct at 800-518-4453. The Acxiom Corporation can be reached at P.O. Box 2000, Conway, AR 72033. Send the letter to Attn: Opt-Outs.

You can also contact one of the Big Three credit bureaus — Equifax, Experian, and Trans Union — and ask to be taken off the mailing lists it sells. If you do, your name will be removed from the lists of all three. Chapter 7 provides telephone numbers for each of the Big Three.

Another approach is to contact the Direct Marketing Association to get your name removed from most, but not all, national telemarketing lists: Telephone Preference Service, P.O. Box 9104, Farmingdale, NY 11735. You can also get your name removed from most national direct-mail lists by contacting the Direct Marketing's Mail Preference Service, P.O. Box 9008, Farmingdale, NY 11735.

Talking Taxes: Avoiding Entanglements with Uncle Sam

They say that two things are certain: death and taxes. Yes, like clockwork, you're legally required to file a federal tax return with the Internal Revenue Service (IRS) and report your income for the previous year every April 15. And by *income,* the IRS means all your wages, fees, commissions, royalties, rental income, interest income, business income, and dividend income. The IRS also counts alimony payments, unemployment income, pension or annuity income, estate or trust income, and income from a life insurance payoff.

If you win the lottery, don't be surprised when the IRS comes calling with its hand out. Income from winning a lottery, sweepstakes, or wagering pool, if it amounts to more than $5,000, is taxable. And don't forget to report those few dollars you receive for doing your civic duty — the IRS counts jury fees as taxable income. No, we're not kidding!

Although you may not count any money you make through illegal means as income when you're completing your federal tax return, you will be required to amend your return if the IRS learns about it, and that income will be subject to taxation. Of course, depending on how you made the money, potential tax debt could be the least of your problems!

You can file your taxes the old-fashioned way, by using paper forms, or you can file electronically. Instructions for how to file online arrives with the tax return information and forms that the IRS sends just after the start of the new year. If your income tax calculations show that you owe the IRS money, the agency expects you to pay that debt at the same time you file your return. You can pay with a check or money order, or you can pay with a credit card by calling 888-272-9829.

When you pay with a check or money order, make sure that you make it out to the United States Treasury, not the IRS. If you ignore this advice, your payment may be returned to you, and you may be liable for interest and penalties because the IRS will treat you as a late payer.

Phone numbers and Web addresses to keep handy

You can find helpful information for your tax questions at 800-829-1040. To receive help from a Taxpayer Advocate, call 877-777-4778. To order IRS forms and publications, call 800-829-1040 or go to the agency's Web site, www.irs.gov. To order IRS forms only, call 800-829-3676.

The IRS does not like non-filers. Therefore, if you ignore your filing obligation, you'll create problems for yourself. If the IRS catches up with you (it will — it's only a matter of when), you will be obligated to file your taxes and pay any taxes you owe, together with interest and late penalties. The interest and penalties begin to accrue on April 16 of the year your tax payment was due. The interest is compounded daily, and the penalties are assessed each month. Over time, these charges can really increase your overall debt to the IRS.

Getting more time to file

The IRS understands that life sometimes gets in the way, and you simply don't have enough time to complete your return and file it by April 15. Therefore, it allows you to request an extension of your filing deadline. To make that request, you must complete IRS Form 4868, *Application for Automatic Extension of Time to File U.S. Individual Income Tax Return.* Assuming you make it before April 15, you automatically get an extension to August 15. You can find a sample IRS automatic extension form on Form 11-2 of the CD.

An extension to file your tax return is *not* an extension to pay your taxes! You must pay your estimated tax liability at the time you request the extension.

Still need more time? You can apply for a second extension by filling out IRS Form 2688, *Application for Additional Extension of Time to File Individual Income Tax Return.* That form appears on the CD as Form 11-3. The extension is not automatic, however; whether you get it is up to the discretion of the IRS. If you do get it, you have until October 15 to file your return.

What to do if you can't pay your taxes

If you can't pay your taxes, don't hide your head in the sand hoping that Uncle Sam won't notice. He will, sooner or later. And while you're waiting, your tax debt grows because interest and penalties are mounting. For example, at some point after the tax payment due date, the IRS starts sending you letters asking for the money you owe. If you don't respond to the IRS by paying the money or making some other arrangement, those letters continue and gradually become more threatening. You receive a similar series of letters if you don't file your tax return. If you have a masochistic streak and insist on ignoring the IRS, consider that in addition to garnishing your wages, the IRS may

- **Freeze your bank account and take your money.** The IRS can block your access to your own accounts. If negotiations with the IRS fail, or if you're foolish enough to ignore the agency's threat, your bank gives the IRS the money it demanded.

- **Place a lien on one or more of your assets.** You have 30 days to protest the lien with the manager of the IRS revenue office that executes the lien. The notice the IRS sends you informing you of the lien also tells you how and where to protest. If your protest is denied, you can file an appeal with the IRS appeals office. The section in this chapter entitled "Appealing things" tells you how the appeals process works. If your appeal is denied, you can sue the IRS to stop the lien. Read on if you want to find out more about suing the IRS.

- **Threaten to seize one or more of your assets, including your home.** The IRS sells the seized assets and applies the proceeds to your tax debt. If your home is sold, you have a period to buy it back. To stop a seizure, you can file an appeal, and you can sue the IRS.

Knowing what to do if a threatening letter arrives

If the IRS sends you a threatening letter about the money it says you owe, the notice instructs you to call an automated collection systems staff person for help resolving your delinquency. You can call the number yourself, or you can ask your CPA or tax attorney what to do. If you owe a lot of money, get professional help; don't call the IRS staff person. If you do make that call, don't agree to do anything you feel uncertain about until you consult a CPA or tax attorney. You don't want to complicate your situation by agreeing to do something you can't carry through.

If you agree that you owe the IRS money but you let the agency know that you can't pay it right away, the IRS may be willing to delay its collection efforts for a couple of months. However, interest and penalties accrue on your tax debt.

If you don't have the money you need to call off the IRS, and if it's unlikely that you'll be able to come up with that money anytime soon, bankruptcy may be your best option. Bankruptcy calls a halt to the IRS's collection efforts and buys you time to figure out how to deal with your tax debt. However, as Chapter 9 explains, filing for bankruptcy is a double-edged sword. Although it can help you hold on to important assets, it also seriously damages your credit record. If you're considering bankruptcy, consult a bankruptcy attorney.

Knowing the better way

The best way to deal with a tax problem is not to wait for the IRS to track you down. Instead, face up to the problem, evaluate your options for dealing with it, perhaps with the help of your CPA or a tax attorney, decide which option is best for you, and then pursue it.

The sooner you begin a productive dialogue with the IRS about the money you owe, the likelier the IRS will be ready to cooperate with you. Stalling and avoidance tactics only alienate the agency and in the end are counter-productive. Remember, too, that the longer you wait to address your problem, the bigger your tax debt becomes.

Remember, if you and your spouse file a joint return and you don't believe that you should be liable for the taxes, penalties, and interest that the IRS says that you and your spouse owe, apply for innocent spouse relief by filing IRS Form 8857, *Request for Innocent Spouse Relief.* If the IRS grants your request, you are excused from the liability. You can find this IRS form as Form 11-4 of the CD.

Knowing your options

You have two basic options for dealing with your tax obligation when you owe money to the IRS: negotiate an installment payment plan or make an Offer in Compromise (OIC). If you don't have enough cash to pay your tax debt in a lump sum, you could pay with a credit card.

Arranging an installment plan

The IRS is amenable to letting you pay your tax debt over time, assuming that you don't owe more than $15,000 and that the installment plan you propose eliminates the debt within three years. Here are some other prerequisites for getting the IRS to okay an installment plan:

- ✔ During the previous five years, you filed each of your tax returns, paid your taxes, and did not negotiate any installment plans.

- ✔ You're willing to submit financial statements to the IRS so that it can be absolutely sure that you can't pay your tax liability in full now.

- ✔ You agree to meet all your tax obligations while your installment plan is in effect.

To apply for an installment plan, complete IRS Form 9465 (Form 11-5 on the CD). If the IRS approves your plan, you must pay $43 to set it up. This fee comes out of your first installment payment. If you later need to revise the plan for some reason and the IRS okays the change, you must pay an additional $24. If you and the IRS can't reach an agreement about an installment plan, you have a right to appeal its decision and even sue the IRS.

Your installment payments are due on time — you don't get a grace period. On the bright side, when you pay your tax debt in installments, the IRS reduces by half the size of the monthly penalty you would ordinarily pay on an outstanding tax balance.

Be sure that you can afford the plan you agree to. Lowering your monthly installments costs you money each time you do it. If you can't make your payments and you don't let the IRS know about your cash shortfall, it begins the collection process after providing you with several opportunities to pay up.

Playing Let's Make a Deal!

Although making a deal with the IRS is not as much fun as appearing on a game show with Monty Hall, getting the IRS to agree to accept less than the full amount of the taxes you owe is another way to settle your tax debt. To initiate the deal, you must make the IRS an Offer in Compromise (OIC). Consult with your CPS or tax attorney before you get the process going.

Getting an OIC approved used to be quite a challenge. However, as part of its effort to become more consumer-oriented and to show a little heart, the IRS has made the process easier and is approving more OICs than in the past.

Apply for an OIC by completing IRS Form 656, *Offer in Compromise.* To figure an appropriate amount of money to offer the IRS, use the IRS-provided worksheet and guidelines that come with that form. The worksheet, guidelines, and the form itself appear as Form 11-6 on the CD.

As part of the OIC request process, you must also complete IRS Form 433-A, *Collection Information for Individuals.* This form asks you for information about your finances. The IRS uses it to decide whether your OIC is reasonable or whether you should pay more. This IRS form appears as Form 11-7 on the CD.

Note: When you ask for an OIC, your finances are closely scrutinized. So if you have any skeletons in the attic, you could develop additional problems with the IRS. Also, if your request is approved, the ten-year statute of limitation on tax collections is automatically extended.

An IRS offer examiner evaluates your OIC and recommends whether to accept it. As part of the decision, the examiner takes into account an IRS formula that considers the amount of equity you have in your home and your car, as well as what the IRS thinks you should be able to pay. If you did not file one or more tax returns in the past, the examiner asks you to file them now so that any taxes you owe for those years can be factored into the total amount of your tax liability when the examiner decides how much your OIC should be.

Although the IRS is trying to speed up the process, getting an answer on your OIC could take up to a couple of years. Meanwhile, interest and penalties add up.

You can ask the IRS to let you pay your OIC over time in installments. You might get as long as ten years to pay what you owe. However, during the life of the installment plan, you have to pay interest on the unpaid balance of your tax debt, and the IRS has the right to place a lien on one or more of your assets. It must file a *Notice of Federal Tax Lien* to do so.

The IRS lets you know by mail whether it accepts your offer and also lays out the terms of its acceptance. You must let the IRS know in writing whether you accept the terms. If you violate any of the terms of your OIC agreement, you can be held liable for all your unpaid taxes, and the IRS can take action to collect the taxes you owe, minus whatever you have paid on your debt so far.

If the IRS rejects your OIC, you get that news in writing, too. The notice explains why your OIC was rejected. You have three options when the IRS rejects your OIS: You can make another offer; you can appeal the agency's decision within 30 days of the date of the IRS rejection letter; or you can do nothing. If you go this route, the IRS uses wage garnishment, levies, asset seizures, and so on to get what it's legally entitled to.

You may be eligible for an OIC when "exceptional circumstances" would create an economic hardship in your life if you had to pay the taxes the IRS claims you owe. IRS Form 656 (Form 11-6 on the CD) tells you how to make an offer based on exceptional circumstances. Follow the same advice if you want to base your offer on your contention that having to pay the taxes the IRS says you owe would be unfair.

When you can't live up to your agreement

If you're paying your taxes in installments, or if you've made some other agreement with the IRS to pay the taxes you owe, changing circumstances might make it difficult or even impossible for you to live up to the agreement. Get in touch with the IRS as soon as possible after you realize that you're having problems and before you miss a payment. Otherwise, you risk the IRS declaring you in default of your agreement and using wage garnishment, levies, property seizures, and so on to collect its money.

The IRS has the right to change or terminate its agreement with you. However, it must give you at least 30 days' prior written notice and tell you in writing why it's doing what it's doing.

Surviving an audit

If you are like most taxpayers, being audited by the IRS probably ranks as one of your worst nightmares. Some audits happen because the IRS randomly looks for tax errors. Other audits occur because the IRS believes that some aspect of your tax return is incomplete or inaccurate or because the IRS thinks that you should have paid more taxes than you did. For example, an audit might ask you to clarify a few things on your return, justify your deductions, or substantiate specific information.

When you're audited, you hold the burden of proof to show that the information the IRS is questioning is correct, accurate, and complete.

If the IRS questions a substantial amount of money, or if your financial affairs and tax return are complicated, get your CPA or tax attorney to help you with the audit. If you know that you filed a false return or did something else illegal, professional help is essential. As a result of the audit, the IRS may send you written notice that you need to change your tax return in some way. The change may or may not mean that you owe more taxes, but usually it does.

When the IRS decides that you owe more money in taxes, it sends you a Notice of Deficiency stating just how much. You can appeal the agency's decision, and you can also take the IRS to court to change or overturn the decision. IRS audits are conducted through the mail or in person at an IRS office. Although rare, sometimes audits take place at a taxpayer's home. Following are short descriptions of how mail and in-person audits work.

Audits by mail

Audits by mail are usually quite simple, although they can lead to something more complicated. If the IRS tells you by mail that it wants additional information about something, provide it within the established deadlines. If you have any questions about an IRS request, or if you need more time to locate information, call the telephone number on your IRS audit notice. You can also get your questions answered by scheduling a face-to-face meeting with an IRS examiner. But before you do, consider contacting your CPA or tax attorney. You want to be sure that you don't say or do anything that could land you in hot water.

In-person audits

If the IRS wants to audit you in person, you're required to visit an IRS office near you with the financial records and other information the IRS asks for and whatever records and information you need to prove that your return is correct. Before you schedule the audit, talk to your CPA or tax attorney. You may also want her to go with you to the audit or to attend in your place.

When you schedule an audit, give yourself enough time to pull together all the information you need for it. Don't feel pressured to schedule it as soon as possible (although the IRS won't wait forever). You don't want to go into your audit unprepared.

What to do if you think the IRS owes you money

If you think you paid too much in taxes, penalties, or interest to the IRS and you want a refund, complete IRS Form 843, *Claim for a Refund and Request for Abatement*. A copy of this form with IRS instructions for completing the form appears on the CD as Form 11-8. Generally, you must file IRS Form 843 with the IRS no later than three years from the date you filed your tax return, or two years from the date you paid your taxes, interest, and penalties — whichever is later. If the IRS denies your request, you can appeal the decision or sue the agency.

The IRS is usually obligated to pay you interest on the refund you're entitled to if it doesn't send you that refund within 45 days of the date that you filed your refund request.

Appealing

If you and the IRS don't see eye to eye about the results of an IRS audit, you can use the IRS appeals process to try to get the agency to change its mind. Here's how the process works:

- ✔ Initiate an appeal through your local IRS appeals office. This office is separate from the office that made the decision you disagree with. Be sure to file the appeal by the date indicated in the letter you received from the IRS informing you of its decision. Otherwise, you forfeit your right to appeal. You can talk with the IRS about the what and why of your appeal via telephone, through the mail, or during an in-person appeals conference.

- ✔ If you request an appeals conference, you may have to complete and file a formal written protest with the IRS by a certain date. The IRS tells you whether you do after you initiate your appeal. You need a CPA's or tax attorney's help to file a written protest because you must provide the IRS with very specific information. For example, you must list all the things you're contesting and explain why you don't think the IRS is correct. You must also provide facts to support your positions and cite the laws or other legal authorities on which you base your positions. Providing the IRS with accurate and complete information can help you win your appeal.

IRS literature says that you do not need a professional to represent you during an appeals conference. That's true, but it's usually a good idea either to keep a CPA or tax attorney by your side at the conference or to let that professional attend in your place. If you want your tax professional to act on your behalf during an appeals conference, you must file IRS Form 2848, *Power of Attorney and Declaration of Representative*. It is Form 11-9 on the CD, and it's the same form you complete if you want a tax professional to act on your behalf in an audit.

You may be eligible to file a small case request rather than a formal written protest if the total amount of money you're disputing for a given tax period is no more than $25,000. The letter you received notifying you about your audit outlines the process for making a small claims request.

Taking the IRS to court

If you're unhappy with the outcome of your appeal, or if you want to skip the appeals process entirely, you may be able to take your case to the U.S. Tax Court, the U.S. Court of Federal Claims, or the district court that has jurisdiction in your area. The appropriate court depends on the subject of your disagreement with the IRS.

✔ For disagreements related to the additional income tax the IRS alleges you owe, file your lawsuit with the U.S. Tax Court. First, the IRS must issue you a form letter stating how much you owe or a Notice of Deficiency. After you receive it, you have 90 days to file your petition with the court. Then your case will be scheduled for trial in a Tax Court near you.

If you don't file your petition within the 90-day period, you receive a bill from the IRS for the taxes it says you owe. If your dispute with the IRS involves no more than $50,000 for a given tax year, the U.S. Tax Court offers simplified procedures. For information about those procedures, talk with a tax attorney or contact the Clerk of the Tax Court, 40 Second St. NW, Washington, DC 20217.

✔ If your problem relates to a tax refund, you can take your case to the U.S. District Court in your area. Generally, you can file in these courts only if you have paid your taxes and filed a claim for a refund with the IRS.

If you win your lawsuit against the IRS, you may be able to recover some of your legal and administrative costs from the IRS. However, the IRS limits how much it will pay out. For example, your attorney's fees can't exceed $125 per hour. Also, the IRS doesn't reimburse you for anything unless you used the appeals process before you sued the agency and unless the IRS believes that you gave it all the information it needed to resolve the lawsuit.

You've got a friend

If you can't resolve a tax problem through the channels outlined in this chapter, you may want to consult the Taxpayer Advocate's Problem Resolution Office. This office is independent of the rest of the IRS and reports directly to the National Taxpayer Advocate. Each state and IRS service center has at least one local taxpayer advocate.

A taxpayer advocate also may be able to help you if

- Application of the tax laws will cause you to suffer a significant hardship, an irreparable injury, or a long-term adverse impact, or will force you to incur significant expenses, including fees for professional representation.

- You're facing an immediate threat of an IRS adverse action.

- You're trying to resolve your IRS problem, but the IRS has dragged its feet for more than 30 days.

- The IRS did not get back to you by the date it promised.

- All the established IRS problem-solving systems or procedures have failed to operate as intended.

Consulting the taxpayer advocate service is not a substitute for using established IRS procedures or the formal appeals process. Also, an advocate can't reverse an IRS tax determination.

To formally request assistance from a taxpayer advocate, file Form 911, *Application for a Taxpayer Assistance Order.* IRS Form 911 is available on the CD as Form 11-10. Among other things, be prepared to provide a short description of the problem you're having with the IRS or of the hardship you're experiencing or anticipate you will experience. Also, be prepared to provide a summary of your efforts to resolve your IRS problem and information about the IRS offices you have dealt with so far.

Once the taxpayer advocate office has received your application for assistance or a written statement that includes all the required information, it determines whether your problem merits its intervention. If it decides that it does, the office decides on a course of action. To make its decision, it considers your opinions and ideas.

Periodically, local IRS offices schedule problem-solving sessions, often on weekends, where taxpayers can get IRS help resolving their tax problems. The schedule for these sessions is available at www.irs.gov/hot/prob-solv.html. You can also call your local IRS or taxpayer advocate office to find out when a problem-solving session is scheduled for your area.

Secret agent man (or woman)

You're in big trouble if an IRS special agent pays you a visit. Special agents conduct criminal investigations for the IRS. If the agent who visits you starts asking questions, *don't answer them,* even if the questions seem harmless. You might unknowingly give the agent information that can be used against you later, and answering the questions might cause you to lose some of your legal rights. When an agent asks you questions, politely but firmly respond that you will not answer the questions and that your lawyer will be in touch with the agent soon. If you don't already have a tax attorney, get one! The sidebar "You need a tax attorney if . . ." provides a list of other tax-related problems that warrant a tax attorney's help.

The conversations you have with your tax attorney are confidential because they're protected by the attorney-client privilege. However, what you tell your CPA is wholly another story. The IRS can force your CPA to disclose what you said about your taxes if it decides to prosecute you.

Hire a tax attorney when the IRS tells you that you're being investigated for tax fraud, or when you're going to be audited and you know that you were not 100 percent honest when you completed your tax return. You will need an attorney's assistance when you're going to be audited and you don't have the information you need to back up your return.

If you receive a note from the IRS saying that you owe a lot of money or that you owe any amount of money you can't pay, call an attorney. If you haven't filed an income tax return for several years, call an attorney.

Paying taxes on the property you own

Most local governments expect you to pay taxes on the real estate you own — land and buildings. The amount you must pay is called your *tax assessment*. The appraised value of your property coupled with the tax rate in your area determines that amount. A tax assessor or board of assessors sets your home value for tax purposes.

In a few states, if you refuse to let a tax assessor walk around your property or enter your home, you might lose your rights to appeal your tax appraisal.

Depending on where you live, you may be obligated to pay taxes to several taxing entities, including your city and county governments, local school district, hospital district, and water district. They use tax income to help fund the services they provide, including police and fire protection, parks, garbage collection, public libraries, public education, and health care.

If you fit in the right category, your tax obligation is reduced somewhat. For example, depending on your state, you may be eligible for an exemption on your property taxes if you're older than 65. You may also be eligible for a property tax reduction on the home you declare to be your *homestead* — the home you live in most of the time.

Knowing what to do if you don't agree with an appraisal

The *tax assessor* may be an elected or appointed official who is authorized to collect taxes. An *appraiser* is someone who works for the tax assessor to help determine property values for tax purposes.

When you find out how much your home or some other property you own is being appraised for, you might think that the appraisal is too low or undervalues your asset. More likely, however, you will object because you think the appraisal is too high, and you'll want to get it lowered so you don't have to pay as much in property taxes. Either way, the first thing you should do is visit your tax appraisal office to discuss your property's appraisal. Ask to see all the information the appraiser used to set its value. When you do, make sure that the appraiser used accurate and current information.

During your visit, you can also try to convince the appraiser that your property's appraisal is wrong. However, it's up to you to prove your argument. Therefore, bring with you any information that's helpful to you — such as the recent selling price of comparable homes or property near yours. Simply telling a tax appraiser that you don't think your appraisal is fair will not do.

If you don't get the results you want from your visit to the tax appraisal office, you have a right to formally challenge your tax bill. However, you must do so within a certain time frame and follow specific procedures. Your tax bill should either provide this information or tell you how to get it. Although the property tax appeal process works differently in every state, usually you must appeal your tax bill to a county office and then file a new appeal with your state if the local appeal fails. You can also go to court.

Hiring a lawyer who has experience in resolving tax disputes can help you get the results you want from an appeal or lawsuit. If the deadline for paying your taxes has passed, interest and penalties start adding to your tax debt.

What to do if you can't pay your property taxes

If you can't pay your property taxes, you may be able to apply for a tax extension and get extra time to pay the taxes or apply for a tax deferral or exemption based on the financial hardship you and your family would suffer if you were forced to pay them. However, you can't get out of your property tax obligation just because you don't have the money. Check with the office that sent your tax bill to learn about your options.

Chapter 12

Being Car Smart

1 t's legendary: Americans love their cars. In fact, for countless drivers, cars represent far more than transportation. For a teenager, having a car to drive was an important milestone along the road to adulthood. Adults view the cars they own as reflections of their identity and their financial success.

Given what a car represents, buying on impulse and ending up with a car that doesn't fit your needs or that breaks your budget is all too easy. If you buy a used car without doing the necessary homework, you could end up with a clunker or even with a stolen car. When purchasing a new car, you may be at a disadvantage when negotiating a price if you're unprepared for all the issues involved. If you can't keep up with your car payments, your car could be repossessed with little or no warning from the company financing its purchase. (Chapter 8 discusses how repossessions work.)

This chapter takes some of the angst out of shopping for a car by explaining your legal rights, defining key terms, warning you about things to look out for, and helping you rationally compare your options. It also tells you a thing or two about leasing as an alternative to buying a car. And because every car, no matter how well it runs, needs routine maintenance and occasional repairs, this chapter fills you in on how to find a good mechanic or auto repair shop.

Note: Although this chapter talks in terms of *cars,* most of its information applies to trucks, vans, and SUVs as well.

Buying a New Car

It's easy to fall in love with a shiny new car parked at a car dealership. In fact, if you're not careful, after a quick spin around the block and some encouraging words from a salesperson, you might throw caution to the wind and buy more car than you need — without haggling about price or reading the paperwork. Later, however, you might have regrets about your impulsiveness. Your car might turn out to be a gas-guzzler, or you may find that your car payments put a crimp in your lifestyle.

New-car lingo

Car dealers speak a language all their own. To get a good deal on a car, you need to speak their language, too. Here are some of the most important words and phrases you should know:

✔ **Invoice sticker price:** Also known as the *dealer invoice price* or *factory invoice price.* It represents the manufacturer's initial price to a dealer. This is the price to focus on when you negotiate a purchase price for the car you want to buy. However, dealers often end up paying considerably less than the amount of the invoice sticker price because they take advantage of manufacturer rebates, allowances, discounts, and so on. By the way, the invoice sticker price always includes freight charges, or "destination and delivery" costs, so be sure that your contract does not include a separate charge for destination and delivery.

✔ **Base price:** This is the price of the car without options, but with standard equipment and factory warranty. This price is printed on the Maroney sticker.

✔ **Maroney sticker price, or MSRSP (manufacturer's suggested retail sales price):** The federal Automobile Information Disclosure Act says that every new, unsold car must have a Maroney sticker on its windshield. This sticker lists a car's make, model, and vehicle identification number; its base price; the manufacturer's installed options, along with the manufacturer's suggested retail price; the manufacturer's transportation cost; and the car's fuel economy — the average number of miles it gets from a gallon of gas. The law prohibits a dealer from modifying the information on a Maroney sticker or removing the sticker. Federal Maroney law does not apply to pickup trucks or SUVs.

✔ **Dealer sticker price:** This smaller sticker is usually located next to the Maroney sticker. Typically, it reflects the Maroney sticker price plus the suggested retail price for dealer-installed options such as dealer preparation, additional dealer mark-up (ADM), additional dealer profit (ADP), undercoating, rust prevention, fabric protection, and so on. When you negotiate a purchase price, tell the dealer that you are ignoring everything on this sticker.

The Edmunds.com Web site (www.edmunds.com) provides sticker price information for specific vehicles.

Doing your new car homework

There's no magic secret for how to get a good deal on a new car — it's simply a matter of going into the dealership prepared. You need to be practical (no ego purchases or impulse buying); you need to know your budget ahead of time; you need to have researched the cars in advance; and you need to know the lingo the salesperson will throw at you when you walk through the door.

The Internet has made shopping for a new car much easier by offering consumers a wealth of car-buying information. Studies show that consumers who use the Internet to research cars and prices pay less for cars than those who don't. The Web is home to numerous independent car-buying sites such as AutoWeb.com, Autobytel.com, CarPoint.com, and Cars.com, and manufacturers such as Ford, General Motors, and Chrysler have their own Web sites that feature links to local dealerships. The sidebar "New car caches on the Information Superhighway" describes some of the independent sites. It also offers information about other Web resources that can come in handy when you want to get the best deal.

Shopping online

The Internet is a great place to shop for a car, but it's not necessarily the best place to buy one. Although many consumers assume that when they buy a car online, they're getting it factory-direct at a super-low price, most new car Web sites act as intermediaries between car buyers and dealers. In fact, depending on what you buy and the Web site you buy through, you might actually pay more than if you purchased the car directly from a dealer.

Dealers featured on car-buying Web sites pay to be there. If you limit your negotiations to just those dealers, you might miss the dealer in your area who can give you the lowest price.

Getting down to details

After you complete your new car homework, zero in on the car you want, decide on the options you're willing to pay for and test drive the car. You should also ask to see the car's warranty. Read it carefully, and ask for clarification on anything you find confusing.

If you still feel positive about the car, it's time to talk money. You can shop for the best price over the phone by calling dealers in your area who sell the car you want, or you can use an auto-buying Web site to get a best-price offer from a dealer in your area. Of course, you can also haggle over a purchase price the old-fashioned way, by visiting dealers in your area and negotiating face-to-face. Remember to ask the dealer about any rebates.

New car caches on the Information Superhighway

When you're in the market for a new car, check out these Web sites. They can help you zoom in on the best car for you and figure out how much to pay for it. Some of these Web sites also provide used car information:

✔ **Autobytel.com** (www.autobytel.com): Submit a detailed list of your new car criteria to this Web site, and one of the dealers in your area that is affiliated with this site will give you its best price within 24 hours.

✔ **Auto Site** (www.autosite.com): You can use this site to price and compare vehicles and dealer prices. You can also use it to purchase the car you choose.

✔ **Autoweb.com** (www.autoweb.com): Go to this comprehensive site for information and advice on buying a new or used car and keeping it in working order, no matter what its age. Also, you can give this site your criteria for a new car, and in return, it gives you information and photos of cars that are available from dealers in your area.

✔ **Carpoint** (www.carpoint.msn.com): This Web site fills you in on dealer prices and rebates. You can also get quotes from participating dealers for the make and model of car you want.

✔ **Car Price Network** (www.w2.com/car1.html): Go here to get the scoop on a car's invoice and list prices.

✔ **Consumer Reports Online New Car Pricing Service** (www.consumerreports.org): This site provides an online version of the new car ratings that are a popular feature of the well-respected *Consumer Reports Magazine.*

✔ **Consumers' CHECKBOOK** (www.checkbook.org/index/cars&trucks.htm#buying): This nonprofit consumer information and service center offers car-buying advice and assistance, among other things. The site is not affiliated with any car dealerships. *CarBargains,* one of its services, frees you from the hassle of shopping for the car you want and haggling over a price. Submit a car's make, model, and style to *CarBargains,* and dealers respond with bids that are above or below the car's factory invoice price. Then CarBargains confirms the low bids and sends you quote sheets with each dealer's asking price and the name of the dealership manager to contact. You take it from there. The cost of *CarBargains* is $165. However, if you subscribe to the magazine published by Consumers' CHECKBOOK, you pay $145.

✔ **Edmunds Consumer Advice and Information** (www.edmunds.com/edweb/consumer.html): This site features general new car buying advice, information, and pricing data by make and model, including the all-important dealer invoice price. You can also use this site to search for vehicles that meet your specifications.

✔ **The Insurance Institute for Highway Safety** (www.highwaysafety.com) **and the National Highway Traffic Safety Administration (NHTSA,** www.NHTSA.dot.gov**):** Check out a car's safety record at these sites.

✔ **Kelley Blue Book** (www.kbb.com): This Web site offers pricing information for both new and used cars.

Don't be reluctant to bargain on price. Most dealers expect it, and some may be willing to bargain on their profit margin — the difference between the manufacturer's suggested retail price and the invoice price. Use the worksheet on Form 12-1 of the CD to plan your negotiations. It asks you to record dollar figures related to a car's invoice price and the manufacturer's suggested retail price on the Maroney sticker.

Also, stick to your guns once you determine how much you want to spend. If you're willing to walk away without a deal, the salesperson you're negotiating with might agree to meet your price or to come close to it.

Car salespeople rely on sales commissions for most of their income. They have a strong incentive to sell you a car for as much money as possible and to get you to purchase options and other extras you don't need and didn't plan on buying. If the car you want is not in stock, don't accept a substitute. Ask the dealer to order the car for you.

Don't discuss the possibility of a trade-in until you know the value of your old car and until you're satisfied with the purchase price you have negotiated for the new car. Use the *Kelley Blue Book* to find out the car's trade-in value. Your local library should have a copy, or you can access the *Kelley Blue Book* online at www.kbb.com.

You might come out ahead by donating your old car to charity rather than trading it in. When you donate it, you can use the vehicle's fair market or retail value as a charitable tax deduction.

Signing your new car contract

Once you have negotiated a purchase price for the car you want to buy, in every state but Louisiana, the car dealer must formalize the sale with a written contract that both you and the dealer sign. Before you sign it, make sure that the contract includes all of the following information:

- ✔ A description of the car you're buying, including the vehicle identification number (VIN).
- ✔ The terms of sale, including the price agreed upon and all conditions of the sale.
- ✔ The trade-in terms if you're trading in a vehicle.
- ✔ The financing terms if the dealer has arranged financing for you. The terms should include the amount being financed, the amount of your deposit, the trade-in allowance, the loan's APR (annual rate of interest), the amount of each loan payment, and so on.

Form 12-2 on the CD features a sample new car contract. Although your contract may look somewhat different, this sample prepares you for the kinds of information and phrases your contract will contain. You're asking for trouble if you sign a contract without reading it from start to finish first, understanding everything in it, and ensuring that every blank is filled in.

Some shady car dealers trick unsuspecting consumers into signing contacts that obligate them to lease, not buy, a car. Before you sign a "sales" contract, read it carefully, looking for terms that tip you off. Among other things, those telltale signs include discussions of a balloon payment or base mileage.

Deciding whether a service contract serves your interests

Be prepared: The salesperson may try to convince you that you should buy a service contract for your new car. A service contract is essentially an insurance policy that covers repairs to your car and replacement of parts. Some service contracts also pay for such things as towing and car rentals when your car is in the shop.

In some states, service contract providers are subject to the same requirements and restrictions as insurance companies. Your state insurance commission or department can tell you whether that's the case in your state.

Another phrase for a service contract is *extended warranty*. However, the term is a misnomer because a service contract is not a true warranty. By federal standards, a warranty comes with the cost of the car; it is not something you have the option to buy.

If you're interested in a service contract, consider purchasing one just before the warranty that comes with your car is due to expire. If the salesperson tells you a service contract is a great deal, don't take her word for it. Find out for yourself by reading the contract and comparing it with the new car warranty. As you do, consider these things:

- ✔ What is the difference between the warranty coverage that comes with the car and the coverage the service contract provides? If there's a lot of overlap, or if the service contract covers things you doubt you'll need, a service contract is probably not a good idea.
- ✔ What repairs are covered?
- ✔ How likely is it that your vehicle will need the repairs and other services covered by the service contract?

✔ How much does the service contract cost? Service contracts range in price from a couple hundred dollars to more than $1,000. Usually, the cost is based on a car's make and model, the comprehensiveness of the contract coverage, and the contract's duration.

✔ Is there a deductible, and how much is it?

✔ How long does the service contract last?

✔ Who backs the service contract? It may be the dealer, the auto manufacturer, or an independent company.

✔ Who will repair your car? Can you have the repairs made elsewhere?

✔ Who will process your claims under the service contract? Sometimes, companies that offer service contracts hire independent administrators to act as contract claims adjusters. You deal with the independent administrator if you're unhappy with the way a claim that you filed under the service contract is handled.

For service contracts that involve both a dealer and an independent administrator, check into the reputation of both companies before purchasing one. Ask for references, and check them out with your local Better Business Bureau, the consumer affairs office of your state attorney general's office, and your local and state automobile dealers associations.

✔ What repairs does the service contract not cover? The more it covers, the better. Are there things that the contract pays only under certain conditions?

✔ Do you have to pay a fee every time you get your car serviced or repaired under the service contract?

✔ Who pays for the labor and the parts?

✔ Does the service contract cover problems with your car that occur when you use it to travel out of town? Does it remain in effect if you move to a different town or state?

✔ What are your responsibilities in regard to the service contract? For example, before you can get your car repaired, do you have to get the repairs authorized? Do you have to perform certain routine maintenance activities to keep the contract in force?

✔ Can you cancel the contract? Under what conditions can you get a refund of the money you paid for the service contract?

✔ Can the contract be transferred if you sell your vehicle before the term of the service contract is up?

✔ What happens if the company that backs the service contract goes belly up?

✔ Is the service contract underwritten by an insurance company? Some states require this. If the contract is underwritten by an insurance company, check with your state's insurance department or commission to make sure that the insurance company is financially solvent and that no complaints have been filed against it.

Don't be pressured into making an on-the-spot decision whether to buy a service contract. Take the service contract home with you, and after you have had a chance to review it, contact the dealer if you want to buy it.

You can save money on an extended warranty by purchasing it online directly from a warranty company. By doing so, you eliminate the dealer's mark-up, which can be as high as 200 percent. Here are a few extended warranty Web sites to get you started:

- ✔ **Certified Car Care** (www.certifiedcarcare.com): This site claims to be the "consumers' #1 choice in new and used car extended service warranty contracts." You can also call Certified Car Care toll-free at 888-222-0078.

- ✔ **New Car Alternative** (www.newcaralternative.com): Fill out the online form at this Web site, and an agent will contact you to discuss your new and used car extended warranty needs and to provide you with price information. You can get the same information by calling 800-548-4671.

- ✔ **Warrantybynet.com** (www.warrantybynet.com/index.asp): This company claims to offer the most comprehensive and reliable extended warranties available for new and used vehicles. You can get an online quote at this site. If you prefer to get your information over the phone, call 877-239-8363.

If you have problems with a service contract and you can't resolve them with friendly means, you may have grounds for a breach-of-contract lawsuit. Talk to an attorney.

Handling warranty woes

The manufacturer's warranty that comes with your new car is supposed to cover the repair of the car's problems. It usually covers both parts and labor. Typically, you can have the warranty repairs performed by the dealer who sold you the car or by another dealer who sells that make.

As great as a warranty might sound on paper, you may discover that you have trouble getting a dealer to provide you with prompt and competent warranty coverage. In that case, after you express your dissatisfaction to the dealer's service manager, do the following:

- ✔ Call the factory manager nearest you and ask that you, a factory representative for your area, and the dealer's service manager meet as soon as possible. You can find the factory manager's telephone number in your warranty booklet.

✔ Send a letter about your problem to the main office of your car's manufacturer if the meeting does not resolve your problem. In your letter, describe the problems you have been having, how you have tried to resolve them, what the dealer and the factory manager offered, and how you want things to be resolved. Attach copies of any documents that substantiate the problems you're having with your car and your efforts to get them taken care of under the terms of your warranty. If you have an attorney, you may want to copy the attorney on your letter in the event that you decide to take legal action and need the lawyer's help.

Send the letter via certified mail with a return receipt requested. Model your letter after the one on Form 12-3 of the CD. For the car manufacturer's addresses and phone numbers, go to page 66 in the *2001 Consumer Resource Handbook* on the CD.

✔ Consider suing the manufacturer or the dealer if you get nowhere. You may want to sue in small claims court, depending on the circumstances of your case and the rules of the court in your area.

Knowing what to do if your car is a lemon

Every state has a *lemon law* — a law that protects consumers when they buy new cars. Most lemon laws also apply to SUVs, trucks, motorcycles, and motor homes, and in a growing number of states, they apply to used cars.

Most lemon laws give you the right to a replacement or a refund if the car you buy has a serious problem that can't be corrected or that keeps reappearing, or if your new car has many small problems. The problems can affect your ability to use your car, your ability to drive it safely, and your car's value. To qualify for protection under your state's lemon law, you must meet certain criteria:

✔ Your car's problems must have occurred within a certain period of time after you purchased it — usually within one year.

✔ During that period, your car must have been in the shop for the same problems a certain number of times (usually at least four times within the year after you purchased the car) or out of service for a certain number of days (usually at least 30). The days do not have to be consecutive.

For the lowdown on the lemon law in your state, call the consumer protection office of your state attorney general. This office can tell you what you must do to qualify for a replacement vehicle or a refund. The warranty information you received when you bought your car should also fill you in. Then, if you think your car is a lemon, call your dealer. If the dealer is not helpful, talk to an attorney.

The warranty that came with your new car may provide information about your state's lemon law. In some states, dealers must give you a copy of the lemon law when you buy a new car.

If you think your car is a lemon, save all your repair orders and receipts. Each repair order should be dated and should indicate the nature of the problems your car is having, along with the mechanic's diagnosis.

After you have the proof you need according to your state's criteria, write to the manufacturer of your car to request a refund or a replacement car. Model your letter after the Lemon Letter on Form 12-4 on the CD. Send it via certified mail, return receipt requested. Depending on the law in your state, your letter may trigger an arbitration process that determines whether you get a refund or a replacement vehicle.

The refund you're entitled to may amount to the total of all of the following, less a deduction for wear and tear on the car while you owned it:

- ✔ The car's purchase price, including sales taxes and finance fees
- ✔ The cost of registering your new car
- ✔ The total cost of your repairs
- ✔ A reasonable amount for mileage

If you meet the criteria of your state's lemon law and the manufacturer refuses to give you a refund or a replacement vehicle, consult with an attorney. The law may require that you go to arbitration before you can sue the manufacturer. The arbitration may or may not be binding. Either way, you need a lawyer.

If you sue and win, you may be entitled to twice the amount you paid for your car and twice what you spent on repairs. You're also entitled to be reimbursed for your attorney's fees and court costs.

Buying a Used Car

The fundamentals of buying a used car are no different from buying a new car. You do your homework; you decide what you can afford to spend on a car; you figure out how you will pay for the car; you shop around; you test drive a car in a variety of situations; and you negotiate. However, buying a used car does differ from buying a new car. One of the most important differences is that you must take extra precautions to ensure that the car you buy is not a clunker.

Federal law does not obligate dealers to give you a three-day cooling-off period — a period of time when you can return the car, no questions asked — when you buy a used car. If a dealer tells you that you can return the car if you're not happy with it, get the promise in writing.

Deciding whom to do business with: A dealer or an individual seller

Should you buy from a dealer or from an individual who has a used car to sell? There's no right answer to that question, because each option has its pros and cons. An individual seller does not have to use a buyer's guide sticker. You will probably spend more on a used car from a dealer rather than an individual seller.

An individual seller has fewer obligations to you than a dealer does if the car you buy has problems. Some state laws give extra protection to used car buyers. You're more apt to get a warranty when you buy from a dealer. Also, when you purchase from an individual seller, you're not protected by the implied warranties of state law.

You're usually better off buying a used car from a large reputable dealer that sells mainly new cars than from a used car lot. Large dealerships that take trade-ins and sell them as used cars want to protect their reputations. Therefore, they're apt to fix a trade-in's problems before they sell it, and they're more apt to stand behind that car. The owners of used car lots may not have such high standards for themselves or the cars they sell.

No matter who you end up buying from, if you do everything on the following list before you pay any money or sign any paperwork, you're more apt to end up with a used car that's a gem, not a gyp:

- ✔ Check the title to ensure the seller is the registered owner of the vehicle.

- ✔ Examine the car's service records, if available.

- ✔ Get a written statement of the number of miles on the car you're interested in. Compare the number on the statement to the number on the car's *odometer* — the thing on a car's dashboard that shows how many miles the car has been driven. If you see a discrepancy, look for another car.

    Federal law says that used car dealers must provide buyers with a written mileage disclosure statement.

- ✔ Test drive the car in traffic and on the highway.

- ✔ Examine the car in the daytime when you can see the quality of the paint and whether the car has any dents.

✔ Check out the repair record of the car you're interested in by going to Consumer Reports Online (`www.consumerreports.org/Categories/CarsTrucks/index.html`).

✔ Research the value of the car so that you don't pay more than you should. Check prices at the library with the *NADA Official Used Car Guide* or with a used car pricing service. You can also go to the *Kelley Blue Book* Web site (`www.kbb.com`) or Edmunds.com (`www.edmunds.com`) to find a car's value. Base your offer on a used car's market value, not on the seller's asking price.

Knowing the importance of buyer's guides

The Federal Used Car Rule requires dealers who sell six or more used cars per year to affix a buyer's guide sticker to the windshield of each car they offer for sale. You can find out what the sticker looks like by going to Form 12-5 on the CD.

The buyer's guide sticker becomes a part of your sales contract when you purchase a used car, and when there is a discrepancy between the contract and the buyer's guide sticker, the sticker information prevails. For example, if the contract says that you're buying a car "as is" and the buyer's guide says that the car comes with a warranty, the dealer is legally obligated to warranty the car according to the terms of that sticker. Be sure that the sticker reflects any changes in warranty coverage that you and the dealer negotiate. Also, when you sign the sales contract, be sure to get the original sticker or a copy of it.

By law, the buyer's guide sticker must

✔ Indicate the car's make, model, year, and VIN.

✔ Indicate whether a car has a warranty. If it has no warranty, the buyer's guide must indicate that the car is being sold as is. That means the dealer makes no promises about it and is under no obligation to fix any problems the car has.

Some states, including Connecticut, Kansas, Maine, Maryland, Massachusetts, Minnesota, Mississippi, New Jersey, Rhode Island, West Virginia, and the District of Columbia, don't allow certain used cars to be sold as is. When this is the case, the words "Implied warranty only" must be printed on the car's buyer's guide sticker. Louisiana, New Hampshire, and Washington require different disclosures than those on the buyer's guide.

✔ Reflect the percentage of the repair costs that the dealer will pay for if the car has a warranty.

✔ Include a statement that you should let the dealer know if you want to have the car inspected by the mechanic of your choice.

✔ List the car's major mechanical and electrical systems and the common major problems you should look out for.

✔ Suggest that you hold on to the buyer's guide for future reference.

Some buyer's guides come with a signature line and a disclosure statement that reads, "I hereby acknowledge receipt of the buyer's guide at the closing of this sale." This feature is optional, but when it does appear, a car buyer is asked to sign to acknowledge receipt of the sticker.

Using used car warranties and service contracts

State laws hold dealers responsible if the cars they sell don't meet "reasonable quality standards." This is called an *implied warranty*. However, in most states, dealers can include the words "as is" or "with all faults" in a written statement to eliminate the implied warranty. If the buyer's guide for the car you want comes with an implied warranty, the warranty is one of two types:

- **Warranty of merchantability:** This is the most common type of used car warranty. It promises that the car you buy will do what it's supposed to do — run. However, it does not promise that the car will be problem-free.

- **Warranty of fitness:** This warranty applies when you buy a car because the dealer says that it's suitable for a particular purpose — to drive across the Sahara Desert or to haul your travel trailer, for example.

Ask the dealer for a copy of the warranty documentation. Read it carefully, noting the repairs covered by the warranty, how to get repairs, whether the warranty covers labor, what the warranty excludes, how long the warranty lasts, and who is legally responsible for fulfilling the terms of the warranty

If a third party, not the seller, is responsible for fulfilling the terms of a car's warranty, check out the company with your state attorney general's office or your local Better Business Bureau. Also make sure that the dealer has checked the appropriate box on the buyer's guide to indicate whether the car's warranty is full or limited, and has included the following information in the warranty section of the sticker: the percentage of any repair cost that the dealer will pay, the specific parts and systems covered by the warranty, the terms of the warranty for each covered part and system, whether there is a deductible, and, if there is, the amount of the deductible

If the dealer tells you that a used car comes with a manufacturer's warranty, read the documents related to that warranty, too. Then call the manufacturer with the car's VIN to verify the terms of the warranty coverage so you can be sure that the warranty is still in effect.

Some used cars come with service contracts. If the car you're interested in has one, unless your state's insurance laws regulate service contracts, the appropriate box should be checked on the car's buyer's guide sticker. If you buy the car and purchase the service contract within 90 days, federal law says that the car automatically comes with an implied warranty, even if you bought it as is. Depending on the law in your state, the warranty may last longer than the service contract.

Being extra cautious when buying from an individual seller

Unless your contract says differently, when you buy from a private seller, it's an as-is deal. The car does not come with a buyer's guide sticker, and in most states your purchase does not come with an implied warranty. In other words, it's up to you to ensure that the car you buy is a good deal mechanically as well as financially. Therefore, getting your car checked out by a good mechanic is essential. It's also advisable to ask for the car's maintenance and repair records. If the seller doesn't have them, ask for the name of the dealer or mechanic who took care of most of the car's repairs, and contact that business to learn about the car's repair history.

Individual sellers in some states must provide buyers with written assurance that the vehicle they're selling will pass inspection. In other states, they must provide a minimum warranty for a car before they can sell it. Contact the consumer affairs office of your state attorney general to find out about the law in your state.

Ask to see the car's title to ensure that it's in the name of the seller. Also run a title check or purchase a comprehensive history for the car. The title check assures you that the seller has a legal right to sell the car, and the history lets you know whether the seller is hiding any ugly secrets about the car that would cause you not to want it. The secret could be that the car has been totaled or was stolen. (It's a good idea to run a title search and order a comprehensive history on a used car you're purchasing from a used car dealer, too.) You can find out about title searches and car histories in the section "Telling the good cars from the bad" on the next page.

If an individual seller tells you that the used car she's selling comes with either a warranty or a service contract, ask to read the warranty or service contract paperwork so you can be sure that the coverage is still in effect and is transferable.

After you and a private seller agree on a price, but before you pay the seller any money, let him know that you want a signed bill of sale. It serves as your sales receipt, and, depending on your state, you may have to present it when you register the car. At a minimum, the bill of sale should indicate the date of the sale; the make, model, and year of the car; the VIN or vehicle identification number; the *odometer reading* (the number of miles the car has been driven); how much you paid for the car and whether you paid it with cash, a check, money order; your name, address, and phone number as the buyer; and the seller's name, address, and phone number.

Form 12-6 on the CD provides a sample bill of sale for a used car purchased from a private seller. It reflects all the information that should appear on the one you sign.

Telling the good cars from the bad

A used car may look pristine, but if only it could talk! Despite its appearance, it may have a rather checkered past. For example, it may have been badly damaged in a wreck, flood, or fire and rebuilt to look like new, or it may be a stolen car. Although most state laws require the words "Salvaged" or "Rebuilt" to be stamped on the car's title, if a car has been rebuilt after a wreck or a flood, some sellers ignore the law. Other sellers knowingly sell damaged and stolen cars to unsuspecting car buyers who are looking for inexpensive cars to drive.

Rebuilt and salvaged cars can be unsafe to drive! If you're going to buy one, have a good mechanic thoroughly check out the car.

The federal Anti-Tampering Odometer Law outlaws tampering with a car's odometer so that the car appears to have fewer miles on it than it really does. Unscrupulous used car sellers may tamper with a car's odometer so that they can ask for more than the car is really worth.

By knowing a car's 17-digit VIN (vehicle identification number), you can find out whether the seller is trying to conceal the car's past. For example, your state's motor vehicle department can use the VIN to run a title check on the car. The check tells you whether the seller is the car's legal owner and there-fore has a right to sell it. Better yet, with the VIN you can purchase a compre-hensive history on the car from CarFax. For $19.95, CarFax compares the car's VIN, not just against state motor vehicle records but against police and fire department records, insurance company records, and the records of emission inspection stations and automobile auctions as well. You can call CarFax at 888-422-7329 or access its services at www.carfax.com.

Most VINs are located on car dashboards, but sometimes they're inside the driver's side door, on the passenger's door, on the car's engine, and so on. The VIN may be stamped on a metal plate, engraved onto the car itself, or printed on a sticker.

If a used car seller claims that its VIN has already been checked out, ask for a copy of the results. But to be on the safe side, get the car's VIN and run a check yourself. (Doing so is less important if you're buying a used car from a new car dealer that sells trade-ins.)

You might have the basis for a lawsuit under your state's unfair or deceptive trade practices law if you can prove that the seller of the car you buy deliber-ately withholds information from you or gives you misleading information — and that you would have acted differently if you had known the truth. This law also applies to new and leased cars.

Leasing a Car

Leasing a car almost always costs more than buying one. Even so, a growing number of consumers are leasing. Why? Because, among other things, you may not have to put any money down when you lease a car. If you do, the amount of money you have to pay up front may be less than what you would have to pay as a down payment on a car purchase. You may be able to lease a more expensive car than you can afford to buy. Your monthly lease payments are apt to be lower than your car payments. And leasing eliminates the hassle of having to sell your car or negotiate a trade-in when you want a new one.

Interested in leasing? If you are, it pays to shop around, because some leases are better than others. But before you do, get familiar with leasing lingo. Get a quick vocabulary lesson by reading the sidebar "Leasing lingo." You should also figure out what you can afford to spend each month on a leased car and know how leasing works.

Use the worksheet at *Family Money Magazine*'s Web site (`www.familymoney.com/calc.htm`) to compare whether you're better off leasing or buying a car.

Knowing the two types of leases

There are two different kinds of leases:

- **A closed-end lease** is the most common type of car lease. When the lease is up, you return the car to the *lessor* (the company that leased it to you) and walk away. However, under certain circumstances, you have to pay end-of-lease costs. These costs may apply if you put more than the usual wear and tear on the leased car or if you drive it more than the number of miles specified in your lease — usually between 12,000 and 15,000 miles a year. Pay close attention to these costs and how they're calculated when you negotiate the terms of your lease, because they can really drive up its overall cost.

- **An open-end lease** assumes that the car is worth a certain amount of money at the end of the lease — its *residual value*. If the leasing company determines that the car is worth less than the residual value when your lease is up, you must pay the shortfall, which could cost you a bundle if the estimated residual value is too low. You may also have the right to buy the car at the end of the lease. If you don't, you may be charged a disposition fee to reimburse the lessor for the cost of selling the car, often in an auction.

Check with your state attorney general's office of consumer protection before you begin shopping for a car to lease. Some states have laws that govern car leases and give you rights that may not be reflected in your lease agreement.

Shopping for a lease

The federal Consumer Leasing Act (CLA) makes it easier for you to shop for and negotiate a lease by requiring that a leasing company disclose up front certain information about a lease. To see a CLA disclosure form for a closed-end lease, and for an explanation of the information it presents, go to Form 12-7 of the CD.

Among other things, the CLA disclosure form you receive from a leasing company should tell you

- ✔ How much, if anything, you must pay up front. Those up-front expenses may include a security deposit, a capitalized cost reduction or down payment, an acquisition fee, the last month's lease payment, taxes, title, license, and registration fees, a processing fee, and freight or destination fees

- ✔ The amount of your monthly lease payment, as well as the date each payment is due and the number of monthly payments you make during the term of the lease.

- ✔ The insurance you must purchase for the car. Depending on the lessor's requirements, you could spend more for insurance on a leased car than on a purchased one.

- ✔ Who has responsibility for maintaining and servicing your car.

- ✔ The leasing company's standards for wear and tear on the car you're leasing.

- ✔ The terms of cancellation if you decide to end the lease early, including the cost of cancellation.

Ending your lease before it's up will probably cost you an arm and a leg, because leasing companies make money by keeping you on your lease. Also, when you signed your lease agreement, you entered into a legally binding contract with the leasing company, so even if you no longer want to lease your car, you're still obligated to meet your lease obligations. The earlier you end your lease, the more you have to pay. So before you sign a lease, make sure that you can afford the payments and that you're happy with the other terms of the lease.

- ✔ Whether the lease comes with an express warranty.

- ✔ Whether you can buy the car you're leasing, and the terms of purchase if you can.

If you lease a car without all this information, the CLA gives you the right to sue the leasing company for 25 percent of the total amount of the payments you have made so far, up to $1,000. You can also sue for actual damages. If you win, you can collect your attorney fees and court costs. You have only one year after the end of your lease to sue the leasing company.

Leasing lingo

When you shop for a good car lease, it pays to have at least a passing knowledge of key auto leasing terms. Here are definitions of the most important terms:

✔ **Adjusted capitalized cost:** The gross cost of your lease less your down payment and any credit you receive as a result of rebates, a trade-in, and so on.

✔ **Capitalized cost reduction:** Essentially, the down payment on the car. The more you put down, the lower your monthly payments.

✔ **Capitalized cost:** The actual cost of your auto lease after negotiations.

✔ **Disposition charges:** Money you may have to pay the lessor at the end of the term of your lease to compensate it for the cost of selling your vehicle.

✔ **Lease rate:** The interest rate associated with your lease. Make sure that this rate is included in the lease you're asked to sign.

✔ **Manufacturer's suggested retail price (MSRP), also called list price or sticker price:** You find this price on the sticker of the car you want to lease.

Leasing a car for its MSRP is like buying a car for its full sticker price. Negotiate!

✔ **Money factor:** A figure used to calculate your lease payment. There are different money factors for different types of car models and leases. Also, different leasing companies have different money factors. Usually, if all other terms are the same, a lower money factor means lower payments.

✔ **Purchase option:** The right to buy the car you lease at the end of the lease term for a predetermined price.

✔ **Residual value:** The amount the leasing company estimates the car you lease will be worth at the end of your lease.

Negotiating the terms of your lease

When you're negotiating the terms of a lease, take the following factors into consideration. These factors should be spelled out in whatever lease you sign:

✔ The length of your lease, the amount of your monthly lease payments, and the interest rate associated with the lease.

✔ The agreed-upon value of the leased vehicle. The lower its value, the lower your monthly lease payments should be.

✔ The car's gross and adjusted capitalized costs and any other up-front costs for which you are responsible.

✔ The amount of the security deposit you have to pay, whether it's refundable, and under what circumstances.

✔ The car's residual value for an open-end lease.

✔ A precise definition of normal wear and tear for a closed-end lease.

✔ The number of miles you can put on the car during the lease without having to pay for excess mileage. This provision applies to closed-end leases only.

✔ The price per mile you're charged if you exceed the maximum mileage. You may want to contract for additional miles if you're concerned that you will exceed the number of allowable miles stated in the lease. You'll pay dearly if you exceed your allotted mileage.

✔ The size of the end-of-lease charges you have to pay, and the amount of the lease termination fee.

✔ The insurance you are responsible for and whether the lease includes gap insurance.

Gap insurance protects you if your leased car is stolen or wrecked in an accident. Without it, the leasing company treats the loss as an early lease termination, and that costs you dearly. If gap insurance is not included in your lease, ask for it.

Having Your Car Repaired

If you're clueless about the stuff under your hood, getting your car repaired can be an unnerving experience. Given your lack of knowledge, it's difficult if not impossible to evaluate a mechanic's diagnosis and recommendations, much less tell whether the quoted price is realistic.

If you want to tackle simple car maintenance and repair tasks yourself, visit the AutoSite Web site (www.autosite.com/garage/garmenu.asp). It takes you on a tour of what's under your car's hood, defines everyday auto mechanic terms, offers troubleshooting tips, and tells you about the ins and outs of common repairs. The site also tells you when it's time to call a pro.

Finding a mechanic before you need one is the best way to alleviate the anxiety and hassle of getting your car repaired and to ensure that the mechanic you hire does good work and is reasonably priced. Start by asking your family, friends, or coworkers for mechanic references. You can also look up auto repair shops in your local Yellow Pages. Try to find shops that specialize in your particular type of car.

If your car is covered by a warranty or service contract, you may or may not have a choice about who wrenches on your wheels. If you have a choice, make sure that the repair shop you choose honors your warranty or service contract.

You might invalidate your car's warranty if you do not perform the maintenance it requires. You can screen auto repair shops by phone or in person. However you do your screening, find out how each shop prices its work. Some charge a flat fee for labor based on an estimate of how much time it takes to complete a particular type of repair. Others charge based on the actual amount of time a mechanic spends repairing the car. Find out whether the shops' mechanics have experience working on your particular make and model of car. Ask about any certifications. For example, a shop with an Automotive Service Excellence (ASE) certification employs mechanics who possess basic skills and knowledge in specific technical areas.

If you visit auto repair shops, check whether they display a current license, assuming that your local or state government requires licensing. When you call, ask for a license number. Then call the government office that issued the license to make sure that the license is current and problem-free.

Before you hire an auto repair shop to work on your car, check it out with your local Better Business Bureau and the consumer protection office of your state attorney general.

Undoing the damage: Getting it in writing

When your car needs fixing and you bring it to a repair shop, ask for a signed, written estimate of how much the repairs will cost. The estimate should identify the problems to be repaired, identify the parts needed, include an estimate of labor costs, and state that before the shop does any work on your car that exceeds a given amount of money, it will get your approval. Some state laws require this approval. The written estimate should also reflect the odometer reading on your car when you bring it in and indicate the date the repair order is completed.

To repair your car, the repair shop might use new parts (parts generally made to original manufacturer's specifications); remanufactured, rebuilt, or reconditioned parts (parts that have been restored to sound working order); or salvaged parts (parts taken without alteration from other cars). Depending on your state, a repair shop may be required to tell you if it doesn't put new parts in your car. Also, if a shop is going to put rebuilt parts in your car, make sure that your warranty covers the labor involved. It might cover only the cost of the replacement parts.

If the cost of a repair is substantial, or if you're not sure that you trust a repair shop's diagnosis of what's wrong, get at least one more diagnosis and estimate. However, you may have to pay a diagnostic fee if you get an estimate from one shop and then hire another to do the repairs.

Knowing how your car works and how to identify common car problems is a good way to ensure that you maintain your car properly and steer clear of auto repair rip-offs. The FTC brochure *Taking the Scare Out of Auto Repair* is another good resource. You can find an online version of the brochure at www.ftc.gov/bcp/conline/pubs/autos/autorpr.htm, or you can order it by calling toll-free, 877-382-4357.

After your car has been repaired

When you go to the repair shop to pick up your car, be sure to get a repair order describing everything that was done to your car. It should list each repair done to your car, each part used to accomplish the repairs, the cost of each part, the labor charges, and your car's odometer reading when you brought it in and after the repairs were completed. Ask the shop to show you the parts that were removed from your car. Some states require this.

Handling disagreements with the auto repair shop

When you and the auto repair shop disagree about whether your car's problem has been fixed, and you want to take your car home or to another repair shop, in most states, you can't take your car until you pay the repair shop. This is because the shop has a *possessory lien* on your car. In most states, the repair shop has you over the proverbial barrel. If you need your car, you have to pay your bill, even if you don't think that you should have to. However, you can then take the auto repair shop to court to try to recover the money you paid. While your car is at the repair shop, the shop may have the right to charge you for storage.

In a few states, you can get your car back by paying the money you owe to a court official, who puts the funds in an escrow account, where it stays until your dispute is resolved.

To bolster your case in court, when you pay an auto repair shop bill that you dispute, write "I Dispute This Bill" on it. Another option is to pay with a credit card. Then, according to the Fair Credit Billing Act, you can dispute the charge and withhold payment on it.

If your car's problem is fixed but recurs a short time later, you can expect the auto repair shop to repair it again for free. However, the repair shop might see it another way and tell you that it will charge you more to fix it again. In most states, whether the repair shop has the right to expect more money from you depends on whether the auto mechanic used "reasonable skill" when repairing your car or whether your car's problem is particularly difficult to diagnose or fix. If the recurrence of your car's problems is the mechanic's fault, you shouldn't have to pay to have your car fixed again; otherwise, the cost of the additional repairs must come out of your pocket. The dilemma for you, of course, is how to know whether the mechanic used "reasonable skill." The best way is to ask at least one other auto repair shop to look at your car and give you its opinion in writing.

Chapter 13

Arming Yourself with Insurance

· ·

In This Chapter

▶ Understanding how insurance works

▶ Evaluating insurance companies

▶ Knowing how insurance companies evaluate you

▶ Shopping for insurance

▶ Getting your claims paid

· ·

*L*ife is full of risks, and most of them are unpredictable: car accidents, ill-nesses, disabling injuries, theft, fire, flood, and even death. Your life can be humming right along, and all of a sudden, *whammo,* seemingly out of nowhere, you have a serious and potentially costly problem to deal with. That's why having insurance is a good idea and, sometimes, absolutely necessary.

Insurance costs money. Right now, you may not be able to purchase all the types of insurance described in this chapter; depending on your age and cir-cumstances, you may not need it. An insurance broker or agent can help you evaluate your current insurance needs and reassess them as your family grows, your assets increase, your work situation changes, you grow older, and so on. It's also a good idea to consult your financial advisor to find better ways to provide yourself and your family with the protection that certain kinds of insurance can buy.

Understanding Insurance

Insurance provides you with a financial and legal suit of armor by protecting you and your family against financial loss. For example, homeowner's insur-ance protects you against the possibility that your home will be damaged or destroyed and helps pay for the cost of repairing or rebuilding it. Health insurance protects you from the financial impact of having to assume the full cost of your medical bills. And life insurance helps you provide, among other things, financial resources for your family after you die.

You can purchase insurance for just about anything you can imagine. However, the most common types of insurance are auto, homeowner's, health, life, disability, and long-term care.

You may purchase your insurance through a group plan or as an individual. If you purchase individual rather than group insurance, the insurer sends you a policy that is a legally binding contract between you and the company. Among other things, the policy spells out your insurance benefits and your obligations as the policyholder, including the amount of your annual premium. You may have to pay the premium in a single lump sum, or you may be able to pay it in monthly or quarterly installments.

You can also purchase insurance to protect yourself from the financial impact of being sued over an auto accident or an accident that happens in your home. This kind of insurance is called *liability insurance*. You can purchase it as part of your home or auto insurance package.

When you're sued and you have liability insurance, your insurance company foots the bill for your legal defense. In exchange, you give up control of how you are represented. Your insurance company chooses your lawyer, has the ultimate say regarding the strategy for your defense, and can even okay an out-of-court settlement of the lawsuit. Yes, you can contribute your two cents, but in the end, the insurance company has the right to make most of the decisions. If you lose the lawsuit, your insurance company also pays for the court judgment, up to the amount of your coverage. The balance, if any, is your responsibility.

If you're sued and you do not have liability insurance, you have to pay the full cost of your defense, and you're also liable for the full amount of the judgment, assuming the judge or jury decides in favor of the plaintiff. If you can't pay it, the judgment creditor can use the collection process to collect the judgment, which means that you could lose some of your assets. Given the frequency with which people sue one another these days and the size of the monetary awards judges and juries award plaintiffs, liability insurance can mean the difference between financial solvency and bankruptcy.

Think twice about purchasing a minimal amount of homeowner's or auto liability insurance. It may not be enough. For example, if you injure someone seriously in an auto accident, consider the expenses you could face if you were sued because of it. Minimal liability coverage might provide just a drop in the bucket compared to the size of the judgment.

One option is to purchase an umbrella liability insurance policy that provides at least $1 million in additional coverage. Usually, however, the company that sells you this additional coverage requires that you purchase a minimum amount of regular liability insurance.

If the plaintiff in a lawsuit sues you for multiple damages and your policy does not fully cover some damages, your insurance company is not legally obligated to pay those damages if you lose the lawsuit. Before the lawsuit begins, your insurance company might send you a reservation of rights letter stating that although it is defending you, it reserves the right not to reimburse you for certain losses, depending on the outcome of the lawsuit.

Finding the best insurance company

When you're in the market for insurance, do business with a company that's financially sound so that the company will be there for you when you need it. A financially shaky company might be unable to pay your claims and might even go out of business, leaving you without the financial safety net you thought you had. Every state has a special fund to pay insurance claims when a company goes belly up; however, this safety net has its limits and may not be able to pay your claim in full.

The easiest way to judge a company's financial stability is to find out how it's rated by companies that evaluate the finances of insurance companies. Those companies include A.M. Best, Standard & Poor's, Moody's Investors Services, Duff and Phelps, and Weiss Ratings, Inc. If your insurance agent or broker recommends a company to you, ask her how it's rated and what the rating means. Purchase your insurance from a company with a high rating.

When you compare insurance company ratings, make sure that you don't compare apples to oranges. In other words, although all the rating companies use letters to signify a rating, the meaning of those letters can vary from company to company. For example, one company might use AAA to signify its highest ranking, whereas another might use A++ or A+.

If you buy your insurance directly, without an agent's assistance, the insurance company's written information should tell you how the company is rated. Over the years, an insurance company's rating can deteriorate. You should periodically check the rating of your insurance company.

Knowing how insurance companies rate you

A key consideration when an insurance company is deciding how much it will charge you is its assessment of how much risk it thinks it assumes by covering you. The greater the risk, the more it will probably have to pay out in insurance claims. Because insurance companies want to minimize the amount of risk they assume, if they consider you to be a bigger risk than others, you will probably have to pay more for insurance than someone it believes represents a lower risk. Some people are considered so risky that it's difficult for them to get insurance.

Getting the scoop on rates

Here's a list of the major companies that rate insurance companies. Call them or visit their Web sites to find out how they rate the insurance company you're thinking about working with. A few of these companies charge for their information:

✔ A.M. Best Co.: 800-424-2378, www.ambest.com. Cost: $2.94 plus $4.95/rating if you order by phone. The information is free if you order it at the company's Web site.

✔ Duff & Phelps Credit Rating Co.: 312-368-3198, www.dcrco.com. Free by phone or online.

✔ Moody's Investors Service: 212-553-0377, www.moodys.com. Free by phone or online.

✔ Standard & Poor's Ratings Group: 212-438-2000, www.standardpoors.com. Free by phone or online.

✔ Weiss Ratings Inc.: 800-289-9222, www.weissinc.com. Cost: $15/rating by phone or online.

In most states, if a company refuses to sell you insurance, it must provide you with a written explanation for its refusal. There are legal limits on the factors an insurance company can take into account when it sets its rates. If it wants to charge you a higher-than-normal rate, the company must have a legitimate reason, and that reason must relate to risk. When the term of your insurance policy is up, your insurer usually has the right to increase the size of your premium if it decides that your risk has increased.

Insurance companies are prohibited from selling you insurance at a higher-than-usual rate because of the your race, national origin or ancestry, gender, or religion. In some states, depending on the type of insurance you want to buy, this list might also include your marital status, occupation, sexual orientation, the language you speak, where you live, and any physical or mental impairment you have.

Some insurance companies charge different rates for the same amount or type of coverage, depending on whether you're male or female. However, a handful of states prohibit this distinction when it comes to auto insurance, and a couple bar gender distinctions in setting insurance rates for all types of insurance. To find out whether your state is one of them, call your state insurance commission or state department of insurance.

Buying insurance

Before you sign on with an insurance company, pay careful attention to the details of the coverage you're being offered. If you don't, you might face some unpleasant surprises. For example, when you file a claim, you might discover that your policy gives your insurance company the right not to pay it, that your deductible is higher than you realized, and so on.

If you don't understand something in the policy, ask your agent to explain it. If you're unhappy with the terms of the insurance you're being offered, speak up. Your agent may be able to find you a better policy. When you read a policy, be sure to note the following:

- ✔ **The term of the policy.** How long it will be in effect?

- ✔ **The provisions for cancellation and nonrenewal.** Usually, an insurance company has the right not to renew a policy; however, for auto and home insurance, most states require that a policyholder receive written notice of nonrenewal at least 30 days prior to the end of the policy.

- ✔ **The amount of the deductible.** This is the amount you must pay out of pocket before your benefits kick in. Some policies have different deductibles for different types of coverage.

- ✔ **The size of the caps.** A *cap* represents the maximum amount of money an insurance company pays out over time on certain types of claims.

- ✔ **The exclusions.** *Exclusions* are the things a policy does not cover.

- ✔ **The grace period.** This is the amount of time you have to pay your premium after its due date before your policy is cancelled.

- ✔ **The time limits.** Policies have certain time limits for taking certain actions. For example, a homeowner's policy specifies how quickly you must report property damage or loss to your insurance company. Depending on the policy, waiting too long could give the company the right not to pay the full amount of your claim, or not to pay anything at all.

- ✔ **The special requirements.** Ignoring a policy's special requirements could mean forfeiting the right to be reimbursed for certain expenses or missing out on other policy benefits. For example, your medical insurer might require that you get certain kinds of medical care and treatment preapproved. Also, your homeowner's policy might say that you must notify the police after your home is burglarized within a certain number of days. If you're shopping for an individual insurance policy, check out your options at Quotesmith.com, or call 800-556-9393.

Getting Paid at Claim Time

Most states have laws that govern how quickly a claim must be processed and either paid or denied. Usually, it's between 30 and 60 days. In some states, these laws apply to all insurance, but in other states, they apply only to specific types of insurance. A list of state insurance regulators can be found at page 66 in the *2001 Consumer Resource Handbook* on the CD.

If your insurance company offers to settle with you for less than what you believe you're entitled to, you're under no obligation to accept its offer. To expedite the processing of your insurance claim, follow the insurance company's instructions for completing the claim paperwork and for filing the claim.

If you think that your insurance company is taking too long to process your claim, talk to your insurance agent. If you don't have an agent already, call the company's customer service number to find out the status of your claim. If you don't like the answer you get, write a complaint letter and ask for a written response within a certain period of time. Call your insurance company to find out to whom to write — politely insist on a specific name. Use the sample letter in Form 13-1 on the CD to write your complaint letter. If your letter doesn't get results, you may want to consult a lawyer about what to do next.

You may have problems getting your insurance company to pay a claim. You might be denied because you haven't met your deductible; you waited too long to file your claim; your insurance company believes that your claim is false; or your insurance company made a mistake. Yes, it happens!

If you file a false claim, you open yourself to criminal prosecution. No matter what the reason, your insurance company must provide you with a written explanation for a denial. The explanation must also indicate the policy terms or provisions on which the company based its denial.

Dealing with a denied claim

If you think that your insurance company should pay a claim it has denied, or that your insurance company should pay more on a claim than it's paying, read your policy first. The insurance company may be entitled to do what it did. If you have an insurance agent or broker, ask him to contact your insurance company about your claim. If you don't, call your insurance company's customer service number to find out what you can do (if anything) to get the company's decision reversed. You may be told to resubmit your claim with additional information. If you're having trouble with your insurance company, call the National Insurance Consumer Hotline at 800-942-4242 for advice.

You can send your insurance company a letter indicating why you believe your claim should be paid. Make sure to direct it to a specific person. Attach to the letter copies of supporting documentation, such as medical records, receipts, photographs, a police report, and so on. If the amount of money at stake is substantial, and particularly if you believe that you have the basis for a lawsuit against your insurance company, hire a lawyer to help you with the letter — you want to be sure that the letter will help and not hurt the lawsuit. Form 13-2 on the CD features a sample letter.

You can also file a complaint with your state's insurance department or commission. Sometimes, just knowing that you're reporting it to your state's insurance regulator can make an insurance company change its mind about your claim. If you have trouble getting your insurance company to reimburse you fairly for damage done to your home or auto, consider getting an independent appraisal of the damage, and if the appraisal supports your argument, send the appraisal to your insurance company.

Don't delay acting on a claim, thinking that your state insurance department or commission will go to bat for you. Those offices rarely, if ever, intercede on behalf of an individual, although they do act on behalf of multiple consumers if they receive a lot of complaints about a particular company or insurance industry practice.

If your letter does not clear up the problem you're having with your insurance company, your policy probably requires that you use the company's dispute resolution process to settle the matter. Your policy should explain how the process works and how to use it. The process may include mandatory arbitration.

If you receive health, life, or disability insurance through your employer's group plan, the federal Employees Retirement Income Security Act (ERISA) limits your appeal rights. This law preempts or substitutes for the laws of your state. Efforts to make ERISA more consumer-friendly and less pro-insurance-industry have failed so far. If you have serious problems with your coverage and the plan administrator (usually your employer) is unable to resolve them for you, consult with a lawyer who specializes in ERISA.

Suing your insurance company

If your insurance company's dispute resolution process does not resolve the problem with your claim, you can file a breach-of-contract lawsuit against your insurance company in civil court. If you win, you're entitled to a reimbursement plus interest.

Depending on the circumstances of your case, you might also want to file a "bad faith" lawsuit. To win this lawsuit, you must prove to the court that your insurance company acted unreasonably when it denied your claim. If you do, you're awarded money above and beyond the amount of your insurance claim. For example, the court might issue a judgment that compensates you for the money you had to spend out-of-pocket because your claim was denied and for the mental and emotional suffering you endured because of the denial. The court can award you punitive damages as well. *Punitive damages* provide defendants with extra punishment for their wrongdoing and are supposed to discourage them from doing the same thing again. Bad faith lawsuits are more difficult to win than lawsuits based on breach of contract.

If you're suing for a relatively small amount of damages — between $1,000 and $10,000, depending on the laws of your state — consider filing your lawsuit in small claims court and representing yourself. Otherwise, hire an attorney with experience suing insurance companies. Insurance law is complicated, and your insurance company will aggressively defend itself if a lot of money is at stake.

Canceling your insurance policy

Usually, you can cancel your insurance policy simply by not paying the premiums. However, you might pay a price for canceling; you may not get back the full dollar value of the number of months left on the policy as of the cancellation date. Also, if you cancel your life insurance policy, you might have to pay a *surrender charge* if the policy was not in effect for a certain number of years and depending on the type of policy. The surrender charge represents the penalty you pay for canceling. It helps reimburse the insurance company for lost income.

Read your policy to be sure that you don't have to cancel your insurance in writing and to learn about any other cancellation requirements. The "Understanding Auto Insurance" and "Owning Homeowner's Insurance" sections of this chapter provide you with additional information about auto and homeowner's insurance and prepare you to make wise decisions when you shop for and use these two types of insurance. For additional information on life, health, disability, and long-term care insurance, read Chapter 19.

Understanding Auto Insurance

Auto insurance is an obligation, not a choice, because all states mandate that you maintain a minimal amount of bodily injury and property damage insurance when you own a car. Your state may require that you purchase other kinds of insurance coverage as well.

In some states, if you don't have the legally required insurance and you cause an accident, you can be fined or even arrested. In other states, if you're involved in an auto accident, whether or not the accident is your fault, you're legally required to prove that you are "financially responsible" — that is, that you can afford to pay for any damages. If you can't provide that proof, your driver's license can be suspended or your vehicle registration revoked. Some states do not let you register your vehicle or obtain new license plates for it unless you can prove that you have insurance.

If you borrowed money to purchase your vehicle, the lender requires that you protect its interest in your vehicle by purchasing at least a minimum amount of insurance. The lender tells you what the minimum is.

Knowing the five types of auto insurance

You can actually buy five different types of auto insurance coverage. Exactly what you buy depends just as much on the requirements of your state and the bank financing your vehicle as on what you can afford.

- **Liability insurance — bodily injury and property damage.** Bodily injury insurance protects you if you're responsible for an auto accident that results in the injury or death. Property damage insurance covers you if you cause another vehicle to be damaged or destroyed. Liability insurance also pays for your legal defense if you're sued over an auto accident.

- **Collision insurance.** This type of insurance reimburses you for the cost of repairing or replacing your vehicle if it's damaged or destroyed in an accident.

- **Comprehensive insurance.** Having this type of insurance means that your insurance company reimburses you if your car is stolen, vandalized, or damaged as a result of theft, fire, vandalism, flooding, falling tree limbs, and other things that are not auto accident-related.

- **Personal injury insurance.** This type of coverage pays for the medical treatment and care that you or passengers in your car may need as a result of an auto accident, even if the accident is your fault. The coverage might pay for lost wages as well. Some states require this type of coverage.

- **Uninsured motorist insurance**. This coverage reimburses you if you are injured in an auto accident and the person responsible for the accident does not have insurance.

Minimizing your insurance costs

Earlier in this chapter, we cover what an insurance company can and can't consider when it decides whether to sell you insurance and how much to charge you for insurance. Other factors that insurance companies takes into account when it comes to auto insurance are your driving record, the age and model of your vehicle, and the ages of the people driving the vehicle. Teenage drivers who drive their own car or who drive a car most of the time are more expensive to insure than other drivers are. They also consider whether you regularly use your vehicle for business purposes or for pleasure. You save money by not using your car to commute to and from work.

 If you're over 60 years of age, you may have a hard time finding reasonably priced auto insurance. That's because older drivers are more apt to experience vision problems, slowed reflexes, and other physical changes that cause them to be involved in traffic accidents more often than younger drivers.

Figuring out fault versus no-fault

Whose fault is it? This is the key question in states that use a "fault" system to determine who pays for car accident-related damages. In these states, the person who causes the accident is liable for damages. Sometimes, there is no question about who is to blame, but when there is, the only way to settle the matter may be a lawsuit. If you live in a fault state, even when an auto accident is relatively minor, you may spend a lot of time and money resolving the issue of who should pay and getting paid if you're not at fault.

About half the states have adopted no-fault systems. In these states, regardless of who is responsible for an auto accident, each driver's insurance company pays her bills. In these no-fault states, a driver who is seriously injured (or the family of someone who is killed) in an auto accident can also sue the driver responsible for the accident.

Aside from the obvious money-saving advice like don't get speeding tickets and avoid accidents, the following tips can help bring down the cost of your insurance premiums:

- ✔ Insure all your cars with the same company, or purchase your auto insurance and your homeowner's insurance from the same company.

- ✔ Let your insurance company know if one of the drivers on your policy attends traffic school after receiving a ticket.

- ✔ Increase the deductible on your collision insurance, assuming you can afford to pay more out of pocket to repair your car if it's damaged. If your car is old, you may want to forgo collision insurance entirely, because the cost of the insurance may be greater than the car's value.

- ✔ Tell your insurance company if you have an antitheft device installed on your car.

- ✔ Pay the full amount of your premium up front rather than in installments.

Owning Homeowner's Insurance

Homeowner's insurance is not an option when you have a mortgage. Your lender requires that you protect its interest in your property — the collateral — by purchasing a certain amount of homeowner's insurance. The lender wants to be sure that if your home is destroyed or damaged, you have the money you need to rebuild or repair it.

Once you pay off your mortgage loan and the lender no longer has a financial interest in your home, whether to purchase insurance is up to you. But practically speaking, you should view this kind of insurance as a necessity, not an option. Why wouldn't you want to protect what is probably your most valuable asset? Without homeowner's insurance, you bear the full financial burden of repairing or rebuilding your home and replacing personal belongings that are damaged, destroyed, or stolen from your home. Having homeowner's insurance simply makes good sense. A homeowner's policy provides for

- Damage done to your home, up to the amount of insurance you purchase. This includes reimbursement for the destruction of your home.

- Any theft of or damage to the personal property in your home, up to the amount of insurance you purchase.

Insure your home and your personal belongings for their replacement value, not for their cash value. Doing so costs you a little more, but you will have the money you need to buy something that's comparable to what you lose. If you file a homeowner's insurance claim, you'll be happy that you did.

- The needs of someone injured at your home because of your negligence, up to the amount of the insurance you purchase, and a legal defense if you're sued by someone injured at your home.

Periodically, review your homeowner's policy to make sure that you have the appropriate amount of coverage. For example, you may need additional insurance if your home increases in value due to market forces, if you make substantial improvements to it, or if you purchase expensive new furniture, artwork, and so on. You can have your home appraised to determine whether it has increased in value. Usually you would get some clue that this is necessary by looking at your tax appraisal each year, or if you hear that your neighbors sold their home for a lot of money. A useful guideline is that you should have enough insurance to rebuild your home from the ground up and to replace all the items that are really important to you.

Also, note that the home must be insured for 80 percent of replacement value to have rebuilding coverage rather than original cost coverage. This is important because original cost coverage might not provide enough money to rebuild completely. Your insurance agent can help you assess whether it's time to increase your coverage.

Homeowners are not the only people who should insure their belongings from loss, damage, or theft. Renters should, too. Renter's insurance can protect you if someone is injured at your home or apartment, and it's quite affordable.

Insuring your condo or co-op

When you own a unit in a condominium project, you own the inside of your home but share the project's grounds and facilities — the common areas — with the owners of the other units in your complex. As an owner, you pay regular dues to the condominium's homeowner's association, and part of those dues go toward the cost of insuring the project's exterior and common areas. Usually, the insurance also covers liability for injuries on the project's premises.

The condominium project's insurance will not cover you against the loss or theft of the property inside your unit or protect you if someone is injured inside your home. Therefore, purchase a homeowner's policy specifically for condominium owners.

If you live in a cooperative apartment or co-op, you own shares of the corporation that owns the building and lease the unit that you live in from the corporation. As a shareholder, you're obligated to pay the corporation a monthly maintenance fee, part of which helps insure the building you live in and the common areas you share with other co-op owners. However, because the insurance does not cover the interior of your unit, to protect yourself and your things you need to purchase a homeowner's policy for co-op owners.

Before you purchase a condominium or co-op apartment, ask for a copy of its insurance policy. Review it so you can be sure the policy provides adequate coverage and so you can determine exactly what kinds of coverage you need in your own policy. For extensive treatment of the special insurance needs of condominium owners, see Jack Hungelmann's *Insurance For Dummies* (Hungry Minds, Inc.).

Chapter 14

Disposing of Your Stuff: Wills, Trusts, Living Wills, and More

In This Chapter

▶ Understanding what you can accomplish with estate planning

▶ Knowing what to consider when you write a will

▶ Using an attorney to help you prepare a will

▶ Writing your own will

▶ Planning for the end of your life

*W*hether you are worth millions or just wish you were, and regardless of whether you're age 65 or age 25, estate planning is something you should address if you care about what happens to the assets you own when you die. Estate planning includes writing a will, setting up a trust, giving your stuff away while you're still alive, deciding on the kind of medical care and treatment you want at the end of your life, and a whole lot more.

A cookie-cutter approach to estate planning is dangerous because the planning may not meet your particular needs. Even worse, it could create problems for your loved ones later. Estate planning should be a highly personal process that reflects your goals and objectives, the total value of your assets, and your personal values.

This chapter introduces you to basic estate-planning concepts and tools. The first part of the chapter describes estate planning and covers such topics as writing a will and setting up a trust. It also reviews other estate-planning tools that you may want to use and alerts you to the potential consequences of dying without a will or with a will that's not legally valid. Along the way, you find out how and when to use an estate-planning attorney.

The second part of this chapter tells you about how a living will and a durable power of attorney can give you control over whether you receive life-sustaining treatment and care when you're near death. Doing such planning now helps protect your estate from being eaten up by the cost of life-sustaining measures you may not want if you could speak for yourself.

Defining Estate Planning

What is estate planning? At its most basic, *estate planning* is the process of deciding what happens to all your stuff — your estate — when you die. Depending on what you own, your estate can include your home, other real estate, cars, recreational vehicles, antiques, fine jewelry, collectibles, bank accounts, life insurance, stocks, mutual funds, and so on. Most people want the things they own to go to their spouses, children, and other immediate family members, but you may want to remember your unmarried partner, your close friends, your alma mater, your favorite charities, or even a cherished pet. It's up to you to decide.

The individuals, charities, and so on that inherit your assets are called your *beneficiaries.* Estate planning is also about preserving your estate so that as much of it as possible transfers to your beneficiaries instead of being eaten up by estate taxes and other expenses. Presently, federal estate taxes are only a concern to those whose estates are worth more than $675,000. If your estate is worth this much, Uncle Sam takes between 37 and 55 percent. Ouch! However, the federal Taxpayer Relief Act authorized gradual increases in the estate tax threshold. The increases stop in 2006, when your estate will be liable for federal estate taxes if it's worth more than $1 million.

In 2002, the value of your estate can be as much as $700,000, and it will not be liable for federal estate taxes. In 2004, the number goes up to $850,000, and then up to $950,000 the following year. In 2006, it reaches $1 million and stops.

Your estate may be liable for state estate taxes, too. Estate planning is also about what happens to your young children if both you and your spouse die. The laws in all states say that minor children — children who are under age 18 or 21, depending on the state — can't make their own decisions about major matters such as their schooling and healthcare, and generally need adult guidance and supervision. A will provides you with a legal vehicle for designating the adult you want to raise your kids and make important decisions for them should both you and your spouse die. That person is called a *personal guardian.*

Depending on your state, a will may be the only legal tool you have for designating a legal guardian for your young child. If the worst happens and both you and your spouse die without a will, your state will determine who raises your kids. Although that person is likely to be a relative, there's no guarantee that it will be someone you respect or someone who shares your values.

You can also use your will to name the adult you want to manage the money and other assets you leave your children while they're young, assuming that the value of the assets is greater than your state says minors can own without adult supervision. This person is called a *property guardian.* Again, if you leave no will, your state will decide who manages your children's assets.

Minors can own only a small amount of assets without adult supervision — between $2,500 and $5,000 in most states.

Estate planning helps you die with dignity. It lets you use legal means to take control of the medical care and treatment you receive when you're close to death and not able to make those decisions for yourself. Unless you make such decisions now and formalize them legally, your estate may be consumed by the cost of your end-of-life care.

Where There's a Will . . .

At the heart of all estate planning is a legally binding will. For many people, writing a will is all the estate planning they need to do. Writing a will may be enough if estate taxes are not a concern for you and your assets are relatively simple — just a bank account, a home, and a car, for example. Examples of more complex assets include a closely held business, limited partnerships, oil and gas interests, or stock options, to name a few. Transferring these types of assets to your beneficiaries often takes more than a will. For example, a will can't help you if you want to minimize your estate tax obligation because the total value of your estate is more than $675,000. "Defining Estate Planning" in this chapter tells you more about estate taxes and explains how the federal Taxpayer Relief Act affects estate taxes between now and 2006.

Although some states recognize oral and handwritten wills, most don't, so you should take care to follow legal formalities. Like any other important legal document, your will should be typed. Be sure that the wishes you express in it are clear and unambiguous. If there is confusion about your intentions after you die, your local probate court judge may have to interpret what you meant, and your will could be subject to a contest. The cost of defending the validity of your will comes out of your estate.

Having a written will also minimizes the potential for family squabbles or outright war after you die. Without a clearly written will that details what you want to happen to your stuff, your loved ones may argue over what they think you wanted to happen and what they believe they're entitled to. Those arguments could cause irreparable damage to their relationships.

A will may be enough when you are young and don't own much in the way of assets. But as you begin to earn more money, buy more stuff, get married, have kids, and whatnot, you may need more than just a will. An estate-planning attorney can advise you about exactly what types of estate planning are appropriate for you.

Giving and receiving under a will

You can't give away certain assets with your will. If you include them in it, the wishes you expressed regarding those assets will be ignored. Examples of these assets include life insurance proceeds, pension plan money, and 401(k) money. When you established these plans, you designated a beneficiary for each of them — that designated person receives the plan assets when you die regardless of what your will says.

Other assets you can't give away in your will include assets you don't own. For example, if your name is not on the title to your home, the home is not yours to give away. Also, you can't give away an asset that you gave to someone else as an *inter vivos* gift. An *inter vivos* gift is a gift that you make while you're still alive as part of your estate planning. For information on *inter vivos* gifts, read the section "Discovering Other Estate-Planning Tools" later in this chapter.

Making sure your will stands up in court

State requirements for a legally binding will tend to be pretty similar, although some differences exist. Typically, for your will to be legal, when you write it you must

✔ Be a legal adult — 18 years of age in most states.

✔ Be of sound mind. In other words, you can't be senile, under the influence of drugs or alcohol, insane, or mentally incompetent when you write your will.

✔ Have *testamentary capacity*. This relates somewhat to the preceding item. It means that you must understand what you're doing and the significance of your decisions when you write your will.

✔ Reflect your wishes and desires, not someone else's. In other words, you can't have been forced to write your will, nor can someone have had "undue influence" over what you put in it.

✔ Be typed, not handwritten or oral.

A few states recognize oral wills or handwritten wills, also called *holographic wills*. To be on the safe side, always have your will typed or printed. In it, you should include

- At least one provision that disposes of your assets.

- A statement that the will is yours — that is, "I, Joe Schmoe, . . ."

- Indicate that it is your final statement regarding your wishes for the disposition of your property. Most wills say something like, "This is my last will and testament."

- Be signed and dated. In some states, your signature must appear in a specific place on your will.

- Be witnessed by at least two people, sometimes three, depending on your state. The witnesses can't be beneficiaries of the will. In many states, your will must be notarized, too.

If your will is not legally valid according to the laws of your state, the *probate court* in your area — the court that oversees the distribution of your assets — will throw out your will, and the court will proceed as though you had not written one.

Special protections for spouses

If you're like most married people, you want to leave most of what you own to your spouse to be sure that the person you shared your life with can benefit from your assets after you're gone. But if your marriage has gone south, you may be tempted to leave your spouse out of your will entirely. That's impossible if you live in a *separate property state,* assuming that your spouse did not waive her inheritance rights in a legally valid prenuptial or postnuptial agreement.

Most states are separate property states. In these states, a spouse is entitled to a minimum amount of the estate of the deceased. This amount is called the *elective share* and is usually expressed as a percentage of the estate's value. In most states, the amount ranges from a one-half to a one-third interest. The percentage may be applied to everything you own when you die or just to what was in your will — it depends on the laws of your state. If you don't leave your spouse at least the minimum amount she is entitled to, she has a legal right to take her elective share. If she takes it, your spouse is said to *take against the will.*

Some states have adopted a sliding scale for the legal minimum amount a surviving spouse is entitled to. The scale is based on the length of the marriage — the longer the marriage, the bigger the share.

If estate taxes are a concern, you may want to leave your spouse the full amount of your estate because the federal unlimited marital deduction says that the portion of your estate that's ordinarily subject to estate taxes is exempt from those taxes if it goes to your spouse. However, without the appropriate estate planning, this approach can create a future estate tax problem for your spouse because the deduction only delays payment of the tax.

Dying without a Will

If you die without a will — called dying *intestate* — or if the court invalidates your will, your legacy to your loved ones could be legal hassles and considerable expense. For starters, a probate judge, not you, decides which of your legal heirs inherits the property you own and how much each person gets. The judge's decisions are based on the intestate laws of your state. Most likely, your surviving spouse will share your estate with your children. In fact, depending on the state, your spouse may be entitled to just one-third of everything you own.

If you die intestate, your spouse could face financial problems and might even have to move out of the home you once shared. Furthermore, because the distribution of your assets is based on the laws of your state, not on your wishes, you have no assurance that your property will go to the people you really want to have it. For example, no matter what your state, the law does not consider unmarried partners, close friends, charities, or pets to be legal heirs.

The probate court in your state divides and distributes your most significant assets only. Your family members are left to decide what to do with everything else — your personal belongings and items with sentimental value, for example. Sometimes, deciding how to divvy up "the little stuff" can bring out the worst in a family, creating bad feelings that last for years.

When you die without a will, your state names someone to be the administrator for your estate. That person carries out all the responsibilities that an executor would normally handle. An *executor* is the person you name in your will to oversee the distribution of your assets, pay any debts you owe, and settle all the other matters concerning your estate. "Putting someone in charge of things" later in this chapter tells you more about executors. The administrator charges your estate a fee for his services, which means that less money is left for to your heirs.

Theoretically, intestacy laws are supposed to reflect what you probably would have decided if you had written a will. Therefore, although state intestacy laws vary, it's likely that your assets would be distributed first to your surviving spouse, then to your children, and then to their children. However, your parents, your siblings and their children, and your cousins, nieces, nephews, aunts, and uncles could also end up with some of what you own. And if none of these relatives is still alive when you die, or if the family you left behind is very small, your closest blood relative — someone you may never have met, perhaps — could end up with what you owned. Finally, if the state can't find anyone related to you, it gets your stuff!

Putting someone in charge of things

When you prepare your will, you have more to decide than who your beneficiaries are and what to leave to each of them. You must also designate an *executor* for your estate. This person acts as your legal representative after you die. Among other things, she is responsible for ensuring that the wishes in your will are carried out. She's also responsible for handling any problems that arise during the probate process.

Probate is a court-supervised process that begins with the filing of your will and ends with the distribution of the assets in your *probate estate* — the assets that go through probate. Your estate executor shepherds your estate through probate.

The only assets that go through probate are the ones in your will. Assets that you have already legally transferred to a living trust or that transfer automatically to your beneficiaries — such as the proceeds of your life insurance policy or your IRA — do not go through probate.

Your executor should be someone you trust who also has the trust and respect of your immediate family, because they have to deal with this person during probate. Ideally, your executor has a good head for numbers and is not put off by paperwork, legal forms, and the court. Most people designate a spouse, an adult child, a sibling, or a close friend as executor.

To help you choose the right person for the job, here's a list of the things your executor may have to do on behalf of your estate. This list also provides you with an overview of the probate process. (Depending on your state of residence, some of these steps may not take place.)

✔ Locate your will after you die. Ideally, you will have told your executor where your will is located, and you will have reviewed it with her. If your will has any unusual provisions, be sure that your executor understands why you wrote them. That way, your executor can explain your thinking to your loved ones. Be sure to give your executor a copy of your will.

✔ Initiate the probate process by filing a petition for probate with the probate court in your area and filing your will with the court. Then the court formally appoints your executor and makes sure that your will is legally valid.

✔ Notify all your potential heirs that probate has begun.

✔ Inventory the assets that will be probated and determine their values.

Make your executor's job easier by developing a written inventory of your assets and updating it as necessary. Keep a copy with your will, and be sure that your executor has a copy of the inventory. Use the inventory form on Form 14-1 of the CD to develop your record.

✔ Work with the probate court to make sure that your beneficiaries get what they're entitled to according to the terms of your will.

✔ Notify any potential creditors of your death so that they can file claims against your estate, if necessary, to get your debts to them paid. Each state has its own procedures and time frames for creditors to be notified and for creditors to file their claims.

If the executor does not approve a creditor's claim for payment, the creditor must sue your estate to get paid. In some states, creditors file their clams with the probate court, not with an executor. If your estate does not contain enough money to pay your creditors' claims, state law determines who gets paid and how much each creditor gets.

✔ Use funds from your estate to pay any debts, judgments, taxes, and so on you owed. Your executor also pays the taxes your estate may owe.

- ✓ Receive any payments that are due your estate. Those payments may include tax refunds, dividends, interest income, and so on.

- ✓ Manage the assets in your estate until they can be distributed to your beneficiaries. Depending on the size and complexity of your estate, your executor may invest money, pay bills, cancel your credit cards, sell assets, and so on.

- ✓ Notify Social Security and, if appropriate, the Veteran's Administration, Civil Service, and so on about your death.

- ✓ Help defend your estate against any contests to your will. You can find out more about will contests later in the "Managing will contests" section of this chapter.

- ✓ Keep your loved ones informed regarding the progress of the probate process.

- ✓ Once all creditor claims have been handled, and assuming that there are no contests, prepare a final list of your probate assets, file tax returns as necessary, and take the steps necessary to prepare to transfer the assets to your beneficiaries.

- ✓ Prepare a final report for the probate court and ask it to close your estate and end the probate process. Assuming that no problems are pending, the probate judge formally closes the estate, and your executor's work is over.

Designating an alternate executor in your will is a good idea. This person takes care of things if your first choice dies soon after you do or can't fulfill her responsibilities as executor when the time comes.

If your estate is especially large and complicated, or if your first choice for an executor does not live in your area, consider appointing co-executors. These people share the responsibilities of executor. Be sure, however, that the people you choose can work together cooperatively.

Your executor is entitled to receive a fee for her efforts. The size of the fee i s determined by the laws of your state. In most states, the fee amounts to about 2 percent of an estate's value. Your executor is also entitled to be reimbursed by your estate for any out-of-pocket costs she incurs as your executor.

Many executors, especially family members and friends, waive their rights to receive a fee for their services. However, if you're considering asking your executor to forgo a fee, think about whether your request is fair. If you know that getting your estate through probate and dealing with your family will be time-consuming and emotionally difficult, it might not be fair to ask your executor to do all that for free. However, if your executor does waive his right to a fee, make that fact clear in your will. By the way, if your executor is a financial institution or an attorney, don't even think about asking for a waiver!

Changing your mind

The will you write is not etched in stone; you can change it. In fact, you should review your will and change it as necessary whenever you acquire new assets, sell old ones, remarry, add to your family, move to a new state, and so on. It's important that you keep your will current so you can be sure that it continues to reflect your wishes over the years.

Depending on your state's laws, if you get divorced, the parts of your will relating to your former spouse may be cancelled automatically. When you get divorced, it's time to amend your will or maybe even write a new one.

You can make a minor change to your will by writing a *codicil* — a statement of the change you're making. For the codicil to be legally valid, your state probably requires that it be dated, witnessed, and notarized. Keep the codicil with your will. Form 14-2 features a sample codicil.

If your change is substantial — you add a trust to your will or change your whole gift-giving plan, for example — formally cancel your old will and write a new one. The same holds true if you want to make several relatively small changes to your will. Although there's no legal limit on the number of codicils you can write, as a general rule, it's usually best to limit them to two. Otherwise, when all your codicils are combined with your will, they could create inconsistencies, contradict one another, muddy up your intentions, and so on, making your will vulnerable to a contest or to being tossed out by the probate court.

When you write a new will, make clear in it that you're revoking all previous wills. Also, get back all copies of your old will and destroy them. That way, when you die, there will be no confusion about which will is the valid one. Even if your state law says that you can cancel your will by throwing it away, burning it, writing "cancel" on it, and so on, revoke your former will in your new will. This extra step helps protect your loved ones against costly and time-consuming legal hassles after you die.

If you're going to cancel your old will and codicils and start over with a new will, be sure to note that you're doing so in the new will. Form 14-3 on the CD provides you with sample revocation language.

Managing will contests

If you don't make your wishes crystal clear, or if someone close to you is unhappy with the way he was treated in your will, your will may be contested. Sour grapes are not reason enough for a will contest, however; your will must be proven legally invalid. Unfortunately, if your will isn't carefully drafted or doesn't meet your state's requirements, it may not take much for an attorney to poke legal holes in it.

The probate court in your area hears the will contest. It may uphold the validity of your will, invalidate certain provisions, or invalidate the whole document. If your will is declared invalid, it is as if you never wrote it. No matter what the final decision, with a contest, it takes longer for your beneficiaries to receive the assets you left them. If your executor has to hire an attorney to defend the validity of your will, the cost of that legal help is paid by your estate, leaving less for your beneficiaries.

Using an attorney to write your will

Most people get a lawyer's help to prepare a will. They may write a draft and then hire a lawyer to fine-tune their draft so that they can be sure that the will meets the requirements of their state and does not include any provisions that could cause confusion or trouble after their death. Other people hire an attorney to write their will from start to finish because they have no interest in preparing a draft or don't feel confident about their writing skills.

We're not trying to make estate-planning attorneys rich, but writing your own will without a lawyer's advice and assistance can be risky. For example, if your will is unclear or if it does not meet your state's legal requirements, the wishes you express in it might not be honored; your will could even be declared invalid. Other good reasons to hire a lawyer to help you with your will include the following:

- ✔ To help ensure that you actually get a will written. In our busy world, it's easy to procrastinate when it comes to confronting your mortality and doing it yourself. Be honest; if you have extra time on your hands, which are you more likely to do: write your will or watch TV? Write your will or read a good book? Write your will or go to the beach?

- ✔ To advise you about whether you should do more than write a will based on your estate-planning goals and your finances.

- ✔ To help you minimize your estate taxes.

- ✔ To provide you with information if you want to write your own will and to review your will after you have drafted it. An attorney can make sure that your will covers all the right bases and raise issues that you may not think about.

Luckily, the cost of a lawyer's assistance shouldn't drive you into bankruptcy. You can probably get a qualified attorney to draft a simple will for you — one that doesn't include a trust — for no more than $1,000. However, if you want to do more than write a will, your legal costs increase, depending on the size and value of your estate, your estate-planning goals, the kinds of estate-planning tools you decide to use, and so on.

Writing Your Own Will

If you want to write your own will instead of hiring an attorney to write it for you, read this section first. It provides essential advice for how to do it, including the steps to take to ensure that your final will is legally valid and to achieve your estate-planning goals.

- ✔ **Schedule a meeting with an estate-planning attorney.** Seek professional advice to find out about your state's requirements for a legally valid will and any issues you should consider, given your estate and your family situation. At the very least, call your state's probate court to find out what makes a will legally valid in your state.

- ✔ **Inventory your assets.** Do so by creating a written record of everything you own that's of significant value. Briefly describe each asset; note how you own each asset and whether you own 100 percent, 50 percent, and so on; and then give your share of each asset a market value. *Market value* represents what your share of the asset is worth today.

  If you want to make sure that certain people end up with items that may not be worth a lot but that have special meaning to them, include those items in your inventory, too. They may include such items as a family photo album, a stamp collection, the painting that hung over your favorite armchair, a family brooch, or your mother's old button collection.

  When you create your asset inventory, consider adding to it information that will help your executor during the probate process. This information might include account numbers; the names, addresses, and phone numbers of your bank, brokerage house, and CPA; addresses for the real estate you own, and so on.

- ✔ **Consider your debts.** You may want to include specific provisions in your will for paying them off. Otherwise, these debts are paid from your estate.

- ✔ **Decide on your beneficiaries and what you want to leave to each of them.**

- ✔ **Designate alternate beneficiaries in case a primary beneficiary dies.** Another option is to name a *residual beneficiary* and an *alternate beneficiary* in your will. The alternate beneficiary inherits whatever you left to any beneficiary who died before you did, as well as everything in your estate that you did not leave to a specific beneficiary. Your residual beneficiary also inherits any assets you overlook when you write your will or forget to include when you update it.

- ✔ **Designate an executor for your estate, as well as an alternate executor.** Be sure to speak with these two people first so that you know they're willing to take on the responsibility. When you talk with them, explain exactly what the job entails.

Some states require that an executor be bonded. However, you may be able to waive that requirement in your will. If you don't and bonding is required, the cost is paid by your estate.

✔ **Name a personal and a property guardian for your minor children.** Make sure that the persons you designate are willing to take on these responsibilities. A *personal guardian* raises your children and is responsible for making important decisions about their lives if both you and your spouse die while your children are younger than 18 or 21, depending on the laws of your state. A *property guardian* is the person who manages the money and other assets you leave to your young children, assuming that the total value of those assets exceeds a certain dollar amount. The dollar amount is set by your state.

If you leave assets to a charity, use the charity's exact legal name in your will. Otherwise, it could take longer than usual for the charity to get your gift, or worse, it could go to the wrong charity! To make sure that the charity you want to remember in your will is well run and likely to make responsible use of the money you leave, visit the Web site of the National Charities Information Bureau at www.give.org. The organization's goal is to help people make sound charitable giving decisions.

Draft your own will, modeling it after one of several sample wills on this book's CD. The sample wills include one for a single person with no children (Form 14-4) and one for a single person with minor children (Form 14-5). They also include a sample will for a married person with no children (Form 14-6) and one for a married person with minor children (Form 14-7). Finally, you will find two other sample wills. One is for an unmarried person with a partner who has no minor children (Form 14-8), and the other is a will for an unmarried person with minor children (Form 14-9).

Hire an estate-planning attorney to review your draft will. A lawyer can make sure that your will complies with your state's laws and can tighten up any vague language that could be open to interpretation after you die. The lawyer also may raise important issues you might not think about otherwise. If your will doesn't comply with the laws of your state, it will be thrown out by the court as though you never wrote a will at all. If your will is not tightly worded, your beneficiaries may fight among themselves about what you really meant, and the intent of the wishes you tried to express in your will may be misinterpreted.

Sign your final will, and get it witnessed and notarized according to the requirements of your state. Also, make copies of your will — one for you, one for your executor, and one for anyone else you think should have one. Store your original will in a safe place, such as your home safe or your safe deposit box.

If you decide to use a fill-in-the-blanks will that you purchase at an office supply store or download off the Internet, make sure that it meets the legal requirements of your state. Also, be sure that it addresses all your concerns. Form wills do not address unusual estate-planning situations or wishes.

Knowing when not to write your own will

Steer clear of a do-it-yourself will if your estate is large enough to be subject to estate taxes; if your assets are complicated; if you want to include a trust in your will, or you want to set up a living trust; or if your family situation is complicated. For example, you have children from at least one previous marriage; you intend to disinherit one of your children; there is bad blood among your adult children or between some of your children and your current spouse; or you want to include your partner in your will, particularly if your family disapproves of your relationship and you're worried that they will contest your will.

Discovering Other Estate-Planning Tools

A will is just one of many estate-planning tools that you may want to use in your estate planning. Some of these solutions cost you little or nothing to use, and others come with important caveats that you need to be aware of. An attorney can help you assess whether you should employ the other tools described here and can help you use them appropriately, including making sure that they work with your will as necessary.

Other estate-planning tools you may want to use in your estate planning include

- ✔ **Assets owned with someone else — usually your spouse or unmarried partner — as joint tenants with the right of survivorship:** As joint tenants, you and your co-owner each own an equal share of the asset, and when you die, your share goes to your surviving co-owner — no ifs, ands, or buts about it! For a quick education on the various forms of legal ownership and how each of them affects your estate planning, check out "Owing up to your ownership options" later in this chapter.

- ✔ *Inter vivos* **gifts:** These are gifts that you make to others while you're still alive. Making this kind of gift is a way to reduce the size of your taxable estate. However, you may want to give away some of your stuff simply because you want the opportunity to watch your beneficiaries enjoy your gifts while you're alive.

For a gift to qualify as *inter vivos,* you must give up all future rights to it when you make the gift. In other words, you can't take back the gift, receive income from the gift, make decisions regarding how the gift is used, and so on.

Unless you change all legal ownership documents related to an *inter vivos* gift and file the new documents with the appropriate court or office as necessary, the asset you think you have given away is still yours from the law's perspective.

Tax-free giveaway

According to federal law, each year you can give away up to $10,000 worth of money, stock, real estate, and so on to as many beneficiaries as you want without having to pay a federal gift tax. In other words, if you have four grandchildren, you can give each of them $10,000 a year, tax-free. However, if you give someone $11,000, you have to pay a gift tax on the extra $1,000.

Your spouse can give away the same amount each year. Every year, for example, you and your spouse can give away a total of $20,000 to each of your grandchildren.

✔ **Life insurance:** When you purchase a life insurance policy, the person you designate as your beneficiary automatically receives the policy proceeds when you die.

✔ **Totten trusts and payable-on-death accounts (POD):** These are inexpensive, easy-to-establish accounts that you set up at a bank or brokerage house. When you establish an account, you designate a beneficiary to receive the account funds when you die. Usually, the accounts are revocable.

✔ **Brokerage accounts:** When you set a brokerage account, you designate a beneficiary for the account assets. The beneficiary becomes the legal owner of those assets upon your death.

✔ **Employee benefits:** These include individual retirement accounts (IRAs), pension plans, 401(k)s, stock ownership plans, and so on. Typically, you can designate who you want to receive the benefits from these assets after you die.

✔ **Custodial accounts:** These kinds of accounts are good vehicles for leaving assets to a minor child. You set one up at a bank or brokerage house in the name of the adult who will be the *account custodian.* Then you transfer into the account the assets you want to give to the child. When the child becomes a legal adult, and sometimes even later, depending on your state, she has full access to them. Form 14-10 on the CD provides you with a sample clause to include in your will when you set up a custodial account.

Every state has adopted either the federal Uniform Gifts to Minors Act (UGMA) or the federal Uniform Transfers to Minors Act (UTMA). The UGMA allows you to transfer money, securities, insurance policies, and annuities into a custodial account. The UTMA is broader — it permits the transfer of both real and tangible property as well as all the types of property covered by the UGMA.

Custodial accounts are irrevocable because they are a special type of *inter vivos* gift. Once you place something in them, you can't take it back. If you decide you need it later, you're out of luck.

✔ **Trusts:** These are complicated legal entities into which you place assets you own before you die or after. There are two basic types of trusts — *testamentary* and *living* trusts — as well as myriad specific kinds of trusts. The next sections of this chapter tell you more about trusts. You can make an *inter vivos* gift to a trust, and you can make a trust the beneficiary of a life insurance policy.

Owning up to your ownership options

There are a number of ways to own the major assets you acquire throughout your life. How you own an asset can affect your estate planning. An estate-planning attorney can provide you with additional information about your ownership options and their impact on your estate planning, but here's an overview of your ownership options:

✔ **Joint tenants with the right of survivorship:** When you own property with someone this way, it doesn't matter what your will says; when you die, the asset automatically goes to your co-owner.

✔ **Tenant by the entirety:** This form of ownership is available to spouses only. If you own property with your spouse this way, the surviving spouse automatically owns the entire asset when one of you dies. Therefore, you don't need to leave it to your spouse in your will, and you can't give it away to anyone else. Not all states recognize this form of ownership. Some states recognize it as an ownership option for certain kinds of assets only.

✔ **Tenant in common:** When you own an asset with someone else as a tenant in common, you and your co-owner do not have any right to the other's share. Therefore, you can leave your share to whomever you want, and your co-owner can do the same.

✔ **Separate property:** If you and your spouse live in a separate property state, the assets you acquire with your own money are yours alone, and your spouse has no legal right to them. You get to decide who receives them when you die, and if you want your spouse to get them, you must leave them to her in your will, in a trust, or by some other type of estate planning. Most states are separate property states.

✔ **Community property:** In a very limited number of states, you and your spouse own equal shares of the assets you acquire during your marriage, even if only one of you is on the title. Depending on your state, your spouse may not automatically inherit your share when you die. You must use estate planning to make sure that it happens. Arizona, California, Idaho, Louisiana, Nevada, New Mexico, Texas, Washington, and Wisconsin are community property states.

Putting your faith in a trust

A *trust* is a legal entity into which you transfer assets that you own. Depending on the kind of trust you set up, you can place the assets in it while you're alive or after you die. Trusts have become a popular estate-planning tool because they're very flexible (you can set up a trust to do just about anything), they give you a lot of control over your gift-giving, and they can help you minimize the size of your taxable estate. For example, you can set up a trust that

✔ Limits your child's access to the assets in the trust you set up for him until he reaches certain milestones — turns 30 years of age, finishes his college education, gets married, and so on.

✔ Requires your beneficiary to use the trust's assets for one purpose only.

✔ Provides for the needs and care of your developmentally disabled child after you die.

✔ Minimizes your estate taxes or reduces the amount of your estate that goes through probate so that your beneficiaries can receive the trust assets sooner rather than later.

✔ Ensures that your cat has plenty of catnip after you die and that your dog has plenty of bones to gnaw on.

Types of trusts

There are two basic types of trusts: a testamentary trust and a living trust. A *testamentary trust* is set up within your will. While you're alive, it exists on paper only, but when you die, the trust is activated, and the assets earmarked for the trust are transferred into it. Compared to a living trust, a testamentary trust is easy and inexpensive to establish and administer. It also provides estate tax advantages. However, because a testamentary trust is part of your will, its assets go through probate.

When assets are transferred into a trust, the trust owns the assets, pays taxes on them as appropriate, files a tax return as necessary, and so on. A trust has its own legal identity much as a corporation does.

A *living trust* is more complicated. It's considerably more flexible than a testamentary trust, and its assets do not go through probate. When you place an asset in a living trust, make sure that the legal ownership of the asset has been legally transferred from you to the trust. Otherwise, the trust doesn't own it, and your state determines who ends up with it. A living trust can be revocable or irrevocable. As its name implies, a *revocable trust* is something you can change after you set it up. You can move assets into and out of it, add or subtract beneficiaries, and even cancel the trust. The downside of a revocable trust is that it doesn't give you any tax advantages. Therefore, if estate taxes are a concern for you, you may want to set up an *irrevocable trust.* After you set up this kind of trust and place assets in it, you can't modify the trust or cancel the transfers. Some irrevocable trusts can help protect your estate from creditor collection actions after you die.

Taxation without exasperation

Your estate may have to pay estate taxes when you die, depending on its value. In that case, your executor must file IRS Form 706. Your estate may also have to pay estate taxes to your state as well as to Uncle Sam. Form 14-11 on the CD shows you what a federal estate tax form looks like. Because your death marks the end of your final income tax year, your executor may have to pay federal taxes on the income you earned. Your executor may also have to pay state income taxes on that income.

Most states have a personal income tax. Your estate may also have to pay state income taxes. Finally, after you set up a trust, the assets you place in it may earn income. If that happens, the trustee must report the income and pay any taxes that are due by filing IRS Form 1041, an Estates and Trusts income tax return. Depending on when the income is generated, the trust could begin paying taxes while you're still alive. You can find a copy of the tax form on Form 14-12 of the CD.ZZ

You must draw up a trust agreement to set up a trust. The agreement covers all of the following:

- ✔ The purpose of the trust.

- ✔ The names of the trust's beneficiaries.

- ✔ The name of the trustee. The *trustee* manages the assets in the trust according to your instructions. The trustee can be an adult, an attorney, or a financial institution.

- ✔ The powers and responsibilities you give to the trustee.

- ✔ How you want the trustee to manage the trust assets, including what you want done with any income the assets generate.

- ✔ When you want the trust's beneficiaries to gain full control over the assets in the trust. The trustee's responsibilities end at that point.

- ✔ Anything else you want the trustee to know or do.

Trusts are complicated! Don't try setting up one on your own. You need a lawyer's help.

Looking before you leap into a living trust

Although living trusts are often touted as the answer to estate planning because of their benefits and flexibility, they're not for everyone. For one thing, they're relatively expensive to set up, and there may be less expensive ways to achieve your estate-planning goals. Setting up an irrevocable living trust costs at least $1,000, and even more if you want a revocable trust. Plus, a living trust doesn't eliminate the need for a will. You need a will to transfer any assets you don't place in a trust and to designate personal and property guardians for your minor children. Therefore, before you purchase a living trust, consult with an estate-planning attorney.

If you conclude that a living trust is the best thing since sliced bread, steer clear of living trust scam artists. Instead, hire someone reputable to set up your trust. Ordinarily, that's an estate-planning attorney. In fact, some states do not allow anyone other than attorneys to sell them.

If you purchase a living trust in your home or somewhere other than at the seller's place of business, the federal Cooling Off Rule applies, giving you the right to cancel the transaction within three business days of making it. Also, when you make the transaction, the living trust company must provide you with a cancellation form. To avoid being ripped off when you purchase a living trust, watch for these telltale signs of a scam:

- ✔ The living trust salesperson wants to sell you a standardized trust agreement. Do not purchase a trust unless the agreement is going to be tailored to meet your particular needs. Avoid fill-in-the-blanks agreements.

- ✔ You're contacted about buying a living trust over the phone or via a direct-mail solicitation.

- ✔ You attend an estate-planning seminar, and the sole purpose of the seminar is to get you to buy a living trust.

- ✔ The person who tries to sell you a living trust does not seem to care about whether you really need one or about how it will work with your will and with any other estate planning you may have done. Instead, the salesperson either touts a trust as an estate-planning panacea or tries to scare you into buying one by exaggerating the time it will take for your estate to get through probate and how much probate will cost. Truth is, depending on your state and on the thoroughness of your estate planning, the probate process may not be nearly as time-consuming as some people want you to believe. Furthermore, the cost of establishing and administering a trust may not justify the advantage of avoiding probate.

Planning for the End of Your Life

The cost of life-sustaining medical care and treatment can be astronomical. Even with good insurance, it can eat up every extra penny you have, leaving little or nothing of your estate to pass on to those you care about. Therefore, a growing number of people are making end-of-life planning part of their estate planning.

End-of-life planning lets you take control of your own death. By completing the appropriate legal forms, you can dictate the kinds of medical treatment and care you want and don't want when death is near and you can't speak for yourself. Such planning spares your loved ones from the possibility that they may have to make those gut-wrenching decisions for you.

Accomplishing such planning is surprisingly easy. All it takes is writing a living will and preparing a durable power of attorney for healthcare. You may also want to arrange for your organs to be donated to someone else or for your body to be used for medical research or training.

The generic term for a living will and a durable power of attorney for healthcare is *advance directive*.

Having the last word

A living will gives you the opportunity to have the last word about the medical care and treatment you receive when you're too ill or injured to speak for yourself and death is near. The typical living will addresses issues related to life support and forced nutrition, but it can deal with much more. At a minimum, your living will should address the following:

- ✔ Do you want to be resuscitated or hooked up to a respirator or mechanical ventilator?

- ✔ Do you want to be fed through tubes? What about hydration tubes?

- ✔ Do you want invasive surgery? Under what circumstances do you want or not want such surgery?

- ✔ Under what circumstances do you want such treatments as chemotherapy, radiotherapy, and so on?

- ✔ Do you want to receive blood transfusions, kidney dialysis, or cardiopulmonary resuscitation?

- ✔ What are your desires regarding pain medication?

Your living will can also indicate whom you want (or don't want) to be with you when you die, what personal items you want in view of your deathbed, and where you want to die.

The federal Patient Self Determination Act says that hospitals that accept Medicaid and Medicare funds, as well as health maintenance organizations (HMOs), nursing homes, and home healthcare providers, must inform their patients about their right to make their own end-of-life treatment decisions.

Sources of living wills

You can write your own living will; you can hire an attorney to draft one for you; or you can use a fill-in-the-blank living will form. If you write your own, make sure that you comply with your state's requirements for a legally valid living will. Usually, those requirements mirror the requirements for a legally valid will. For example, your living will must be witnessed and notarized.

If you use a fill-in-the-blanks living will, be sure that it's specific to your state. If it isn't, the document you end up with will not be legally binding. You may be able to purchase such a form at your local office supply store or get one for free from your doctor, local hospital, or area agency on aging.

Form 14-13 provides a Partnership for Caring sample living will for Texas, and Form 14-14 provides one for Connecticut.

Two excellent sources for a fill-in-the-blanks living will are Partnership for Caring and Aging with Dignity, both of which are national nonprofit organizations. Their forms are available online.

Partnership for Caring offers legally valid state-specific living will forms, as well as durable power of attorney for healthcare forms, for all 50 states and for the District of Columbia. You can download both by going to www. partnershipforcaring.org/ad.htm. You can also order a package of both forms for your state by calling 800-989-9455 or 410-962-5454. You must pay $5 plus the applicable state tax if you don't order online.

Aging with Dignity has created an exceptionally detailed "Five Wishes" living will that is legally valid in most states. Find out more about this particular living will by reading "An option to consider" later in this chapter. You can also learn more by going to the organization's Web site at www.agingwithdignity.org or by calling 850-681-2010.

If you have a vacation home in a state other than the state where your primary residence is located, or if you spend a lot of time in another state, you should prepare a legally valid living will for each state.

Knowing what to do with your living will

Once you have a living will, make copies of it and give one to your spouse, to other close family members, to your unmarried partner, to whoever has durable power of attorney for your healthcare, and to anyone else you want to know about your wishes. Make sure that your doctor has a copy. If you end up in a nursing home, hospital, or some other care facility, it should have a copy of your living will on file. Store your original living will in an accessible but safe location — not in your bank safe deposit box. That way, if it's needed, your spouse, adult child, or whoever can get to it right away.

To avoid the potential for problems when it comes time to activate your living will, sit down with the people who are closest to you and walk them through it. (You should have this same conversation with the person to whom you give a durable power of attorney for your healthcare, and with your doctor.) Explain why you made the choices you did and answer their questions. Open, honest communication about your living will can make it easier for your loved ones to accept your wishes and act on them when the time comes. Such a meeting also minimizes the potential for conflict among your loved ones about your end-of-life desires and minimizes any guilt your loved ones might have if your living will is activated. Talking about these things helps get your living will activated if your doctor refuses to comply with its directives. Family members may have to hire an elder law attorney and use the courts to get this done.

Some states prosecute doctors who refuse to obey the wishes a patient has expressed in a living will. However, all states exempt doctors from prosecution if a patient dies because doctors complied with her living will.

Revisit your living will every year or so to ensure that the wishes you expressed when you wrote it still stand. Some states require you to periodically prepare a new living will to maintain the validity of your end-of-life wishes.

In many states, your doctor must get a second opinion before acting on your living will. Both doctors have to certify in writing that you are unable to make your own decisions and are near death with no possibility of recovery. If your doctor is uncomfortable with your living will requests, he must bring in a doctor who is willing to follow through on your wishes.

If you don't have a living will

If you don't have a living will and you become terminally ill or injured and can't speak for yourself, your doctor's inclination may be to try to keep you alive at all costs. However, your doctor will consult with your spouse and other members of your immediate family, or maybe with a close friend if you have no family. As you might imagine, if that happens, making life-and-death decisions on your behalf without direction from you is likely to be extremely difficult for those who care about you.

If your family and your doctor disagree about what should be done, your family may have to initiate a lawsuit to get their wishes acted on. Even worse, what your family wants could run contrary to what you would have indicated if you had written a living will.

An option to consider

Aging with Dignity (www.agingwithdignity.org) is a national organization that deals with end-of-life issues. It has developed an exceptionally clear and detailed living will form that it calls "Five Wishes." Those five wishes are

1. Who should make medical decisions for you when you can't make them for yourself?

2. What you do want and don't want in the way of medical treatment?

3. How comfortable do you want to be? For example, do you want to be pain-free even if the necessary medication will make you drowsy?

4. How do you want people to treat you? Do you want people to be with you when you die if possible, and do you want your hand held? Do you want prayers said at your bedside, and do you want to die at home if possible?

5. What do you want your loved ones to know? For example, are there relatives with whom you want to make amends? Do you want your loved ones to make peace with one another before you die?

To read more about the Five Wishes and to order a copy of the living will form, call Aging with Dignity at 850-681-2010. The form will cost you $5 plus handling and shipping.

Changing your mind

You can cancel or modify your living will whenever you want, even if you are extremely ill or injured. Before you do, however, find out your state's requirements so that you can be sure that your revocation or change is legally valid. Depending on your state, to cancel your living will, you may be able to tear it up, write "revoked" or "cancelled" across the top, verbally state that you are canceling it, or signal with a hand gesture that you do not want your doctor to abide by your living will.

 When you cancel your living will, make sure that you get back any copies from other people as well as a hospital, nursing home, and so on. Then rip them up or run them through your home shredder.

Durable Power of Attorney for Healthcare

A durable power of attorney for healthcare is a legal document that gives someone else the right to make healthcare decisions on your behalf if you are unable to. You do not need to be terminally ill for this person to make those decisions.

This document should express the kinds of medical treatment and care you do and do not want. It can also address your values and desires regarding pain and other quality-of-life issues at the end of your life. The more specific you are, the better, because there's less room for conflict over what you really want, and you provide the person who has power of attorney with the guidance she needs to make difficult decisions for you.

When you prepare your durable power of attorney document, make sure that you explicitly state that it's durable. It's a good idea to prepare this power of attorney at the same time that you write your living will and to make everyone who knows about your living will familiar with this other legal document as well. The person you give durable power of attorney for healthcare can

- ✔ Take steps to activate your living will if your doctor or a family member interferes with it. This action can include going to court.

- ✔ Make medical and health decisions for you when you're dying. In some states, this person can also make those decisions for you when you are incapacitated but expected to recover.

- ✔ Arrange for you to be moved to a hospital, nursing home, or hospice.

- ✔ Move you to another state if you expressed that wish in your living will or power of attorney document.

- ✔ Release your medical files and apply for medical benefits on your behalf.

Obviously, the person to whom you entrust decisions related to your life and death should be someone you trust and you believe has good judgment. It goes without saying as well that this person should be willing to accept the responsibility. You may not want to give this responsibility to your spouse or unmarried partner because it may be difficult, if not impossible, for him to push for the enactment of your living will when the time comes.

In addition to giving someone a durable power of attorney for healthcare, you may want to give someone a durable power of attorney. The person with this kind of power of attorney has decision-making powers over your financial and business affairs, not over your health. This person manages your affairs if you became too ill or incapacitated to do so yourself.

Every state has its own requirements regarding what makes a durable power of attorney for healthcare legally binding. The same resources that provide information about living wills can fill you in on the requirements for this legal document. Partnership for Caring and Aging with Dignity (see the preceding section) are sources of this information. Each organization also offers fill-in-the-blanks forms that you can use.

Some states restrict to whom you can give durable power of attorney for healthcare. For example, they may prohibit you from choosing your doctor or your residential caregiver.

To avoid confusion, the instructions in your power of attorney regarding end-of-life care should mirror those in your living will. If you write your own durable power of attorney for healthcare, be sure to have a lawyer review it so that you know it meets the letter of the law in your state and the lawyer can reword anything unclear or ambiguous.

If you have already prepared your living will and you hire an attorney to either write your durable power of attorney for healthcare or review your draft, give her a copy of the living will so she can make sure that the documents complement one another. If they conflict, the validity of one or both could be questioned.

After you prepare a durable power of attorney for healthcare

It's a good idea to periodically review your durable power of attorney for healthcare to make sure it continues to express your wishes. If you want to change something in it, make the change in accordance with the laws of your state. If you want to cancel it, prepare a formal revocation notice. Be sure that you get back all old copies of the durable power of attorney, and if you change it, ensure that everyone gets the new, revised power of attorney document.

Benefiting the world even after you're gone

The federal Uniform Anatomical Gift Act allows anyone 18 years and older to donate his organs and tissues when he dies so that they can be transplanted into someone else or used in a medical teaching hospital or in scientific research. To become an organ donor, you fill out a donor card, sign it, and have it witnessed. Then you keep it with you at all times. Some states allow you to become an organ donor when you get or renew your driver's license. In those states, your wishes are printed on the back of your license.

When you die, even if you have a signed and witnessed organ donor card, your family must sign a consent form allowing your organs and tissues to be donated. To help ensure that they sign this form, make them aware of your wishes before you die and address any reservations they have about respecting them.

Part IV
Home Matters

The 5th Wave   By Rich Tennant

"I swear, Frank, it's not a pyramid scam. You help a few guys with their home improvements and then, after you bring in ten friends, you'll be enjoying each and every Saturday as much as I do."

In this part . . .

Putting a roof over your head is no simple matter, whether you're already a homeowner, you want to become one, or you're content to rent. Chapter 15 guides you through the home-buying process, from finding a real estate agent or broker to closing the deal. Chapter 16 gives you the information you need to get a good deal on a mortgage. If you already own a home but want to make it bigger or better, read Chapter 17 before you hire a contractor to help you. Chapter 18 is for those who want to rent rather than buy a place to live. It gives you the lowdown on leases and advises you about the best way to deal with conflicts, including evictions.

Chapter 15

Buying or Selling Your Home

· ·

· ·

*B*ecoming the official owner of a new home or receiving the money you're entitled to for selling your home is a momentous occasion. But the process that gets you to that day can be confusing, stressful, and full of potential stumbling blocks and legal perils.

As with other important financial transactions, understanding the basics of the home-buying and -selling process, and knowing what to consider at each decision-making milestone, can help minimize your anxieties and increase the likelihood that you make wise choices. This chapter walks you through these processes, tells you the ins and outs of making a deal, and explains what happens at a real estate closing or settlement. It also highlights the services a real estate agent can offer and explains how to find a good agent.

Compared to sellers, buyers tend to have more to do and more issues to consider. Therefore, a lot of this chapter focuses on buyers, but it offers sellers plenty of information, too. For example, we tell sellers about listing agents and listing agreements and provide advice about how to sell their homes without the help of a real estate agent.

Buying or Selling a Home: The Steps

Every residential real estate transaction follows a fairly predictable path. Sure, you may experience twists and turns along the way, but in the end, before you can get the keys to your new home or count the dollars you made on the sale of your home, you must take certain steps.

The specific steps you take along the path depend on whether you are a buyer or a seller. Buyers take more steps because they not only have to locate a home to buy, but also have to apply for and obtain a mortgage.

Moving toward homeownership

Buyers, here's an overview of the basic steps you take toward homeownership:

- ✔ Decide what you want in a new home and how much home you can afford to spend.

    Asking a mortgage lender to prequalify you for a loan helps you zero in on what price range of home you can afford. You're not obligated to apply for a mortgage with the lender who prequalifies you.

- ✔ Decide whether you want to work with a real estate agent.

- ✔ Research your mortgage and mortgage lender options.

- ✔ After you find a home to buy, make the seller a written purchase offer, negotiate the terms of your offer, and sign a purchase agreement with the seller.

- ✔ Apply for a mortgage and do everything your contract obligates you to do by the stated deadlines.

- ✔ Go to your real estate closing.

- ✔ Enjoy your new home.

Selling your home

Sellers have it easy compared to buyers. They have to find someone to buy their home, usually with the help of a real estate agent, and to prepare for the real estate closing according to the terms of the purchase contract. At the closing, the buyer becomes the official owner of the home. Sellers, here's the least you must do to get your home sold:

- ✔ Decide whether to sell your home yourself or hire a real estate agent to do it.

- ✔ Put your house on the market.

- ✔ Negotiate the details of your sale with a qualified buyer, and then sign a purchase agreement with the buyer after you iron everything out.

- ✔ Meet all your contractual obligations.

- ✔ Prepare for the real estate closing so that the ownership of your home can be legally transferred to the buyer.

- ✔ Count your money.

Form 15-1 on the CD provides an overview of the responsibilities you assume when you sell your own home.

Working with an Agent or Going It Alone

Most people hire a real estate agent to help them with the nuts and bolts of buying or selling a home. However, you may feel comfortable handling everything yourself. Before you decide which option is better for you, it's a good idea to understand the services a real estate agent provides. A real estate agent can help a buyer

- ✔ Define your new home wants.

- ✔ Find homes for sale that fit your needs and your budget.

- ✔ Prepare a written purchase offer when you find a home to buy.

- ✔ Present your offer to the seller in the most favorable light.

- ✔ Negotiate the terms of your purchase with the seller.

- ✔ Find a home inspector, mortgage lender, and so on.

- ✔ Prepare for the real estate closing — the last step in the home-buying process.

A real estate agent can help a seller

- ✔ **Set a realistic asking price for your home.** To do so, the agent should perform a comparative market analysis (CMA) for your home. This analysis takes into consideration the state of the economy in your area — whether it's improving or slowing down, whether a lot of people are moving into your community, and how much homes like yours have been listed for and sold for recently. The analysis also reflects anything unique about your home — a newly redone kitchen, exceptional landscaping, a pool or tennis court, and so on.

- ✔ **Market your home.** Most likely, your agent will post a "For Sale" sign in your yard and list your home on a local Multiple Listings Service (MLS) database, which may also include a listing on the Internet. The agent should also advertise your home in the real estate section of your local paper. Your agent might also post photos and a description of your home on her real estate agency's Web site, advertise it on another real estate Web site, host an open house, or feature your home in a direct-mail piece.

- ✔ **Show your home.** The agent should give prospective buyers tours of your house. If you're like many sellers, you may feel uncomfortable having a bunch of strangers parade through your home while you're there, asking questions, making critical comments, and so on.

✔ **Select buyers.** Your agent should screen out buyers who aren't serious about your home or who don't have the financial capacity to buy it. This is important because some people may want to see your home out of curiosity, not because they're really in the market for a home like yours.

✔ **Provide the proper paperwork.** The agent should make sure that you provide buyers with all the necessary legal disclosures.

✔ **Negotiate the sale.** The agent should negotiate the nitty-gritty terms of a contract for sale with an interested and qualified buyer.

Your agent is legally obligated to show you all offers, even the ridiculous ones.

✔ **Help clean up.** Your agent should help you meet all your contractual obligations to the buyer by the agreed-upon deadlines, including delivering a clear title to the buyer and taking care of all your closing-related responsibilities.

Selling Your Own Home

If you decide to join the ranks of the estimated 15 percent of homeowners who sell their homes on their own, it's important to take special precautions to ensure that you sell your home for a fair price and protect your legal interests. Those precautions include

✔ **Hiring a real estate attorney.** The attorney can brief you on your legal responsibilities, tell you how the selling process works in your area, and help ensure that the purchase agreement you sign protects your interests. The attorney can also help you negotiate the agreement with the seller and represent you at the real estate closing. In some areas, real estate attorneys are rarely used in residential real estate transactions. Even so, if you're selling your own home, it's a good idea to consult with one to ensure that your home sale goes smoothly.

✔ **Getting your home appraised so you know how much to ask for it.** A professional appraisal costs between $200 and $400. Other ways to arrive at a realistic asking price include

- Looking in your newspaper's real estate classifieds section to see how much homes comparable to yours are listed for.

- Using the Web to get an approximate value for your home. Some sites to check out are SmartHomeBuy (www2.smarthomebuy.com), Homeadvisor.com (homeadvisor.msn.com), RealHome.com (www.realhome.com/shr/reg/reg00006.cfm), and Realtor.com (www.realtor.com).

In some regions, real estate brokers offer a *broker price opinion,* which is like an appraisal but is less expensive.

✔ **Marketing your home.** Purchase a "For Sale" sign for your yard, buy ads in the real estate section of your local newspaper, let your friends, family, and coworkers know that you're selling your home, and produce a simple flyer that provides basic information about your home that buyers would want to know. You may also want to use the Internet to market your home. The sidebar "Home sites" highlights real estate Web sites that you may want to check out.

Real Estate Agent, Broker, Realtor: Who Are These People?

If you decide to work with a real estate agent, one of the things you will notice almost right away is that some refer to themselves as real estate agents, and others call themselves brokers or Realtors. Although the words are often used interchangeably, they do not mean the same thing.

A *real estate agent* is someone who sells real estate. She has taken a certain number of hours of real estate classes and has passed a standardized state test to become licensed as an agent by her state. Agents must work under the supervision of a broker.

A *broker* is a licensed real estate agent who has earned the right to own and manage his own real estate business or brokerage. A brokerage can be an individual, a large national company such as Caldwell Banker, or a smaller local real estate company.

The standards for becoming a broker vary among states, but they're more stringent than the requirements for becoming an agent. They usually include taking additional higher-level real estate classes and passing a second state exam.

Every state has an office that sets licensing requirements for real estate agents and brokers, regulates their activities and actions, and disciplines agents and brokers as necessary. In most states, this office is called a *real estate commission,* but it may have a different name in your state. Want to contact your state's real estate commission? Form 15-1 on the CD provides state-by-state contact information.

A *Realtor* is a real estate agent or broker who is a member of the National Association of Realtors (NAR). NAR members are expected to live up to the organization's code of ethics. Consumers who have a complaint against a NAR member can file the complaint with their local NAR organization as well as with their state's real estate commission.

Home pages

The Internet is becoming a powerful tool for buyers and sellers. Real estate Web sites provide useful information about the buying and selling process, let sellers reach many more buyers than they could ever hope to reach with just a yard sign or a traditional real estate ad, and allow buyers to shop for a home any hour of the day or night by using their home computers.

Real estate companies and local real estate organizations are increasing their use of the Internet. Many now have their own Web sites where they provide educational information as well as listings. For example, many local real estate boards have a version of their MLS that consumers can access online. Although the following Web sites are just a drop in the bucket when it comes to real estate Web sites, they're a good place to start when you want to buy or sell a home.

- **Buyityourself.com** (http://buyityourself.com). You can post up to five color photos of your home on your own Web page at this site. Your Web page can include a phone number that interested buyers can call to learn more about your home or to schedule a time to see it.

- **The Home Buyer's Information Center** (www.ourfamilyplace.com/homebuyer). This site provides you with helpful home-buying hints, to-do lists, and a lot of information about finding and working with an agent, getting a home inspected, and applying for a mortgage.

- **Homes.com** (www.homes.com). This site offers buyers more than 700,000 homes to

choose from, plus comprehensive neighborhood and property reports.

- **The Home Seller's Information Center** (www.ourfamilyplace.com/homeseller). At this site, you can find advice and information about selling your own home, working with an agent, valuing your home, preparing it to sell, and so on.

- **Owners.com** (www.owners.com). This site claims to have the greatest number of for-sale-by-owner homes on the Web. Buyers can search for a home to buy by specifying the area of country they want to live in, the size of home they're looking for, the number of bedrooms they need, and their price range. Sellers can market their homes by purchasing virtual tour ads and posting Owners.com "For Sale" signs in their yards, among other things. Other features of this site include community and school reports, maps, and a kit to help sellers hold their own open houses.

- **Realtor.com** (www.realtor.com). The National Association of Realtors Web site has something for everyone. Use it to educate yourself about the buying and selling process, to locate a home to buy, to price comparable properties, and to find a Realtor.

- **4salebyowner.com** (www.4salebowner.com). This Web site may be just what you need. You can post color photos of your home on your own Web page ad and turn your ad into a sales flyer. This Web site claims to be the busiest for-sale-by-owner site on the Internet.

If you want access to your area's MLS, work with an agent who is a member of your local Board of Realtors. Agents who are not members do not have access to that information.

When deciding whom to hire, you should be less concerned about titles, and more concerned about the experience and qualifications of the real estate professional you hire and whether you feel comfortable with the person.

Listing your home for sale

The agent you hire to sell your home is referred to as your *listing agent*. The agent will require that you sign a listing agreement or legally binding contract that spells out the terms of your relationship.

Read the agreement carefully to be sure that it protects your interests, minimizes your out-of-pocket expenses, and provides the agent with a strong incentive to sell your home. Most likely, the agent will use a standard fill-in-the-blanks form. At a minimum, the agreement should reflect

- ✔ **Duration:** Most agents want a listing that lasts at least 6 months, but they usually try for a listing with a duration of at least 12 months. The drawback of a long listing agreement is that if you become unhappy with the job your agent is doing for you during the term of the agreement, you may have to pay a substantial penalty to break the contract.

  Don't sign a listing agreement that automatically renews when its term is up.

- ✔ **Cancellation penalty:** Depending on the terms of the listing agreement, you may have to pay a penalty if you cancel the agreement before its term is up.

- ✔ **Price:** The agreement should specify your asking price as well as how much you're willing to accept if you can't get it.

- ✔ **Sales commission:** Most agent commissions are between 5 and 7 percent of the selling price. Also include when the agent is entitled to receive a commission. Usually, the commission is not payable unless your home is sold.

- ✔ **Showing:** The contract should address who can show your home. Usually, the best deal for you is an agreement that allows other agents besides the listing agent to show your home to potential buyers. The more qualified buyers who see it, the more likely your home will sell quickly.

- ✔ **Self sale:** The contract should address whether you can sell your home yourself, and if you can and you find your own buyer, what portion of the sales commission, if any, your listing agent is entitled to.

Consider all the provisions in a listing agreement negotiable. However, be careful not to negotiate such favorable terms for yourself that you take away your agent's incentive to work hard to sell your home.

The terms of your listing agreement can mean more or less money in your pocket when you sell your home. Therefore, before you sign the agreement, it's a good idea to pay a real estate attorney to review it to point out things to change and add. However, don't look to an attorney for advice about how much to ask for your home or for other terms of sale. Those matters do not fall within the typical attorney's areas of expertise. However, the attorney can help you be sure that the listing agreement adequately protects you before you sign it.

Agents, agents, and more agents

It used to be that when you looked for a home to buy, the agents you dealt with, as helpful and nice as they might be, actually represented the seller, not you. Therefore, they were legally obligated to look out for the seller's best interests, which included maximizing a home's selling price. Furthermore, because the agent's commission was tied to the selling price, the agent had a financial incentive to sell the home for as much as possible. As a result, buyers were ultimately on their own when they negotiated to buy a home.

Things are beginning to improve for buyers. For example, a new kind of agent is increasingly common — a buyer's agent. This agent works only with buyers. Also, a growing number of states now permit an agent to represent either the buyer or the seller in a real estate transaction, as long as the agent discloses up front who he is representing. Yet another improvement for buyers in many states is a requirement that an agent let a buyer know up front whether he works for the same real estate agency as the seller's listing agent. Agents who fail to make the appropriate disclosures are breaking state law and will be penalized.

When you're looking for an agent to help you, you may encounter a couple other types of agents.

✔ **Dual agent:** This person represents both the seller and the buyer in a real estate transaction. Working with this kind of agent may not serve the interests of either party, because it's difficult, if not impossible, for most dual agents to truly look out for the interests of both the buyer and the seller. Conflict arises when the buyer wants to get as good a deal as possible on a home and the seller wants to make as much as possible from the sale of her home. Depending on your state, a dual agency relationship could also exist if you and a seller each have your own agents but they both work for the same broker. Because of the inherent potential for conflict in a dual agent relationship, dual agents are illegal in some states.

In states where dual agents are legal, dual agents must disclose their role to buyer and seller so that both parties have the option of finding another agent to represent them if they feel uncomfortable working with a dual agent. Although state laws vary, a dual agent may be prohibited from sharing certain information with one or the other parties in a real estate transaction without getting written permission from the other party first.

✔ **Transactional agent:** Depending on your state, you may also have the option of working with a *transactional agent*. In some states, this is another term for a dual agent, but in other states, a transactional agent is a little different. This person is a neutral party who represents neither the seller nor the buyer. She is legally obligated to treat both of you fairly and is prohibited from revealing your confidences to the other. If you're frustrated by this arrangement because you need advice or information from someone who's looking out for your interests only, go to the agent's broker and ask to have someone assigned to work with just you. You can do the same thing if you're in a dual agent relationship.

If your state does not require disclosures, be careful about the information you share with an agent. If it's helpful to the seller, the agent might pass it on.

Using a buyer's agent

If you're buying in a state where most agents work for sellers, hiring a buyer's agent is a good idea. You are *numero uno* with this kind of agent. The agent gives you the full scoop on the home you like and helps you negotiate the most advantageous terms of purchase.

Be sure to get a written contract from the buyer's agent you want to hire. At a minimum, the contract should address

✔ **Payment arrangements:** The agent can charge a flat fee, bill you by the hour, or take a percentage of your purchase price. Make sure that the contract spells out under what conditions you are legally obligated to pay the agent.

A buyer's agent who takes a percentage of your purchase price may not help you negotiate a low price. However, most buyer's agents are reputable professionals who look out for their clients' best interests.

If you don't have the cash you need to pay your buyer's agent, your lender may be willing to let you finance the cost, or you can include a provision in your purchase offer requiring the seller to pay it.

✔ **Services:** The contract should specify the specific services the agent will provide to you.

✔ **Duration:** Most buyers' agents expect a six-month to twelve-month contract. Anything less may not give them adequate time to find you a home that meets your needs.

✔ **Cancellation:** The contract should address how to cancel it and the amount of the cancellation penalty.

If you don't work with a buyer's agent, hire an attorney to help you prepare a written purchase offer when you find a home to buy. The attorney can help you make sure that your interests are protected.

Hiring the best agent

A good real estate agent can make just about everything easier when it comes to buying or selling a home. A bad agent can be a waste of money. Therefore, whether you are a buyer or a seller, look for a real estate agent who is

✔ **Experienced.** Hire an agent who has worked full-time in the real estate profession for at least a couple of years — the more experience, the better.

✔ **Known for handling properties like the one you want to buy or sell.** Agents tend to handle certain kinds of homes in certain types of neighborhoods — older or newer homes, inner-city or suburban neighborhoods, and so on. They also tend to handle homes in a particular price range. Therefore, if you want an older home in a downtown neighborhood and you can spend up to $200,000, don't hire an agent who sells homes in suburban subdivisions priced in the $50,000 range.

✔ **A subscriber to your local Multiple Listing Service (MLS).** The MLS is a computerized database of homes for sale that other subscribers can access. If you're a seller, it's a cost-effective way to advertise your home to a broad number of agents with potential buyers. If you're a buyer, the MLS is an easy way to find out about the homes that are available to you.

✔ **Sensitive to your needs and concerns.** When you feel comfortable with an agent, the buying or selling process is a lot less stressful.

✔ **Reputable in the local real estate community.** An agent with a reputation for professionalism and integrity can facilitate your negotiations and sometimes help you get the mortgage you need.

The best way to find a good real estate agent is to get references from friends or family members who have bought or sold homes recently and who liked the agents they worked with. You can also get agent names from the real estate listings in your local newspaper, from real estate "For Sale" signs in your neighborhood or in the neighborhood where you want to live, and from real estate Web sites. Meet face to face with the agents you're referred to so you can judge them for yourself.

If you're looking for a listing agent, the agents should visit your home so they can assess its strengths and weaknesses, determine a realistic asking price, and suggest things you can do to make your home more saleable. Each of them should also provide a written marketing plan that spells out exactly what they intend to do to sell your home.

Don't let an agent's flashy marketing plan cloud your judgment. What will get your house sold is how hard the agent works to sell your home, her experience, and the kind of networks and connections she has.

Handling problems with your agent

If you're unhappy with the real estate agent you hire, politely let the agent know what's bothering you. If the agent is unresponsive, write a letter to the agent's broker. You can find a sample complaint letter on Form 15-2 on the CD. If the agent works for a large real estate firm, you may want to let the broker know that you want to work with a different agent.

Your other options are to find a new agent after your contract expires or to break your contract. Consult a real estate attorney before you break a contract so you do it in a way that minimizes the potential for a lawsuit.

If you feel that a real estate agent has treated you unfairly, or you believe that an agent has broken the law, contact your state's real estate commission or whatever department licenses real estate professionals in your state. If the agent is a Realtor, you can also contact your local association of Realtors. It may help you resolve your problem and even discipline the agent if it decides that the agent acted unethically.

Making the Deal

You've found a home to buy. Now what? You prepare a written purchase offer and present it to the seller. A *purchase offer* is a multi-page document stating how much you're offering to pay for the home, plus all the other terms and conditions of your offer.

Depending on your state, a purchase offer may be called a purchase contract, binder, purchase agreement, earnest money contract, escrow contract, or deposit receipt.

If you're working with an agent, he helps you prepare your offer and also meets with the seller's listing agent to present it and to answer any questions. Rather than start from scratch, if the agent is a Realtor, he probably uses a fill-in-the-blank purchase offer that complies with the laws of your state. You can find a sample purchase offer on Form 15-3 of the CD.

To be sure that your purchase offer fully protects your interests, have a real estate attorney review it before your agent submits it to the seller. Involving a lawyer is especially important if the agent you're working with is representing the seller and not you. Your attorney can also help you decide how to respond to any counteroffers the seller makes.

Before you make an offer on a home, consider how much you have to spend on property taxes and home maintenance. High property taxes and maintenance expenses can make a reasonably priced home unaffordable. If you can't afford to maintain your new home, it deteriorates and loses value. Maintenance expenses are particularly important when you buy an older home. Depending on the terms of your mortgage, your property taxes may be rolled into your monthly mortgage payment and deposited in a special escrow account. The lender uses those funds to pay the taxes for you when they come due. Therefore, the amount you pay each month for your mortgage is higher than if your loan payments do not include taxes.

If you're making an offer on a home in a brand-new subdivision, your agent might present your offer to a subdivision salesperson, not to a listing agent.

The seller can accept your offer, reject it, or come back with a counteroffer that includes a higher price and different terms of sale that are more advantageous to him. If the seller counters, it's your turn to decide on a response. Back-and-forth negotiations continue until you and the seller agree on every term of sale or until one of you refuses to negotiate any more. If you and the seller come to an agreement, you both sign your agreement offer and enter into a legally binding contract with one another.

In some areas, when a buyer and seller come to an agreement, they sign a *binder,* which outlines the most basic terms of their deal — purchase price, closing date, address of home, and so on. You pay the seller a small deposit when you sign the binder. A binder is a symbol of your intention and the seller's to enter into a contract with one another. After you sign the binder, you negotiate the details of your deal.

Covering all your bases with a good offer

Your purchase offer spells out the terms of your deal with the seller. Although it's easy to focus all your attention on how much money you're going to pay for the home you want to buy, other terms of your offer are equally important. They provide you with legal and financial protections and affect the amount of money you pay at closing.

Furthermore, an informed seller considers more than just how much you want to pay for his home when evaluating your offer and deciding how to respond to it. The seller also takes into account the closing costs you want him to pay, how quickly you can close, whether your offer is all cash, what your offer is contingent upon, and so on.

Although you can add provisions, your purchase offer should include all of the following:

- Your name, the seller's name, the street address of the home you want to buy, a legal description of the home, and your proposed purchase price.

- The specific items you want to convey with the home. They may include kitchen appliances, a custom-made chandelier, a portable storage shed, and so on. (Doorknobs, built-in furniture and lighting, drapes, and blinds, among other things, are generally assumed to come with a home, so they aren't addressed in an offer.)

- Whether you're making an all-cash offer or your offer is subject to your obtaining a mortgage.

- Who is responsible for the title search — you or the seller. The section "Easing your mind with escape clauses" later in this chapter tells you about the title search.

- How much cash you put down as *earnest money,* who will hold the money until the closing, and under what circumstances you can get the money back. You pay earnest money to the seller to demonstrate that you're serious about buying the home. This money is payable to the seller when you make your offer and tells the seller that you're a serious buyer. Typically, once you pay the earnest money, the seller stops showing his home to other potential buyers. If your purchase goes through, the money is applied to your down payment. Your deposit may be held by the seller's listing agent, an escrow or title company, or an attorney.

- How you and the seller share prepaid expenses such as property taxes, water and sewer charges, utility bills, and condominium or co-op fees. Ordinarily, you are responsible for only the portion of those expenses that applies once you become the home's owner.

- Who pays for a property survey to determine the legal boundaries of the home you're buying.

Don't assume that a fence line, a wall, or shrubbery accurately defines where the property you want to buy begins and ends. That assumption could cause you problems later. For example, after you cut down a tree that you thought was on your property, suppose your neighbor informs you that the tree belonged to him. Or suppose your neighbor's new deck extends onto what you thought was your property, destroying your privacy. Unless you and your neighbor can work out your difficulties, you could become estranged and even end up suing one another. To help minimize the potential for such problems, ask the seller who owns the fence, wall, and other features that appear to be on the property. Also, find out who is responsible for the upkeep of these features, who can take them down, and so on.

✔ **Who pays for pest inspections.** The seller pays if there is an outstanding mortgage on their property. Some standard purchase-offer forms require sellers to provide buyers with written proof that they recently inspected their home for pests. At closing, your mortgage lender may require that you present proof that the home you're buying is free of termites and other pests.

✔ **Who pays to test for environmental hazards** such as radon, lead, asbestos, leaking underground oil tanks, and so on, and what happens if any hazards are found. Your local or state government may mandate certain tests and even require sellers to handle the necessary cleanup.

Lead-based paint can cause neurological damage in young children. Federal law says that for a home built before 1978, the seller must tell you anything he knows about the existence of lead-based paint. However, the seller may not be aware of any such paint. It's important to test for lead in a home. Federal law gives you ten days after you sign a purchase agreement to cancel your offer and get your money back if lead-based paint is found. Some state laws go even further. They say that a seller must clean up lead-based paint before she puts her home on the market.

The seller or seller's agent must give you an EPA brochure titled *Protect Your Family from Lead in Your Home* or an EPA-approved publication on the subject.

✔ **How you share closing costs with the seller.** In some regions, it's customary for sellers to pay certain costs, but you can suggest any arrangement you want. Your agent can tell you who usually pays what.

✔ **A proposed date, time, and location for your real estate closing.** Turn to the section "Closing the Deal" later in this chapter to find out about closings.

✔ **When you want to take possession of your new home.** It usually happens at closing.

✔ **Your right to a final inspection or walk-through.** This happens just before closing.

✔ **All the contingencies that you want to apply to your offer.** The section "Easing your mind with escape clauses," on the following page, discusses contingencies.

✔ **Whether you're buying the home as is** or you want the seller to warranty, or guarantee, that all the home's systems and other components are free of defects when you take possession.

✔ **What happens if the home you're buying is damaged or destroyed before you take possession.** The damage could occur because of vandalism, fire, bad weather, an earthquake, a flood, or some other act of nature. Your options include reserving the right to cancel your purchase, requiring that the seller repair the damage up to a certain dollar amount, or buying the house as is.

✔ What happens if you or the seller cancels your contract. Usually, if the cancellation happens because an agreed-upon contingency was met, you or the seller can get out of the deal, no questions asked.

If you withdraw your offer after you have a legally binding contract, the seller can sue you for breach of contract. You face the greatest risk for such a lawsuit when the seller's listing agreement says that she must pay her listing agent a sales commission when the seller accepts a purchase offer, not when the sale is actually completed.

Easing your mind with escape clauses

Most purchase offers include several different contingency clauses. Each clause provides a reason for a buyer to cancel his contract with the seller and get his deposit back. The most common contingency clauses include a financing contingency clause giving you the right to cancel your purchase if you can't get a bank to give you a mortgage commitment that meets the criteria for a loan that you spelled out in your offer. Usually, those criteria cover the amount of money you're borrowing, the kind of mortgage you're applying for, the duration of the loan, the maximum interest rate at which you're willing to borrow the money, and the date by which you will have a written loan commitment. Your offer may be cancelled automatically if you don't meet that deadline, or the seller may have the option to give you more time to arrange your financing.

For an idea of how to word this contingency clause, read Form 15-4 on the CD.

In some states, no matter what kills your real estate deal, it takes the signatures of both the seller and the buyer or a court action to liberate escrow monies.

Inspection contingency clauses

Another typical escape clause relates to inspections. It may allow you to get out of the deal if a professional inspection of the home uncovers serious problems, or it may obligate the seller to clear up any problems so that your deal can go though.

An inspection contingency clause gives you the right to have the home you're buying professionally inspected for defects. The clause should state what happens if defects are found. The seller may get a certain amount of time to correct them, but you may prefer a clause that gives you the right to cancel your deal and get your deposit back. Form 15-5 provides a sample inspection contingency clause.

For added protection, your inspection contingency clause can address a general inspection as well as any specialized follow-up inspections that are necessary. You may want to include separate inspection contingency clauses for pests, environmental hazards, and so on.

Title contingency clauses

A good title contingency gives you the right to cancel your purchase if a title search turns up problems with the home's title. The results of the title search may be presented in an abstract of title. You should receive a copy of the abstract, which tells you who owns the home and the form of legal ownership and provides you with its ownership history. The search might also turn up outstanding liens or restrictive covenants on the home. It's important to buy a home with a problem-free, or good, title. Otherwise, you could be prevented from using it as you want, and you could have problems borrowing against the equity in your home or even selling it. Plus, a bad title can diminish the home's value.

Even if a search indicates that the title to the home you're buying is good, your mortgage lender will insist that you purchase title insurance. It protects you and your lender in the event that title problems surface after you buy the home.

A restrictive covenant places legally binding restrictions and requirements on a homeowner. For example, the covenant could impose landscaping requirements, prevent you from running a business from your home, forbid you from renting out your home, and so on. Condominium projects and subdivisions often have restrictive covenants.

Your title contingency clause could give you the right to cancel your home purchase in the event of a bad title, or it could give the seller a certain period of time to clear up the title defects. It's customary for the seller to pay for the title search.

Attorney approval contingency clause

An attorney approval contingency clause gives you the right to have an attorney review the final agreement before you sign it and to change your offer or even cancel it, depending on your lawyer's recommendations. In some states, the standard purchase offer gives you this right.

Although it's important to protect yourself by including in your written offer whatever contingency clauses you believe are necessary, the more you add, the more reasons you may be giving a seller to reject your offer. This is particularly true in a hot real estate market, also known as a *seller's market.* Don't omit the most important contingencies just to get a house, however. You may find that your haste was costly.

Being covered by state disclosure laws

Depending on the laws of your state, you may be responsible for finding out about any serious defects in the home you're buying. In these states, before you make an offer to buy a home, you should ask the seller and his agent a lot of questions about the home and include an inspection contingency clause in your purchase offer. Form 15-6 provides a list of questions you may want to ask.

A growing number of states have passed seller disclosure laws in an effort to help buyers make more informed decisions, although the laws vary widely in terms of their specifics. Some, for example, require sellers to answer specific questions about their homes and to share their written answers with buyers. Others just require sellers to tell buyers about any *material defects* they may be aware of that a buyer may not notice, and that may influence a buyer's decision to buy, as well as how much the buyer would offer to pay for the home. Material defects could include a water problem in the basement, a leaking roof, septic tank problems, or a multi-story parking garage scheduled to be built down the street. Yikes!

Some real estate companies require sellers to complete a disclosure form as a condition of listing their home, even if there is no seller disclosure law in their state.

If your state does not have a seller disclosure law, create your own disclosure form and ask a seller to complete it. You may even want to make completing the form a condition of sale. Form 15-7 on the CD provides a sample form.

Having the Home Inspected

A home inspector should check out the heating and cooling systems and the plumbing and electrical systems in the home you want to buy. He should also assess the condition of its roof, foundation, windows, exterior walls, and basement, among other things. A professional inspection does not highlight cosmetic problems in a home — such as dirty carpeting, grimy walls, damaged wood floors, or outdated lighting.

If you're buying a home in a brand-new subdivision, don't assume that a professional inspection is unnecessary. Some new homebuilders do shoddy work, so brand-new homes can have problems, too.

Whenever possible, be present when the inspection takes place. That way, if the inspector finds problems, you can see them for yourself and find out how serious they are and how much it can cost to repair them. Being there can also provide you with an on-the-spot education regarding the construction of the home you're buying, home maintenance issues, and so on. The opportunity to get to know your future home from the inside out is invaluable.

If an inspector prefers to work without you looking over his shoulder, arrange to meet him at the home immediately after the inspection so you can discuss what he found and see any problems for yourself.

The typical home inspection costs between $200 and $500. However, it could cost you more if the home you're buying is larger than average or has unusual features.

Finding a home inspector

Don't hire just any old home inspector; hire a good one. A good inspector is

- ✔ **Experienced.** He should have worked as an inspector for at least a couple of years and should conduct numerous inspections each year (the more, the better).

- ✔ **Familiar with problems that may be unique to your area due to weather, terrain, soil conditions, local building materials, and so on.**

- ✔ **Accredited by the American Society of Home Inspectors (ASHI).** To become a member, an inspector must complete a certain number of inspections, take a written exam, and pass muster with a committee of his peers. The Society's Web site is www.ashi.com.

- ✔ **Licensed as an engineer or contractor.** If your state licenses home inspectors, the inspector should have a current license. (Only a few states license inspectors.)

- ✔ **Insured and bonded.** It's best to hire an inspector who has *errors and omissions insurance*. This insurance protects you if the inspector fails to detect a significant problem in the home you purchase.

To find a reputable home inspector, get references from anyone you know who has recently purchased a home in your area, your real estate agent, your lender, or a real estate attorney. You can also find the names of inspectors in the Yellow Pages of your local phone book under "Building Inspection Services" or "Home Inspection Services."

Before you hire an inspector, ask him to provide a written statement of exactly what he inspects. It will probably be a standard statement, not something that's prepared just for you. The inspector should check the house from top to bottom, inside and out. However, some inspectors inspect roofs, foundations, security systems, sprinkler systems, pools, hot tubs, septic systems, and so on or charge extra to inspect those things. You can arrange separate, specialized inspections for whatever the home inspector does not check. Also, ask whether the inspector provides a written report of his inspection results, and don't work with an inspector who won't.

Local inspectors tend to rely on local real estate agents for a steady stream of business. There is potential for conflict in this relationship because an inspector may be reluctant to be a deal killer by reporting all the problems a home has, knowing that he may not get business from the agent again.

Warranties

You may have an opportunity to purchase a home service warranty when you're purchasing a home. Most warranties cover the repair and replacement of a home's major appliances and systems, including its central air and heating systems, plumbing, and electrical systems. You may have to pay extra to have the warranty cover the home's roof and foundation as well as such things as its garage door opener, garbage disposal, trash compactor, doorbells, and hot tub.

Don't buy a warranty without reading all the warranty documents so that you can be sure it's worth your money. Check out

- ✔ **What the warranty covers.** Among other things, the warranty should cover any preexisting problems in the home — problems that existed when you bought it.

- ✔ **Whether the appliances, systems, and so on in the home are covered by their own warranties.** There's no point in paying for duplicate warranty coverage.

- ✔ **What restrictions apply to the warranty.** An overly restrictive warranty may not be worth your money.

Warranty coverage for an existing home is usually more limited than what new home warranties offer, even though things are more apt to wear out and need fixing in an older home.

- ✔ **The cost of the warranty, including its service fee.** You must pay this fee every time you request that something in the home be repaired or replaced under the warranty. Most warranty service fees are in the $25 to $35 range, but some are a lot higher.

Some state insurance commissions regulate home warranty companies. If your state does, contact your state commission to find out whether consumers have had problems with the warranty company you're considering. You can also check out the company with your local Better Business Bureau and the consumer protection office of your state attorney general. A brand-new home probably comes with a one-year builder warranty. Most likely, the warranty covers the home's appliances and mechanical systems, but it may also cover its foundation and roof.

If you're buying a home in a new subdivision, ask residents of the neighborhood who own homes built by the same builder how satisfied they are with the quality of their homes and their warranty service. If a seller says that she has a home warranty and that she can transfer it to you for a price, read the warranty paperwork to ensure she is correct and to determine whether the warranty is worth paying for.

If you want the seller to pay for a home warranty, include that requirement in your purchase offer. Be sure to specify that you, not the seller, will choose the warranty plan.

Land-use matters

When you're looking for a home to buy, it's human nature to focus on a home's appearance, size, and neighborhood and not consider whether it's subject to public or private land-use restrictions that could limit your ability to use it as you want.

Local zoning laws and easements create public restrictions. Subdivision covenants and condominium or co-op association bylaws can impose private restrictions on homeowners. In fact, private restrictions can prohibit you from doing things that your local government does not ban. The sidebar "Cooperatives and condominiums: What's the difference?" explains how condominiums and co-ops work.

Zoning

Local zoning laws limit where commercial, retail, and multi-family development can occur in a community. Among other things, the laws help protect homeowners' property values. Your local zoning laws may also restrict what you can do with your home — whether you can operate a home-based business, keep chickens in your backyard, turn your garage into a rental apartment, and so on. Some communities have much more restrictive zoning laws than others.

Ask your real estate agent how the home you want to buy is zoned. Also ask about the zoning of nearby property, because it can affect the value of your home. For example, suppose a large, undeveloped lot up the street from the home you want to buy is zoned "commercial." After you move in, a retail strip shopping center appears on the lot. The noise and traffic on your street that the shopping center generates may bring down your property value.

If the zoning laws in your area allow you to operate a home-based business, be sure you understand any restrictions that apply. They can include limits on the kinds of businesses you can run out of your home, the hours you can do business, the kind of signage you can display, and so on. If you don't comply with the restrictions, your local government could fine you, force you to change the way you do business, or even order you to close your home-based business.

Zoning changes

Once you purchase a home, you can apply to your local government for a zoning variance if you want to do something that's not normally permitted by the way your home is zoned. However, you have no guarantee that your variance request will be granted.

Call your local government's zoning or planning department to find out how to initiate a variance request. After completing certain paperwork, you'll probably have to attend a public hearing about your request. Supporters of your request, as well as opponents, can speak at the hearing. If you don't anticipate a lot of opposition and feel comfortable representing yourself, you may not need to hire an attorney to help you with your variance. However, if you want legal help, hire an attorney who's familiar with your area's zoning laws and who has a successful track record getting variances approved.

Another option you have when local zoning laws stand in your way of doing what you want with your home is to change the zoning on your property. If you go this route, you need the help of an experienced attorney, not to mention the support of the property owners who will be affected by the change you're seeking.

Prior to making a variance or zoning change request, try to get your neighbors on your side by letting them know what you want to do and addressing their concerns. Otherwise, they could block approval of the change.

If you're unhappy with the outcome of your variance or rezoning request, you can appeal. To win your appeal, you may have to show that no one in your neighborhood would be harmed by the change you're seeking, and that without the change you will be unfairly denied your right to use your property, among other things. To find out about the appeals process, contact your local government's zoning or planning department. If you're already working with an attorney, she should be familiar with the process.

If your appeal is denied, you can sue your local government, but the lawsuit process is time-consuming and costly. Also, your odds of winning are probably poor because courts tend to give local governments considerable leeway when it comes to their interpretation of their own laws.

Easements

An *easement* gives someone permission to use someone else's property for a specific purpose. For example, your future next-door neighbors may have an easement to use your driveway to get to their property, or the local utility company may have an easement to run lines through the backyard of the home.

Easements are usually created by written agreements and come with the property. In other words, an easement is not cancelled when a home is sold. A title search indicates the easements that come with a home.

Getting Ready for the Closing

Once you satisfy all the requirements in your purchase agreement and your financing is in place, it's time for your real estate closing. But before the closing, you have a few final but important details to tend to:

- ✔ **Decide how you want to hold title to your new home.** Don't treat this decision casually. It can have important estate-planning implications. The "Deciding how to hold title to your home" section on the following page explains your options.

- ✔ **Schedule a final walk-through or inspection.** This final inspection gives you a chance to make sure that any defects the seller agreed to fix and any cosmetic changes the seller agreed to make as a condition of the sale are complete, and that all the items your contract says convey with the home are still in place. It also lets you ensure that the seller has moved out or is in the process of moving.

  Final walk-throughs are rare in some areas of the country. Instead, sellers prove to buyers that they addressed the defects and cosmetic changes that the buyers agreed to make as a condition of the sale by providing the buyers with receipts.

- ✔ **During the walk-through, test out all the appliances that are conveying, flush the toilets, make sure that all the faucets are working, test all the light switches and ceiling fans, and so on.** This is your last chance to make sure that the seller has lived up to her end of the bargain, so go over the house with a fine-tooth comb. Your agent should participate in the walk-through as well. If you find that the seller did not do something that was promised in your purchase agreement, your agent should let the seller's agent know that your closing will not happen until those things are taken care of.

- ✔ **Purchase homeowner's insurance.** Chapter 13 discusses homeowner's insurance in detail.

- ✔ **Review your HUD-1 Settlement Statement.** The federal Real Estate Settlement and Procedures Act (RESPA) says that whoever conducts your closing must provide you with a completed copy of this statement one day before your closing. It lists all the expenses you and the seller are obligated to pay, all the payments you're being credited for, and how much you and the seller must pay at the closing. Although your eyes may blur in the process, review this statement line by line, before your closing, to make sure that you understand all the numbers and that there are no errors. If you have any questions, ask them. A sample HUD-1 form is on the CD at Form 15-9.

RESPA is enforced by the Department of Housing and Urban Development (HUD). If you want more information about your RESPA rights, visit www.hud.gov/fha/res/repa_hm.html or call 800-217-6970.

Deciding how to hold title to your home

How you hold title to your home is an important decision with estate-planning and tax implications. It can also be important if you're sued, file for bankruptcy, or get divorced. Yet most buyers spend little or no time deciding which ownership option is best for them.

When you're buying a home on your own, you don't have a lot of options for how to hold title to it. Most likely, you will own the home as a sole owner. However, you may want to consider setting up a living trust and letting it own the home. Consult an estate-planning attorney about the pros and cons of a living trust. (Chapter 14 explains living trusts.)

You have several options when you're buying a home with one or more people. Depending on your state, you and your co-owners can own the home as

- ✔ **Joint tenants with the right of survivorship.** You and your co-owners own equal shares of the home. When you die, your shares automatically transfer to your surviving co-owners, regardless of what your will says. Therefore, joint tenancy with the right of survivorship is a good option for spouses and unmarried partners.

- ✔ **Tenants in common.** You and each of the other owners own an undivided interest in the value of your home, but the interests may not be equal. For example, you can own 55 percent of the house, and your co-owner can own the remaining 45 percent. You and your co-owners can do whatever you want with your own share — sell it, borrow against it, or leave it to anyone you want in your will. You must use estate planning to ensure that your share goes to your spouse or unmarried partner at your death. It does not transfer automatically.

- ✔ **Tenants in the entirety.** Only spouses can own homes this way. As tenants in the entirety, you and your spouse each own one-half of your home. Neither of you can sell your share or use it as collateral without the other's agreement. Also, your individual halves automatically transfer to one another when you die. Many states do not offer this form of ownership.

If you own your home one way and then decide later that you would rather hold title in some other way, ask your attorney to prepare a new deed that reflects the change and to record it with your local recorder of deeds office.

If you live in a community property state, when you and your spouse purchase a home, you each of you owns one-half of that asset, no matter whose name is on the title. Your half does not automatically transfer to your surviving spouse when you die. Therefore, you must transfer it through your estate planning. Arizona, California, Idaho, Louisiana, Nevada, New Mexico, Texas, Washington, and Wisconsin are community property states.

You and your spouse can modify your community property rights in a legally binding prenuptial or post-nuptial agreement. Each of you should consult with your own attorney if you're interested in drafting such an agreement. In some states, legal representation is required.

Taxation without perspiration

Selling your home can cost you money — federal and state taxes, to be exact — although not as much since the passage of the federal Taxpayer Relief Act in 1997. The law says that if you are married and file a joint return, you can realize up to $500,000 in profit on the sale of your home without having to pay federal capital gains tax, assuming that the home was your primary place of residence for at least two of the five years prior to the sale. If you're single, you can exclude up to $250,000. Unlike the old rules, you don't have to purchase a new home of equal or greater value to benefit from this exclusion.

If you do have to pay capital gains taxes on the profits you earn from the sale, the tax rate is 20 percent unless you owned the home for more than five years. If that's the case, the rate is 18 percent.

Good record keeping is key to minimizing the amount of capital gains taxes you have to pay. Your record keeping should include the amount of money you spend on capital improvements to your home — improvements that increase its value — as well as all the money you spend related to the sale. Those expenses can include the commission you pay to your real estate agent, attorney's fees, appraisal fees, cosmetic improvements, and so on.

If you're worried about how the sale of your home affects your tax situation, talk to your CPA or tax attorney before you put it on the market. Presale tax planning can help minimize any potential tax impact.

You don't have to purchase mortgage insurance unless your loan down payment is less than 20 percent. You can find out more about mortgage insurance in Chapter 16.

Closing the Deal

A real estate closing is the final step in the home-buying process. At your closing, you sign the mortgage paperwork, pay your share of the closing costs, and pay the seller. In most states, you must go through the closing to become the legal owner of your new home.

In some regions, you don't become the legal owner of your new home until some time after closing. Your closing will probably take place at the office of the title or escrow company that conducted the title search and issued the title insurance for the home you're buying. However, depending on what's customary in your area of the country, the closing can occur at an attorney's office, the office of the seller's listing agent, the office of your mortgage company, or somewhere else.

In some states, an *escrow closing* substitutes for the more formal traditional closing. An escrow agent processes all the paperwork, arranges for the buyer and seller to sign the necessary documents, collects and disburses funds, and gives the new homeowner the keys to the home.

Your closing may be crowded with people or may include only a few people in attendance. The person who's running the closing, you, and anyone else involved in buying your home will be there. Others who might attend include your agent and the seller's listing agent, your real estate attorney and the seller's attorney, and the seller.

If you can't attend your closing, give someone you trust a power of attorney so that she can act on your behalf at the closing. First, however, check with your lender to confirm that it allows you to close this way. You may have to sign the closing documents ahead of time.

Signing stuff

You have to sign a pile of documents at closing. They relate to what is probably the single biggest financial transaction of your life, so it's important to read them carefully before signing them. You want to be 100 percent sure that they're accurate and that you understand exactly what you're agreeing to. The documents include

- ✔ **A mortgage note.** This document shows the amount of money you're borrowing, when and where your monthly payments are due, the amount of your monthly mortgage payments, and the penalty you have to pay if you're late making a payment.

- ✔ **A mortgage.** This document gives your mortgage lender a lien on your home, which means that if you don't live up to the terms of your mortgage agreement, the lender can take possession of your home.

- ✔ **The final purchase contract between you and the seller.**

Some states are *deed of trust states,* not mortgage states. In these states, lenders do not use a mortgage to secure their loan, and you don't actually hold title to your home. A neutral third party does until you pay your mortgage loan. If you default on your mortgage loan in a deed-of-trust state, you can lose your home relatively quickly because the lender doesn't have to use the same legal foreclosure process required in mortgage states.

After you sign everything, be prepared to give the closing agent a certified check or cashier's check for the amount of money shown on line 103 of your HUD-1 Statement. No cash or personal checks, please! The seller may have to pay money, too. The closing agent distributes the funds according to the HUD-1 Statement.

Finally, after signing all the paperwork documents and paying a bundle of money, you're the owner of your new home and the seller is a lot richer.

Before you leave the closing, find out who has responsibility for recording the deed to your new home. The title company might do it for you, or it might deliver the deed to you soon shortly after closing. Then you have to take the deed to your local recorder of deeds so that it can become part of the public record.

Avoiding post-closing problems

After you're living in your new home, you may discover problems that you believe the seller should have told you about. If that happens, you may have grounds for a lawsuit against the seller and possibly against his real estate agent. But first, check your purchase agreement and your inspection report. You may have the right to expect the seller to repair the problem if

- ✔ Your state has a seller disclosure law, and you have reason to believe that the seller knew about the problem at the time you made your purchase offer.

- ✔ When he signed your purchase agreement, the seller warrantied that everything in the home was in working order to the best of his knowledge.

- ✔ You specifically asked the seller whether the problem existed and the seller told you "No."

On the other hand, you may have to resolve the problem on your own if your home inspector should have discovered the problem, or the inspector noted the problem in his inspection report and you ignored the information, or you bought the house as is.

Meet with a real estate attorney if you believe that you're entitled to have the seller fix the problems in your new home. She can advise you about your best course of action given the laws of your state and the details of your purchase contract. If filing a lawsuit is an option for you, weigh the cost of the lawsuit and the probability that you will prevail against the amount of money you have to spend fixing the problem yourself. Your home warranty may cover some of your new home's problems.

Chapter 16

Getting a Mortgage

. . . .

In This Chapter

▶ Understanding the different kinds of mortgages

▶ Working with a mortgage broker

▶ Applying for a mortgage

▶ Dealing with denial

. . . .

*U*nless you have made a fortune from an IPO or the lottery, you have to finance the purchase of your new home with a mortgage loan. If you are like most homebuyers, this loan is the biggest financial obligation you ever make. To get that loan, you must first and foremost, find a home to buy. Then you must decide exactly what kind of mortgage loan best meets your needs. After that, you need to locate a lender and apply to the lender for the loan. Assuming your loan application is approved, you become the official owner of your new home after a real estate closing. Then, all you have to do is pay, pay, pay.

When a lender gives you a mortgage, it secures the loan by putting a lien on the home you are buying. If you do not meet the terms of the loan, the lien gives your lender the right to foreclose on your property. The lien is released once you pay off the mortgage. Chapter 8 describes the foreclosure process.

Many different mortgage lenders offer a wide variety of different types of mortgages. The type of mortgage you choose and the lender you decide to work with affect not only the size of your monthly mortgage payments and the amount of interest you pay over the life of your loan, but also how much you have to pay at your real estate closing. Therefore, both decisions are extremely important. However, once you sign a contract to buy a home, you don't have a whole lot of time to make either choice. The purchase contract you sign likely includes a deadline by which you must have your financing arranged. Miss that date, and you may lose your chance to buy your dream home.

For all these reasons, it's a smart move to begin investigating your lender and mortgage options as soon as you begin shopping for a home. This chapter helps you get started by providing the background information you need to do that research. It also informs you of your rights when you apply for a mortgage and after you begin making your loan payments, and it educates you about how home equity loans work. Sounds pretty dry, huh? Well, learning about mortgages is probably not the most exciting thing you have ever done, but consider the payoff — owning your own castle, cave, or whatever!

Knowing Who's Got the Money

Getting the kind of loan you want for the least amount of money takes some homework. Banks, savings and loans, credit unions, and mortgage companies all make mortgage loans, but they may differ in regard to the types of mortgages they make, the fees they charge to make their loans, and the terms of credit they offer. To begin, compile a list of lenders from the following sources:

- ✔ Your real estate agent or broker.
- ✔ The financial institutions listed in your area's Yellow Pages under the heading "mortgage" or "mortgage lending."
- ✔ Friends or family members who recently obtained a mortgage loan.
- ✔ Mortgage-related advertisements in your local paper. You are most apt to find them in your local newspaper's business and real estate sections.
- ✔ The Internet. Click your mouse on some of the mortgage loan Web sites highlighted in the sidebar "The Web can be a loanly place."

If you call about a mortgage-related ad you saw in your local paper and the number you call reaches a pager, not someone in an office, you may be calling a fly-by-night operation. These outfits are likely to charge you an application fee and then disappear.

Some Web sites let you apply for a mortgage online. Attractive as it may sound, however, you might not get the absolute best terms on a mortgage if you limit yourself to online lenders. Especially if you're a first-time buyer, you might overlook key details regarding the terms of a loan if you read about it on your computer screen, rather than get it explained to you by a mortgage lender or mortgage broker.

If a lender has already prequalified or preapproved you for a mortgage loan and you liked dealing with that lender, be sure to include it on your list. If you have an established relationship with a financial institution, put that lender on your list, too, because it might be willing to give you a mortgage loan with better-than-average terms. Being preapproved for a mortgage loan can help make you more attractive to a seller.

It is important to remember the difference between mortgage prequalification and mortgage preapproval. To get prequalified for a loan, you provide a mortgage lender with certain information so it can tell you how large a loan you can qualify for. Being prequalified can help you focus your search for a home to buy. However, prequalification does not guarantee that you will actually qualify for a loan in that price range. On the other hand, if a mortgage lender preapproves you for a loan of a certain amount, you can get a loan of that size.

Once you assemble a list of possible lenders, schedule a meeting with a loan officer at each so you can ask them important questions that will help you select the right lender. If you do not have time for in-person meetings, you might be able to get most of your questions answered over the phone. The next section of this chapter, "Asking a mortgage lender the right questions" tells you what questions to ask. Use the worksheet on Form 16-1 of the CD to compare the information you get from the lenders you speak with.

The Web can be a loanly place

You can shop for a loan and even apply for a loan online at a wide variety of Web sites. Most local lenders have their own web sites and other sites are hosted by Internet companies, or by mortgage brokers. Here are some to start with:

✔ **MonsterMoving.com.** mortgagequotes. monstermoving.com This site claims to offer the largest source of mortgage information in the Web. It provides continuously updated rate information from more than 1,400 lenders,

✔ **Lycos Real Estate.** www.lycos.com realestate/mortgages.html At this Web site, you can shop for a mortgage loan by type of loan and by the number of points you want to pay.

✔ **Countrywide.** www.countrywide.com The Web site of this national lender not only provides you a good education about buying a home, but also features a wide variety of mortgages.

✔ **InterestRatesonline.com.** www. interestratesonline.com/ shopforthebestrate/index2.html When you fill out the loan application at this Web site, various viewers look at your information and offer you their best mortgage, and then you can compare your options and select the loan you want.

✔ **E-loan.com.** www.e-loan.com This site covers 70 lenders in 50 states but makes no guarantee that its rates are the lowest you will find.

✔ **Homeadvisor.com.** homeadvisor.msn. com/default.asp?toss=done This home site has it all. Not only can you shop for and apply for a mortgage loan online, but you can also find a home to buy, organize your move, and use this site to sell your home when you are ready to move to a new one.

If a financial institution offers you a mortgage loan at a rate of interest that is substantially below what other lenders are offering, make sure that the lender is reliable. Ask for references, and check out that lender with your area's Better Business Bureau and with your state attorney general's consumer protection office. Your research might show that the lender has a history of questionable practices or shoddy customer treatment.

Asking a mortgage lender the right questions

There is a lot to consider and compare when you shop for a mortgage. For example, to help ensure that you get a good deal, find out what kinds of mortgage loans lenders make, what interest rates they offer, whether the rates are fixed or adjustable, and so on. Although you may want to add questions of your own to the following list, to help you decide which mortgage lenders should go on your short list, ask them the following questions.

- **What types of mortgage loans do you offer?** If a particular kind of mortgage sounds interesting, find out more about it. For example, if a lender offers an adjustable rate mortgage, ask how often the interest rate is adjusted and how much the interest rate can be increased or decreased. "Mortgage Loan Smorgasbord" section of this chapter covers the various types of mortgage loans.

- **What are the current interest rates for the loans?** Are the rates fixed or adjustable? Ask only about the mortgage loans you are interested in.

- **How many points, if any, will I have to pay?** Find out how much money the points equate to. For more information on points, read the section "Tending to the terms" later in this chapter.

- **What are the annual percentage rates (APRs) for the loans?**

- **How much is the loan application fee?** If I'm denied the loan, can I get any of the fee back?

- **What other fees do I have to pay?** How much is each fee, and when is it due? Also, how much would I have to bring to closing?

- **Given my finances (describe them briefly) and the amount I want to borrow, do you think I will have any problem qualifying for a mortgage loan with you?**

- **Approximately how much will my monthly mortgage payments be?**

- **Will I have to purchase mortgage insurance?** How much will it cost?

- **Can I lock in an interest rate?** When does the lock begin, and how long does it last?

   ✔ **Do you charge a prepayment penalty for your loans?**

   ✔ **How quickly can my loan be processed?**

One of the most common reasons people file for bankruptcy is to save their home when they can't make their mortgage payments, and their lender is threatening to take back the home. Therefore, when you are mortgage shopping, look for a loan that you believe you can pay in bad financial times as well as good. That way, if your finances take a turn for the worse, your home will not be in jeopardy.

If your credit is stellar, you have plenty of cash, and you want to close on a loan ASAP, ask the lenders about *low doc* loans. This type of loan involves an abbreviated application process. The lender may check only your income and your job. A key benefit of this kind of loan is that because there's less information for the mortgage lender to process, your loan can close quickly — within two weeks depending on the lender. The downside of a low doc loan is that you must pay a larger than normal down payment. You may have to pay as much as 30 percent of the purchase price. You may also have to pay more in points.

Understanding the benefits of a portfolio lender

When you shop for a mortgage lender, be aware that some lenders make loans to keep in their own portfolio of investments. Others however, make loans with the intention of making additional money by selling the loans, often to the Federal National Mortgage Association (Fannie Mae) or to the Federal Home Loan Mortgage Corporation (Freddie Mac). These two organizations are the leaders in the secondary home mortgage market. They sell the loans they buy to investors.

What your lender does with your loan is important to you for a couple of reasons. For one, loans sold to Fannie Mae or Freddie Mac are harder to qualify for than other loans because both organizations place strict limitations on the types of loans they buy. Therefore, it tends to be easier to qualify for a loan from a lender who plans to keep it in their own portfolio, since the lender is not concerned about selling it to Fannie Mae or Freddie Mac. If your finances are a bit iffy, if you don't have a lot of money for a down payment, or if the home you're buying is not in great shape, you have a better shot at getting approved for a mortgage if you apply to a portfolio lender or to a lender who plans to make your loan part of its portfolio. To find out whether a lender sells its loans to Fannie Mae or Freddie Mac, simply ask the loan officer you interview. The downside to limiting your mortgage search to portfolio lenders is that they tend to offer fewer mortgage options than other lenders. Also, they tend to be somewhat more expensive.

Mortgage Loan Smorgasbord: Distinguishing among Loans

You can choose from so many mortgage loan options that you might find sorting through them somewhat bewildering. It's like standing before a sumptuous buffet table wondering which platter of food you will like best. The loans you have to chose from vary in regard to their interest rate — whether the rate is fixed or changes over time, whether you have to come up with a large balloon payment at the end of the loan, the number of years the loan lasts and so on. However, this section should help you hone in on the particular type of mortgage that best meets your needs. Your real estate agent, mortgage broker, or the loan offer herself can offer valuable guidance.

Fixed-rate mortgage: The interest rate on a *fixed-rate mortgage* is set at the start of the loan and stays the same until you pay it off. Usually, a fixed-rate loan is your best bet when interest rates are low. However, if interest rates get even lower after your loan is in place, don't worry; you can always refinance to benefit from the downward trend.

Adjustable-rate mortgage or ARM: The interest rate on an *adjustable-rate mortgage loan*, commonly referred to as an ARM, moves up or down periodically depending on the interest rate of the index it is tied to. Different lenders use different indexes. As a result, your monthly payments go up or down. Your interest rate is adjusted annually or more often, depending on the terms of your mortgage. When rates are high, an ARM is more attractive than a fixed-rate loan, especially if you believe that rates are on their way down.

Waning interest

When you make your mortgage loan payments, you are actually paying off two things — the principal on your loan, which is the amount of money you borrowed, and the interest on the loan. In the beginning years of your loan, your payments primarily go toward paying the interest. Even though the dollar amount you pay each month stays the same, the amount that the lender applies to the interest and the amount it applies to reducing the principal change over time. As time goes on, you begin paying more toward the principal and less toward interest.

Over time, as you whittle down your loan balance, the equity in your home increases. Equity is the difference between your home's market value and the balance on your loan. Equity is important because you can borrow against it. For information on home equity loans, read the sidebar "Special information about home equity loans" at the end of this chapter.

If interest rates really drop after you get an ARM, consider converting it to a fixed-rate loan if you can, or refinancing to a fixed-rate mortgage. Before you apply for an ARM, make sure it includes limits on how much the interest rate on the loan can increase or decrease, as well as how much the interest rate can be adjusted over the life of the loan.

A loan that combines elements of a fixed-rate loan and an ARM comes in two basic flavors:

- A loan that features fixed mortgage payments for a limited number of years — for three, five, seven, or ten years — and then converts to an ARM

- A loan that starts out at a fixed rate of interest and then, after a certain number of years, moves to a higher fixed interest rate

Balloon mortgage: Balloon mortgages have two categories. One lets you make interest-only payments for a period of time and then requires that you pay off your loan balance with a single large payment. Another type requires that you start out paying a certain amount of money each month that includes interest and principal; after a period, you must make one large payment to pay off your loan.

When you opt for a balloon payment loan, you are gambling that you will have the money you need to make the lump sum payment when it comes due. If you can't come up with the bucks, you will be in default of your loan.

Assumable loan: With an *assumable loan,* you may be able to save time and money by taking over the seller's current mortgage loan rather than applying for a new one. However, the seller's lender must qualify you to assume it.

FHA (Federal Housing Administration) loan: An FHA loan can be an attractive option if your credit record is iffy or if you don't have much money for a down payment. When you opt for a conventional loan — a loan from a private lender — the traditional down payment is 20 percent of your purchase price. With an FHA loan, your down payment can be as small as 5 percent. A smaller-than-usual down payment comes with a catch, however: You have to purchase mortgage insurance, which can be quite expensive.

Although FHA loans are available to anyone, not just to low-income home-buyers, there are limits on how much you can borrow when you choose FHA. The maximum mortgage you can apply for is based on the kind of residential property you are buying — single family home, duplex, and so on — and where the property is located. More expensive areas of the country have higher loan limits than other areas.

Veteran's Administration loans: VA loans are available to qualified veterans and are administered by the U.S. Department of Veteran's Affairs. If you qualify, you may not have to make a down payment at all. However, you will have to pay a VA funding fee, which increases the cost of a VA loan.

Owner financing: You may find a seller willing to provide you with the financing you need to buy his home. In essence, the seller becomes your mortgage lender. Owner financing can be attractive for several reasons. Usually, the loan can be finalized more quickly than a conventional loan. You probably do not have to pay any points. This kind of loan probably comes with a lower interest rate than other kinds of loans.

If the owner of the home you're buying agrees to finance your purchase, use a real estate attorney to draft an agreement that spells out all terms of your relationship.

Counting the years

An important consideration, no matter what kind of loan you apply for, is the length of the mortgage. Do you want a traditional 30-year loan, or would a 15-year mortgage make more sense? Depending on the lender you choose, you might also have the option of a 40-year, 25-year, 20-year, or 10-year mortgage loan.

Longer and shorter loans each have pros and cons. For example, if you have a 15-year loan, each of your mortgage payments is higher than if you opt for a loan of the same amount and pay it off over 30 years. On the plus side, however, a 15-year loan usually comes with a lower rate of interest than a longer loan. Also, a shorter loan lets you build equity in your home faster.

Usually, it is easier to qualify for a longer-term loan than for a shorter-term loan. A 30-year mortgage is a good option if you want to minimize the size of your monthly loan payments or you plan on living in your new home for a long time.

If you have a 30-year mortgage, you can achieve some of the benefits of a 15-year loan by making one or more extra loan payments each year. Another option is to make larger-than-usual loan payments when you can afford it. Be sure to instruct the lender to apply the additional dollars toward your loan principal. Yet another option is to get a loan that lets you make biweekly rather than monthly loan payments. This option saves you a considerable amount of interest expense.

However, a 15-year mortgage makes a lot of sense if you expect to be in your home for only a few years, or if you want to pay off your mortgage as fast as possible — perhaps because you're thinking about your retirement or you want to have your house paid for before your kids go to college — and you can afford the larger monthly payments.

Tending to the terms

Lenders can offer the same kinds of loans with different terms of credit. Because the terms of credit affect the overall cost of the loan you apply for, pay close attention to lenders' terms of credit when you are shopping for a loan. Some of the most important terms of credit to note follow:

✔ **What is the interest rate?** Lenders are legally obligated to provide written information about a loan's APR, or annual percentage rate. For a mortgage loan, this percentage takes into account the loan's basic interest rate as well as such charges as your closing costs and other fees.

The federal Truth in Lending Act says that lenders, including mortgage lenders, must disclose the APR up front. For the full scoop on APRs, read Chapter 6.

✔ **What points will you pay?** A point is equal to one percentage of the total amount of a loan. For example, one point on a $100,000 loan is $1,000. Points are pre-paid interest and you pay them in full at closing and are deductible from your federal taxes. When you get a mortgage loan, you might be asked to pay between one and three points. The specific number of points you have to pay can vary, depending on the lender you work with and the type of mortgage you apply for. For example, you can expect to pay more in points for a $100,000 fixed-rate loan than for a $100,000 ARM. Usually, the lower the interest rate on a loan, the higher the points.

If you can afford it, you might want to lower the interest rate on your loan, and your monthly payments, too, by paying extra points. This can be a good option if you plan to stay in your home for a long time, because paying extra points saves you a considerable amount of money over the life of the loan. If you are not sure whether paying extra points is a good idea for you, ask the lender to provide a comparison of the cost of a loan with and without extra points.

✔ **What is the size of your down payment?** If you are applying for a conventional loan, the traditional down payment is 20 percent of the home's purchase price. However, some banks offer low or zero down payment loans. FHA and VA loans are other options when money is tight.

Making a smaller-than-normal down payment brings some drawbacks. First, your loan will probably come with a higher rate of interest. Usually, the smaller the down payment, the higher the interest rate. Second, you might have to purchase mortgage insurance to protect your lender against a possible default. Typically, the lower the amount of your down payment, the higher your insurance premiums are. However, other factors such as the type of loan, the size of your mortgage, and the insurance carrier also affect costs.

Don't hesitate to try negotiating the terms of a loan, especially if you want to work with a particular lender, but its terms are not as attractive as those of another lender. If the lender really wants your business, it might be willing to work with you.

Getting the Loan: Show Me the Money

You may work with a number of different professionals when you shop for a mortgage loan and go through the loan application process. For example, you may hire a mortgage broker to help you sort through your mortgage options, locate a mortgage lender, and get you through the loan application process.

Although a good mortgage broker knows which lenders are making what kinds of loans, the broker does not make loans. That is the job of a loan officer. The loan officer provides you with the loan application paperwork, answers questions related to the loan you apply for, takes whatever steps are necessary to initiate the application process, informs you or your broker about the outcome of the process, and prepares the loan paperwork for the real estate closing, assuming that the loan is approved.

Mortgage brokers

If you find the process of shopping for a mortgage loan just plain overwhelming, or if you simply do not have the time to compare and contrast, consider working with a mortgage broker. The broker does the mortgage shopping for you after assessing the state of your finances, helps you pull together all the information you need for your loan application, and submits the application to the lenders she believes can best meet your mortgage needs.

Working with a mortgage broker can also be a good idea if you are concerned that you might have difficulty qualifying for a mortgage. An experienced mortgage broker knows how to package your application information to maximize your attractiveness to potential lenders. Because he has contacts with many different mortgage lenders, he may be able to arrange a more attractive loan for you than you could get on your own.

Some lenders work with mortgage brokers only. In other words, they do not accept your loan application directly. The mortgage broker charges a fee for her services. The fee is not due until you close on your loan. Usually, the fee is a percentage of the value of your loan. Form 16-2 on the CD has a checklist of questions to ask a potential mortgage broker.

Applying for a Mortgage Loan

Applying for a mortgage loan concerns more than just filling in some blanks on an application form. In addition to completing a multipage application that asks about your income, debts and assets, and employment history as well as the home you want to buy, you also have to provide the lender with a lot of documentation to corroborate your application information. If you have a co-borrower, he must also provide this information. You can find a sample mortgage loan application on Form 16-3 of the CD.

If you are working with a mortgage broker, you work with the broker, not a lender, to complete the application process. At a minimum, you probably have to provide the following backup documentation:

- ✔ Copies of your W-2 forms for the past two years, and a month's worth of pay stubs.

- ✔ Copies of your tax returns for the past two or three years as well as a current balance sheet and a year-to-date profit and loss statement, if you are self-employed. If you are in a partnership or your business is incorporated, the lender will want to see copies of your business federal tax returns for the past two years.

- ✔ Lease agreements and mortgage statements for any rental properties you might own.

- ✔ Three months' worth of statements (or your three most recent statements) for each of your bank accounts, IRAs, 401(k)s, money market funds, brokerage accounts, and so on.

- ✔ A comprehensive list of all your debts, including creditor names, account numbers, account balances, and monthly account payments.

- ✔ Proof of any Social Security, spousal support, or child support payments you might be receiving.

If you are not honest when you fill out a mortgage loan application, you risk being charged with loan fraud. You also have to provide the lender with a copy of your signed home purchase agreement, and you're required to pay a nonrefundable loan application fee. The amount of the fee depends on the lender.

Picking a lock

When you apply for a mortgage loan, the lender asks you whether you want to "lock in" the current interest rate or let it float. If you lock in the rate, your loan will have whatever interest rate is in effect at the time of your application. If you let the rate float, you gamble that when you close on your loan, interest rates will have decreased and, therefore, your loan will be at a lower rate.

If you lock in a rate, the lender wants to know how long a lock you want. You might have the option of a lock that lasts anywhere from 15 days to 120 days, depending on the lender.

However, the longer the lock, the higher the interest rate. Therefore, don't ask for a longer lock than you really need. To make that determination, find out when the lock goes into effect — when you submit your mortgage loan application or when the lender approves your loan.

If you agree to a lock, make sure that you do everything you can to get all of your loan paperwork processed quickly. Otherwise, the lock could expire before you are ready to close, and your loan would be made at the current interest rate, which could be higher than the rate you locked in.

After you submit your loan application to a lender, the lender orders a copy of your credit record from one of the three national credit bureaus discussed in Chapter 7. Reviewing your credit record helps the lender assess how good a credit risk you are. Chapter 7 also explains what lenders can learn about you by reading your credit record.

Before you apply for a mortgage loan, order a copy of your credit report from each of the three major credit bureaus. That way, you can take care of any problems in your credit report that could cause you to be denied the loan you want. To find out how to order your credit report and how to correct credit record problems, return to Chapter 7.

The lender also schedules an appraisal of the home you want to buy to compare its appraised market value to the dollar amount that you want to borrow. This comparison is called an LTV, or loan-to-value ratio. Depending on the lender and the state of your finances, if your LTV is too low, a lender can refuse to lend you as much money as you want to borrow, or it may only agree to give you a loan if you purchase mortgage insurance or make a larger down payment.

If you are concerned about what the home you want to buy will appraise for, your agent might be willing to provide the appraiser with information that could help get you the appraisal you want. If the appraisal comes in too low, ask your agent to provide the appraiser with market data that supports the price you agree to pay for the home you are buying. The lender might require you to pay for either or both the credit report and the appraisal when you submit your loan application or at your closing, assuming your loan is approved. Federal law entitles you to a copy of the appraisal report. Put your request in writing before or just after the appraisal has been conducted, and direct it to the lender, not the appraiser.

Getting full disclosure

The federal Real Estate Settlement Procedures Act (RESPA) places a variety of requirements on mortgage lenders. The purpose of the law is to give home-buyers more power in the real estate closing process and allow them to become better shoppers for settlement services.

Prior to its passage, title or settlement companies, real estate agents, bro-kers, lenders, and others involved in the real estate settlement business, commonly referred business to one another in exchange for a kickback. The cost of these kickbacks was passed on to homebuyers, increasing their settle-ment costs. After the passage of RESPA, kickbacks are prohibited. Those who pay or accept a kickback may be fined and jailed.

RESPA makes additional requirements of the company that services your loan once your closing is history. It says that the company must provide you with a yearly escrow account statement. The statement summarizes all of the deposits made into the account and all of the payments made out of it. It also alerts you to any account shortages or surpluses in the account and tells you what the servicing company plans to do about them.

If your mortgage lender services your loan initially and later decides to sell servicing rights to some other company, it is obligated to send you a notice about its plans at least 15 days before the change will occur. The notification must provide you with the name and address of the new servicer, the date when you must begin sending your mortgage payments to it, and a statement that the transfer of servicing rights will not affect any of the terms or condi-tions of your mortgage, except those that directly relate to the servicing; it must also provide a phone number you can call for additional information, among other things.

After the transfer occurs, RESPA gives you a 60-day grace period during which you do not have to pay a late fee if your mortgage payment is late because you sent it to the company that used to service your loan and not to the new servicer. Your account can't be reported late to credit bureaus during this time. RESPA also requires that you receive certain information before, during, and after the closing process. Here is a rundown of the what's and the when's of the required disclosures:

✓ **A copy of a HUD's *Buying Your Home: Settlement Costs and Helpful Information* booklet.** You can read this booklet on Form 16-4 of the CD.

✓ **A written good faith estimate of your closing costs.** This estimate includes all fees due before closing, all expenses to be paid at the closing, and any escrow account costs. Depending on the terms of your purchase agreement, you might have to pay all these expenses, or the seller might pay some of them.

You should receive this estimate from your lender or mortgage broker when you apply for your mortgage, or no later than three business days after. Review this estimate carefully for anything you don't understand, or for expenses that are larger than what you had anticipated. If you have questions, raise them with your lender or your real estate agent. Keep the estimate so you can compare it to your final closing costs.

✓ **A servicing disclosure statement.** This statement tells you who will service your mortgage loan — your lender or some other company. This is the company you send your mortgage payments to. This statement must also tell you how to resolve any problems you may have with the loan servicing.

✓ **Affiliated business arrangement disclosure statement.** Sometimes, one large parent company owns several affiliated companies, all of which provide settlement services. Therefore, RESPA says that if your real estate agent, mortgage broker, lender, or someone else involved in the closing process refers you to one of its affiliated companies, you must receive a statement indicating this relationship and letting you know that you are free to use some other company.

✓ **A HUD-1 settlement statement.** This statement details all the loan-related services you received and all the fees you're required to pay. It also provides the same information for the seller. Although the numbers can be a little different, the statement provides the same information as the good faith estimate you received at or soon after you applied for your mortgage. You can review your HUD-1 settlement statement the day before your closing if you ask to. You will also see it at your closing. A sample HUD-1 form is in Form 15-8 on the CD.

Looking at the HUD-1 statement ahead of time gives you an opportunity to make sure all of the information is accurate and to get any last minute questions answered. If you live in an area with no formal real estate closing process, your HUD-1 settlement statement is mailed to you, and you're not entitled to look at it ahead of time.

✓ **Escrow account disclosure statement.** If the terms of your mortgage loan allow your lender to establish an escrow account for the payment of the liability insurance and property taxes due on your home throughout the life of your loan, RESPA says that whoever services your loan must provide you with an initial escrow account statement at closing or within 45 days of the closing.

You fund the escrow account at closing, and each of your mortgage payments includes an additional amount for the account as well as a cushion, just to make sure it contains enough money when it's time to pay the insurance and taxes. RESPA limits the amount of the cushion. By the way, the money in your escrow accounts probably do not earn interest.

Under certain circumstances, your mortgage lender can waive its right to set up a property tax escrow account — if you make a down payment of at 30 percent or if you agree to keep a certain amount of money in a savings account, for example. Ask your lender about its waiver requirements.

Protecting your RESPA rights

If you believe that your RESPA rights have been violated, send a letter to your lender or to the company who is servicing your loan — whoever committed the violation. Describe the violation, and provide the name of the lender or servicer as well as the company's address and phone number. Include your own phone number as well. Attach to your letter copies of any documentation you have that helps you prove your points. Be sure to include your mortgage loan number in your letter. Form 16-4 provides a sample complaint letter.

Some scam artists make money by sending out phony mortgage loan transfer letters instructing borrowers to begin sending their mortgage payments to them. To avoid getting ripped off by one of these cons, do not start sending your mortgage payments to a different address unless your lender sends you an official servicing transfer statement. If you receive such a statement and want to confirm that it is legit, call your mortgage lender. Want still more information about RESPA? Visit HUD's RESPA Web site at www.hud.gov/fha/sfh/res/respa_hm.html.

Do not send your complaint letter with your mortgage payment. It might never end up where you want it to go, or it might take a long time to get to the right person's desk.

The company must respond to your complaint in writing within 20 business days of receiving it. In addition, within 60 business days, it must either correct the problem or let you know that it has concluded that your RESPA rights were not violated. Be sure to continue making your loan payments while you are waiting for your problem to be resolved. Use this same process if you find an error in one of your escrow account statements.

If you're unhappy with how your mortgage lender or servicer responds to your letter, you can file a complaint with the consumer protection office of your state attorney general's office, as well as the federal Department of Housing and Urban Development (HUD). To file a RESPA complaint with HUD, write to

Director, Interstate Land Sales/RESPA Division
Office of Consumer and Regulatory Affairs
Office of Housing and Urban Development
451 7th Street, SW, Room 9146
Washington, DC 20410

You may also want to consult a real estate attorney. Depending on the specific nature of your problem and the strength of your case, you may be able to sue for actual and punitive damages. Don't delay meeting with a lawyer. You may have a relatively short time to sue depending on the subject of the lawsuit.

Chapter 17

Improving Your Home: Working with Contractors

*O*nce you buy a home, it's usually only a matter of time before you want to make it bigger and better. That may mean adding on, building up, taking down, putting in a pool. To maintain the value of your home, you also perform periodic home maintenance projects. They could include replacing the roof on your home, painting your home's interior and exterior, repaving your driveway, fixing plumbing problems, and so on.

When it comes to doing these things, most homeowners lack three essentials: the know how and skills, the right tools and equipment, and the time. Therefore, you will probably hire a professional to do the work for you. Depending on your needs, that person might be a jack-of-all-trades handyman, a home contractor, or, for really big jobs, an architect. Whomever you choose, choose carefully. Problems with home improvement professionals, such as contractors and handymen, rank high on the consumer complaint lists maintained by government agencies and nonprofit consumer organizations.

Among other things, consumers complain about poor quality work, unfinished work, such as having the roof of your home torn off and not replaced (Yikes! What a nightmare!), or projects that seem to escalate in cost almost daily. Consumers who hire home improvement professionals without a written agreement or contract are particularly vulnerable to problems, as is anyone who is not familiar with the federal and state laws that can protect them from unscrupulous businesses.

This chapter helps decrease the potential for homeowner hassle and heartbreak by educating you about how to select a professional to work on your home. It describes what should be included in the contract you are asked to sign, how to structure a payment schedule, how to protect yourself from the threat of a mechanics lien, and how to spot a home remodeling scam artist. The advice and information in this chapter applies to home repair pros as well as to home contractors because they handle bigger, costlier projects and, therefore, expose you to greater risk.

Picking the Right Professional for the Job

If you want to remodel your home and you don't want to do it yourself, you have three options. You can hire a handyman, a general contractor, or an architect and general contractor. Which option is right for you depends on the extent and the complexity of the work you want done, how much you have to spend, and how much of your own time you can devote to your home improvement project.

Handymen can handle simple home remodeling and construction projects, but usually they lack specialized building skills and the large project management skills of a general contractor. In addition, handymen might not be licensed, bonded, or insured. Although handymen charge less for their services than most general contractors, they are usually not appropriate for large scale or complicated home projects. Hire handymen to handle relatively routine home maintenance and repair work.

If you have a specific need that requires a special skill, hire a home professional with that specific skill. For example, if you want cabinets built for your kitchen, hire a cabinetmaker or skilled carpenter; if your roof needs replacing, hire a roofer; if you need work done on your heating and air-conditioning system, hire a company that does that kind of work; and so on.

Hire general contractors to handle the big stuff. They manage all of the nuts and bolts of getting the job done, making home remodeling and construction projects relatively trouble-free, assuming you hire the right contractor, of course. A general contractor will hire, fire, and manage all the people who work on your home project. They may include basic laborers as well as specialists such as carpenters, cabinetmakers, tile workers, sheet rock hangers, plumbers, electricians, and heating and air-conditioning specialists. She will also obtain all the government permits your project may require; schedule government inspections of your project as necessary; and work hand-in-hand with your architect, if you hire one to design your home project and draw up blueprints.

Reputable general contractors are usually licensed, bonded, and insured. You find out the significance of those three words in the next section of this chapter, "Getting the good, avoiding the bad."

You should consider involving an architect in your home improvement project if it is relatively complicated and involves a considerable amount of money. For example, an architect can help when you want to put an addition on your home, or you are totally redoing your kitchen or another important room in your home. Among other things, an architect works with you to create a design for your project and draws up plans for your project that a contractor can execute. Architects can also recommend a home contractor. Some general contractors provide architectural services through in-house architects or relationships with outside architects.

Getting the good, avoiding the bad

Because you are more apt to use a contractor rather than an architect and a contractor, too, and because contractors are usually hired to handle bigger projects than handymen, the rest of this chapter focuses primarily on contractors. When you are in the market for one, look for a reputable, experienced, and reliable professional who can work within your budget, but don't rush into a decision; shop around. A good contractor can help appreciate the value of what is probably your biggest asset and add to the pleasure that you get from living there, but a bad one can mean a boatload of trouble.

The best way to find a general contractor is to get names from people you trust who were happy with the contractors they hired to handle projects similar to yours. Bankers and real estate agents are also good sources. If you are already working with an architect, she should be able to steer you in the direction of some good contractors.

The classified ads section of your local paper can be a resource for names of small but qualified general contractors who charge less than the big guys who purchase expensive display ads.

Asking the right questions

Once you have names of contractors, call them to tell them in general terms what you want done to your home, and how much you can afford to spend. From your phone conversation with a contractor, you should determine whether he seems interested in your job, how quickly he can start, whether his answers to your questions were direct and helpful, and whether he returned your phone call in a prompt and courteous manner.

Meet in person and get written bids from at least three contractors. Provide each of them with a written statement of exactly what you want done to your home; be as specific as possible. The statement should also include the budget you have established for your project. Giving each of the contractors a copy of this statement means that when they bid on your project, they all use the same information, making it easier for you to compare their bids. After you have received their bids, read each one line-by-line. Ask the contractors to explain any differences in their prices, in the materials they propose using, in the amount of time they say it will take to complete their work, and so on. Form 17-1 on the CD contains a list of questions you should ask each potential contractor.

Don't automatically hire the contractor with the lowest bid. Cheap and good do not necessarily go hand in hand when it comes to home remodeling. Spending a little extra on a contractor who has a reputation for honesty and quality work is worth the money.

Before you make a final decision about a contractor, check out the company with your state's consumer protection office. If your local and state governments license contractors, make sure those offices have no complaints on file about the contractor. Also, check out the companies with your local Better Business Bureau.

To be extra sure that the contractor you hire is reputable and financially stable, contact the small claims clerk in your area and the clerk for your county court to find out whether any lawsuits are pending against the company or whether there are any judgments against the contractor. You can also call the federal bankruptcy court in your district to learn whether the contractor has ever filed for bankruptcy. Contact information for all federal courts can be found at the Federal Judiciary home page at www.uscourts.gov/allinks.html.

An absence of complaints against a contractor is no guarantee that the company is 100 percent reputable. Some shady contractors change their names frequently or do business under several names to avoid trouble and continue ripping off consumers.

Get names, addresses, and telephone numbers of previous clients who have worked with this contractor before. Also, make sure that the contractor performed for the references work similar to what you want done. For a list of the questions to ask a contractor's references, check out Form 17-2 on the CD.

Steering clear of crooked contractors

Although most home improvement businesses are reputable and do good work, there are reasons why so many appear on the complaint lists of government agencies and nonprofits. Some of them are pretty darn shady, including home contractors. When you are in the market for one, avoid businesses that seek you out via mail, e-mail, telephone, or knocking on your door. Avoid companies that offer a far cheaper price than all of the other bids you get or offer exceptionally long guarantees. Steer clear of a company that offers you discounts for finding new customers or just happen to have materials left over from another job. Form 17-9 on the CD provides a list of red flags to watch out for when dealing with contractors.

Getting the Essentials: A Written Contract

The contractor you hire should provide you with a signed, written contract. The contract may be a single page or multiple pages, depending on the complexity of your project. It should include the date and the contractor's name and physical address (not a P.O. box), phone number, and license number, if required. Be sure to read the contract thoroughly; ask about anything you do not understand. For a sample contract, go to Form 17-3 on the CD.

Do not let work begin on your home until you have a signed contract from a contractor.

Financing: If your home project cannot proceed unless you get it financed, be sure that your contract includes a provision stating that the agreement will not be binding on you if you are unable to secure the financing you need.

Scope: The contract should address the scope of work. You or the contractor can either fill in the work to be completed or note that the contractor's proposal is attached to the contract. If you are using an architect, you can refer to the architect's drawings.

Materials: This section of the contract should spell out all of the materials to be used, including, as appropriate, the color, make, model, and size of certain products. If you are not sure about the specific lighting fixtures, plumbing fixtures or other finish items you want, the contract can include an allowance for those things. Then, you can shop around for the various items while work on your home is going on.

Dates: The contract should also include an estimated start and completion date. Motivate a contractor to complete all but the small finishing details for your home improvement project by adding either a carrot or a stick to the contract. The carrot rewards the contractor if the company meets or beats the date for completion. The stick penalizes the contractor for each day that the completion date is missed. The sample contract takes the carrot approach. If you prefer the stick approach, use Form 17-4 as a model for the penalty clause you add to the contract.

Costs: The contract also needs to state the total cost of the project and how cost overruns will be handled. Unless you decide to handle them differently, your contract should say that any overruns will be absorbed by the contractor.

The contract should also address potential cost savings. Some contractors will agree to pass along any savings on your project or to split the savings with you.

Payment: Also included in the contract should be the payment schedule. Some contractors will ask for money up front or a down payment. However, as a rule, you should never pay for work not completed. All payments should be tied to the contractor's meeting certain deadlines and accomplishing certain phases of work. If the contractor needs money for materials, request that they be delivered C.O.D or execute a joint check agreement. Your bank can help set this up.

If you obtained a bank loan to pay for your home remodeling project and the cost of the project is substantial, the bank will probably allow the contractor to request a construction draw on the funds. The draws are paid as the work is completed. Normally, a bank pays 90 percent of the completed work and retains 10 percent until the project is completed.

Make your last payment as large as possible so that the contractor has a strong incentive to finish your job on a timely basis. Also, do not make the final payment or sign an *affidavit of final release* until you are sure that all work on your project has been completed and passed inspection, until the contractor has lived up to all the provisions in the contract, and until you have written proof that all the subcontractors and suppliers who worked on your job were paid. When you sign this affidavit, you are stating that all the contractor's obligations were met. Do not sign such a document until you are certain that the contractor *has* met his obligations.

Some states limit the amount of money a contractor can require as a down payment. Contact your state attorney general's office to find the law that applies where you live.

If you pay too much money up front, disreputable contractors are likely to take your money and run.

Subcontractors: Attached to the contract needs to be a list of the sub-contractors and suppliers who will work on your project, including their names, addresses, phone numbers, and Social Security or employers information numbers: This information is particularly important on big projects that involve multiple subcontractors and suppliers — in most states, if one of them is not paid by your contractor, the subcontractor can place a mechanic's lien on your home. To release the lien, you must either pay the subcontractor yourself or get the contractor to pay the subcontractor.

To protect yourself from the legal and financial ramifications of a mechanic's lien, ask your contractor to get a signed, *unconditional lien waiver* from each subcontractor and supplier every time one is paid. This document states that the subcontractor was paid and has no claim against your property for nonpayment. This obligation should be specified in the contract. Form 17-5 provides you with sample language to add to the contract, and Form 17-6 provides a sample release or waiver of lien form you can ask the contractor to use.

Any time you change something in the contract or add something to it, you and your contractor should both initial it. Another way to protect yourself from mechanics' liens is to pay the subcontractors and suppliers yourself rather than have the contractor do it. That may or may not be practical for you and your contractor.

Permits: The contract needs to address the contractor's obligation to obtain all necessary building permits, to comply with all relevant building codes and zoning requirements, and to arrange for all required government inspections: The contract should also indemnify, or hold you harmless, if the contractor fails to do any of those things. Otherwise, you would be held legally liable if a problem developed related to a permit, building code, and so on and the contractor had not lived up to your agreement. Your contract should also make clear who is responsible for paying for any necessary water or sewer taps or other required fees.

Change Orders: Changes to the original contract may be necessitated by the unavailability of a particular product, or technical complications, or simply because you change your mind about how you want things done. For example, you decide that you want wood floors not carpeting. Because change orders can affect the overall cost of your project and its completion date, unless you have a formal process for dealing with them, the cost of your project could skyrocket, and you and your contractor are apt to end up in conflict. Form 17-7 provides a sample clause to add to the contract if it does not already include a provision requiring change orders.

Your state might have a law that limits the amount by which your contractor's final bill can exceed the amount of the estimate you were given unless you okay the increase.

Most contractors have fill-in-the-blanks change order forms, but just in case, Form 17-8 on the CD gives you a sample change order form that you can ask your contractor to use and attach as an addendum to the contract. As an alternative, your contract can state that any change in the scope of work must be spelled out in writing as amendments to the contract and signed by both you and the contractor.

Cleanup: Your contract needs to address who will be responsible for daily and end-of-the-job cleanup. This is particularly important for big jobs that take a lot of time. However, even a relatively small home project can create quite a mess. Your contract should show that the contractor will be responsible for cleaning up the work site, taking care of any spills and stains, and hauling off trash and debris. This is called a *broom clause.*

Warranties: All warranties the contractor is providing, including their type, their duration, and any limitations associated with them. Be sure that the contract includes the names and addresses of the parties who will honor the warranties and that it says you will receive copies of all warranties.

Theft: State who has responsibility for the theft of any building materials or equipment from the job site.

Damage: It is important to state that it is the contractor's responsibility for any damage the contractor or any subcontractors might do to your home (inside and out).

Disputes: The contract must state how contract disputes will be handled. Most misunderstandings will probably be pretty minor; however, if things heat up and you reach a stalemate, you will be glad you have a provision in the contract that spells out how your problem must be resolved. For information about resolving problems, see Chapter 3.

Breach and Cancellation: The contract should also address breach of contract and contract cancellation provisions.

Finally, make sure that all written bid and estimates and any plans for your project are attached to the final contract before you sign it.

Changing your mind

Once you have signed a contractor's contract, you have a *cooling off* period of three days to back out of the deal if you signed the contract somewhere other than in the contractor's office. This cooling off period is called the *right of rescission* and is mandated by the federal Truth in Lending Act (TLA). To preserve your right of rescission, never sign a contract at the contractor's business location. You also have three days to rescind if the contract implies that the contractor has any financial claim to your home, or if you financed the project and repaying the loan will take four installments or more.

After you sign a contractor's contract, the contractor should give you a copy of the signed contract and two copies of a notice of rescission, a document that you fill out if you wish to rescind the contract. If you have a change of heart about the contract, you must sign one of the two copies and return it to the contractor before the three days are up. For more information about the Truth in Lending Act, turn to Chapter 6.

If a contractor violates the TLA, you have the right to rescind your contract for up to three years from the date that you signed it, or until you transfer interest in or sell your home.

Knowing your payment options

When you pay for a home remodeling project, pay with a check, credit card, or through draws on a construction account set up by your bank. Don't pay with cash. If you pay with cash and subsequently discover that the work is shoddy or unfinished, there might be little that you can do to get your money back or get the work done right. However, if you pay with a check, you can stop payment on it if you act quickly. If you pay with a credit card, you can refuse to pay the charge. For additional information on your Fair Credit Billing Act rights when you pay for merchandise or services with a credit card, read Chapter 6.

If you need a loan to finance your home remodeling project, your contractor might be able to arrange the financing, or you can apply for a bank loan. A loan through a contractor probably costs you more. However you get your loan, be sure that you're charged a fair interest rate and that you feel comfortable with your monthly loan payments. If you can't make them, the lender probably has a right to put a lien on your home.

Keeping records

Keep all paperwork related to your project in one place. This includes copies of the contract, change orders, and correspondence with your contractor. It's also a good idea to keep a log of all the phone conversations you have with your contractor — or at least of all the important ones. If your project will be completed over a period of weeks or even months, you might also want to take photographs as it progresses. At a minimum, use photos to document work not being done according to the terms of your contract — shoddy work, a trashed-out work site, and so on.

These records can be helpful if there is a problem between you and your contractor. You also need them if you are making a capital improvement to your home — one that increases your home's tax value. When you sell your home, the cost of the capital improvements decreases the amount of capital gains you must pay, assuming you sell it for more than you paid for it.

Tying up loose ends

Don't make your final payment to the contractor until you are sure that the contractor has done everything in the contract and in the change orders. Review each provision item by item. Also make sure all work meets the standards spelled out in the contract. Get written warranties for materials and workmanship according to the terms of the contract. Be sure to have proof that all subcontractors and suppliers were paid. And make sure the project job site is clean and no construction-related tools, equipment, or supplies remain at your premises.

Handling Contractor Conflicts

Not every contractor-homeowner relationship is made in heaven. In fact, the bigger the job, the more likely you are to have conflicts along the way. If you have chosen your contractor carefully, your disputes will probably be minor, but there is always the potential for bigger problems. Here is a rundown on how to deal with all eventualities.

At the first sign of trouble, talk to your contractor, by telephone or in person. Bring the contract violation to the attention of your contractor without being accusatory or confrontational. More often than not, this step will clear up the problem. If it does, follow up the conversation with a letter that summarizes the agreement you reached. Send it by certified mail, and request a return receipt. Keep a copy for your files.

If the contractor is unresponsive, you might want to pay an attorney to write a second letter for you. Receiving a letter on law firm letterhead is usually a pretty effective way of getting a contractor's attention. However, if the letter does not resolve your problem, review your contract to see whether it requires mediation or arbitration.

When mediation or arbitration does not settle things, you may want to consider a lawsuit. Before you do, however, compare the cost of suing to the likelihood that you will win your lawsuit and that you will be able to collect any damages, or get the contractor to make good on your contract. There's no use throwing more good money after bad if you don't have a strong case, if you're suing for a relatively small amount of money compared to your legal costs, or if the chances of getting a judgment enforced are slim to none.

You should also file a complaint against the contractor with your state attorney general's office of consumer protection or consumer affairs. If your local government has a consumer protection office, file a complaint there, too. Also file complaints with your local Better Business Bureau and your state or local Builders Association and Remodelers Council if the contractor belongs to either of these.

Chapter 18

Being a Tenant

. . . .

In This Chapter

▶ Reviewing the lease

▶ Renting with a roommate

▶ Getting your landlord to fix things

▶ Moving out before your lease is up

▶ Dealing with eviction

. . . .

Most landlords are fair and reasonable. Renting a place to live is usually a no-sweat proposition. However, even if your landlord-tenant relationship begins on a high note, problems could develop later, and if you deal with them the wrong way, you could face eviction.

This chapter provides the information you need to find a good landlord, to deal with landlord-tenant problems, and to protect your legal rights from the day you sign a lease to the day your lease is up. Among other things, this chapter highlights the most important provisions in the typical lease, tells you how to protect yourself if you rent with a roommate, gives you the full scoop on security deposits, advises you about what to do if your landlord refuses to tend to necessary repairs, and explains how evictions work.

Finding a Place to Hang Your Hat

Before you begin looking for a place to rent, figure out how much you can afford to spend each month. Also, decide what neighborhoods you want to consider and what kind of rental property you would like — a single-family home, duplex, garden apartment, high-rise apartment, efficiency, and so on.

Then, look for rental properties that fit the bill by reading the real estate section of your local newspaper, checking out the apartments for rent publications you can find for free in your local grocery and drug stores, by driving around neighborhoods looking for "For Rent" signs, and by putting out the word that you are in the market for a new place to live. Make appointments to see the places that interest you. You schedule them directly with the landlord or with the landlord's property manager.

You may want to let a rental locator company find a place for you to rent. The company presents you with rental options that it thinks fit your needs and sells you to the owner or the property manager of the rental property you want to rent. Usually, the landlord pays the rental locator company a fee for finding it a tenant; you do not have to pay the company anything. However, make sure of this before you agree to work with a locator company. Also, if the company confirms that the landlord pays the fee, check to make sure that the fee is not being passed on to you as an extra charge in your new lease.

After you find a place, ask for a rental application and a blank copy of the lease you're expected to sign if you move in. Read the lease carefully to make sure that it protects your interests and to identify anything that you want to add, modify, or delete. Also, note anything that you do not understand so you can ask about it later. The "Looking for Mr. Goodlease" section of this chapter reviews the basic lease provisions to look for.

If any of the properties you see are dirty or rundown, you can probably conclude that if you move in, you face a tough time getting your landlord to respond to your maintenance and repair requests.

If you are new to town or unfamiliar with the landlord's reputation, check it out by contacting your local Better Business Bureau. And if you're really a stickler for detail, take a trip to your county courthouse and check in with the clerk's office to find out whether the landlord has ever been sued by tenants or by your local or state government. For example, former tenants may have had to sue the landlord to get back their security deposits, or your municipal government may have sued because the landlord refused to meet local building code standards.

You need the legal name of the landlord to look him up in the court records. That name might actually be the name of a corporation or business partnership and not the name of the complex where you want to rent or the landlord's first and last names. The "Playing Business Name Detective" section of Chapter 4 shows you how to find out the legal name of a business.

Completing the rental application

Unless you are renting a place to live from a personal friend or family member who already knows all about you, a prospective landlord asks you to complete a rental application. The application asks about your rental history, recent employment history, and your finances. You probably have to provide references, too. The landlord reviews your application information to determine whether she wants to rent to you.

Landlords are prohibited by federal law from asking you about your race, religion, national origin, gender, age, or familial status. This includes prohibiting questions about whether you are pregnant or have children younger than age 18. Landlords are also barred from asking you if you have a physical or mental disability, including whether you are a recovering alcoholic or drug addict. Your state or local government may also have laws governing what can and can't be asked on a rental application. Those laws may mirror or expand on the federal law. To find out about those laws, call your areas tenant council or fair housing agency.

Looking for Mr. Goodlease

Most states permit oral leases assuming the term of the agreement is no longer than a year. However, as with any other important agreement, you're asking for trouble if you don't get a written lease from your landlord that clearly spells out your rights and obligations as a tenant, and your landlord's responsibilities. If the landlord won't give you one, find another place to rent.

Don't move into the place you're renting until you and your landlord have signed the lease. If another adult will be responsible for helping to pay the rent, she should sign the lease, too. Form 18-1 on the CD provides you with a sample lease. In reading it, you'll notice it is very landlord-friendly. Most are, because the landlord provides them. However, the sidebar "Lease loopholes" highlights some specific landlord-friendly provisions you should try to avoid.

There are two basic types of leases. The most common type gives you the right to live in a place for a certain amount of time — usually a year. When your time is up, you may be able to renew the lease, and your landlord usually has the right to set new terms for the lease if he agrees to renew it. The second type of lease automatically renews from one period to the next — most often month to month. Usually, if your landlord chooses not to renew, he does not have to give you a reason. Form 18-14 provides a checklist of terms your lease should address.

The lease you sign probably obligates you to pay your landlord's attorney fees and court costs if you sue him and lose. Be sure to consider these potential costs when you are deciding whether a lawsuit is worth your time and money. Use a pen when you strike though something in a contract, write in a new provision, or add just a few words. Before either of you sign the contract, you and your landlord should initial all the changes.

If you rent a condo, you are responsible to two masters — your landlord and the condominium association. If you ignore either your landlord's rules or the rules of the association, you may have to find a new place to live.

Lease loopholes

It's a fact of life for most tenants that the lease they sign probably favors their landlord. That's because landlords provide the leases. Even so, some leases are less tenant-friendly than others, and you are best off avoiding them when possible. Here are some lease provisions to watch out for:

✔ A clause that says your landlord is not responsible for maintaining or repairing the property you are renting.

✔ A clause that says the landlord is not responsible for any injuries you might suffer because your rental property is poorly maintained or because necessary repairs were not completed.

✔ A clause that prohibits you from withholding your rent if your landlord refuses to fix a problem that threatens your safety, health, security, or ability to enjoy living in the place you are renting.

✔ A clause that gives your landlord the right to enter your residence for any reason or with little or no notice.

✔ A clause that requires you to continue paying rent even if your rental property burns down or gets destroyed by a flood or some other natural disaster. Luckily, this clause is illegal in most states.

Documenting problems before you move in

Don't sign a lease until you and the landlord together walk through the place you are renting and make a list of anything that is damaged, dirty, or defective in some other way. For example, during the inspection you may notice marks on the walls, stained countertops, a broken dishwasher, or a burn hole in the carpet. Use an inspection checklist to document the problems you find. If your landlord does not provide one, create one yourself by using the form on Form 18-2 of the CD.

If the place you are renting is furnished, the inventory should also note the condition of each item. Depending on your state, your landlord may be legally required to give you a written statement of the condition of your rental unit before you move in. The statement should include a list of all existing defects. You may have a right to follow up with an inspection of your own to ensure that the landlord noted every problem.

Inventorying the condition of the place you are renting before you sign a lease is important for two reasons. First, if your landlord claims that when you move out, he is entitled to deduct from your security deposit the cost of fixing problems in your rental that you believe existed when you moved in, the signed written inventory helps you make your argument. Second, it may be easier to get the landlord to agree to take care of the problems in the place you're renting if you and he document them together and you can talk about them on the spot.

Your landlord is legally obligated to correct any problems in your rental unit that could affect your safety, health, or security. However, your landlord is not obligated to address any cosmetic shortcomings in the property you are renting. So if you hate the green shag carpeting in your new apartment, you may have to live with it. However, your landlord might be willing to let you make some changes yourself, probably at your own expense. Get his permission first.

If your landlord promises to repair or replace something or to make cosmetic improvements to the place you're renting, ask him to put those promises in writing and to indicate a date by which he will make good on them.

Getting the scoop on security deposits

When you sign your lease, you will probably have to pay a security deposit. Usually, the deposit is equivalent to one or two months rent. Your local or state government can limit the amount of your security deposit and also require that your landlord keep it in a special bank account, possibly one that earns interest. You are entitled to the interest income.

If your rental unit is spic and span and problem-free when you move out, and you always pay your rent on time, you're probably entitled to get back all of your security deposit. However, if your unit is damaged and the damage goes beyond normal wear and tear, don't expect to get back all of your security deposit. Your landlord is entitled to use your deposit to help pay to repair the damage. Examples of damage that are probably considered beyond normal wear and tear include stains in the carpeting; a child's handwriting on the walls; fish tank water stains on the wood floors; a rotten floor from a problem with the plumbing upstairs that you never reported to your landlord. Your landlord can also deduct from your security deposit any money you may owe him. That might include past due rent, late fees, and so on.

In most states, a landlord must refund a tenant's security deposit within a certain period of time — usually, no later than 30 days after a tenant moves out.

When you move out, if your former landlord does not return all of your security deposit, ask for a written list of the expenses that were deducted from your deposit. Some states require this statement.

Getting your security deposit back

If you are like most renters, you count on getting all of your security deposit back. You may need it to rent a new place to live, help pay some bills, finance a vacation, and so on. Keep in mind the following tips. They can help you get back as much of your deposit as possible:

✔ Understand your lease obligations and live up to each one of them.

✔ When you first move into the place you are renting, take photos of any preexisting damage. Write the date you took the pictures on the back of each photo.

✔ Treat the place you rent as you would treat your own home. Keep it clean; contact your landlord in writing right away about anything that needs to be repaired; do not let your children, roommates, or visitors misuse the appliances, cut on countertops, write on walls, or flick ashes onto your floors; and so on.

✔ Handle minor repairs yourself if you have the skills and your lease allows it. Small problems can grow into big ones over time.

✔ Bring any problems in your rental unit to your landlord's attention right away so that any damage is minimal. Also, explain the cause of the damage. You're less apt to have problems getting your security deposit back if you're forthcoming about the damage and if your landlord clearly understands that the damage is not your fault.

✔ Clean your rental unit before you leave. If you are not good at cleaning or you only have time to do a superficial job, hire a cleaning service.

✔ If your landlord discovers problems during his final inspection, consider asking your landlord whether you can fix them yourself. If the damage is relatively easy to repair and if you are handy with a paintbrush, hammer, nails, and so on, you may be able to take care of the damage yourself for little or nothing.

✔ Know what your state law says about security deposits.

If your landlord does not refund the full amount of your security deposit after you move out, write and ask for an explanation. Model your letter after the one on Form 18-3. If your landlord is violating the law in your state, be sure to indicate that in your letter. If your landlord does not respond or continues to maintain that she acted legally, consider suing your landlord in small claims court, assuming the amount of money at stake qualifies for that court. Depending on your state, you can also sue your landlord if she refuses to pay you interest on your security deposit or does not return your deposit within the required time.

If the amount of your security deposit does not cover the cost of the damage you did to your rental unit while you were living there, your former landlord may send you a demand letter asking you to pay for the additional damage by a certain date. If you do not respond or refuse to pay the extra money, the landlord may take you to court to try to get the money.

Renting with a Roommate

You have special issues to consider when you rent with a roommate. First, make sure that both of you are on the lease. Otherwise, you are legally liable for paying all of the rent each month, and for any damage your roommate might do to the place you share, even if you each agree to share all expenses 50/50.

In landlord-speak, your roommate is your co-tenant. If you are renting a place to live by yourself and then you decide that you want a roommate, whether he is your new love interest or your best friend, ask for your landlord's permission first. Otherwise, depending on the terms of your lease, your landlord may have the right to evict you. For example, your lease may say that only you can live there.

Your landlord will probably want your roommate to complete a rental application just as you did. Then, assuming your roommate passes muster, your landlord will probably require that you both sign a new lease that makes you co-tenants with the same legal rights and responsibilities. Putting both of you on the lease gives your landlord the right to come after either one of you if you are late on your rent, or violate the terms of your agreement.

If you and your roommate sign a new lease, your landlord might take the opportunity to raise your rent and increase the size of your security deposit.

Avoiding litigation limbo

An ounce of prevention is worth a pound of cure when you have a roommate, even if your roommate is your best friend or your fiancé. It is always a good idea, before you sign your lease, to come to an agreement regarding your obligations to one another as roommates. Put your agreement on paper, date it, and sign it.

When you and your roommate are on good terms with one another, preparing such an agreement may sound like a waste of time. But you may be glad you have it if your relationship sours later and you have trouble sharing a bathroom sink, much less sharing responsibility for the rent. Among other things, your roommate agreement should address:

- ✔ How you will share your living expenses — rent, payments, utilities, groceries, home and yard maintenance expenses, and so on.
- ✔ How you will share household chores such as cleaning the house, cooking, grocery shopping, mowing the lawn, shoveling snow, and so on.

✔ If you don't want to be roommates any more, which of you has the right to stay where you are living.

✔ If one of you wants to move out before your lease is up, the amount of notice you must give one another, and the responsibilities of the person who moves out. Legally, the person who is moving out is breaking your lease and therefore, is responsible for paying her share of the rent and other expenses until your lease is up, or until you have a new roommate.

When your co-tenant moves out before your lease is up, she is breaking your lease and officially, your landlord has the right to evict you because you and your roommate are equally responsible for meeting the terms of your lease. In reality, however, assuming you have been a good tenant, your landlord will probably let you stay, assuming the rent checks keep coming.

✔ If one of you wants to move out before your lease is up, how you will deal with any damage done to your rental unit while both of you were living there.

Use the sample roommate agreement on Form 18-4 to iron out all of your differences before they happen. If your roommate moves out before your lease is up and ignores her lease obligations, leaving you to scramble to come up with the full amount of the rent, write your ex-roommate a polite letter asking her to pay her share of the rent, utilities, and so on. If worse comes to worse, you can sue your roommate. However, dealing with one another in court is apt to be extremely difficult for both of you, and collecting your money if you win your lawsuit could be even more problematic.

If your landlord says that you can remain where you are once your roommate moves out, but you do not want to pay the full amount of the rent yourself, you have two options: Find a new roommate, or ask your current roommate to find someone to sublease to, assuming your lease permits subleasing. Your lease may permit subleasing, prohibit it, or allow subleasing only with your landlord's permission. It may also give your landlord the right to approve whomever you want to sublease to.

If your lease says that subleasing is not permitted, consider asking your landlord about it anyway. Your landlord may agree if he feels good about the person you would sublease to. Also, subleasing saves your landlord the hassle of advertising for a new tenant once you move out, readying your place for someone new, and so on. From your perspective, the advantage of a sublease arrangement is that your current lease remains in effect and that you have someone to share your rent expenses. From your roommate's perspective, the sublessor pays his share of the rent and assumes all his other obligations.

Protecting yourself with federal law

Federal law prohibits discrimination on the basis of race, color, national origin, sex, familial status, or handicap status. For supplemental information on the Federal Fair Housing Act, see Form 18-11 on the CD. An excellent HUD brochure on housing discrimination is on the CD at Form 18-12. A sample complaint letter is on the CD at Form 18-13.

Being aware of sublease shortfalls

Subleasing may sound like an easy answer to the question of what to do about your lease responsibilities when your employer transfers you, when you want to move into your new sweetie's place, when you buy a home, or when you just want a change of scenery. But (and it's a big but) there may be a catch. Depending on state laws and the terms of your lease, you may be legally responsible for paying the rent until your lease is up if the person you sublease to doesn't. Plus, you could be held legally liable for any damage that the sublessor does to the rental property.

The best way to protect yourself from the negative consequences of subleasing is to sublease to someone you know to be trustworthy and financially responsible. Also, as an extra measure of protection, consider asking the sublessor to sign an agreement with you that spells out the terms of your relationship. Form 18-5 on the CD provides a sample agreement to model your own after.

Getting Things Fixed

Repair and maintenance issues create conflict and bad feelings between many landlords and tenants. The conflict may arise because a landlord does not believe that he's legally obligated to take care of the problem his tenant complains about, because the landlord charges his tenant for the cost of a repair, because a tenant thinks that her landlord is taking too long to fix a problem, and so on.

Leveraging the lax landlord

Your landlord is not required to make cosmetic improvements and changes to your rental unit, such as painting your walls so they match your new furniture or replacing the current carpeting with something you like better. However, if your walls are dingy and your carpeting is worn from years of use, your landlord may be willing to spruce up your place or to let you handle some of the redecorating yourself, assuming your landlord approves your plans first.

Here are four keys to minimizing the potential for conflicts over rental repairs and maintenance:

- ✔ Rent a place to live that's in good shape. A well-maintained place is less likely to need repairs than one that looks rundown.

- ✔ Rent a place with a decor that you like and that works with your furniture so that you're less likely to become dissatisfied with the color of the walls, the kitchen tile, the carpeting, and so on.

- ✔ Be clear about your landlord's obligations and your rights and responsibilities when it comes to repair and maintenance activities. That way, you don't set yourself up for disappointment and frustration by asking for things from your landlord that you're not entitled to. Read what your lease says about repairs and maintenance and become familiar with the local and state laws regarding your landlord's responsibilities to fix and maintain the place you're renting.

  If you want advice regarding your repair and maintenance rights and responsibilities, call your local tenant's organization or council, or contact a lawyer who specializes in landlord-tenant matters.

- ✔ Follow the process outlined in your lease when you want your landlord to take care of a problem in your rental unit. Your lease probably dictates that you put your request in writing. It is a good idea to include in your letter a date by which you would like the problem taken care of; 10 to 14 days is probably reasonable. Same-day or next-day service is unrealistic except in the case of an emergency repair. However, your local or state government may have a law that dictates how quickly your landlord must respond to you.

If a problem with your apartment (a water leak or fire, for instance) causes damage to your personal property, your landlord's property insurance probably does not protect you. This is also true if your personal property is stolen. Therefore, protect yourself from loss by purchasing renters' insurance. See Chapter 13 for more on insurance.

When you prepare your repair or maintenance request, you may increase the likelihood that your landlord will do what you are asking for in a timely manner if you include the following two items in your letter:

✔ Clearly explain why your request is necessary and important.

✔ Speak to your landlord's self-interest. For example, most landlords want to clear up any problem that creates even the slightest risk of a lawsuit — someone could get hurt if he falls through the hole in your front porch — or that could put a really big dent in their wallets if ignored (because your living room ceiling will need to be replaced if the upstairs water leak is not fixed).

Model your letter after the one on Form 18-6 of the CD. Keep a copy for yourself, and if you want proof that your landlord received it, send the letter certified mail and ask for a return receipt.

Handling the unresponsive landlord

If your landlord does not respond to your repair or maintenance request, call him and write a follow-up letter. In your second letter, reiterate what you asked for in your previous letter, and set a date by which you want a response. Form 18-7 provides a sample follow-up letter.

You have several options if your landlord continues to ignore you or refuses to do what you ask. Each option is described in this section. Before you pursue any of them, however, read your lease so you can be sure that your actions will not create more problems for you by giving your landlord a reason to sue you for eviction. Also, check with a landlord-tenant attorney and with your local tenants' organization to find out whether your local or state government prohibits any of these options. These resources can also indicate any special requirements you must meet if you pursue a particular option. For example, you may have to provide your landlord with specific notifications if you want to withhold rent, take care of repairs yourself, move out, and so on.

When your landlord refuses to live up to his repair and maintenance responsibilities, you may be able to

✔ **Withhold your rent:** Send your landlord a letter alerting him to the fact that you are exercising your legal right to withhold rent. Form 18-8 provides a sample letter to send to your landlord.

Your local or state government may prohibit rent withholding. In areas where it's allowed, a law may limit how much you can withhold. You may be required to deposit the rent that you withhold in an escrow account or with a neutral third party, such as the court, until your landlord completes the repairs you are asking for.

✔ **Pay less rent:** You may be entitled to make lower rental payments until the repairs and maintenance problems are taken care of. The amount of rent you pay must reflect the value of your rental unit without the repairs.

Do not withhold rent until you have spoken with a landlord-tenant attorney or to your local tenants organization about the circumstances that entitle you to take this step and about how much money to withhold. For example, you cannot withhold rent just because your landlord refuses to paint your apartment a different color. Notify your landlord in writing about your plans to reduce the amount of rent you pay. In your letter, describe the specific repairs you want done, indicate a deadline by which you want them completed, and state exactly how much of your rent you will withhold each month as long as the repairs go undone.

✔ **Take care of the repairs yourself:** You may have the right to make the repairs yourself or hire someone to take care of them for you and then deduct his cost from your next month's rent. The term for this is *repair and deduct.*

Your lease may set a dollar limit on the cost of the repairs that you can handle on your own and deduct from your rent. If you exceed that limit, you may have to absorb the extra cost yourself.

✔ **Break your lease:** If your landlord's failure to attend to necessary repairs or maintenance is a violation of your lease, you may have a legal right to cancel your lease agreement. However, before you take this step, consult with a landlord-tenant lawyer or with your local tenants' organization. Either of them can help you ensure that you accurately interpret your lease, act within the law, and follow the appropriate process for breaking your lease. For example, before you break your lease, you may be required to try to resolve your problem in other ways.

If you do not have a legal right to break your lease and you do anyway, your landlord might sue you to force you to meet all of your remaining lease obligations. He may also sue you for the damages he alleges you caused him to suffer as a result.

✔ **Report your landlord:** You can report your landlord to your local building, health, or fire department. Which department to contact depends on the nature of your complaint. Most local governments have building, housing, and fire codes that establish minimum standards for things such as wiring, heating, plumbing, sanitation, water supply, elevators, and so on. They may also require that landlords install certain types of locks on doors and windows, install smoke detectors, and so on. These codes are established to protect tenants' safety, security, and health.

✔ **Move out:** When your living conditions are so intolerable that you have no choice but to move from where you are living, the law gives you the right to vacate your premises without being penalized by your landlord.

The legal term for such a move is *constructive eviction*. Depending on the local or state laws, you may be entitled to reimbursement for your moving expenses, the cost of staying in a hotel or motel while you look for a new place to live, and so on.

✔ **Sue:** Depending on your state, you might be able to sue your landlord to force him to do what you have asked or for breach of contract. If you file a breach-of-contract lawsuit, you may be able to ask your landlord to reimburse you for the rent you paid while the necessary repairs and maintenance went undone; pay to repair or replace the personal property you lost or had damaged because of the problems; and reimburse you for your medical expenses if your landlord's negligence caused you to become ill or be injured. Your lawsuit may be heard in your area's small claims court, in a landlord-tenant court, or in a regular trial court. That depends on the nature of the lawsuit and the amount of money you're suing for.

Breaking Your Lease

Generally, you're not legally entitled to break your lease unless your landlord significantly violates the terms of your agreement, refuses to make necessary repairs, continually enters your rental unit without giving you the proper notice, and so on. Before you break your lease, review what it says about the consequences you face. If getting out of your lease will cost you a lot and there isn't a lot of time left on it, you may want to consider staying put until the lease is up. Your lease may require that you pay your landlord a penalty if you move out early. Most likely, it says that you must continue paying your rent just as you did while you were living there, until your landlord finds a tenant to replace you. Your lease might also state that your landlord has the right to sue you if you break it.

The laws in most states prohibit *double-dipping* — a landlord may not collect rent from the tenant who broke her lease while collecting rent from a replacement tenant in the same apartment.

Depending on the terms of your lease, an alternative to breaking your lease can be subletting the place you are renting to someone else. You should also review your lease to see whether it tells you how to break it. Most likely, it requires you to provide your landlord with a 30-day notice. Even if it does not, to protect yourself, notify your landlord of your plans in writing at least 30 days before your intended move-out day. Do not just fly the coop. Your landlord is more apt to sue you if you do. Form 18-9 provides a sample letter that you can send your landlord to notify him of your plans.

Getting Evicted

If your landlord defaults on your lease agreement, you might be able to break your lease and move out without suffering any negative consequences. However, if you are the one in default, your landlord can ask you to move out, and if you don't, she can ask the court for permission to evict you or force you to move. Examples of things you might do that could cause you to be in default of your lease include not paying your rent, vandalizing your property, having more people living with you than your lease allows, playing loud music into the wee hours of the morning, and keeping a dog when your landlord has a no-pets policy.

Compared to other legal procedures, an eviction lawsuit can proceed very quickly. To protect tenants, landlords in every state are required to take very specific steps before they can get the court's permission to evict. Among other things, your landlord must tell you in writing that you are in default of your lease and give you a chance to cure the default by a certain date. The notice also lets you know that if you don't take appropriate action, you have to move out or you face eviction. Don't ignore this notice! If you do, your situation will surely go from bad to worse. Instead, decide how to respond. To figure out what to do, you may want to speak with a landlord-tenant attorney or with your local tenants organization, especially if you don't believe that your landlord is justified in making the demands he has made of you.

If you have proof that your landlord is wrong — receipts, cancelled checks, letters, photos, and so on — pull it together just in case you need it. If you're able to cure the default, let your landlord know and provide her with a deadline by which you will take care of the problems she highlighted in her notice to you. Summarize your conversation in a letter and send it to your landlord after making a copy for yourself.

If you and your landlord are able to work things out, summarize your agreement by using the letter on Form 18-10 of the CD. If you disagree with what your landlord accuses in his notice, let your landlord know in a letter. Now is when those receipts, cancelled checks, and so on come in handy! The attorney or tenants organization you consult can help you be sure that your letter is phrased correctly and that you cite any local or state laws that may apply to your situation. Under certain conditions, your landlord can send you an *unconditional quit notice.* (It may be called something different in your state.) This kind of notice essentially tells you that it's time for you to go!

When you receive an *unconditional quit notice,* you have no opportunity to cure your default. Usually, your landlord can't send this notice unless you have repeatedly violated your lease or are using illegal drugs or selling drugs in the place that you rent. If the eviction process moves forward and your landlord files an eviction lawsuit against you, you are formally notified of the lawsuit via a summons, and probably given a court date at the same time. The lawsuit is heard in a formal trial court, in a small claims court, or in a special court set up just to resolve landlord-tenant problems, depending on your state.

Unless you feel fully capable of representing yourself in court and are prepared to lose the lawsuit and be forced to move, or unless your case is being heard in a small claims court that does not permit plaintiffs or defendants to use attorneys, hire an attorney to represent you if you are being evicted.

The legal processes and procedures in small claims court are fewer and less formal than in other courts, and most cases are resolved in one relatively brief hearing. Some small claims courts do not allow attorneys. After you receive the summons, you can

- **Offer to settle with your landlord in exchange for his dropping his lawsuit.** Chapter 4 explains how the settlement process works, including the importance of putting your settlement agreement in writing.

- **File an answer by the deadline on the summons.** In your answer, you can deny all or some of what your landlord alleges in her complaint, move to end the lawsuit, or countersue.

- **Do nothing.** If you do not file an answer or show up in court on the trial date, the court will probably award your landlord a default judgment that means your landlord gets the right to evict you. The court might also give him the right to collect back rent, damages, and so on from you. Your landlord may be awarded attorney fees and court costs. Most likely, they come out of your security deposit. If your security deposit will not cover all of the costs, your landlord may sue you for the balance.

- **Simply show up for your day in court.**

If you're unhappy with the court's decision, you can appeal it. You need an attorney to help you with your appeal because the appeal is heard by a higher, more formal court than the one that issued the judgment against you. Your eviction is put on hold pending the outcome of the appeal.

If the court gives your landlord permission to evict you, even if you move out prior to the official eviction date, the eviction becomes part of the court record. It might also show up on your credit record, possibly jeopardizing your ability to rent future housing and even get a good job.

If you decide not to appeal, or if you lose your appeal and you do not move voluntarily, your eviction moves forward. However, your landlord cannot show up at your door and start throwing your stuff onto the sidewalk. She must pay a county sheriff, marshal, or constable to notify you in writing about when the eviction will happen and to execute the eviction on the scheduled date unless you have moved out by then. Your landlord is breaking the law if she tries to get you to move by cutting off your utilities, changing your locks, threatening you, and so on. If that happens, get in touch with a landlord-tenant lawyer right away. In most states, you can sue your landlord for forcible eviction, and if you win, your landlord might be liable for both actual and punitive damages.

Part V
Personal Matters

The 5th Wave   By Rich Tennant

"Included with today's surgery, we're offering a manicure, pedicure, haircut, and ear wax flush for just $49.95."

In this part . . .

Check out this part when it's time to address insurance matters: life insurance, disability insurance, health insurance, and long-term care insurance. Chapter 20 addresses those who are eligible for federal Medicare insurance benefits and those who are helping someone else deal with the Medicare system.

Chapter 19

Insuring Yourself and Your Loved Ones

. . . .

In This Chapter

▶ Shopping for health coverage the right way

▶ Taking advantage of COBRA

▶ Dealing with disability insurance

▶ Protecting your assets with long-term care insurance

▶ Understanding how the Medical Information Bureau can affect you

. . . .

*L*ife, health, and disability insurance are all about "what ifs." What if you die and your family is left destitute because they can't afford to pay their bills and take care of their daily expenses? What if your child becomes seriously ill and you face medical bills that are bigger than you ever imagined? What if you injure your back in a freak accident and you're unable to work for months? How would your family meet its financial obligations?

Although you may want to believe that none of these situations could ever apply to you, all you have to do is read the paper, listen to the news, or live long enough and you realize that life is unpredictable and that bad things can happen, no matter how careful you try to be. Life, health, disability, and long-term care insurance shields you and your loved ones from the full impact of those consequences. You may hate paying money for insurance that you may never use, but we guarantee that you'll be glad you did if one of those "what ifs" happens to you or to someone in your family.

This chapter gives you the rundown on how life, health, disability, and long-term care insurance works and what to consider when you shop for a policy. It also directs you to resources you can use to get information about a particular type of insurance or to compare policies and rates. The chapter also gives you a peek at the Medical Information Bureau (MIB), explains how this little-known organization can affect your ability to get the insurance you want, and tells you how to find out whether the MIB is storing information about you.

Insuring Your Health: Protecting Your Finances

The United States is facing a health insurance crisis. Too many people do not have health coverage. Many of those without insurance can't afford to buy health coverage themselves and do not get it as an employment benefit. Other people can only afford to purchase coverage that protects them if they're hospitalized or experience some other major medical problem. Therefore, they must pay out of pocket for their preventive care and for the treatment of relatively minor health problems.

Doing without health coverage or not having adequate coverage can be financially devastating if you or someone in your family becomes seriously ill or is badly injured. In fact, heavy medical expenses have become one of the primary causes of consumer bankruptcies in this country.

Check out these resources if you have trouble finding health coverage

If you're hitting a brick wall in your search for health coverage, or for a health plan that will cover a pre-existing condition, here are some options to explore. None is ideal, but they all offer some form of health coverage.

✔ **Blue Cross and Blue Shield:** The "Big Blues" are large insurance companies that often insure people whom other companies refuse to touch. Go to the Web site of the Blue Cross/Blue Shield Association (www.bluecares.com) to get the full scoop on what these companies have to offer. You can also use the Web site to locate a Blue Cross/Blue Shield insurance company in your area.

✔ **Your state insurance commission:** This government office can tell you whether your state has an insurance-buying pool that you qualify for. Participating in the pool may bring health coverage within your financial reach. If you're having a hard time finding insurance because of your medical problems, you may be able to purchase insurance through your state's high-risk pool. However, buying insurance this way can be quite expensive. A few states require insurance companies to insure anyone who is willing to pay their price.

✔ **The Medicaid program:** If you have a low income, no matter what your age, you may qualify for medical coverage through the federal/state Medicaid program. The federal government sets broad national guidelines for this program, and each state sets its own eligibility standards and determines the type, amount, duration, and scope of the health benefits it offers. Each state also administers its own Medicaid program. For more information about Medicaid, including the toll-free number to call for information about eligibility standards in your state and how to apply for benefits, go to www.hcfa.gov/medicaid/meligib.htm.

Choosing group or individual

Most people obtain medical insurance through their employers as part of their benefits package. However, if you are a part-time employee, you might not be eligible for that benefit, and if you work for a small business, your employer might not be able to afford that employee benefit. When a small business does offer a group health insurance plan, it's apt to be less comprehensive than what a larger company offers.

In these instances, and when you are self-employed, assuming that you're not on a plan offered by your spouse's employer, you must purchase individual coverage if you want health coverage. You will pay a lot for this coverage. Also, you're more apt to end up with a policy that excludes any pre-existing health conditions you have. Typically, the exclusions last for between six and twelve months, but sometimes they last forever. If a pre-existing condition is making it difficult for you to find coverage you can afford, check with Blue Cross/Blue Shield. They are more apt to cover people with health problems.

Knowing the difference between health insurance and managed care health plans

When you shop for health coverage, you have to decide whether you want to purchase a fee-for-service insurance plan or prefer to get your health coverage through a managed care plan. *Fee-for-service insurance* is the traditional type of health insurance. With this kind of coverage, you can see the healthcare providers you want, and you submit your medical bills to your insurance company for reimbursement. Once you satisfy your annual deductible, the company reimburses you for all covered expenses. A *deductible* is the amount of money you must pay out-of-pocket before your insurance plan will begin sharing the cost of your medical care with you. Usually, the insurance company pays 80 percent of each bill, and you pick up the remaining 20 percent. For most people, the high cost of medical care has made fee-for-service insurance too expensive.

Legitimate insurance companies use underwriting to determine whether they want to sell you insurance. Some companies, however, practice post-claim underwriting. Those companies sell you insurance, collect your insurance premiums, and then, once you file an insurance claim, come up with a reason for not paying the claim. Post-claim underwriting is illegal in many states.

Managed care health plans are an alternative to traditional fee-for-service policies. They're intended to control the cost of healthcare in the U.S. One of the ways they do so is by contracting with certain healthcare providers to provide services to their members, and by controlling consumers' access to healthcare.

Generally, a managed care health plan costs less than a traditional fee-for-service insurance policy. Also, over time, the cost of such a health plan tends to increase less than the premium for a health insurance policy.

When you enroll in a managed care plan, you probably have to make a small copayment each time you receive healthcare services. It is your share of the cost of the medical care or treatment you received. It is either a percentage of the total charges or a fixed amount of money. Copays eliminate the need to file reimbursement claims as you do with fee-for-service health insurance. However, you still have a yearly deductible to satisfy. Copays are supposed to discourage you from getting care and treatment you don't really need.

Managed care plans include Health maintenance organizations (HMOs), preferred provider organizations (PPOs), and point of service plans. Here are descriptions of each:

- **Health maintenance organization (HMO):** Usually, when you enroll in an HMO, you must designate a primary care doctor who either is an employee of the HMO or has a business relationship with the HMO as part of its provider network. Typically, the HMO pays this doctor a set amount of money to treat you regardless of how much time she spends with you. This doctor not only provides you with medical care and services but also acts as your *gatekeeper,* determining when you should be referred to a specialist, receive certain tests, and so on.

  The doctor also provides you with referrals to other doctors and medical care providers within the HMO network. Depending on the HMO, you may be able to use its services free of charge in exchange for paying an annual fee, or you might make a small copayment each time you access medical care and services. You may have to go to a certain location to obtain the care and services, or you may be able to choose an HMO provider and visit the provider's office to get the care you need. If you get medical care or services from a provider outside your HMO, the plan does not cover the cost.

  Although you must deal with a considerable number of restrictions when you enroll in an HMO, you pay less for your insurance coverage than if you purchase traditional health insurance.

  If you want to make the most of your HMO, it pays to be your own advocate. Passive patients are apt to get less care and treatment than patients who stand up for themselves and state their wishes.

- **Preferred Provider Organizations and Point of Service plans:** Usually, participating in one of these types of managed care plans costs you more than enrolling in an HMO. Two important reasons for the added cost are that you don't have to deal with a gatekeeper and that you can access services from providers both inside and outside the plan's provider networks. However, if you go outside the network, you are reimbursed at a lower rate than if you use network providers.

Internet sources of insurance information

When you shop for affordable health coverage, don't overlook the Web. Some of the following sites let you comparison-shop for health coverage. Many of them also offer useful general information:

✔ Health Insurance Resource Center (www. healthinsurance.org).

✔ Health Insurance Association of America (www.hiaa.org/cons/cons.htm).

✔ eHealthInsurance (www.ehealthinsurance. com). This site provides you with low-cost or no-cost state-sponsored insurance for children.

✔ WellnessWeb (www.wellweb.com/ INSURANCE/ health_insurance_ index.htm).

Challenging the decision of your health insurance company or health plan

If your health insurer refuses to reimburse you for a claim, if your health plan does not cover the cost of the medical care or service you received, or if your HMO gatekeeper will not refer you to the care or treatment you believe you need, you have the right to appeal the company's decision. However, be sure to act quickly, or you may lose that right. Most health policies and plans establish a limited period for submitting a written appeal. They also spell out the specific steps you must follow to file an appeal, and each step may have its own deadline.

The process for challenging a decision varies from company to company. It also depends on the requirements of the law in your state that regulates health insurance companies and plans.

If you have a lot of money at stake, or if you believe that the medical benefit or service you're being denied could save your life or is critical to maintaining the quality of your life, hire an attorney to help you with your appeal. If your appeal heads to arbitration, or if you believe that the only way to resolve your problem is to file a lawsuit, an attorney is essential. Without one, you will be legally outgunned.

Chapter 11 discusses what to do before you appeal an insurance company's decision, no matter what kind of insurance is involved.

Losing your medical insurance

As with other types of insurance, your health insurance coverage can't be cancelled willy-nilly. The insurer must have a legitimate reason for canceling —

for example, you failed to pay your premiums, or you lied on your insurance application and the insurer wouldn't have sold you health coverage if it had known the truth.

In some states, if you have already received benefits for a health problem, your insurer must continue covering that problem even if it cancels the rest of your coverage.

Canceling your coverage: Read this first!

If you currently have health coverage and are thinking about canceling it and purchasing new coverage, don't take that step until after you receive written confirmation that you have replacement coverage. This step is particularly important for people who are not moving from one group plan to another. Here are some of the dangers associated with not following this warning:

✔ You may not be able to obtain new coverage, particularly if you developed medical problems while you had your old coverage.

✔ While you're without coverage, you could become seriously ill or be seriously injured. Without medical coverage, you are legally responsible for all your medical bills.

✔ If you find a company willing to sell you health coverage, it may not be willing to cover any pre-existing conditions that developed during or after the time that you had your old coverage.

Hip, HIPAA, hooray!

The federal Health Insurance Portability and Accountability Act (HIPAA) protects you when you leave a job that provides you with health coverage. Before its passage in the late 1990s, many people felt trapped in jobs that provided them with health coverage because they feared that if they changed jobs, their new employers' health insurance policy or plan would not cover them. Others feared doing without insurance if they were laid off or wanted to quit their jobs.

HIPAA alleviates some of these fears. For example, it says that if you had employer-sponsored health coverage at your former job and your new employer also offers that benefit, you must be covered even if you have a pre-existing health condition. This requirement also applies to your family members. By the way, HIPAA says that pregnancy can't be treated as a pre-existing condition.

Under HIPAA, you may have to wait up to a year to have your pre-existing conditions covered when you change jobs. HIPAA also protects you if you lose or quit your job and have reason to believe that you will not have health coverage for a period of time. In such a circumstance, it says that you can choose COBRA coverage, assuming that you had group coverage for at least 18 months. You must do so within 60 days of being informed of your rights to that coverage.

If you opt for COBRA, you can remain on your former employer's health policy or plan for up to 18 months after you leave your job, and for up to 29 months if you leave your job because you became permanently disabled and can't work again. However, you have to pick up the full costs of the coverage, plus a 2 percent surcharge. COBRA coverage applies only to employers with at least 20 employees.

If you are not eligible for COBRA, consider purchasing a short-term, temporary insurance policy. Most likely, the policy will cover only hospitalizations and other major medical matters. Your dependents can also receive COBRA coverage. Your former spouse can also continue coverage under COBRA for up to 36 months after you leave your employer.

Dealing with disability insurance

Disability insurance provides you with an income safety net when illness or injury makes it impossible for you to work for a period of time. Although this insurance is expensive, having it can make the difference between staying current on your bills and being forced to file for bankruptcy.

Some disability policies cover illness or injury but not both. Policies that cover both are the most expensive. There are three basic types of disability insurance:

- **Insurance that can't be cancelled.** This insurance comes with a fixed premium. You pay a bundle for the peace of mind that this kind of insurance provides.

- **Insurance that comes with a guarantee of renewal.** If you have this kind of disability insurance, your insurer can't refuse to renew your policy, but it can increase your premiums, as long as you are not singled out for the increase. In other words, the increase must affect everyone in your same class or category.

- **Insurance that gives the insurer the right to refuse to renew your policy, the right to increase your premiums, and the right to cancel your insurance for one or more of the reasons stated in your policy.** This is the least expensive of the three types of disability insurance.

Depending on your financial needs, you may want to supplement the disability coverage available to you through your employer's plan with your own insurance. If your employer does not offer disability insurance as part of your benefit package and you need to shop for your own coverage, here are some of the factors to consider when you compare policies:

- ✔ **When are you considered disabled?** Some policies treat you as disabled if you can't perform your current occupation but you can work at a related, lower-paying job. This is the most expensive type of disability insurance. Other policies do not consider you to be disabled if you can't work in your own specialty area but you can work in a related field. Still other disability policies are even more restrictive.

  Some disability policies link disability with income. For example, if you're working in your same occupation but you're earning less for some reason, you can collect disability income.

- ✔ **How disabled do you have to be before you can collect benefits?** With some policies, you must be 100 percent disabled to receive benefits. Other policies pay you benefits if you are partially or temporarily disabled.

  When your employer pays the premium on your disability insurance, you must pay tax on any benefits you receive.

- ✔ **Does the policy pay for the education or rehabilitation you may need to prepare yourself for a new career?**

- ✔ **How are your policy benefits calculated?** Disability benefits are set either as a percentage of income or as a fixed dollar amount. If you receive Social Security disability payments, your insurance company might take them into account when determining how much your insurance benefits will be.

  If your disability is the result of alcoholism, drug addiction, or a suicide attempt, your insurance company might refuse to cover your disability or limit your benefits.

- ✔ **How long do you have to wait after you are disabled to begin collecting benefits?** The longer you wait, the cheaper your premium will be.

- ✔ **How long do you receive benefits?** The benefit period can depend on whether your disability is due to an injury or an illness.

- ✔ **Is the policy renewable after you turn age 65?** Many policies are not guaranteed renewable once you turn that age. Those that are might reserve the right to increase your premium at that milestone.

- ✔ **Does the policy offer other benefits besides disability payments?** Some policies for example pay for the cost of the education or rehabilitation services you may need to prepare yourself for a new career.

Try to avoid purchasing a disability policy that requires you to get an annual physical exam. You are less apt to lose your insurance.

Long-Term Care Insurance

It's impossible to predict, but you may need nursing home care toward the end of your life. If you do, the cost of that care could use up every bit of your financial resources, because the nursing home benefits offered by the federal Medicare program are extremely limited, and most private medical insurance policies do not pay for nursing home care. Therefore, most people who end up in a nursing home pay out-of-pocket. Many of them liquidate their assets one by one until they are poor enough to get help paying for their nursing home stay from the federal Medicaid program.

For hard-working people who spent years building their assets and who planned to pass them on to their loved ones, having to deplete those assets in order to qualify for government assistance is demoralizing. Furthermore, the process of liquidating assets to pay for nursing home care often means that the spouse of the person in the nursing home must spend the rest of her life in diminished circumstances or move in with relatives.

If you're concerned that a nursing home stay will eat up your hard-earned assets and leave little or nothing for your surviving spouse and other heirs, you may want to consider buying long-term care insurance. Usually, this insurance also pays for home healthcare and other related services. Although the price of this kind of insurance is declining, it is still quite expensive and has many limitations and restrictions.

Buying long-term care insurance

Assuming that you're in good health and that your immediate family does not have a history of health problems that required nursing home care at a relatively early age, wait until your late 50s or early 60s to purchase a long-term care policy, even though the cost of the policy increases the older you get. For most people, long-term care insurance is simply too expensive to purchase earlier, especially considering that with luck, they will never need to take advantage of their policy benefits.

One potential benefit to holding off on the purchase of your long-term care policy is that as the Baby Boomer generation ages, you can anticipate an improvement in the kinds of long-term care policies available as well as in their costs. Over the past ten years, more affordable and generous long-term care policies have already begun to be available.

If you purchased a long-term care policy several years ago and would like to take advantage of the features available in a newer policy, ask your insurance company if you can upgrade.

Some employers offer group long-term care insurance. The cost of this insurance tends to be considerably less than what you would pay for an individual policy. If you can purchase your insurance through your employer, it may make financial sense to take out a long-term care policy sooner than your early 60s, depending on your circumstances. Your employer's benefits administrator should be able to help you make this determination.

Knowing what to look for in long-term care insurance

The cost of long-term care insurance is coming down, but it is still expensive to buy and comes with many limitations and restrictions. Therefore, it's important to shop carefully to find the best long-term care policy you can afford. When you compare your options, consider these factors:

- **The cost of the insurance:** Prices vary widely, depending on the insurance company and the policy benefits. To get the most for your money, don't buy a policy with more bells and whistles than you really need.

- **The daily benefit amount:** This is the heart of a long-term care policy. Ideally, you want a policy that covers the daily cost of your stay in a nursing home and the cost of each day that you need at-home care. Most policies pay more for nursing home care than for home health care and assistance.

- **Protection against inflation:** You want a policy that increases the amount of the daily benefit each year. At a minimum, the increase should keep up with inflation. Otherwise, you risk buying a policy at age 45 that sounds generous but discovering when you're 85 and living in a nursing home that the daily benefit amounts fall far short of the daily cost of your stay there.

- **When the benefits begin:** Some long-term care policies do not pay benefits until you're dependent in two or more activities of daily life. Those activities are considered to be eating, bathing, and dressing. Other policies are less restrictive. For example, they might pay benefits if you need help performing a specific activity as spelled out in your policy, or if you just need general assistance taking care of yourself. Avoid policies that will pay only for nursing home care if it is preceded by a hospital stay.

 Look for a plan that pays benefits when you become mentally impaired. Alzheimer's is an example of a mental impairment.

- **How the policy treats pre-existing conditions:** When you are old enough to be benefiting from a long-term care policy, you probably have a pre-existing condition or two. Ideally, your policy should not deny coverage for such conditions, but at the most, it should exclude them for just six months.

Long-term care insurance resources

A growing number of resources are available to help you understand your long-term care insurance options and determine which one is best for you. Here is a sampling of what you can find online:

✔ Take advantage of the free long-term care insurance decision-making and policy rate comparison service offered by the American Academy of Long Term Care Insurance Professionals at `clay.gta-tech.com`.

✔ Go to the Web site of the Health Insurance Association of America (HIAA) at `www.hiaa.org/cons/cons.htm` to read an online version of its informative brochure, "The Consumer's Guide to Long-Term Care Insurance," and to use its national directory of HIAA members who sell long-term care insurance. For information about ordering

printed copies of these publications, call 800-828-0111.

✔ Check out MetLife's easy-to-understand online brochure about long-term care insurance at `www.metlife.com`. The brochure features a worksheet for comparing policies before you buy. There you will also find an online version of "An Educational Guide to Long-term Care Insurance" prepared by MetLife for the American Association of Retired Persons (AARP). The publication provides helpful advice and information about how long-term care insurance works and how to shop for a policy. You can also order a copy of AARP's Long Term Care Insurance Information Kit at this site. For additional information on long-term care, check out the AARP's Web site at `www.aarp.org`.

✔ **How quickly your benefits start:** Policies vary in the number of days you must be in a nursing home before you can begin receiving benefits. The longer the waiting period, the less expensive the policy. Generally, a 100-day waiting period is too long, but a policy with a less than 20-day waiting period will be too expensive.

✔ **Renewability:** The policy you buy should be guaranteed renewable. Most are these days. The only reason your long-term care insurer should be able to cancel your policy is for nonpayment of premiums.

Living with Life Insurance

If you have young children or a spouse to support, purchasing life insurance and naming a loved one as your beneficiary — the person who receives the insurance benefits when you die — is one way to help ensure that they are financially cared for after you pass away. If your family relies on your spouse's income to help pay the bills and put food on the table, then both of you should purchase life insurance and name one another as your policy beneficiaries. You can purchase an individual life insurance policy, or you may be able to participate in a group policy — through your employer, trade or professional organization, union, and so on. Compare the costs and benefits of the insurance you can get through a group plan to what you can purchase on your own. You may find a better deal.

Employers are not legally required to guarantee the benefits of a group life insurance policy. Therefore, the death benefits could end up being less than what you anticipate, or they could even be eliminated. Relying on your employer's policy to take care of your family is usually not a good idea.

There are some other good reasons to purchase life insurance, depending on your situation. For example, the proceeds from your life insurance policy can

✔ Help you ensure that there is adequate money to pay the taxes on your estate after you die. Estate taxes can represent a financial burden to your loved ones if you acquire a substantial amount of wealth while you are alive. Chapter 14 provides more information on estate taxes.

✔ Ensure that there is money to pay off your debts after you die.

✔ Provide your beneficiaries with cash. If you have more than enough money to live on, you may want to purchase a cash-value insurance policy as part of your estate planning. Speak with an estate-planning attorney about whether this option makes sense for you. Cash-value policies are explained in "Understanding the different flavors of life insurance."

Some life insurance polices pay off your home loan after you die or if you become disabled. Most life insurance policies pay out benefits after the policyholder's death. However, it's also possible to purchase life insurance that pays benefits when you reach a certain age or that can be either paid out over time or cashed out in a lump sum while you're alive.

Periodically, assess whether you have the right amount of life insurance. Your insurance needs are likely to change over time. For example, if your family expands, you may want to purchase a larger policy. This is something you should discuss with your financial advisor or your insurance agent.

Understanding the different flavors of life insurance

There are two basic types of life insurance:

✔ **Term life insurance:** This is life insurance pure and simple, with no bells or whistles. It simply pays your beneficiaries a fixed amount of money — a *death benefit* — after you die, assuming that the policy is still in effect. Term life insurance is an inexpensive way to purchase life insurance when you're young; however, as you grow older and your risk of death increases, the premiums on a term life policy increase.

Once you retire and your income comes not from the sweat of your brow but from your savings, retirement plan, Social Security, and any other investments you may have made, you may want to cancel your term life policy. You no longer need it, because the money you and your family are living on now keeps coming whether or not you are alive. Remember, the basic purpose of most life insurance policies is to replace your lost paychecks when you die.

When you shop for a term life policy, look for one that renews automatically every year and that can be renewed for as many years as you want. You should also try to find one that guarantees that your policy premiums stay the same for a certain number of years — the longer the better. Finally, just to keep your options open, look for a term life policy that you can convert to a cash-value policy at standard rates, and without having to take a physical at any time, up until you turn age 65.

✔ **Cash-value life insurance:** Cash-value insurance couples a death benefit with a built-in tax-deferred savings account. Some policies allow you to set up a tax-deferred investment account. Your premiums pay for your insurance and help fund the savings account. When you die, the insurance company uses the money that has accumulated in the account to help pay your death benefits.

   This kind of insurance is initially more expensive than term life insurance; however, over the years, your premium does not increase, or it increases relatively little. Also, once you accumulate a substantial amount of money in your savings or investment account, you can borrow against that money at a relatively low rate of interest. If you do not repay the loan, the amount that your borrowed is subtracted from the policy proceeds when you die. There are many different types of cash-value life insurance policies including whole life, universal variable life and so on. Sorting through all your options can get confusing pretty darn quick. To help you decide which type is best for you if you are in the market for cash-value insurance, talk to your insurance agent or financial advisor. Another excellent resource for insurance information is Jack Hungelmann's *Insurance For Dummies* (published by Hungry Minds, Inc.).

Before you borrow against the money in your insurance savings or investment account, understand the terms of the loan and be clear about its cost compared to other borrowing options. You may be able to find a cheaper source of borrowed money. For example, although your insurance company pays interest on your cash-value policy every year, it pays less interest on the cash that you borrow against. Therefore, your true cost of borrowing is higher than the stated interest rate for the loan.

The Insurance Guide at www.insure.com can help you make sure that the company you purchase life insurance from is financially solid and has a good track record. Use this site to search for insurance companies by state and by type of insurance. This site also provides information on complaints received by the company you are investigating.

Beware of an insurance agent who urges you to cancel your existing term life policy and replace it with a cash-value policy. He may be more interested in earning a commission on the sale than on making sure that you have the policy that best meets your needs.

Figuring out what affects the cost of your life insurance

The cost of your life insurance policy is based in part on the insurer's assessment of your risk of death. To make this assessment, the company considers, among other things, your age and gender.

Several states bar insurance companies from distinguishing between men and women when setting life insurance rates, even though actuarial data shows that women live longer than men. Insurance companies also review your height, weight, and medical history including the medical history of your mother, father, and other immediate family members. They also consider whether you smoke, use tobacco, or abuse alcohol; your occupation. Your premiums are apt to be higher than normal if you work at a job or in an industry that's associated with a high rate of disease or a higher than normal risk of death; your income and the number of speeding tickets you have received in recent years. Your hazardous hobbies are also considered — you race cars or motorcycles, climb mountains, or skydive.

Discovering the Medical Information Bureau

Be honest when you complete an application for life, medical, or disability insurance. Your lack of honesty could cost you the insurance you want because the insurance company might check your information with your doctors, hospitals, or with something called the Medical Information Bureau (MIB), assuming that the company is a member of the MIB.

Never heard of the MIB? We aren't surprised. This organization of insurance companies is unknown to most consumers. Yet the medical information it may be maintaining on you can affect your ability to obtain the insurance you need.

When the insurance companies who belong to the MIB underwrite an application for insurance, they report to it information they learn about the applicant that could affect his health and longevity. That information can include health and medical information as well information about the applicant's driving record, participation in a hazardous sport, and so on. The medical conditions that are most apt to be reported include being overweight, having high blood pressure, and electrocardiogram results. The MIB then shares this information with other member insurance companies to help protect them from selling insurance to someone who is not 100 percent honest when she applies for insurance.

If the insurance company you apply to wants to find out what information the MIB may have on you, the Federal Fair Credit Reporting Act requires it to get your written permission first. At the same time, it must also provide you with information about how to correct any misinformation that may be included in your MIB record.

Most likely, you do not have an MIB record. The organization estimates that only about 15 to 20 applications out of 100 result in information being added to its database. However, if you want to find out whether you are in that minority, you have the right to ask the MIB to search its database and to provide you with a copy of your report if your name turns up. The cost of the search is $8.50. Once the MIB receives your request, it must disclose any information it has on you within 30 days. To request a search, write to

Medical Information Bureau
P.O. Box 105
Essex Station
Boston, MA 02112

Form 19-1 on the CD provides you with a sample request letter and reflects all the information that you must provide to the MIB. You can also request a search by downloading a request form at the MIB's Web site, www.mib.com. The site provides detailed ordering instructions. The request form lets you indicate how you want to learn about any information the MIB may have on you. You can indicate that you want a written report, that you would like to set up a personal meeting with MIB personnel (assuming you live close enough to the MIB for such a meeting to be practical), or that you would like to have the information disclosed to you over the phone. If the phone call is long-distance, you must give the MIB permission to reverse the charges so that you, not the MIB, pay for the call. If you have questions about ordering or about your report after you receive it, call the MIB at 617-426-3660.

You can obtain a free copy of your MIB report every 12 months if you can certify to the organization when you make your request that you are unemployed and will be seeking employment within 60 days; you are on welfare; or your MIB report is inaccurate due to fraud. Contact the MIB to find out about the certification process.

If you are denied life, health, or disability insurance because of MIB information (or you are charged an extra premium), you are entitled to a free copy of your report if you request it within 60 days of the denial. Be sure to include a copy of the denial notification you receive from the insurance company when you make your request. Form 19-2 provides you with an example of the kind of request letter.

If you are denied the insurance you want because of information in your MIB file, the insurer must give you the name and address of the company or individual that provided the information, as well as the name of any MIB member that received a copy of your MIB report during the 12 months preceding your request for disclosure.

Chapter 20

Accessing Your Medicare Benefits

Countless Americans are involved with the federal Medicare program, a national health insurance program for people 65 and older. Some of them receive Medicare benefits. Others are too young to be enrolled in the program yet, but help their parents deal with the Medicare paperwork and ensure that they receive the benefits they are entitled to.

Although Medicare helps countless Americans pay for their medical care and treatment, like other government programs, it can be confusing and difficult to manage. Furthermore, Medicare's consumer-oriented brochures and the information on its Web site are not always easy to understand, so they do not always clear up confusion and help Medicare enrollees and their families cut through the bureaucratic red tape. For these reasons, many Medicare partici-pants do not get the healthcare and treatment they need and are entitled to, and others pay more than they should for their medical care. Bottom line: Although enrolling in the Medicare program is easy to do, getting what you are entitled to can take time and effort.

The goal of this chapter is to help you understand your Medicare rights (or your parents' rights) by cutting through the program's bureaucratic lingo and confusing rules and by directing you toward additional sources of information and help. The chapter explains the Medicare enrollment process, provides an overview of your insurance benefits and their associated costs, and steps you through the appeals process available to you when you dis-agree with the treatment of your Medicare claims. Because Medicare does not provide comprehensive coverage, this chapter also explains your options for filling the gaps.

Meeting Medicare

Medicare is a federally sponsored health insurance program for older Americans. Most people become eligible for it when they turn 65. However, some people who are younger than 65 also qualify, including disabled individuals and people with end-stage renal disease (kidney failure). The Medicare program is managed by the Healthcare Financing Administration (HCFA), which is part of the Department of Health and Human Services, in cooperation with the Social Security Administration. Medicare provides two different types of health insurance coverage:

- ✔ **Part A Medicare or hospital insurance:** You automatically receive this insurance when you turn age 65, assuming you meet certain criteria. Most Americans do. Also, most people with Part A coverage get it for free; they pay no monthly insurance premiums.

- ✔ **Part B Medicare or medical insurance:** You pay a monthly premium for this insurance, the cost of which is deducted from your monthly Social Security check.

Most people who are eligible for Medicare enroll in the traditional Medicare fee-for-service health insurance plan that probably comes to mind when you hear the word *Medicare*. However, you can also get your Medicare coverage by enrolling in a Medicare managed care plan. These plans must offer the same coverage that you would get if you enrolled in the fee-for-service Medicare program, but they can offer you additional coverage as well. We discuss Medicare managed care plans later in this chapter in the section "Medicare Managed Care."

Although Medicare's information booklets say that you can receive your Medicare benefits by setting up a Medicare Medical Savings Account (MMSA), the truth is, at the time this book was written, no companies offered MMSAs. Therefore, it is not really an option.

If you're enrolled in the traditional Medicare program, when you file your Medicare claims or have questions about them, you deal directly not with Medicare but rather with one or more private companies hired by the program to process claims. A company that processes Part A claims is referred to as an *intermediary,* and one that processes Part B claims is called a *carrier*.

Dealing with Medicare and keeping track of the status of your claims can be a nightmare if you aren't organized and don't keep track of every single piece of paper you send or receive. For example, your claims and your reimbursements might cross in the mail, or the information you receive related to a claim might be incorrect. Do you have a headache yet?

One source of assistance when your eyes are blurring over and you're ready to throw up your hands in frustration is your state's Health Insurance Counseling and Advocacy Program (HICAP). (It may be called something different in your state.) Federal law requires every state to have such a program.

Don't confuse Medicare with Medicaid. Although both are national health insurance programs, Medicare is a 100 percent federal program, and Medicaid is a federal program that's administered by each state. Furthermore, although Medicare is automatically available to most Americans 65 years and older, regardless of their financial status, Medicaid is for low-income people only, regardless of age.

Being eligible

The eligibility criteria for Medicare depend on whether you are applying for Part A or Part B Medicare. If you want Part A Medicare coverage, you must be at least 65 years of age in most cases, and be eligible to receive Social Security retirement benefits based on your work history or on your spouse's. Eligibility for Railroad Retirement benefits or federal civil service retirement benefits also makes you eligible for Medicare. However, this chapter focuses on retirees who are eligible for Social Security benefits only. If you are eligible for Railroad Retirement or federal civil service benefits and want to get specific information about how Medicare relates to you, call 800-633-4227 or go to Medicare's Web site at www.medicare.gov.

When you work at a job that's covered by Social Security, your employer deducts a certain amount of money from each of your paychecks to pay into the Social Security System. Most Americans contribute enough money to the system throughout their work life to make them eligible for Part A coverage at age 65. If you are at least 65 but your or your spouse's work history does not qualify for Part A coverage, you may be able to sign up for the coverage and pay a monthly premium. The less you or your spouse contributed to the Social Security System throughout your work life, the more you pay for the coverage.

To qualify for Part B Medicare coverage, you must be a citizen of the U.S. or a legal resident for at least five consecutive years and be at least 65 years old.

Becoming part of the program

The process for enrolling in the Medicare program depends on whether you are already collecting Social Security retirement benefits when your 65th birthday approaches. If you are, enrollment in the program is automatic and your Medicare coverage begins when you turn 65. In fact, about three months before your birthday, the HCFA mails you a red, white, and blue Medicare card.

If you aren't receiving Social Security benefits yet, but you are about to turn 65, you can enroll in the Medicare program by visiting the Social Security office in your area. You find the address of that office in the blue pages, or government listings section, of your local phone book, or you can locate it on the Social Security Administration's Web site at www.ssa.gov.

Be sure to apply for your Medicare benefits during your *initial enrollment period*. Otherwise, you have to wait until the following January to enroll and your coverage does not begin until the following July. Your initial enrollment period begins three months before the month of your 65th birthday and ends three months later.

Like a growing number of seniors, when you turn 65 and become eligible to begin receiving the full amount of your monthly Social Security retirement benefits, you may decide to delay collecting those benefits and continue working. If you do, you can still enroll in the Medicare program

If you have general questions about your Medicare eligibility or about how to enroll in the program, call Medicare's toll-free hotline at 800-633-4223 from 7:00 a.m. to 7:00 p.m. EST, Monday through Friday. If you're hearing- or speech-impaired, call 877-486-2048. The lines are busiest early in the week and early in the month, so avoid calling at those times. You may also be able to get the information you need at Medicare's Web site, www.medicare.gov.

Opting in or out of Part B

When you participate in the Medicare program, Part B is optional. If you enroll in Medicare at your local Social Security office, you can choose what you want to participate in — Parts A and B or just Part A. You may not want Part B coverage because you do not want to pay for it or because you have comparable coverage through another insurance plan.

If your enrollment in Medicare is automatic, however, the government signs you up for both Parts A and B, and your Medicare card shows that you are participating in both. Then, if you don't want Part B coverage, you must let Medicare know during your initial enrollment period. To do that, fill out the form that came with the packet of Medicare information you should have received along with your card. On the form, check off the box that follows the statement, "I do not want medical insurance." Then return the form in the envelope that came in the same packet. Medicare sends you a new enrollment card showing that you have Part A coverage only. If you wait until after your initial enrollment period has ended, you'll probably end up having to pay some Part B monthly premiums while you wait for your name to be removed from that part of the Medicare program.

You can sign up for Part B coverage later if you want, but it costs you more money than if you sign up during the initial enrollment period. Your Part B premiums increase 10 percent for each 12-month period that you were eligible for Part B but did not participate in it.

If you have group health insurance based on your own or your spouse's current employment, you're not financially penalized if you sign up for Part B after your initial enrollment period. You don't have to wait until the start of the next open enrollment period to enroll, either. This exception does not apply if you're participating in the group health program because it's part of your retirement benefits.

Paying claims: How much Medicare pays

Medicare is a complicated program, so in large part, your ability to deal effectively with it depends on understanding how it operates. Here are some of the quirks of the Medicare program that you should recognize, although there are a lot more:

✔ Medicare only pays for medical care and treatment that it considers "medically necessary and appropriate."

✔ Medicare only pays for stays at hospitals and at skilled nursing facilities that are Medicare-approved. The same is true for home health agencies and hospices.

✔ Medicare only covers the cost of the medical care or treatment you receive from a doctor or other medical provider who accepts Medicare.

✔ As a means of cutting costs, Medicare determines in advance how much it will pay for a particular medical procedure, treatment, office visit, and so on. That amount is referred to as the *Medicare-approved amount.* It might be less than the actual cost of the care or treatment you received.

✔ When you're in a hospital or skilled nursing facility, Medicare Part A reimburses the cost of your stay based on how many days you were an inpatient during a particular *benefit period.* This is another term for a period of illness. For example, when you're hospitalized in a Medicare-approved facility, your benefit period begins on the first day you enter the facility as an inpatient and ends after you have been out of the facility for 60 consecutive days. During the first benefit period associated with a particular illness, Part A pays 100 percent of all covered costs once you meet your deductible. If you're hospitalized for the same illness during a second benefit period — days 61 through 90 — you must contribute a daily copay toward the costs of the Medicare-covered services and treatments you receive. Medicare pays 100 percent of the balance. There's no limit to the number of benefit periods you can have.

If you leave a hospital or skilled nursing facility and then are readmitted during the 60-day period, it is treated as one benefit period.

Knowing the Benefits

You're entitled to very specific benefits when you participate in the Medicare program. This section provides an overview of what you are entitled to depending on whether you are enrolled in Part A or Part B Medicare. However, to understand the full scope of your benefits, including all the restrictions that apply, order a copy of the most current edition of the HCFA's publication *Medicare & You* by calling 800-633-4227. If you're already enrolled in Medicare, you're sent a new edition of this publication every year. You can also get information about your benefits at www.medicare.gov.

Part A Medicare

The Part A hospital insurance part of the program pays for the cost of the following:

- ✔ A stay in a semiprivate hospital room, including the medical care, hospital meals, services, and supplies you receive while you are there. Part A does not pay for the cost of a private room, a private nurse, a television, or a telephone in your room.

- ✔ A stay in a semiprivate room at a skilled nursing facility, including meals, drugs, and medical supplies as well as skilled nursing and rehabilitation services. The stay must follow a hospitalization.

For Medicare to cover your stay in a skilled nursing facility, you must satisfy three different requirements. You must have been hospitalized for at least three consecutive days. (You can't count the day you're discharged as one of those three days.) Your stay in the skilled nursing facility must occur within 30 days of your being discharged from the hospital. You must be in the nursing facility because the doctor ordered it.

- ✔ Home healthcare, including part-time skilled nursing care, physical therapy, home health aid services, speech therapy, the cost of a wheelchair, walker, hospital bed, oxygen, and other durable medical equipment and supplies, and so on.

- ✔ Hospice care if your doctor does not expect you to live longer than six months. Covered services include medical and support services, drugs to control your symptoms and treat your pain, short-term respite care, and so on.

Most likely, you do not have to pay a monthly insurance premium for your Part A coverage. However, each benefit period, you have to satisfy a deductible and you have to pay a daily copayment. Presently, the deductible is $792, and the copay amounts are $198 per day for days 61 through 90 in a benefit period and $396 per day for days 91 through 150. The copays for skilled nursing facility care are different. These numbers increase every year.

For a more complete review of your Part A benefits and their associated costs, read the information in *Medicare & You 2001* on Form 20-1 of the CD. However, because the details of this coverage can change from year to year, you'll want to contact Medicare or visit its Web site to get the most up-to-date information about Part A.

Medicare Part B

Medicare Part B is the medical insurance part of Medicare. Part B helps pay for

- ✔ Doctor services and care, including diagnostic tests and laboratory services

- ✔ Outpatient hospital care, including emergency room visits

- ✔ Medical equipment such as a wheelchair or hospital bed, casts and splints, prosthetics, pacemakers, and so on

- ✔ Mammograms, Pap smears, pelvic exams, screenings for colorectal cancer, bone density tests, and prostate cancer screenings

- ✔ Doctor-prescribed blood-glucose testing supplies for diabetics

- ✔ Doctor-prescribed physical and speech therapy

- ✔ Doctor-prescribed therapy from a social worker or clinical psychologist, under limited conditions

- ✔ Medically necessary ambulance services to and from a hospital or skilled nursing facility

- ✔ Doctor-prescribed skilled at-home nursing care and therapy, assuming that you meet certain conditions

- ✔ Flu shots and pneumonia vaccines

With some exceptions, once you meet your annual Part B deductible, Medicare pays 80 percent of the approved amount of the medical care and services you receive. The remaining 20 percent is your responsibility. In 2001, the amount of the deductible is $100, but it changes annually. You must also pay a monthly deductible of $50. It is taken out of your monthly Social Security checks. The amount of your deductible increases each year. For a good overview of your Part B Medicare benefits and their associated costs, see *Medicare & You 2001* on From 20-1 on the CD.

Knowing When Medicare Doesn't Pay

At first glance, it may appear that Medicare Parts A and B cover a lot. However, if you look at what Medicare does *not* pay for, you will probably draw a different conclusion. Although having Medicare insurance is certainly better than nothing, the coverage is full of holes. For example, Medicare Part A focuses on acute care at the expense of medical care for chronic conditions.

If you're concerned about how to pay for the cost of long-term care should that care become necessary, don't look to Medicare for help. Depending on your finances, purchasing a long-term care policy may be a good option. Chapter 19 explains how this insurance works.

Part B is even holier, and we're not talking religion. What we mean is that Medicare Part B pays for very little preventive care and does not pay for prescription drugs, even though both are critical to maintaining good health and overall physical well-being. See for yourself. Here is some of what Medicare Part B does *not* cover:

- Routine or yearly physical exams. Medicare does not cover the cost of a physical just because you want to monitor your health. However, it does pay for a doctor's exam if you think that something is wrong with you. Therefore, when you call your doctor to schedule an exam, be specific about any physical problems you are having. Being specific can make the difference in getting Medicare to help pay for the exam.

- The drugs and other medications you take at home.

- Routine eye exams, routine eye care, and hearing exams.

- Eyeglasses, contacts, and hearing aids under most circumstances.

- Most dental care.

- Routine foot care and custodial care — help bathing yourself, dressing, eating, and so on — either at home or in a nursing home.

Filling the Gap with Medigap

Many people fill the gaps in their Medicare coverage with Medigap insurance. You purchase this insurance from a private insurance company, not from Medicare. Another term for a Medigap policy is *Medicare supplemental insurance.* That term must be clearly marked on any Medigap policy you purchase.

In most states, Medigap policies must be one of ten different standardized policies authorized by Medicare. The policies range from the least expensive, which is a bare-bones plan, to the most expensive, which has a lot of bells and whistles, including preventative healthcare services and screenings and coverage of prescription drug costs. However, companies that sell Medigap policies are free to set their own eligibility standards, premiums, exclusions for preexisting conditions, and so on, so shop carefully.

For maximum choice in Medigap policies, purchase your policy no later than six months after the first day of the month in which you turn 65. Got that? During this period, you can't be turned down for a Medigap insurance policy because of a current or past health problem, nor can you be charged more because of that problem. Under most circumstances, if you wait until later to purchase Medigap insurance, you can be denied the policy you want, or you may have to pay more for it.

Although a Medigap policy helps fill the gaps in Medicare coverage, it only reimburses costs that are not covered by Medicare. Therefore, if you're looking for broader coverage, you may want to consider a Medicare managed care plan. For additional information about Medigap policies, including advice about buying and using one, call 800-633-4227 and order a copy of Medicare's *Guide to Health Insurance for People with Medicare.*

Medigap shopping tips

Medigap policies vary widely in terms of costs and coverage, so it pays to shop around when you're in the market for one. Here are some shopping tips:

- Do not buy more policy than you really need.
- Be clear about exactly what the policy will and will not cover, including preexisting condition exclusions.
- Be aware of your maximum benefits under the plan.
- Compare the cost and benefits of a Medigap policy with the Medicare managed care plans available to you.
- Never pay for a Medigap policy with cash and don't be pressured into buying a Medigap insurance plan you're not sure you want.
- Beware of insurance salespeople who claim that the federal government sells, services, or guarantees the Medigap policy they're selling. The federal government does not do any of those things for Medigap policies.
- Steer clear of unsolicited Medigap policies that you receive in the mail or that claim you must purchase the policy no later than a certain date before the insurance offer expires. Usually, these policies are bad deals. If one of them looks attractive, however, contact your state insurance commission to make sure that the company selling it is on the up and up.

When you're not rolling in dough

If your income is low, it may be tough for you to afford the cost of your Medicare premiums, deductibles, and copays. However, you can be eligible for state assistance. To qualify:

- ✔ You must have Medicare Part A.

- ✔ Your annual income level must be at or below the federal poverty guidelines. The guidelines take into account the number of people in your household. For example, the federal poverty guideline in the year 2000 is $11,250 for a family of two and $17,050 for a family of four. (The guideline amounts are higher for people living in Alaska and Hawaii because it costs more to live in those states.) The Census Bureau updates the federal poverty guidelines annually. For the most current information as well as links to information about the federal poverty guidelines go to www.rxassist.org/federal.htm.

- ✔ You can't own more than $4,000 in easily liquidated assets if you are single or widowed, or more than $6,000 if you're married. These assets include bank accounts, stocks, and bonds. They do not include your home or your car.

Assistance may be provided through one of the following programs:

- ✔ **QMB:** Qualified Medicare Beneficiary program, also known as the Medicare Buy-In program. It pays for your Medicare premiums, deductibles, and most of your copayments.

- ✔ **SLMB:** Specified Low-Income Medicare Beneficiary program. This program pays only for the cost of your monthly Medicare Part B premiums.

- ✔ **QI:** Qualifying Individual program. This program pays for all or part of the cost of your monthly Medicare Part B premiums.

To find out whether you qualify for any of these programs, contact your state's Medical Assistance office. If you need financial assistance paying for your Medical care, consider applying for Medicaid.

Using Medicare Managed Care

Besides getting your Medicare benefits the traditional way, you can enroll in a private Medicare managed care plan such as an HMO or a PPO. This can be an attractive option because

- ✔ There are no Medicare claims forms to handle.

- ✔ Not only do you receive the same basic coverage offered by the fee-for-service Medicare program (Medicare requires that), but also the

Medicare managed care plan might offer additional coverage, including prescription drug and dental coverage.

✔ A Medicare managed care plan can be an attractive alternative to a Medigap policy because it offers you the same benefits as Medigap but usually at a slightly lower cost.

Participating in a Medicare managed care plan does have some potential drawbacks:

✔ Depending on the plan you enroll in, you may be limited to certain doctors, hospitals, and so on.

To keep their costs down, managed care plans come with many restrictions. Chapter 19 explains them.

✔ All managed care plans must sign one-year contracts with Medicare. After the year is up, a plan is free to end its association with Medicare, which could mean that you're left without Medicare coverage. However, you may be able to find another Medicare managed care plan to enroll in. Otherwise, you can enroll in the traditional Medicare program and possibly purchase a Medigap policy as well.

Enrolling in a Medicare managed care plan is an option only if you

✔ Have both Medicare Part A and Part B.

✔ Are willing to continue paying your monthly Part B premiums even after you are in a managed care plan. In other words, you must pay the Medicare Part B premium as well as the managed care plan's premium, if it charges an additional premium.

✔ Live in the service area of a Medicare managed care plan. Some people do not live in an area served by this kind of plan. You can get a current list of all the plans that serve your area by calling 800-633-4227, or you can get that same information by going to www.medicare.gov. Both also provide information on how these plans rate in regard to quality and consumer satisfaction.

✔ Do not have end-stage kidney failure. However, if you develop this disease and you're already in a Medicare managed care plan, you can stay in it if you want.

If you enroll in a Medicare managed care plan and then move out of its service area, you must leave the plan. Then you can either join the traditional Medicare program or enroll in a new managed care plan that serves the area where you are living.

When you're shopping for a Medicare managed care plan, compare your options at the Web site of the National Committee for Quality Assurance, an independent nonprofit organization that evaluates managed care plans. If you need help comparing your options, contact the Health Insurance Assistance Program in your state. You can find the telephone number to call in your copy of the *Medicare & You* brochure that you receive when you first become eligible to participate in Medicare and each subsequent autumn for the next year.

As a member of a Medicare managed care plan, you can leave the plan at any time. However, write to the plan itself or to the Social Security Administration and let them know what you're doing. To be on the safe side, write to both. When you leave the plan, you're automatically enrolled in the Medicare fee-for-service plan unless you join another managed care plan.

Starting in 2002, you may be able to leave a plan only at certain times. You can learn the conditions by calling 800-633-4227. If you have a Medigap policy when you join a Medicare managed care plan, you can keep the policy, but you cannot use it. Even so, keeping it is a good idea if you think that you might return to the traditional Medicare plan at some time. If you don't keep it and you do leave the plan, under certain conditions, you might have just a short time to purchase a new Medigap policy. For information on the restrictions that apply to purchasing a new policy, call 800-633-4227 or order a copy of the free Medicare booklet "Medicare Supplemental Insurance (Medigap) Policies and Protections" at this same phone number.

If you're in a managed care health plan when you become eligible for Medicare and you want to stay in it, let the plan know so it can switch you to its Medicare coverage, assuming that it offers that coverage. Be sure to contact the plan at least three months prior to the date of your eligibility for Medicare. That way, if the plan doesn't offer Medicare coverage, you have time to find a managed care plan that does during your initial enrollment period.

Filling the gaps other ways

If you have health coverage through your or your spouse's employer, former employer, or union, you may want to maintain that insurance in addition to enrolling in Medicare. It could be financially advantageous for you to combine it with Medicare rather than leave the plan and purchase a Medigap policy or enroll in a Medicare managed care plan. Ask the benefit administrator with your current health plan to help you determine your best option.

If you keep your employment or retirement-based insurance, depending on your circumstances, Medicare may require that you file your claims with that company before Medicare pays your claims.

Getting Medicare to pay the bill

If you're enrolled in the traditional fee-for-service Medicare program, the process for filing your claims and getting reimbursed depends on whether you have a Part A or a Part B claim.

Most likely, if your medical expense is covered under Part A of the Medicare program, the provider of the care or treatment you received — a hospital, skilled nursing facility, home healthcare company, and so on — files a claim on your behalf with the appropriate Medicare intermediary. You do not have to handle any of the claim-filing paperwork yourself, and Medicare reimburses the healthcare provider directly. The provider accepts however much Medicare pays as payment in full. In other words, the provider does not bill you for any additional money. However, it can bill you or your Medigap insurer for the cost of any care and treatment you received that was not covered by Medicare and for any deductible or copays you may owe.

The Medicare intermediary sends you a Medicare Summary Notice (MSN). This notice tells you the following:

- ✔ The service or treatment claim that it relates to. In parentheses next to the description of the service or treatment, you see a numerical code for that particular expense category.

- ✔ The total amount of the claim.

- ✔ How much of the claim is Medicare-approved and what Medicare paid.

- ✔ How much you or your Medigap insurance company must pay.

- ✔ How much of your deductible has or has not been met.

- ✔ Whether a copy of the MSN was sent to your Medigap insurer, assuming that you have one.

If you look on the reverse side of the MSN, you find general directions about how to appeal the claims decision if you disagree with it. Curious about what an MSN looks like? Take a gander at a www.medicare.gov/Basics/ msn_a.asp For a sample MSN Part A. For a sample MSN Part B, go to www. medicare.gov/Basics/msn_b.asp.

If your claim is for a service or treatment covered by Part B Medicare, things get a bit more complicated. For example, some doctors and other medical providers file your claims for you, but some don't. Also, some *accept assignment* of the Medicare-approved reimbursement amount for the services they provide to you, and others don't. Accepting assignment means that a doctor or other healthcare provider promises not to charge his patients more than the Medicare-approved amount for the services and treatment they receive from that doctor. Some doctors and healthcare providers accept assignment on a case-by-case basis only. Others let Medicare know ahead of time that they accept assignment for all Medicare patients. In turn, Medicare awards these doctors by reimbursing them at a slightly higher rate than other doctors.

When your doctor accepts assignment, all that you or your Medigap insurer may have to pay out of pocket is the cost of any services or treatment you received that was not covered by Medicare, any portion of your annual deductible that remains unpaid, and your copay. However, if the provider does not accept assignment, you or your Medigap insurer might also have to pay the difference between the provider's usual fee and the Medicare-approved amount. Federal law caps the additional amount of money that the provider can charge you at 15 percent.

You receive an MSN for each of the claims you file or that a provider files on your behalf. The notice provides the same kind of information as a Part A MSN.

Federal law says that doctors treating patients who receive Medicaid and Medicare, or who receive Medicare as well as QMB assistance, must accept assignment for those patients. If you're enrolled in a Medicare managed care plan, you don't have to deal with all this confusing Medicare paperwork. Phew! All you have to do is pay your plan's premiums and copay amounts and deal with the plan's paperwork.

Receiving a Medicare Summary Notice

When an MSN arrives in the mail, read it carefully. Be sure to note problems such as Medicare not paying as much as you think it should have or Medicare being billed for services you didn't receive. Also look for instances where Medicare refuses to pay for the treatment or care you received.

If you have a general question about the information on an MSN, call the telephone number indicated in its upper-right corner. This is not a number for Medicare. It is the number for the Medicare intermediary or carrier that is handling your claim.

If the MSN shows that Medicare was billed for a service or treatment that you did not receive, call the healthcare provider who filed the claim. The charge may be an innocent mistake. On the other hand, the provider may be trying to defraud the Medicare program. If you suspect fraud or abuse, call the telephone number in the upper-right corner of the MSN. You can also call the inspector general's hotline to report Medicare fraud at 800-447-8477.

Appealing a decision about your claim

If you're unhappy with or unclear about a decision related to a Part A or Part B claim, you have a number of avenues of appeal. The first and simplest avenue is a telephone call to the customer service office of the Medicare carrier who sent you the MSN. The number to call is in the upper-right corner of the MSN. If the person you speak with agrees that your claim should have been handled differently, you are sent a new MSN reflecting the correct information. Ordinarily, the only claims you appeal yourself are Part B claims. Hospitals and other Part A medical providers handle appeals related to Part A claims. Therefore, the rest of this chapter deals with Part B claims only.

When you call your Medicare carrier, be prepared to provide your Medicare number and the date of the MSN you're calling about. Here is some advice about what you should do before making this call, depending on the nature of your problem:

✔ If you think that the reimbursement amount is too low because of the way the treatment or service you received was categorized, contact the medical provider who filed the claim to find out how it described the treatment or service on the claim form it submitted for reimbursement. If you spot a discrepancy between its description and how the service or treatment is categorized on the MSN, ask the provider to contact the Part B Medicare carrier to clarify things. If it won't, make the call yourself. If a phone call to the customer service office resolves your problem, you receive a corrected MSN in the mail.

Sometimes, if a medical provider resubmits a claim and describes the treatment or care differently, Medicare pays the second time around even though it didn't pay the first time.

✔ If Medicare didn't pay a claim because it says that the care or treatment you received was not medically necessary or appropriate, before you call the Part B Medicare carrier, ask the doctor who provided the care or treatment or who ordered it whether she will write a letter on your behalf justifying its medical necessity and appropriateness. Ask the doctor to send you the letter along with a copy of all related medical records. Then, when you call the carrier's customer service office, explain why you believe the claim should be reimbursed. Also, let that person know about your doctor's letter and medical records. You may be asked to mail in that information, or the carrier or intermediary might call your doctor.

No matter what stage of the appeal process you're in, getting your doctor involved can be extremely helpful because she can use your medical records as well as her own knowledge and expertise to help make your case. In fact, your doctor is your best advocate.

Asking to have your claim reconsidered

If a telephone call doesn't resolve things to your satisfaction, complete the information on the reverse side of the MSN for the claim you are disputing. Send it to the customer service address indicated on the front of the MSN. When you do, you're formally requesting a reconsideration of the claim.

Check the date in the upper-right corner on the first page of the MSN. You must file your request for a reconsideration no later than six months after that date. The second page of each MSN also indicates the date by which you must file it.

You may also want to write a letter to accompany the standard form, particularly if the space on the form doesn't give you enough room to make your case. For example, if Medicare is refusing to pay for the doctor's care you received, explain why the care was necessary and ask the Medicare carrier to review its decision. Be sure to include your Medicare number, your name exactly as it appears on the MSN, and the date of the MSN in your letter. Use the sample letter on Form 20-2 of the CD to draft your own letter.

It's is also a good idea to ask your doctor to write a letter on your behalf. Be sure your doctor understands why Medicare is not paying the claim, or not paying as much as you think it should, so he knows what argument to make in his letter. Make two copies of your doctor's letter and the medical records that relate to the claim. Attach one copy of each to the letter you send to the Medicare carrier, and put the other copies in your file together with a copy of your own letter. Send the letters, the standard request form, and all your backup material to the address in the upper-right corner on page one of the MSN.

If your doctor is too busy to write a letter on your behalf, she may refuse to write one or agree and then not write the letter soon enough — or she may charge you to write a letter. In all three instances, include your doctor's name and telephone number on your letter and ask the carrier to contact her before it makes its decision.

After the carrier receives your request for reconsideration and any additional information you send along with it, it reviews its records. It may also call your doctor. Then the carrier sends you a written *notice of determination* indicating what it has decided about your claim.

Copy your doctor on any letters you send to the Medicare carrier and send a copy of the letter to your doctor. He may need it if Medicare follows up with him.

Appealing a Part B claim

If the notice of determination shows that nothing has changed and your claim relates to Part B of the Medicare program, you can request a hearing with the Medicare carrier as long as the total amount of the claim is at least $100. Put your request in writing no later than six months from the date of the notice. If you want to attend the hearing, include that information in your letter so that the carrier can let you know when and where the hearing will take place. Send your request letter to the address on the notice. Attach to it copies of any doctor letters, medical records, or other documentation you have that support your request.

To reach the $100 threshold, you can combine different claims. However, each of the combined claims must have gone through the reconsideration process during the last six months. When you want to request that the carrier hold a hearing on your Part B claim, use the sample letter on Form 20-3 of the CD.

If the date of the hearing is not convenient for you, ask for a new date. A week or so before the hearing date, call to make sure that the carrier has received your doctor's medical records. If it hasn't and if there's not enough time to get them to the carrier, ask for a new hearing date.

Handling the hearing

The hearing is conducted in an informal matter, unlike a court hearing. It is presided over by a neutral hearing officer. If you attend, the officer might ask you questions about why you believe that the carrier's decision is wrong. Make sure that the hearing officer has all of your letters and backup documentation. Bring extra copies with you in case he does not.

After the hearing is over, you receive a written notice of the hearing officer's decision. It may be as long as six weeks before you receive it. If the hearing goes your way, you receive a new, correct MSN. If it doesn't, don't give up! Depending on the amount of money at issue, you might have a couple more avenues of appeal left.

Other appeal options

If the hearing related to your Part B claims does not go your way, you can request a hearing before an administrative law judge, assuming that the amount at issue is at least $500. Request the hearing no later than 60 days after receiving written notice of the hearing officer's decision. To make your request, you can fill out a special form that's available at your local Social Security office. You can find a sample request form on Form 20-4 on the CD. You can also write a letter requesting the hearing.

You can combine claims to reach the $500 threshold, assuming that each claim went through the Medicare carrier hearing process. Get your ducks in a row before the hearing! For example, find out whether your doctor will testify on your behalf. Her testimony could be persuasive. At the least, ask your doctor to write a letter on your behalf.

If you strike out with the judge, appeal his decision to the Social Security Appeals Council (SSCA). You have 60 days to file an appeal. If your claim is for at least $1,000 and you lose your appeal with the SSAC, file a lawsuit in federal district court no later than 60 days after the appeals court's written decision. You need a lawyer with experience in handling Medicare-related lawsuits. Don't do it alone. Depending on the strength of your case, the attorney may take your case on a contingency basis.

Part VI
The Part of Tens

The 5th Wave   By Rich Tennant

"My portfolio's gonna take a hit for this."

In this part . . .

No . . . *For Dummies* book, no matter what the subject, would be complete without the Part of Tens. The first chapter in this part, Chapter 21, directs your attention to ten legal Web sites where you can find additional information about the legal aspects of your money matters. The second chapter, Chapter 22, highlights ten organizations to which you can turn for information, advice, and assistance when you need help with a legal matter that concerns your finances.

Chapter 21

Ten Resources You Can Rely On

*W*hen you need reliable information to make an important money-related decision, or when you want to resolve a legal problem outside of court and without an attorney's help, don't overlook these ten resources. Some of them offer unbiased, easy-to-understand information. Others can help you cut through bureaucratic red tape and even work with you to try to resolve your problem. Add these ten resources to your personal database so that you know where to find them when you need them.

Bankrate.com

When you have to make an important financial decision, you can count on Bankrate.com for timely information and advice. Its award-winning Web site features current interest rates for a wide variety of types of credit, how-to advice and guidance about borrowing money, using credit cards, and taxes, and columns written by a variety of money experts. You can also calculate your loan payments, participate in online chats, and sign up to receive a free Bankrate newsletter. Check out this Web site at www.bankrate.com.

National Foundation for Credit Counseling

The National Foundation for Credit Counseling (NFCC) is a national nonprofit network of 1,450 financial counseling offices called Neighborhood Financial Care Centers, which can help you climb out from under the pile of bills burying you. It has been offering low-cost assistance to consumers in financial crisis since 1951. Contact the NFCC by calling its national toll-free crisis hotline at 800-388-2227. You can also get help by visiting the Neighborhood Financial Care Center nearest you or by pursuing online counseling at the NFCC Web site, www.nfcc.org.

The Legal Aid Society

Check out the Legal Aid Society at www.lsc.gov. Congress established this private, nonprofit organization in 1974 to help ensure that all Americans, regardless of income, have access to legal help and representation. The Legal Aid Society does not deliver legal services itself; instead, it funds independent local programs in each state. In turn, these offices provide legal assistance and advice to low-income people, including students and seniors. Each program sets its own priorities for the kinds of cases it handles based on local needs and priorities. None of them, however, handles criminal cases. To reach the Legal Services Corporation, call 202-336-8800 or write to

The Legal Aid Society
750 First Street NE, Tenth Floor
Washington, DC 20002-4250

Your Local or State Government Consumer Protection Office

Call a consumer protection office when you want to find out about your legal rights and how to protect them, or if you believe that a business or organization has trampled on those rights and has violated a local or state law in the process. Staff members at these offices can provide you with basic information and advice, although they can't act as your lawyer; depending on the office you contact, however, they may be willing to mediate your complaint. If mediation doesn't work, they investigate and may take steps to punish the company or organization, assuming that your complaint helps establish a pattern of abuse.

Federal Information Center

Confused about which federal office to call? Know the office but can't find the right number? The Federal Information Center (FIC) can save you hours of frustration and wasted phone calls. Dial 800-688-9889 to reach an FIC representative.

The FIC is open from 9 a.m. to 5 p.m. local time, except in Alaska and Hawaii. Alaska's hours are 8 a.m. to 4 p.m., and Hawaii's are 7 a.m. to 3 p.m.

National Fraud Information Center

The National Fraud Information Center (NFIC) is dedicated to fighting telemarketing fraud. It sponsors a national toll-free hotline that consumers can call to get advice about the telephone solicitations they receive and to report instances of suspected telemarketing fraud. You can reach the hotline at 800-876-7060. You can also ask questions about a company that uses telemarketing and report suspicions at the organization's Web site, www.fraud.org/info/aboutnfic.htm.

Federal Trade Commission

The Federal Trade Commission (FTC) is on your side. Among other things, the FTC enforces many federal consumer protection laws and produces informative publications related to those laws. For example, its publications address such topics as dealing with credit and debt, protecting your identity and your financial information, purchasing consumer products and services, investing your money, buying a home, and selling a car. When you go to the FTC's Web site at www.ftc.gov, you can read these publications online or download them to your computer. You can also order copies by writing to

Consumer Response Center
Federal Trade Commission
600 Pennsylvania, NW, Room H-130
Washington, DC 20580-0001

If you believe that your consumer rights have been violated, don't take it sitting down. Tell the FTC. Although it won't file a lawsuit on your behalf, your complaint might spur the FTC to take action against the business or organization you have a beef about. For general questions and information about the FTC, call 202-326-2222 or 800-382-4357.

Call for Action

Call for Action is an international nonprofit organization of consumer hotlines that use trained volunteer professionals to help consumers resolve problems with businesses, government agencies, and other organizations through mediation and education. The organization's hotline help is free and confidential, and each Call for Action office is associated with a local radio or television station. Call for Action also distributes consumer publications related to debt, credit, scams, online shopping, and so on. For a list of its publications, call 301-657-8260 or write to

Call for Action
5272 River Road, Suite 300
Bethesda, MD 20816

You can also read online versions of the publications at the Call for Action Web site, www.callforaction.org.

Council of Better Business Bureaus

The Council of Better Business Bureaus, a national nonprofit organization founded in 1912, is dedicated to fairness in the marketplace. The Council is the umbrella organization for the nonprofit Better Business Bureau (BBB) system. Look to your area's BBB for dispute resolution services and for publications intended to make you a more informed consumer. Go to the Council's Web site, www.bbb.org, for advice about what to do before you buy and how to handle problems with your purchases. You can also use this Web site to file an online complaint against a company or organization and to locate the BBB office nearest you. For more information about the Council, contact

Council of Better Business Bureaus
4200 Wilson Boulevard, Suite 800
Arlington, VA 22203-1838
703-276-8277

Elected Officials

When government bureaucracy, red tape, or simple incompetence is hijacking your legal rights, ask your local elected representative or your state or national senator or representative to intercede on your behalf. Assuming that you have a legitimate gripe that's within your elected representative's sphere of influence, asking him or her for help can get you quick results. Remember, your elected representative's job is to represent you, so don't hesitate to ask for his or her assistance.

Chapter 22

Ten Law-Oriented Web Sites to Bookmark

*O*ne of the great benefits of the Internet is that it puts vast amounts of information and resources just a click away. Today, you don't have to be a lawyer to gain at least a basic understanding of your legal rights and responsibilities.

You can click on a wide variety of legal Web sites. Many offer easy-to-understand information about everyday legal matters, as well as the opportunity to get answers to basic legal questions. Some of them can even help you find a lawyer in your area. (We don't recommend locating a lawyer online, but it is an option.)

AllLaw.com

At www.alllaw.com, you can find general information about a limited range of legal topics, including bankruptcy, estate planning, and taxes, as well as information about dispute-resolution methods and advice about hiring an attorney. This Web site also features sample legal forms, articles about various legal subjects, and links to state resources and legal resources.

Court TV

www.courttv.com is the Web site of the cable network that O. J. Simpson helped put on the map. If you're addicted to the trials on Court TV and you miss any trial testimony, you can visit this site to find out what happened. You can also share your thoughts and comments about trials and events by sending e-mails to the Court TV reporters and legal experts, and you can participate in online chats about the legal issues of the day. This site also links you to the FindLaw Web site.

FindLaw

www.findlaw.com is the leading Web portal focused on government and the law. Click to the Public Channel for a wide variety of self-help legal guides related to consumer matters, including housing, autos, money, and Medicare. While you're there, check out FindLaw's legal references, which include dictionaries, law directories, and libraries. You can also connect to federal and state legal resources, visit Findlaw's community message boards, and locate an attorney in your area.

Free Advice.com

www.freeadvice.com covers 100 different legal topics using a question-and-answer format. The questions reflect the kinds of things you might ask a lawyer during your initial meeting. Although this site offers many of the same features that you find at other legal Web sites, it has some interesting extras. For example, its State Law Center provides links to an extensive collection of state-specific information and resources, and it offers FreeAdvice Live! Use this feature to talk with a lawyer one-on-one, in real time. The lawyer can help you sort out your options for resolving a legal problem, clarify the legal issues involved, suggest other legal resources to check out, and let you know whether you need to hire a lawyer.

Lawoffice.com

www.lawoffice.com claims to offer pragmatic, thorough, in-depth information for dealing with legal affairs. Although we're not sure that it quite lives up to its claim, the site does have some nice features, including informative lawyer-authored articles about numerous legal topics. It also lets you search for state-specific information on a particular legal topic.

Law Offices of John Ventura

John simply couldn't resist blowing his own horn — and rightfully so, because the legal Web site at www.johnventura.com both educates and entertains. You can learn about bankruptcy, credit rebuilding, estate planning, and much more by reading sample chapters from his books. Because John believes that the law can be entertaining, and even pretty darn funny sometimes, this Web site highlights dumb laws and lawyer jokes. If you're fascinated by the rich and famous, it also features the wills of Elvis, Clark Gable, and Liberace.

Lawsmart.com

lawsmart.lawinfo.com makes it easy to find state-specific legal information and forms. All you have to do is click on a legal topic and then on your state, and you get a short summary of the issues related to that particular subject. With another click of your mouse, you can get the answers to frequently asked questions about that topic. You can also post your own questions at the Legal Forum.

Lawstreet.com

Although www.lawstreet.com was not 100 percent finished when we wrote this book, it shows considerable promise. Calling itself "Your Legal Guide to Life," it has some interesting features, namely an ability to search by state *and* county (not just state) for information about the laws that affect you. The Web site's Please Advise feature provides free answers to your legal questions.

Lawyers.com

www.lawyers.com is sponsored by the *Martindale-Hubbell Law Directory*. Its main goal is to help you locate an attorney by using its online lawyer database. However, that doesn't diminish the quality of the information that this Web site offers. Among other things, you can find detailed information about a variety of legal topics, post your legal questions on a message board, and link up with an array of legal resources, including self-help legal publications, no-cost/low-cost legal services, and government agencies. You can also kick back, relax, and read about interesting and sometimes famous legal cases at *Law Today*.

The Lectric Law

The downright quirky Web site at www.lectlaw.com has both a sense of humor and a big dose of braggadocio. It claims, for example, to host the Internet's largest collection of law-related software and e-books and asserts that its Lawcopedia reference room includes the Net's biggest and best law dictionary. The site offers a plethora of legal information and resources. Visit its Laypeople's Law Lounge to read up on contracts, taxes, landlord-tenant matters, and more, and then move on to its Forms Room to download the legal documents you need. Later, you can peruse the periodicals in its Periodical Reading Room and read analyses of legal issues by representatives of the political right and left. The site also features a bookstore that sells legal software and e-books.

Legalwise.com

Legalwise Online, located at www.legalwise.com/legalwise_online.htm, contains more than 10,000 legal summaries on laws in all 50 states and federal laws, too.

Washlaw

Washburn University School of Law hosts www.washlaw.edu, a Web site that has been called the most influential legal Web site on the Internet. Short on graphics and long on information, Washlaw can direct you to just about any nugget of legal information worth finding. The site includes links to federal and state courts, legal services, various areas of specialization, education sites, and countless more resources that make this Web site an invaluable legal resource.

Appendix

About the CD

. . . .

On the CD

▶ More than 100 sample documents, contracts, and forms

▶ Microsoft and Netscape browsing software to enable you to surf the Web

▶ Internet access software from MindSpring

. . . .

System Requirements

Make sure that your computer meets the minimum system requirements listed below. If your computer doesn't match up to most of these requirements, you may have problems using the contents of the CD.

✔ A PC with a Pentium or faster processor, or a Mac OS computer with a 68040 or faster processor.

✔ Microsoft Windows 95or later, or Mac OS system software 7.6 or later.

✔ At least 16MB of total RAM installed on your computer. For best performance, we recommend that Windows 95-equipped PCs and Mac OS computers with PowerPC processors have at least 32MB of RAM installed.

✔ At least 250MB of hard drive space available to install all the software from this CD. (You need less space if you don't install every program.)

✔ A CD-ROM drive — double-speed (2x) or faster.

✔ A sound card for PCs. (Mac OS computers have built-in sound support.)

✔ A monitor capable of displaying at least 256 colors or grayscale.

✔ A modem with a speed of at least 14,400 bps.

If you need more information on the basics, check out *PCs For Dummies*, 7th Edition, by Dan Gookin; *Macs For Dummies*, 6th Edition, by David Pogue; *Windows 98 For Dummies, Windows 95 For Dummies*, 2nd Edition. (all published by IDG Books Worldwide, Inc.)

Using the CD with Microsoft Windows

To install the items from the CD to your hard drive, follow these steps.

1. **Insert the CD into your computer's CD-ROM drive.**

2. **Open your browser.** If you do not have a browser, we have included Microsoft Internet Explorer as well as Netscape Communicator. They can be found in the Programs folders at the root of the CD.

3. **Click Start➪Run.**

4. **In the dialog box that appears, type D:\START.HTM.** Replace *D* with the proper drive letter if your CD-ROM drive uses a different letter. (If you don't know the letter, see how your CD-ROM drive is listed under My Computer.)

5. **Read through the license agreement, nod your head, and then click the Accept button if you want to use the CD — after you click Accept, you'll jump to the Main Menu.** This action will display the file that will walk you through the content of the CD.

6. **To navigate within the interface, simply click on any topic of interest to take you to an explanation of the files on the CD and how to use or install them.**

7. **To install the software from the CD, simply click on the software name.** You'll see two options — the option to run or open the file from the current location or the option to save the file to your hard drive. Choose to run or open the file from its current location and the installation procedure will continue. After you are done with the interface, simply close your browser as usual.

In order to run some of the programs on the *Everyday Law Kit For Dummies* CD, you may need to keep the CD inside your CD-ROM drive. This is a good thing. Otherwise, the installed program would have required you to install a very large chunk of the program to your hard drive, which may have kept you from installing other software.

Using the CD with Mac OS

To install the items from the CD to your hard drive, follow these steps.

1. **Insert the CD into your computer's CD-ROM drive.** In a moment, an icon representing the CD you just inserted appears on your Mac desktop. Chances are, the icon looks like a CD.

2. **Double click the CD icon to show the CD's contents.**

3. **In the window that appears, double click the START.HTM icon.**

4. **Read through the license agreement, nod your head, and then click the Accept button if you want to use the CD — after you click Accept, you'll jump to the Main Menu.** This action will display the file that will walk you through the content of the CD.

5. **To navigate within the interface, simply click on any topic of interest to take you to an explanation of the files on the CD and how to use or install them.**

6. **To install the software from the CD, simply click on the software name.**

7. **After you are done with the interface, simply close your browser as usual.**

8. **Some programs don't come with installers. For those, just drag the program's folder from the CD window and drop it on your hard drive icon.**

After you have installed the programs you want, you can eject the CD. Carefully place it back in the plastic jacket of the book for safekeeping.

What You'll Find

Here's a summary of the software on this CD arranged by category. If you use Windows, the CD interface helps you install software easily. (If you have no idea what I'm talking about when I say "CD interface," flip back a page or two to find the section, "Using the CD with Microsoft Windows.") If you use a Mac OS computer, you can take advantage of the easy Mac interface to quickly install the programs.

Contract samples and sample forms

The contract samples and sample forms on the CD come in two distinct flavors.

✔ **Rich Text Format Files.** Use this version if you use a version of Microsoft Word prior to Word 95 or if you use another word processor such as WordPerfect, WordPro, or WordPad.

✔ **Adobe Acrobat (PDF) files.** Some files (such as IRS forms and publications) can only be seen if you install the Adobe Acrobat Reader. You cannot modify these forms, but can print them out.

Acrobat Reader

Evaluation version. For Macintosh and Windows. Acrobat Reader , from Adobe Systems, is a program that lets you view and print Portable Document Format, or PDF files. The PDF format is used by many programs you find on the Internet, because it supports the use of such stylish elements as assorted fonts and colorful graphics (as opposed to plain text, or ASCII, which doesn't allow for any special effects in a document).

Once Acrobat Reader is running, you can view PDF files. To learn more about using Acrobat Reader, choose Reader Online Guide from the Help menu, or view the Acrobat.pdf file that was installed in the Help/ENU subfolder of the folder where the program was installed. You can also get more information by visiting the Adobe Systems Web site, at www.adobe.com.

Internet Explorer

Commercial version. For Macintosh and Windows. Internet Explorer, from Microsoft, is one of the best-known Web browsers available. In addition to the browser, this package includes other Internet tools from Microsoft: Outlook Express 5, a mail and news reading program; Windows Media Player, a program that can display or play many types of audio and video files; and NetMeeting 3, a video conferencing program.

If you have a version of Windows 98, 2000, or NT that already includes Internet Explorer 5.5, don't install the CD version. Instead, go to Microsoft's Web site at www.microsoft.com/windows/ie/download/windows.htm and see what updates are available to fix errors and security problems in the version you have.

MindSpring Internet Access

Commercial version for Macintosh and Windows. MindSpring is an Internet service provider (ISP) that has local telephone access from most areas of the continental United States. The software provided by MindSpring on the CD includes and easy-to-use interface to the Internet programs you will want to use, as well as some useful Internet client -programs. Visit the MindSpring Web site at www.mindspring.com.

Before you sign up for an account with MindSpring, check whether it's accessible from your location as a local telephone call. You can check MindSpring availability in your area through their Web site or call their customer service department at 1-888-677-7464.

Mindspring has several plans you can choose from, depending on how much time you need to spend connected. At the time this book was written, MindSpring offered unlimited 56K dial-up Internet access for $19.95 per month. MindSpring also offers residential and business ISDN and DSL service.

If you already have an Internet service provider, please note that the MindSpring software makes changes to your computer's current Internet configuration and may replace your current settings. These changes may stop you from being able to access the Internet through your current provider.

Netscape Communicator

Commercial version. For Macintosh and Windows. Netscape Communicator, from Netscape Communications, is one of the best-known Web browsers available. You also have the option of installing Real Player G2 (to play streaming audio and video files) and Winamp (to play MPEG3 files). You can find information about Netscape Navigator from its Help menu or at its Web site, `home.netscape.com`.

If You've Got Problems (Of the CD Kind)

I tried my best to compile programs that work on most computers with the minimum system requirements. Alas, your computer may differ, and some programs may not work properly for some reason.

The two likeliest problems are that you don't have enough memory (RAM) for the programs you want to use, or you have other programs running that are affecting installation or running of a program. If you get error messages like `Not enough memory` or `Setup cannot continue`, try one or more of these methods and then try using the software again:

- ✔ **Turn off any anti virus software that you have on your computer.** Installers sometimes mimic virus activity and may make your computer incorrectly believe that it is being infected by a virus.

- ✔ **Close all running programs.** The more programs you're running, the less memory is available to other programs. Installers also typically update files and programs; if you keep other programs running, installation may not work properly.

- ✔ **In Windows, close the CD interface and run demos or installations directly from Windows Explorer.** The interface itself can tie up system memory, or even conflict with certain kinds of interactive demos. Use Windows Explorer to browse the files on the CD and launch installers or demos.

  ✓ **Have your local computer store add more RAM to your computer.** This is, admittedly, a drastic and somewhat expensive step. However, if you have a Windows 95 PC or a Mac OS computer with a PowerPC chip, adding more memory can really help the speed of your computer and enable more programs to run at the same time.

If you still have trouble installing the items from the CD, please call the Hungry Minds Customer Service phone number: 800-762-2974 (outside the U.S.: 317-572-3993).

Index

• C •

• M •

IDG Books Worldwide, Inc., End-User License Agreement

5. **Limited Warranty.**

   (a) IDGB warrants that the Software and Software Media are free from defects in materials and workmanship under normal use for a period of sixty (60) days from the date of purchase of this Book. If IDGB receives notification within the warranty period of defects in materials or workmanship, IDGB will replace the defective Software Media.

   (b) IDGB AND THE AUTHOR OF THE BOOK DISCLAIM ALL OTHER WARRANTIES, EXPRESS OR IMPLIED, INCLUDING WITHOUT LIMITATION IMPLIED WARRANTIES OF MERCHANTABILITY AND FITNESS FOR A PARTICULAR PURPOSE, WITH RESPECT TO THE SOFTWARE, THE PROGRAMS, THE SOURCE CODE CONTAINED THEREIN, AND/OR THE TECHNIQUES DESCRIBED IN THIS BOOK. IDGB DOES NOT WARRANT THAT THE FUNCTIONS CONTAINED IN THE SOFTWARE WILL MEET YOUR REQUIREMENTS OR THAT THE OPERATION OF THE SOFTWARE WILL BE ERROR FREE.

   (c) This limited warranty gives you specific legal rights, and you may have other rights that vary from jurisdiction to jurisdiction.

6. **Remedies.**

   (a) IDGB's entire liability and your exclusive remedy for defects in materials and workmanship shall be limited to replacement of the Software Media, which may be returned to IDGB with a copy of your receipt at the following address: Software Media Fulfillment Department, Attn.: *Everyday Law Kit For Dummies*, IDG Books Worldwide, Inc., 10475 Crosspoint Blvd., Indianapolis, IN 46256, or call 800-762-2974. Please allow three to four weeks for delivery. This Limited Warranty is void if failure of the Software Media has resulted from accident, abuse, or misapplication. Any replacement Software Media will be warranted for the remainder of the original warranty period or thirty (30) days, whichever is longer.

   (b) In no event shall IDGB or the author be liable for any damages whatsoever (including without limitation damages for loss of business profits, business interruption, loss of business information, or any other pecuniary loss) arising from the use of or inability to use the Book or the Software, even if IDGB has been advised of the possibility of such damages.

   (c) Because some jurisdictions do not allow the exclusion or limitation of liability for consequential or incidental damages, the above limitation or exclusion may not apply to you.

7. **U.S. Government Restricted Rights.** Use, duplication, or disclosure of the Software for or on behalf of the United States of America, its agencies and/or instrumentalities (the "U.S. Government") is subject to restrictions as stated in paragraph (c)(1)(ii) of the Rights in Technical Data and Computer Software clause of DFARS 252.227-7013, or subparagraphs (c) (1) and (2) of the Commercial Computer Software - Restricted Rights clause at FAR 52.227-19, and in similar clauses in the NASA FAR supplement, as applicable.

8. **General.** This Agreement constitutes the entire understanding of the parties and revokes and supersedes all prior agreements, oral or written, between them and may not be modified or amended except in a writing signed by both parties hereto that specifically refers to this Agreement. This Agreement shall take precedence over any other documents that may be in conflict herewith. If any one or more provisions contained in this Agreement are held by any court or tribunal to be invalid, illegal, or otherwise unenforceable, each and every other provision shall remain in full force and effect.

Installation Instructions

The *Everyday Law Kit For Dummies* CD offers valuable information that you won't want to miss. To install the items from the CD to your hard drive, follow these steps.

1. **Insert the CD into your computer's CD-ROM drive.**

   In a moment, an icon representing the CD you just inserted appears on your Mac desktop. Chances are, the icon looks like a CD-ROM.

2. **Double-click the CD icon to show the CD's contents.**

3. **Double-click the Read Me First icon.**

   The Read Me First text file contains information about the CD's programs and any last-minute instructions you may need in order to correctly install them.

4. **To install most programs, just drag the program's folder from the CD window and drop it on your hard drive icon.**

5. **Other programs come with installer programs — with these, you simply open the program's folder on the CD and then double-click the icon with the words "Install" or "Installer."**

   Sometimes the installers are actually self-extracting archives, which just means that the program files have been bundled up into an archive, and this self extractor unbundles the files and places them on your hard drive. This kind of program is often called an .sea. Double-click anything with .sea in the title, and it will run just like an installer.

   After you have installed the programs you want, you can eject the CD. Carefully place it back in the plastic jacket of the book for safekeeping.

For more information, see the "About the CD" appendix.

FOR DUMMIES
BOOK REGISTRATION

4/0.

...ter
...ook
...n!

We ... from ...

LOOK FOR!
— Books
— Booklets
— Cassettes
⊥ Discs
— Videos
— Maps
— Patterns
— Charts
— ____

Visit **du**... gister ... book ... it!

✔ Get ...

✔ Give ... st,
what ... ... what w... or
and ...

✔ Let u... ... Dummies tool ... ...

Your fee... ... ... book... ... us what
coverag... ... ... wether
we're m... ... ... most
valuabl... ... you h...

Not on... ... ... The
Interne... ... ...ailers
everyw...

Or let u... ... ™
a letter...

For Du...
Dumm...
10475 ...
Indiana...

P...